IN THEIR OWN RIGHT

In Their Own Right

The History of American Clergywomen

by

Carl J. Schneider and Dorothy Schneider

A Crossroad Book
Crossroad Publishing Company
New York

1997
The Crossroad Publishing Company
370 Lexington Avenue, New York, NY 10017

Printed in the United States of America

Library of Congress Cataloging-in-Publication Data

Schneider, Carl J.
    In their own right : the history of American clergywomen / by Carl
J. and Dorothy Schneider.
      p.   cm.
    Includes bibliographical references and index.
    ISBN 0-8245-1653-2 (hcover)
    1. Women clergy—United States—History. 2. United States—Church
history. I. Schneider, Dorothy. II. Title.
BV676.S348   1997
277.3'0082—dc21

97-751
CIP

To Beverly Page and Mary Attridge,
librarians par excellence,
who found the books we needed,
rejoiced with our enthusiasms,
and sympathized in our woes.

Contents

Preface

RESEARCH FOR THIS BOOK has led us into many libraries and odd volumes: books in which solid facts flounder in an ocean of speculative sentimentality; books written in theological jargon that push the envelope of language to bursting; books written by untutored amateurs desperate to preserve the records of women they admired; books perpetrated solely to vent spleen. Sometimes their style reduced us to despair; sometimes it made us chuckle. To wit: "When the Reverend Gober arrived in Sacramento in 1851, he found a mortgaged church and a backsliding congregation. His wife walked the streets and collected money to pay off the debt."[1] But we also found an extensive scholarship of excellence emerging in the field. With facts and theories from all of these we have undertaken to construct a solid scaffolding on which other scholars can stand: the first history of Christian and Jewish clergywomen in the United States, set in the context of religious history and women's history generally.

The task has been complicated, partly because religion in this country is so denominationally fragmented, partly because religion is currently refashioning itself, and partly because of the stage of scholarship. As Rosemary Skinner Keller writes, "all who write and read in this field realize that we are still in the early stages of discovering, analyzing, and integrating women and religion into American religious history. The luxury does not exist to complete the work stage by stage, compiling all the primary source documents, writing all the monographs, integrating all the studies into a new religious and social history and then writing a new comprehensive history of the United States. Research and writing must continue at all these points simultaneously."[2] We look upon our contribution as one step in this ongoing process, a step inevitably stumbling but essential.

We have confined our history to women in the Judaic-Christian tradition who have preached and pastored in the United States. We talk about foreign missionaries only as they have contributed to the progress of clergywomen in their profession. Although we recognize the spread of such other major religions as Buddhism and Islam in our country, we lack the expertise to write about them, and we shudder at the difficulty of defining "clergywomen" in terms suitable to them. We have excluded post-Christianity as being too new and too amorphous for any fruitful investigation on our part. But many clergywomen in the Judaic-Christian tradition, particularly in the New Thought and New Age movements and among Unitarians, have borrowed and are borrowing extensively from those faiths.

We have approached writing this history as objectively as we would that of any other group of professional women. We have tried to discount the adulatory nature of many of the biographies of clergywomen and the distortions inflicted on experience by the fixed patterns of spiritual autobiographies. We assume that clergywomen are humanly prone to error, though we have found our interviewees an extraordinarily bright and attractive lot. Charges of heresy and blasphemy or just plain wrong-headedness in systems of belief belong in other hands than ours; we stand amazed that they are still being pursued with medieval, inquisitorial ardor. In the main we have focused on the development of the profession, using individual experiences to identify and illustrate general trends.

In our research we have interviewed more than seventy-five clergywomen, who graciously talked with us at length, in person or by telephone, about their professional experiences, pleasurable or painful. They represent many denominations and theological beliefs, several ethnic groups, and a wide range of ages. We sought out particularly women who have taught other clergywomen, have done research on them, or have helped them find jobs; they generously shared their expertise. When we have not indicated a source for a quotation, it has come from one of our interviewees.

Many people have encouraged and helped us in this work, including some whom we have never met. Barbara Brown Zikmund of Hartford Theological Seminary, Joshua Crowell of the Essex, Connecticut, United Church of Christ, and Barbara Sicherman of Trinity College helped us give form to an amorphous impulse; Doris Friedensohn of Jersey City State College cheered us on. Our agent Elizabeth Knappmann helped to pound the proposal into shape. Pat Kluepfel of Twenty-Third Publications lent us many books and the benefit of her own experience.

Friends suggested and introduced us to potential interviewees; here we owe particular gratitude to Nancy Schneller, Pat Smith, and Erica Wimber. Sister Katherine McKenna, Rabbi Nina Beth Cardin, and Lt.-Col. Marlene Chase of the Salvation Army read the sections of our manuscript on their denominations and educated us with their insights.

Denominational representatives have found materials for us and given us the benefit of their knowledge, especially Dorothy Emerson of the Unitarian Universalist Women's Heritage Society. Librarians and archivists have sustained us at every turn, particularly Barbara Smith and her staff in Essex, Connecticut, Renee Klish of the Army Chaplains School, and the staff of the wondrous Schlesinger Library. We thank them all for their generous contributions to this sometimes daunting task.

Notes

1. Quoted by Julie Roy Jeffrey, "Ministry Through Marriage," in *Women in New Worlds: Historical Perspectives on the Wesleyan Tradition*, ed. Hilah F. Thomas and Rosemary Skinner Keller (Nashville, Tenn.: Abingdon, 1981), p. 155.

2. *In Our Own Voices: Four Centuries of American Women's Religious Writing*, ed. Rosemary Skinner Keller and Rosemary Radford Ruether (San Francisco: HarperSanFrancisco, 1995), p. 4.

Introduction:
Clergywomen
on the Edge of Time

AMERICAN WOMEN WHO PREACH and pastor at the end of the twentieth century, Christians and Jews alike, stand where women have never stood before. From New England village churches to California synagogues to New York storefronts, clergy-women are changing the face of religion in America. Women pastors are shepherd-ing congregations of Roman Catholics, mainline Protestants, pentecostals and evangelicals, Mormons, and Jews. Women are serving as chaplains in hospitals, schools, industry, the military, and prisons; as district superintendents and bishops in church hierarchies; as theologians and seminary faculty; as evangelists, whether independently or in organizations like the Salvation Army; and as founders of their own churches.

In theological seminaries across the country still more women are preparing for the clergy. A 1992 survey by the Association of Theological Schools shows steady increases in the proportion of women enrolled every year from 1972 to 1992, rising from 10.2 percent to 31.1 percent. At Yale's Divinity School, women constituted an astonishing 61 percent of 1993 recipients of the Master of Divinity, the degree preparatory for ordination.

"I wake up every morning and think, 'Isn't it marvelous that I can do what I'm doing?' It's the only time in all of history that a woman could be doing this," says a rabbi. She's right. But it has taken a long time to get this far—ever since 1656. . . .

1

1

Preaching Women:
Quakers, Methodists, and Independents
1656–1800 🖎

The Seventeenth Century: Quaker Public Friends

HISTORICALLY, NEITHER IN THEORY nor in practice has religion carried the banner of women's rights. Quite the contrary: as religious historian Edwin Gaustad remarks, it has been "the restraining anchor, the unyielding institution, the bastion of male domination that had behind it the force of centuries-old traditions usually reinforced by a 'thus saith the Lord.'"[1] Yet despite this determined opposition, throughout American history three kinds of women have functioned as clergy: (1) women credentialed by their religious organizations; (2) unordained women who operated within their churches or synagogues, sometimes serving in tandem with or succeeding their husbands; and (3) women who evangelized independently of any denomination or founded new denominations of their own.

The history of clergywomen in America formally dates from 1656, when British Quaker "Public Friends" Mary Fisher and Ann Austin landed in the Massachusetts Bay Colony—only to be arrested, imprisoned, examined for marks of witchcraft, and shipped back to England.[2]

Even earlier, religiously assertive women had already upset church and civil authorities. The principle of the separation of church and state had of course not yet been promulgated in America; instead established churches, recognized and supported by government, enjoyed near monopolies—Congregationalism in Massachusetts, Presbyterianism in some of the middle Atlantic colonies, and Episcopalianism in New York and the southern colonies. Colonial government authorities and churchmen often perceived their interests as identical. Certainly they agreed on the patriarchal principle of women's obligation to accept their authority in silence. Anne Hutchinson (1591–1643) challenged that principle.[3]

By no standard a clergywoman—not, that is, a woman who preaches and pastors professionally—the outspoken Hutchinson unawares teetered on the brink. Her effective religious leadership terrified the Puritan civil and church powers of the Massachusetts Bay Colony almost from the moment of her arrival in 1634, four

3

years after the colony's founding. These men were up against the classic dilemma of Protestantism, where authority resides not in a hierarchy but in the empowerment of the ordinary believer by the grace of God. They were trying to hold to several contradictory principles at the same time: the superiority of males, especially ordained clergy, over females; the supremacy of the institutional church over the individual; the equality before God of all communicants, women and men alike; and what Elaine Huber calls the "authority of inspiration" by the Holy Spirit.[4]

Hutchinson's Anglican clergyman father had gone to prison in England for accusing bishops of ordaining unfit men. His daughter followed his rebellious example by questioning the sermons of clergy who preached that people could contribute to their own salvation by their works, whereas Hutchinson fervently believed that only God's grace could save his creatures from damnation. Fortunately for her neighbors, this doctrine did not prevent Hutchinson from doing all sorts of good deeds that endeared her to many Bostonians and undergirded her influence on them. Despite her own numerous family—she bore her husband William fifteen children —she practiced as a skilled midwife and herbalist.

So far, so good. But Anne Hutchinson also adopted an already well-established custom that has led many a woman to professional ministry—holding meetings for the spiritual betterment of women. In her home (the foreroom of which could accommodate sixty to eighty people) she held weekly religious meetings, in which she repeated and explicated the sermons of John Cotton, an exponent of the doctrine of grace whom she admired, and criticized the sermons of clergy who preached the doctrine of works. Her charisma and her comments drew more and more listeners, at first almost all women, many of whom she had succored in illness and in childbirth. Women brought their husbands. Eventually the charismatic Hutchinson had to establish a second session.

The theological disputations by which Puritans sought to comprehend human existence were exacerbated by the natural opposition between Boston merchants and the governing bodies, including clergy, who without a by-your-leave imposed wage and price controls on their businesses. Hutchinson's increasingly anticlerical merchant followers began to proselytize. "I'le bring you to a woman," offered one of them, "that preaches better Gospell than any of your black-coates that have been at the Ninniversity, a Woman of another kinde of spirit, who hath many revelations of things to come."[5]

Her popularity aggravated the tensions among the colonists as they sought to build their New Jerusalem in the New World. They themselves were seeking a religious haven here, but few of them—certainly not Hutchinson—had the faintest conception of religious tolerance. They were worried about the controls England exercised over them. Their governors, their clergy, and the citizenry themselves struggled for power as they painfully defined the nature of their new state, an effort complicated by their desire to make it religiously correct. They feared the neighboring Native Americans. They were experiencing economic woes. And religious differences among them strained relations to the breaking point—witness the banishment of Roger Williams in the winter of 1635–1636, and the nearly simultaneous departure of the Rev. Mr. Thomas Hooker and his group. As Selma Williams remarks, among true believers "a little nonconformity can be a dangerous thing."

In these circumstances, Hutchinson with her growing following inevitably threatened the insecure governors and clergy, all the more so because wealthy, well-established merchants supported her. That a woman headed such a group, when custom, law, and religion all insisted that women be submissive, obedient, and silent, only exacerbated the fears of government and church authorities. These theocrats rated her conduct as both seditious and heterodox. The clergy, wary of competition, accused her of having "rather been a husband than wife, a preacher than a hearer, and a magistrate than a subject."[6] Then as thereafter women constituted a solid majority of church membership, but churches of Hutchinson's day typically provided no leadership roles for women.

In the fall of 1637 a church synod resolved to discourage prayer meetings like the ones Hutchinson conducted as "disorderly and without rule" and forbade church members to question ministers in such a way as to asperse doctrines delivered in their sermons.[7] Civil authorities tried her, found her guilty, and banished her, the sentence to take effect in the spring of 1638 when travel would again become possible. Meanwhile she was held under arrest in a home not her own, only ministers and her family being allowed to visit her. It was a long ordeal. In the spring the church authorities tried her, found her guilty, and excommunicated her: "I command you . . . *as a Leper to withdraw your selfe out of the Congregation."*

Although Hutchinson's esteemed John Cotton had warned the women associated with her to vomit up any evil she had instilled in them and not to "harden her in her Way by pittyinge of her," her friend Mary Dyer put her arm in Hutchinson's and walked with her down the church aisle.[8] Despite harsh measures imposed on them by church and state, others of Hutchinson's supporters also remained loyal even after her expulsion. Women were whipped or excommunicated for publicly defending her.[9] But the Massachusetts Bay Colony had only begun its discovery of the difficulty of subduing women convinced that they were obeying their consciences, their inner light, the voice of God. Many of these women were Quakers.[10]

Even before the organizing of the Society of Friends in 1668, women followers of its founder, George Fox, began to proselytize in the New World, infuriating established churches and state authorities. In 1656 Elizabeth Harris traveled from England to Maryland to preach; four Quaker women and four Quaker men landed in Boston, where they were imprisoned and returned to England; and English missionaries Ann Austin, mother of five children, and Mary Fisher, a twenty-two-year-old servant girl, were imprisoned, stripped, examined for signs of witchcraft, kept without light or writing materials for five weeks, and shipped out of Boston. But the Massachusetts authorities were fighting a flood. Throughout the seventeenth and eighteenth centuries and much of the nineteenth, Quaker "Public Friends" ardently pursued their itinerant ministries.[11]

These were ministers of the Friends, who for their first two centuries employed no professional or "hireling" ministers. Although Quakers did not ordain their ministers, their meetings (churches) validated the individual's call from God to preach by "recording" it; by the end of the seventeenth century they were so authorizing women.[12] Their support for women ministers was theologically based, for they believed in the equality of redeemed men and women. And they put policy into practice by recording significant numbers of women; Joan Jensen believes that by the end of the eighteenth century, as many as half of all Quaker ministers may have been women.[13] At any rate in 1684 Governor Thomas Dongan of New York was already complaining about the presence of "preachers male and female, lots of Quakers (both 'singing Quakers' and 'ranting Quakers') and much besides."[14]

Of course some of these clergywomen spoke more easily, more fluently, and more persuasively than others. But anxieties over styles of delivery were mitigated by the belief that God put words into their mouths. In this belief they were seizing on the same authority that had empowered Hildegard of Bingen (b. 1098) and other authoritative medieval religious women. Usually they expressed this empowerment in terms of a metaphor that indicated that God spoke through them: Hildegard called herself "God's little trumpet." Quakers waited patiently for God's "leading," speaking only when it came. Rebecca S. Turner, traveling with Priscilla Cadwallader, wrote of the occasions on which Cadwallader was "favored to relieve her mind." At other times, Cadwallader could find no relief, though she had much to communicate, and silently "appeared in solemn supplication."[15]

"Itinerating" Public Friends were obligated by duty both to speak the words God gave them and to visit other meetings, check on their spiritual welfare, and bind them into unity with other Quakers. Through these peregrinations the Public Friends held their society together, carrying news from one local meeting to another, and dutifully reproaching members or meetings that they perceived to be backsliding. In these early days meetings frequently authorized specific trips by written "minutes."

Women Public Friends were of all ages, some being recorded as ministers as young as sixteen. Some were single, but more were married. Married women usually completed their childbearing before setting forth, but not always. Margaret Lewis for one miscalculated: on her way to England she discovered that she was pregnant; nonetheless she doggedly rode horseback from town to town, preaching at two or three meetings each day, as well as gathering with Quaker families for prayer and Bible reading, up until two months before her baby was born.[16] In some cases mothers of five or more young children stayed away from home for years at a time. Although many husbands magnanimously cooperated, some objected, but the will of the woman (or, as she saw it, God's will expressed through her), backed up by the approval of her meeting, obtained. In 1699 the meeting to which Jane Biles belonged approved her "concern" to travel, overriding her husband's opposition; he accepted defeat graciously, requesting and receiving permission to accompany her.[17]

Most itinerants covered remarkable distances in this country and abroad in the face of the most difficult and dangerous conditions. As Ann Chapman Parson remarked during her last illness: "I have traveled a pretty deal in my time."[18] They covered the eastern part of North America by foot, on horseback, and in oxcarts and buggies, over Indian trails, through swamps and wilderness, snowstorms and droughts. They insouciantly shuttled back and forth to England, the Continent, Barbados, and South America. Often they had little idea of where they would eat or rest next, and many a time, summer and winter, they slept under the open skies. Usually women Public Friends traveled in pairs, frequently assisted by a male escort or more briefly by men from the local meetings they visited. Meetings sometimes underwrote these trips, but financially able ministers were expected to pay their own way.

It was such indomitable spirits whom the Massachusetts Bay Colony and Virginia were trying to repel when they enacted laws forbidding Quakers to land on pain of imprisonment, lashing, expulsion, and even death. In 1662 when Quakers Mary Tomkins and Alice Ambrose visited Virginia, they were pilloried, given thirty-two lashes each with a nine-corded whip, and expelled.[19] Undeterred, in the autumn of 1663 they were carrying on their work in Maryland. The authorities were slow to learn: they had eyes, but they could not see, nor did they learn from the martyrdom of Mary Dyer in 1660.[20]

Dyer, the faithful disciple of Anne Hutchinson, was an extraordinarily courageous and persistent seeker after religious truth. Her move from the Anglicanism of her English birth to Puritanism carried her to the Massachusetts Bay Colony, where she experienced the traumas first of being called a sinful mother because she bore a malformed baby and then the trial and banishment of Hutchinson, who had acted as her midwife and had tried to protect her against public condemnation. After Hutchinson's exile Dyer went with the Antinomians to Rhode Island, where from 1640 to 1650 she was kept busy bearing and raising babies. She returned to England with her husband in the first years of the Protectorate. There she was converted to Quakerism and at the personal request of George Fox itinerated as a Public Friend for five years.

In 1656 she returned to Boston, where she was imprisoned as a "heretic"—that is, a Quaker. Rescued by her husband, she preached in New Haven, Connecticut, which in its turn expelled her. In 1659 back she went to Boston to visit two imprisoned male Quakers, with the predictable result of another banishment. The next month all three again defied the "bloody laws," this time to be sentenced to death. Dyer pleaded to the court, "In love and meekness I beseech you to repeal these cruel laws, to stay this wicked sentence. . . . But if one of us must die that others may live, let me be the one."[21] On the gallows, a contemporary report says, she "had her Coats tied about her feet, and the Rope put about her neck, with her face covered, and as the Hangman was ready to turn her off, they cryed out to stop, for she was reprieved. . . . She was not forward to come down, but stood still saying she was there willing to suffer as her Brethren did; unlesse they would null their wicked

Law, she had no freedom to accept their reprieve."[22] The men were hanged; Dyer's long-suffering husband carried her away. But in 1660 she came back, for the last time, refusing to save her life by recanting even on the gallows.

Dyer's determined martyrdom spurred on other equally dedicated women. The next year, sixty-one-year-old British Elizabeth Hooten and her companion Joan Brocksopp, frustrated in an attempt to reach Boston by sea because no ship's captain would land them there, journeyed to Virginia, sailed to Rhode Island in a ketch, and went on to Boston. Imprisoned, then led into the wilderness and abandoned, they found their way to Rhode Island and eventually to England. There Hooten regrouped, and in 1662 returned to Boston with her daughter. Under Massachusetts's Cart and Whip Act, they were stripped to the waist, tied to a cart, and led through the towns of Cambridge, Roxbury, Dedham, Salisbury, and Dover, receiving ten lashes in each settlement. Back in England in 1665 and again in prison, Hooten plotted yet another trip to America. She died en route at age seventy-two. By 1667 Quakers Ann Coleman, Mary Tomkins, Alice Ambrose, Catherine Chattam, Deborah Wilson, Margaret Smith, and Margaret Brewster had endured similar punishments.[23]

✐ The Eighteenth Century: Quaker Public Friends ————————

Governmental persecution like this, administered not only in Massachusetts but also in other colonies, largely ended by 1700.[24] Individual objections to women Public Friends of course continued. Supping in a tavern where they were both staying, a Presbyterian minister took it upon himself to reproach Quaker itinerant Ann Moore on the grounds that she was violating St. Paul's instructions for women to keep silence in the churches. She answered trenchantly with scripture authorizing women to prophesy.[25] And Elizabeth Webb, touring New England in 1698, wrote wistfully: "Had I been a man I thought I could have went into all corners of Ye land to declare of it for indeede it is ye Great day of New England's visitation."[26] But some of the seventeenth-century tensions that had animated official persecution eased with eighteenth-century commercial development, economic growth, and increasing prosperity, and accordingly the prohibitions on women's public activity, including preaching, weakened. Economic changes and the development of more affectionate families had slightly eroded patriarchy, giving women a little more freedom.[27] And punishment even unto death simply had not worked: it had failed to stop the dedicated Public Friends.

Their numbers grew in the eighteenth century. Charity Wright Cook (1745–1822), for instance, even before she had finished bearing her eleven children, devoted her life to itinerating, with the full consent and cooperation of her husband, Isaac. He saw himself as a divinely appointed home-keeping partner in her divinely appointed ministry.[28] On one occasion Isaac learned of Charity's return from abroad only when he heard her praying in Quaker meeting. As soon as the prayer ended, he went through the partition door to the women's side, kissed her, then returned to his place. Reprimanded by one of the elders, Isaac replied, "If thee had not seen thy wife in five years I think thee ought to kiss her as soon as thee could."[29]

Itinerating ran in Cook's blood: her grandfather, two aunts, her mother, a sister, and a woman cousin were all Public Friends. She made her first trip at the age of thirty-one, her last at seventy-five. She did her job conscientiously, riding horseback over backcountry roads from Georgia to Massachusetts, visiting in the home of every member of each local meeting. Dangers she welcomed, for she believed that suffering led to salvation. She found aplenty: suspicion of spying, privateers at sea, smallpox, robbery, arrests—and the fury of British Friends whom she criticized for their treatment of their servants. When she was nearly sixty, she swam to shore, fully clothed, after an accident to her wagon in a creek had drowned her two horses.

Like other Quaker ministers, Cook intoned her sermons, breaking words into sharply accented syllables and alternating a low- and a high-pitched voice to produce a rhythmic sing-song effect. For a long time she smoked a pipe, breaking the habit only when she dreamed that the porter refused her entrance to heaven because smoke obscured her name in the Book of Life.

By no means all Quaker women ministers itinerated. Mary Coffyn Starbuck (1644-1717), for instance, labored only on Nantucket. A woman of independent mind, this farm wife left the established church to become something of a leader among local Baptists. Disillusioned with professional ministers, she sought direct communication with the Holy Spirit. On the suggestion of Quaker missionaries to Nantucket, in the first decade of the eighteenth century Starbuck began holding weekly meetings and eventually became the first recorded Quaker minister on the island, where the Society of Friends flourished. Legend (which has contributed more to our "knowledge" of Starbuck than fact) has it that she started many statements, "My husband and I think . . . ." If indeed she did, she used a ploy that has protected many a clergywoman—and many another woman—from a charge of impropriety.

The equally strong-minded Elizabeth Sampson Ashbridge (1713-1755) created herself, or at least our image of her: much of what we know about her comes from her spiritual autobiography, published posthumously and widely read.[30] She was born in England and raised an Anglican. "In my very Infancy," she wrote, "I had an awful regard for religion & a great love for religious people, particularly the Ministers, and sometimes wept with Sorrow, that I was not a boy that I might have been [a minister]; believing them all Good Men & so beloved of God."[31] A "wild and airy" adolescent who wanted to dance and sing and "take my Swing," she eloped at fourteen with a poor stocking weaver, only to be widowed almost immediately. Her lively narrative makes her the heroine of a series of adventures: taking ship for the New World, quelling a shipboard plot of indentured Irish servants to kill the crew and take over the ship, and being forced into indenture herself. After three years she bought her freedom by her labors as a needlewoman, only to enter another "cruel Servitude" by marrying a man who loved her for her dancing.

Amid all these excitements Ashbridge dabbled in one version of Christianity after another. Roman Catholicism repelled her by insisting that all non-Catholics are damned. She just didn't like the Presbyterians she met, and the Seventh-Day Baptists held her interest only briefly. Ministers of various denominations struck her as ill-behaved and hypocritical, some of them motivated by greed: "Surely these and Such like are the Shepherd that regards the fleece more than the flock, in whose mouths are Lies."[32] Priests of the Church of England failed to assuage her depression. As for the first woman preacher she heard, "I looked on her with Pity for her ignorance (as I thought) & Contempt of her Practise, saying to my self, 'I am sure you are a fool, for if ever I should turn Quaker, which will never be, I would not be a preacher.'"[33]

Nonetheless she finally settled on Quakerism, breaking the news to a dismayed husband, who had thought he was marrying a light-footed and light-hearted lass. He played the heavy husband, forbidding her to attend Quaker meeting. "I then Drew up my resolution & told him as a Dutyfull Wife ought, So I was ready to obey all his Lawfull Commands, but where they Imposed upon my Conscience, I no longer Durst; For I had already done it too Long, & wronged my Self by it, & tho he was near & I loved him as a Wife ought, yet God was nearer than all the World to me."[34] So she defied him, walking eight miles to meeting when he wouldn't let her take the horse, tying on her worn-out shoes with string when he wouldn't replace them, finding another meeting when he moved them to another state. Ashbridge carried her obedience to God and defiance of husband to the ultimate by preaching and in 1738 entering the ministry. She rounds out her narrative with his deathbed conversion after he has deserted her and gone for a soldier. Having paid off his debts by needlework and teaching, she married a third husband, a supportive one, from whose narrative we learn that she capped her itineracy by a trip to Great Britain, where she died.

Ashbridge was neither the first nor the last clergywoman to discover the effectiveness of the appeal to the individual conscience—or obedience to God—as a reason for denying male authority. Protestants have a hard time refuting its authenticity, since their theology rests on direct communication with God and individual conscience. A denomination may insist on a woman's obeying her husband—except when he countermands what God or her church tells her is right. God helping her, she can do no other.

Carried another step, that argument has often been used to defend a woman's right to preach: she must preach, because God has told her to. Sophia Hume (1702–1774), a social butterfly converted to Quakerism during the First Great Awakening, under such a divine command took it upon herself to instruct her sister South Carolinians of the evils of worldly indulgences. She defended herself against the disapproval of her children and her friends, as well as accusations of delusion and religious madness: "But notwithstanding . . . that I suffered your Ridicule and

Reproach, . . . I am willing to become more vile in your Eyes. . . . I would not have you imagine that any Consideration, less than [God's] Favour, could have prevailed with me to have appeared thus publickly."[35] And Priscilla Cadwallader "told the people that a curse [?] was pronounced against those who withhold and preached not that which was given them to say, and however hard [her criticism of other Quakers] might seem, she was bound to deliver it."[36]

◈ The Eighteenth Century: Other "Preaching Women" _____

Although Quakers constituted the overwhelming majority of all clergywomen in colonial and revolutionary America, women of other denominations also preached and pastored. Two historical events empowered them (as well as strengthening women Quaker Public Friends): the First Great Awakening (1730s to 1760s), and the disestablishment of American churches (1777–1833).

The First Great Awakening was one of those periods of intense religiosity that have punctuated American history. In William McLoughlin's definition, awakenings "are periods of cultural revitalization that begin in a general crisis of beliefs and values and extend over a period of a generation or so, during which time a profound reorientation in beliefs and values takes place. Revivals alter the lives of individuals; awakenings alter the world view of a whole people or culture."[37] New England felt the impact of the First Great Awakening most heavily.

During the Awakening revival meetings conducted by itinerating evangelists fanned religious passions and enthusiasm. Most ministers supported these revivals as a source of new members and increased ardor, even while deploring their emotionalism. At some of these meetings at least, people cried out, cast themselves prone, and writhed in agony.[38] Rumor whispered of religious ecstasies extending into sexual raptures. "Our presses are forever teeming with books and our women with bastards," Timothy Cutler alleged.[39] But the indomitable respectability of many of the people who conducted and attended these revivals ensures that most of them were hardly hotbeds of sex. They were, however, social occasions that broke up the monotony of women's lives and inspired them to new religious activity—including preaching.

During the Awakening revival sermons sometimes introduced new doctrines, softening Puritan theology, replacing agonizing fear with hope. In that age of frequent infant deaths, they held out promises of heavenly reunions with their babies to mothers anguished by pulpit threats of infant damnation. Evangelicalism portrayed a gentler, more forgiving deity to women all too accustomed to listening to pulpit misogyny, as in this flight of Cotton Mather: "Poor Daughters of *Eve*, Languishing under your *Special Maladies, Look back* on your *Mother*, the *Woman*, who *being Deceived*, was first *in the Transgression*, that has brought in upon us, *all our Maladies*. Beholding your *Affliction* and your *Misery*, in the midst of your *Lamentations* under it, *Remember that Wormwood and Gall* of the Forbidden Fruit; Lett your

Soul have them still in Remembrance, and *be humbled in you.* Under all your Ails, think, *The Sin of my Mother, which is also my Sin, has brought all this upon me!*"[40]

Although the revivals drew many men into church membership, women continued to outnumber men.[41] By encouraging public prayer and public testimony, even from women, revivals inadvertently set women on a slippery slope toward preaching. They validated the direct religious experience of the individual woman, reinforcing her authority, empowering her. For many a religious woman it was no longer a case of "she for God in him," whether father, husband, or clergyman; she had now found a higher authority.

Women analyzed their own religious feelings in journals, in spiritual autobiographies, and in letters to each other. Instead of a duty to submit to ministerial authority, they perceived a duty to discern ultimate truth for themselves, to choose among competing theologies and churches. They consulted their own consciences and each other rather than the ordained clergy. Esther Burr went so far as to engage in "Smart Combat" with a young minister who tried to prescribe how women should talk.[42] This feminization of religious authority among individual women also impacted churches and clergy. Strengthening women meant weakening the power of the male clergy. Differing with, even criticizing the clergy was no longer confined to martyrs like Anne Hutchinson.

Women's meetings of the kind that had embroiled Hutchinson in so much trouble began to multiply. Starting as gatherings for prayer, they might move on to charitable work or even during the Revolutionary War to political activity.[43] Over time these meetings endowed women with greater self-confidence and more spiritual authority.

Early in the Great Awakening, schoolteacher Puritan Sarah Osborn (1714–1796) helped form such a spiritual sisterhood, which met in her home for 50 years. In the 1760s her leadership during a revival and her reputation for piety attracted hundreds of men and women, especially African-Americans.[44] In a letter to a clergy friend she anguished over whether she might overstep the bounds of religious propriety: "I will begin with the Great [problem] respecting the poor Blacks on Lords day Evenings, which above all the rest Has been Exercising to my Mind." She would willingly hand the meeting over to others, but can find no male to assume this responsibility. Since she cannot get help, she has given up leading in prayer and confines herself to reading to those gathered, talking, and singing psalms or hymns with them. "If any disturbance or disorder Should arise Either to the breaking of Public or family Peace, that would immediately Make the path of duty Plain for dismissing *at once,* but on the contrary Ministers and Magistrates send their Servants and approve."[45] What's a lady to do?

Esther Stoddard Edwards, mother of Jonathan Edwards, who regularly held ladies' meetings in her home, also emerged as a natural leader.

> A table always stood in the middle of her parlor, on which lay a large quarto Bible, and treatises on doctrinal and experimental religion. In the afternoon, at a stated hour, such of the ladies of the neighbourhood, as found it convenient, went customarily to her

house, accompanied not unfrequently by their children. Her daughter regularly read a chapter of the Bible, and then a passage from some religious author, but was often stopped by the comments and remarks of her mother, who always closed the interview with prayer . . . . many of [the women present] . . . dating their first permanent attention to religion from the impression here made. In this way she was regarded with a respect bordering on veneration, and was often spoken of by [the local minister] as one of his most efficient auxiliaries.[46]

By all these means the Great Awakening of the eighteenth century not only empowered laywomen but actually produced "a surprising number of black, Indian, and women preachers and exhorters in the years after 1740," as new converts directed the freedom, energy, and power that conversion brought into the only possible channel of public expression for women, religion.[47]

Beginning about 1777, the disestablishment of American churches broke ground for the constitutional separation of church and state and fertilized the growth of new denominations. For many a woman, piety now involved a choice: Which church should she join? Some of the new denominations in their beginnings were open to women's preaching. So in flux was the situation that within these churches it is almost impossible to distinguish between credentialed and uncredentialed women; the situation approached ordination by inadvertence.

Free Will Baptist women held revival meetings all over New England: among them Mary Savage and Sally Parsons, the latter described as "very useful in the feeble churches." Though it never ordained her, the yearly meeting raised money to purchase horse, bridle, and saddle for her. Such semiauthorized, lay/professional ministries were frequent. At the denomination's Elders' Conference of 1801 of those present eight were ministers and *twenty* unordained preachers and exhorters, of whom three were female.[48] Moravian Anna Nitschman traveled by horseback throughout Pennsylvania as a missionary in the early eighteenth century.[49] Dinah Hardenbergh (1725–1807), a Reformed Pietist minister's wife of the Middle Colonies, interpreted texts and explained doctrine to women, so exemplifying sanctification that in her old age ministers took counsel with her.[50] The doings of Baptist women in Virginia horrified Anglicans, who reported that "Shubal Sterns' sister, Martha, even took to the pulpit and on 'countless occasions melted a whole concourse into tears, by prayers and exhortations.'"[51]

The most sizable group of women preachers in the new denominations was Methodists.[52] Methodists understood "preaching women" differently from Quakers. George Fox, founder of the Friends, believed that inequalities between the genders sprang from original sin, that humans can be redeemed from this fallen condition, and that, once redeemed, women and men are equal. John Wesley, founder of Methodism, did not condone women's ordination. But he needed women to proselytize, to conduct meetings, to teach, especially as the first converts in a community were usually women, and women members remained in the majority. He thought that he could limit what they did, to keep them distinct from the male clergy. So he wrote to Mrs. Sarah Crosby (1729–1804) in 1769: "In public you may properly enough intermix *short exhortations* with prayer; but keep as far from what is called preaching as you can: therefore never take a text; never speak in a continued discourse without some break, about four or five minutes."[53]

As Methodism spread farther afield in Britain and in 1760 to the New World, Wesley authorized women to do more and more, from talking and praying with small groups, to praying in public meetings, to giving testimony of their religious experiences, to exhorting, to expounding, to biblical exegesis, to making applications of biblical teachings. Even in the southern colonies, Methodist women led classes and traveled the country conducting prayer and class meetings, teaching and exhorting other women.[54] Wesley justified their activities by asserting in the 1770s that these women had an "extraordinary" call. Extraordinary cases proved more numerous than he had anticipated.

Particularly from 1781 to 1791, when Wesley died, Methodist women preachers increased in numbers and in power. They came from every class and various occupations. Some were well educated, others barely literate. Many were wives of itinerant male clergy, others single or widowed. Christine Krueger argues that eighteenth-century Methodist women gained a hearing among men by a clever compromise, presenting themselves not as a special-interest group arguing the woman's point of view but as harmless "Mothers in Israel," yet proclaiming a subversive gospel. What's more, she says, in a sense they went beyond Quaker women ministers by proclaiming their right and their duty not merely to deliver God's message received through inspiration but also to interpret scripture.[55]

With Wesley's death, though, and with the institutionalization of the church and the formation of a male hierarchy, the Wesleyan Methodist church cast its women preachers out of its pulpits; by 1803 the situation for most of them had become untenable. Some found a place in other Methodist groups, such as the Primitive Methodists. Some transferred to the Society of Friends. And some were silenced. In George Eliot's *Adam Bede* her admirer Seth wants preacher Dinah to join "a body that 'ud put no bonds on Christian liberty." But Dinah, Adam explains, thinks "it right to set th' example o' submitting, for she's not held from other sorts o' teaching."[56]

✑ The Eighteenth Century: Founders

What of women called to preach and pastor outside the Society of Friends and new denominations such as the Methodists and the Baptists? In the last quarter of the eighteenth century, two remarkable women forged their own paths to ministry.

Mother Mary Ann Lee (1736–1784) and Jemima Wilkinson (1752–1819) apparently never met, but these women had much in common besides being contemporaries. Both came out of the Quaker tradition. Both were visionaries. Both endured persecution. Both believed in celibacy. Both tried to restore or insert into Christianity a missing female element. Without actually claiming divinity, each saw herself as called to carry on the work that Christ had left incomplete. Each claimed the most powerful position within the community she founded.

Wilkinson styled herself the Publick Universal Friend—alias the Universal Friend of Friends, the Friend to all Mankind, the All-Friend, the Best-Friend, or simply The Friend.[57] Early on she exhibited more independence than obedience: at her first call in a New England Quaker meeting she continued to talk even after five Friends had asked her to stop.[58] Read out of meeting when she was fourteen for irregular attendance and not using "plain language," this bright, self-educated woman developed a simple theology based on Quaker principles; preached it in southern New England, Pennsylvania, and New York State; attracted several hundred converts; and after many trials and some mob attacks established a community of believers in western New York.

Soon after the Quakers disowned her, Wilkinson began to preach on short trips around Rhode Island. A miracle, she believed, had shown her specially chosen of God, for after an illness she had died and was mourned and prepared for burial. Just as the funeral procession was about to leave the house, however, she came to life.[59] Gradually she extended her travels, roaming the countryside preaching when and where she could, trusting in divine providence and her followers for her daily bread and shelter. They did well by her. In 1778 one devoted convert gave her the use of his house, then built her a fourteen-room addition. Her followers provided her with monogrammed silverware, special china and pewter, fine furniture, and a white leather and blue velvet sidesaddle with silver stirrups. Her lieutenant and close friend Sarah Richards managed business for her. But Wilkinson accepted no salary and held no real estate in her own name.

Sometimes churches invited her to preach; sometimes she spoke in schoolhouses or barns or groves. Wherever she was, she must have made a striking appearance; contemporary accounts credit her with a good figure, dark expressive eyes, regular features, and curly black hair hanging to her shoulders. She dressed rather like a male cleric, in black or white flowing robes, with a man's white kerchief or cravat around her neck and a large gray felt hat that she doffed to preach, in defiance of the custom that required women to cover their heads.

By 1787 Wilkinson had built a following of at least two hundred and, discouraged with the prospects of saving all of society, was planning to withdraw into her own city on a hill. "I am determined," she said, "not to dwell with revilers for I am weary of them that hate peace."[60] In her ideal community each member was to own her or his own land and work as an individual, but to donate some time and substance to support Wilkinson and her household. She indeed founded the largest community in western New York, with 260 people by 1790 and more preparing to come. Defections, property disputes, and neighborly hostility in 1794 forced Wilkinson and some of her society—particularly its poorer members—to move farther west to plant their New Jerusalem by Crooked Lake (Keuka). There she lived for the rest of her life, this new community growing from twenty-five to several hundred. When she sensed the approach of death, recollecting her "resurrection" as a young woman, she warned followers that she might appear dead, but assured them that she would revive and forbade them to mourn or hold a funeral. Only the natural course of events disillusioned them.[61]

A mystic and visionary, this Publick Universal Friend had chosen her title(s) well. Unlike most prophets, she was honored even within her own family. During the Revolutionary War she numbered among her followers Tories, Yankee soldiers, and pacifists. She recognized no color lines, accepting African-Americans in her community and living in peace with her Native American neighbors. Avoiding doctrinal disputation, she preached an uncomplicated moral gospel. She herself practiced celibacy; so did several of her women followers, and a few men.

Yet a woman preacher, even in the form of a Publick Universal Friend, raised the hackles of the orthodox. Attacks on her and her community from without and within grew more frequent and more legally complicated as her community's property increased in value. Nonetheless, well-off people of good standing continued to support her. When in 1799 her enemies accused her of blasphemy, the judge held blasphemy not indictable and invited her to preach before his court and the people attending. But Wilkinson failed to build a lasting organization. Although the last member of her society survived until 1874, her community fell apart after her death.

Mother Ann Lee, founder of the Shakers (the United Society of Believers in Christ's Second Appearing), had a deeper, wider, more lasting impact.[62] Although she never learned to read or write, her creativity, persistence, and passionate dedication built a community that flourished long after her death under the discipline she had prescribed.

She based this discipline on a naïve interpretation of original sin as sexual intercourse, urging the subduing of lust by intercourse with the divinity. (As John Henry Noyes cogently remarked, "Religious love is very near neighbour to sexual love."[63]) Lee's community both benefited and suffered from her theories. By twentieth-century standards Lee was at once sexually hung up and astonishingly acute in her understanding of gender relationships. Hung up in that she demanded celibacy from all her communicants. Psychologically healthy in that she provided not only for equality of the genders but also for satisfying daily communication between them in joyful dancing, singing, community activities, and talking. They worked and played together, for a common cause, and in the conviction that they were leading virtuous, worthwhile lives.

Possibly, as contemporary evidence suggests, Lee detested sex from her girlhood in England; her position as an elder daughter in a large, poverty-stricken family, bearing heavy responsibilities for the care of her siblings, supports such a likelihood; so does her reluctance to marry. But her disastrous marital experience alone could account for her revulsion. In extraordinarily agonizing births she bore four children, three of whom died as infants and the other at the age of six. Lee decided that God had inflicted these sufferings upon her and her husband as punishment for intercourse—carrying just one step farther contemporary Christian teaching that children's deaths evidenced parental sin.

Lee found release from her anguish in the ecstatic forms of worship developed by former members of the Society of Friends Jane and James Wardley: meditation, confession of sins, preaching by Mother Jane, then walking the floor, chanting, singing, shouting, shaking, and dancing. These "Shaking Quakers" by 1770 were recognizing Lee's vocation, especially after a vision came to her while imprisoned in Bedlam that she was commissioned to complete Christ's work. Inspired by revelation and, no doubt, by a desire to escape the persecutions with which the British government and mobs pursued the Shakers, Mother Ann in 1774 led eight followers, including her husband, from England to the New World.

They landed in New York on the eve of the American Revolution. Most of these industrious people at once found work, Lee herself as a laundress. But clearly New York City with its Revolutionary War fervors was hardly the place for pacifists to settle. Within a year (during which Lee's husband deserted her for earthly delights with another woman), they had found a tract of woods northwest of Albany, Niskeyuna, which they leased in perpetuity. In the spring of 1776 they settled there.

And there they built a thriving community, based on a strict regimen of work and worship. Every decision was taken by the community, for the welfare of the community, women and men participating equally. They divided work between the genders more or less along traditional lines, though women, including Lee, helped to clear their lands. When journalist Charles Nordhoff asked if women were allowed to work as blacksmiths, he was told "No, because this would bring men and women into relations we do not think wise."[64] Whatever its nature, work well done was respected as a tribute to the deity.

Worship became their surcease from labor, their refreshment, their re-creation, their equivalent of secular leisure. In their services the Shakers danced and sang, eventually structuring music and movement into rhythmic chants, step songs, and square order shuffles, in which men and women faced each other in straight lines, advancing, retreating, marching, circling, never touching. Worship renewed their bodies and their spirits; it centered their days.

All this Lee undergirded with a theology positing a four-in-one Godhead, in which the Father and Son of traditional Christianity were balanced and completed by a Mother and Daughter in deity. In Mother Ann, her followers believed, Christ had come again in woman's form. "Some of them say, that the woman called the mother, has the fullness of the God Head, bodily dwelling in her, and that she is the queen of heaven, Christ's wife: And that all God's elect must be born through her; yea, that Christ through her is born the second time."[65] Neither she nor Jesus was divine, but her followers regarded her words as the utterances of Christ. As Shaker Aurelia Mace explained, "To us God is Father *and* Mother and has been from the beginning. Jesus was an inspired man. Ann Lee was an inspired woman. Inasmuch as Jesus became the Christ, so may all be in possession of the same spirit."[66] That spirit, basic good sense, and a knack for memorable utterance shaped Lee's words:

"Put your hands to work and your hearts to God." "Do all your work as though you had a thousand years to live, and as you would if you knew you must die tomorrow." "Do all the good you can, in all the ways you can, as often as you can, to all the people you can." "There is no witchcraft but sin." "You must first establish order within yourself." In answer to a rumor that the world was about to end, "I am only concerned with the end of *worldliness*."[67]

Befriended by Native Americans, persecuted by their white neighbors, the Shakers soon stabilized their community enough to begin itinerating to win converts and establish new colonies. In 1781 Mother Ann set out with five of her followers on a trip that lasted two years and four months. Whatever tolerance American colonists of the period accorded Quakers did not extend to Shakers, whose celibacy seems to have roused special fury. Mobs exercised their cruelties against them; local authorities imprisoned them. Once they were driven like cattle for ten miles, while men whipped them across their faces. Always patient, always forgiving, the Shakers endured all, singing as they were beaten, preaching from their prison windows. Eventually, having founded six new colonies, Lee led her people back to Niskeyuna. But her health was broken, and she died the next year.

The Shakers lived on. Although Ann Lee was immediately succeeded by males, remarkably enough as the denomination became institutionalized it developed a cross-gendered pattern of governance: two elders, two eldresses, two deacons, two deaconesses. Beginning in 1796 Lucy Wright led the faithful through a period of expansion. They peaked in numbers just before the Civil War, when six thousand of them owned more than one hundred thousand acres in nineteen communities spread across New England, Ohio, Kentucky, and Indiana. Lee had built soundly. The system she had constructed did not require extraordinary leaders to operate it. But changing cultures and bad decisions can destroy any system, as when the Shakers cut themselves off from mainstream evangelism by turning to spiritualism.[68]

Clergywomen of the seventeenth and eighteenth centuries, whatever brand of religion they professed, were even more peripatetic and migratory than other Americans. Except for the Quakers who served as ministers in their own meetings, a clergywoman could have a church of her own only if she founded a new sect or denomination. Ironically, during these years when society shuddered at women's speaking in public, it nonetheless allowed clergywomen to preach more readily than it gave them opportunity to pastor. This pattern was to persist until the middle of the nineteenth century. Without the Quakers, clergywomen would hardly have existed. Quaker women, empowered by the "minutes" of their meetings, created the precedents. Both Wilkinson and Lee were rooted in the Quaker tradition.

Notes

    1. Edwin Scott Gaustad, *A Religious History of America*, rev. ed. (New York: Harper & Row, 1990), p. 338.

2. Robert Judson Leach, *Women Ministers: A Quaker Contribution,* ed. Ruth Blattenberger (Wallingford, Penn.: Pendle Hill, 1979), p. 11.

3. See Emery Battis, *Saints and Sectaries: Anne Hutchinson and the Antinomian Controversy in the Massachusetts Bay Colony* (Chapel Hill: Univ. of North Carolina Press, 1962); Jean Cameron, *Anne Hutchinson, Guilty or Not? A Closer Look at Her Trials* (New York: Peter Lang, 1994); William Dunlea, *Anne Hutchinson and the Puritans: An Early American Tragedy* (Pittsburgh: Dorrance, 1993); Elaine C. Huber, *Women and the Authority of Inspiration: A Reexamination of Two Prophetic Movements from a Contemporary Feminist Perspective* (Lanham, Md.: Univ. Press of America, 1985); and Selma R. Williams, *Divine Rebel: The Life of Anne Marbury Hutchinson* (New York: Holt, Rinehart & Winston, 1981).

4. Huber, *Women and the Authority of Inspiration,* p. 1.

5. Battis, *Saints and Sectaries,* p. 116, citing Edward Johnson, *Wonder Working Providence of Sions Saviour in New England, 1628–1651,* ed. J. Franklin Jameson (New York, 1910), p. 127.

6. Williams, *Divine Rebel,* p. 2.

7. Battis, *Saints and Sectaries,* p. 173.

8. Ibid., pp. 242–47, passim.

9. Cameron, *Anne Hutchinson,* p. 215.

10. *Reclaiming the Past, Landmarks of Women's History,* ed. Page Putnam Miller (Bloomington: Indiana Univ. Press, 1992), p. 189; and Joan M. Jensen, *Loosening the Bonds: Mid-Atlantic Farm Women, 1750–1850* (New Haven: Yale Univ. Press, 1986), p. 148.

11. On Quaker women, see Margaret Hope Bacon, *As The Way Opens: The Story of Quaker Women in America* (Richmond, Ind.: Friends United Press, 1980); eadem, *Mothers of Feminism: The Story of Quaker Women in America* (San Francisco: Harper & Row, 1986); Jensen, *Loosening the Bonds;* Leach, *Women Ministers;* Glenna Matthews, *The Rise of Public Woman: Woman's Power and Woman's Place in the United States, 1630–1970* (New York: Oxford Univ. Press, 1992); *The Influence of Quaker Women on American History: Biographical Studies,* ed. Carol and John Stoneburner (Lewiston, N.Y.: Edwin Mellen Press, 1986); and *Witnesses for Change: Quaker Women Over Three Centuries,* ed. Elisabeth Potts Brown and Susan Mosher Stuard (New Brunswick, N.J.: Rutgers Univ. Press, 1989), p. 74.

12. Jensen, *Loosening the Bonds,* p. 146.

13. Ibid., p. 151. See also Susan Hill Lindley, *"You Have Stept Out of Your Place": A History of Women and Religion in America* (Louisville, Ky.: Westminster John Knox, 1996), p. 10; and Jacqueline Field-Bibb in *Women Towards Priesthood: Ministerial Politics and Feminist Praxis* (New York: Cambridge Univ. Press, 1991), pp. 292–93.

14. Gaustad, *Religions History,* p. 85.

15. Quaker Library, Swarthmore College, CRG 5 Turner Family Papers Ser. 2, Journal of Rebecca S. Turner traveling in ministry 1850–51.

16. Bacon, *Mothers of Feminism,* p. 36. See also pp. 169–71.

17. Jensen, *Loosening the Bonds,* p. 150.

18. Ibid., p. 151.

19. Julia Cherry Spruill, *Women's Life and Work in the Southern Colonies* (New York: Norton, 1972), p. 250.

20. The most detailed recent account of Dyer is Ruth Talbot Plimpton's *Mary Dyer: Biography of a Rebel Quaker* (Boston: Branden, 1994).

21. Bacon, *As The Way Opens,* p. 18.

22. *A Call from Death to Life,* ed. G. T. Paine (London, 1660), p. 46, cited by Tucker and Liefeld, *Daughters of the Church,* p. 228.

23. *Influence of Quaker Women,* ed. Stoneburner and Stoneburner, p. 415.

24. Jensen, *Loosening the Bonds,* p. 147.

25. Matthews, *Rise of Public Woman,* p. 45.

26. Jensen, *Loosening the Bonds,* p. 160.

27. Matthews, *Rise of Public Woman,* p. 35.

28. Algie Inman Newlin, *Charity Cook: A Liberated Woman* (Richmond, Ind.: Friends United Press, 1981).

29. Newlin, in *Influence of Quaker Women,* ed. Stoneburner and Stoneburner, pp. 179–80.

30. *Some Account of the Fore-Part of the Life of Elizabeth Ashbridge* (1774) in *Journeys in New Worlds: Early American Women's Narratives,* ed. William L. Andrews et al. (Madison: Univ. of Wisconsin Press, 1990).

31. Ashbridge, *Some Account,* p. 148.

32. Ibid., p. 163.

33. Ibid., p. 155.

34. Ibid., pp. 165–66.

35. Sophia Hume, *An Exhortation to the Inhabitants of the Province of South Carolina* (Philadelphia: B. Franklin and D. Hall, 1774), pp. 3–4, quoted in *Second to None: A Documentary History of American Women,* ed. Ruth Barnes Moynihan, Cynthia Russett, and Laurie Crumpacker (Lincoln: Univ. of Nebraska Press, 1993), 1:145.

36. Quaker Library, Swarthmore College, RG 5 Turner Family Papers Ser. 2, Journal of Rebecca S. Turner traveling in ministry 1850–51.

37. William McLoughlin, *Revivals, Awakenings, and Reform: An Essay on Religion and Social Change in America, 1607–1977* (Chicago: Univ. of Chicago Press, 1978), p. xiii.

38. J. M. Bumsted and John E. Van de Wetering, *What Must I Do to Be Saved? The Great Awakening in Colonial America* (Hinsdale, Ill.: Dryden, 1976), p. 89.

39. Cedric B. Cowing, "Sex and Preaching in the Great Awakening," *American Quarterly* 20/3 [Fall 1968]: 624. Scholars are still debating the occurrence of sexual activity at revivals. Accusations of illicit sex flew as freely around them as accusations of communism during the McCarthy era.

40. Cotton Mather, *The Angel of Bethesda,* ed. Gordon W. Jones (Barre, Mass.: American Antiquarian Society and Barre, 1972), p. 233, quoted in *Second to None,* ed. Moynihan et al., 1:125–26.

The term "evangelicalism" here refers to the teachings that emphasize salvation by faith and reject the efficacy of the sacraments alone; it emphasizes the relationship between God and the individual rather than that between the church and the individual. For a discussion of the development of this slippery term, see Lindley, *"You Have Stept Out of Your Place,"* pp. 323–24.

41. Lindley writes: "the Great Awakening in New England, where women had outnumbered men as church members for decades, actually increased the *proportion* of male members. Yet women still outnumbered men in these churches, and the southern forms of the revival seemed to attract more women than men" (*"You Have Stept Out of Your Place,"* p. 42).

42. *Second to None,* ed. Moynihan et al., 1:123.

43. Ibid., 1:124.

44. Matthews, *Rise of Public Woman,* pp. 42–43; see also Lindley, *"You Have Stept Out of Your Place,"* pp. 45–46.

45. Letter to Rev. Joseph Fish, Feb. 28–Mar 7, 1767, Osborn Collection, American Antiquarian Soc, Worcester, Massachusetts, quoted in *Second to None,* ed. Moynihan et al., 1:147–49.

46. Sereno E. Dwight, "Life of President Edwards," *The Works of President Edwards* (New York: S. Converse, 1829), 1:18, quoted in *Second to None,* ed. Moynihan et al., 1:144.

47. McLoughlin, *Revivals,* p. 75.

48. Donald W. and Lucille Sider Dayton, "Women as Preachers: Evangelical Precedents," *Christianity Today* 19, no. 17: 4; Nancy Hardesty, *Women Called to Witness: Evangelical Feminism in the Nineteenth Century* (Nashville, Tenn.: Abingdon, 1984), p. 102; Tucker and Liefeld, *Daughters of the Church,* p. 259.

49. Cathy Luchetti, *Under God's Spell: Frontier Evangelists, 1772–1915* (New York: Harcourt Brace Jovanovich, 1989), p. 46.

50. Tucker and Liefeld, *Daughters of the Church,* p. 235.

51. Gaustad, *Religious History,* p. 48.

52. For Methodist women preachers in this period, see Paul Wesley Chilcote, *John Wesley and the Women Preachers of Early Methodism* (Metuchen, N.J.: Amer. Theological Library Ass'n and Scarecrow Press, 1991).

53. Earl Kent Brown, "Women of the Word," in *Women in New Worlds: Historical Perspectives on the Wesleyan Tradition,* ed. Hilah F. Thomas and Rosemary Skinner Keller (Nashville, Tenn.: Abingdon, 1981), p. 75.

54. Spruill, *Women's Lives,* p. 248. On the history of women in early American Methodism, see also H. K. Carroll, *The Makers and Making of American Methodism: The Customs, Morals, and Social Conditions of the Pioneer Days drawn from the best Historical Sources. . .* (New York and Cincinnati, 1916); Frederick A. Norwood, "Expanding Horizons: Women in the Methodist Movement," in *Triumph Over Silence: Women in Protestant History,* ed. Richard L. Greaves (Westport, Conn.: Greenwood, 1985); and Gaustad, *Religious History,* p. 50.

55. Christine L. Krueger, *The Reader's Repentance: Women Preachers, Women Writers, and Nineteenth-Century Social Discourse* (Chicago: Univ. of Chicago Press, 1992), pp. 5, 82.

56. George Eliot, *Adam Bede* (London: Thomas Nelson, n.d.), pp. 586–87.

57. Herbert A. Wisbey, Jr., *Pioneer Prophetess: Jemima Wilkinson, The Publick Universal Friend* (Ithaca, N.Y.: Cornell Univ. Press, 1964), p. 35.

58. Jensen, *Loosening the Bonds,* p. 156.

59. Hannah Whitall Smith, *Religious Fanaticism,* ed. Ray Strachey (London: Faber & Gwyer, 1928), p. 48.

60. Wisbey, *Pioneer Prophetess,* p. 98.

61. Smith, *Religious Fanaticism,* p. 50.

62. On the life of Ann Lee, see, among others, D'Ann Campbell, "Women's Life in Utopia: The Shaker Experiment in Sexual Equality Reappraised—1810 to 1860," *New England Quarterly* 51/1 (March 1978): 23–38; Nardi Reeder Campion, *Ann the Word: The Life of Mother Ann Lee, Founder of the Shakers* (Boston: Little, Brown, 1976); *Second to None,* ed. Moynihan et al.; and *Women and Religion in America,* ed. Rosemary R. Ruether and Rosemary S. Keller, 3 vols. (San Francisco: Harper & Row, 1981, 1983, 1986). Twentieth-century scholarship rests on such early evidence as Benjamin S. Young, *The Testimony of Christ's Second Appearing* (1808); and *Testimonies of the Life, Character, Revelations, and Doctrines of Our Blessed Mother Ann Lee,* comp. Rufus Bishop and Seth Y. Wells (1816).

63. Ann Lee said, "I have been in fine vallies with Christ as a lover. I am married to the Lord Jesus Christ. He is my head and my husband, and I have no other!" (Campion, *Ann the Word,* p. 44).

64. Campbell, "Women's Life," p. 26. Campbell's fascinating study concludes that the Shakers did indeed achieve a remarkably high degree of success in realizing their ideal of gender equality.

65. 1780 report, quoted in Tucker and Liefeld, *Daughters of the Church,* pp. 275–76.

66. Campion, *Ann the Word,* p. 43.

67. Ibid., pp. 50, 70, 138, 139, 168, 140.

68. Campbell, "Women's Life," p. 37. Susan Hill Lindley suggests, however, that "the period of Spiritualist revival further enhanced the roles of women leaders . . . and drew the female aspect of godhead, Holy Mother Wisdom, into greater prominence" (*"You Have Stept Out of Your Place,"* p. 255). Marjorie Procter-Smith notes that theologically after Lee's death Shakerism developed gender-specific spiritual roles for women and associated them with the origins of sin, even while "the balanced male-female leadership system . . . promoted some women into positions of power and authority, at the cost of the religious autonomy of all Shaker women" ("'In the Line of the Female': Shakerism and Feminism," in *Women's Leadership in Marginal Religions: Explorations Outside the Mainstream,* ed. Catherine Wessinger [Urbana: Univ. of Illinois Press, 1993], pp. 28–31).

2

Crosscurrents
1800–1853 🦅

IN THE FIRST HALF OF THE NINETEENTH CENTURY, in a young nation just actualizing its independence, crosscurrents were at once propelling women into the clergy and pushing them away. The Second Great Awakening (1795–1835) was in full swing, and religious feeling ran high. Mainstream culture still defined itself in terms of Protestant Christianity; people taught their children to form their ambitions in terms of Protestant values; and society paid at least lip service to Protestant ideals. As Alexis de Tocqueville wrote, Christianity exercised "a greater influence over the souls of men" in America than anywhere else. Everyone agreed that women must help to propagate and perpetuate the faith but heatedly disagreed about just how they could be allowed to function.

The ideal of Republican Motherhood, which sprang up around the American Revolution, had emphasized women's role as mothers, displacing the earlier concept of women as primarily "Good Wives." Republican Mothers were to raise their sons as virtuous, informed American citizens; their daughters as virtuous, informed American Republican Mothers. Now the nineteenth-century concepts of True Womanhood and Separate Spheres were engendered by the industrialization then being launched, towing in its wake a shift in values from spiritual to economic welfare and a shift in middle-class women's roles from producers to consumers and dispensers of charity. As men went out to work in their new worlds of business and politics, they perforce spent less time at home and in church. The solution? Separate spheres, offering her the governance of the home and a reputation for moral superiority, him the exclusive control of business and politics. The True Woman would be a self-abnegating wife and mother, bearing the responsibility for child-rearing, family virtue, and family religion. She would embody the virtues of piety, purity, submission, and domesticity. "Everything valuable in human society," wrote pamphleteer Charles Hammond, "depends upon the veneration with which female chastity is regarded . . . . were it not for the influence, which that almost angelic quality exercises over the minds of men, the most polished society would . . . degenerate into a despicable state of barbarism."[1] All this reinforced bans on women's speaking publicly, certainly not as clergy.

But, powerfully as this ethos operated in keeping women silent, passive, and accepting of men's decisions, in its realization every fantasy has its dark, satanic side effect. Some True Women assumed that the moral superiority attributed to them ought to and indeed did lead to moral authority, which entitled them to a voice in all matters moral—and what isn't?[2]

This maddening ambiguity manifested itself at every turn. The religious education of the young was a duty of the True Woman, clearly within her private sphere. In 1801 New Yorker Joanna Graham Bethune brought back from Scotland enthusiastic reports on the potential of Sabbath Schools to save the souls of children. When ministers failed to respond, she took her husband's advice: "My dear wife, there is no use in waiting for the men; do you gather a few ladies of different denominations, and begin the work yourselves."[3] In 1816 Bethune established the Female Union for the Promotion of Sabbath Schools. And in 1838 Rebecca Gratz (1781–1869) started schools on the same pattern among American Jewish congregations.[4]

All these religious schools demanded the services of myriads of volunteer women to teach the word of God outside the home as part of their religious duty. As Ann Douglas has pointed out, with the growth of the Sunday School movement, most children learned their religious ABCs not from a minister but from a laywoman. Some clergy were unperturbed; when Mrs. Ann Rhees asked her Baptist pastor whether she could start a Sunday School, he replied, "Well, my sister, you can but try it: blossoms are sweet and beautiful, even if they produce no fruit." But the elders in Medway, Massachusetts, were not entirely off the mark when they grumbled: "These women will be in the pulpit next."[5] Indeed, as an institution the Sunday School reinforced the idea that religious education was/is mainly a woman's business. In the twentieth century it would give rise to a new profession inhabited largely by women, as directors of religious education—many of whom are now ordained ministers.

Similarly the concept of True Womanhood prescribed church activities for women. The more the women conformed, the more likely they were to stray into areas technically reserved to the clergy. Pious women attended not only Sunday services but also midweek prayer meetings, where their prayers and testimonies veered dangerously close to preaching. In the African Methodist Episcopal Church women organized all-female prayer bands, and some black churches licensed (but did not ordain) women preachers.[6]

The denominational changes of the early nineteenth century were as forceful in keeping women out of the pulpit as the ideas of True Womanhood and Separate Spheres. The early evangelical denominations were becoming institutionalized and in the process were transferring power from women religious leaders to male hierarchies. Baptists were transforming their church from an egalitarian sect into a patriarchal denomination, excluding women from participation in church governance and feminizing sin.[7] Methodists, who had earlier depended on women evangelists to spread their gospel, in 1800 officially banned women from their pulpits.

And yet even in the conservative South, where by 1800 Anglicanism had been overrun by evangelical Methodists, Baptists, and Presbyterians, women evangelized as missionaries and in their own communities. Some bethought themselves of the slaves: in 1825 Ann Page Randolph recognized a solemn Christian duty to care for both their bodies and their souls.[8] A number of Methodist women continued to preach or later accepted a divine call to the ministry after the official ban. Although they were seldom credentialed, their preaching was not only tolerated but, in the case of itinerating evangelists, often invited.

African-American women, both freewomen and slaves, preached. Throughout American history, it seems that, proportionally to their distribution in the population, more black women than white have preached and pastored. C. Eric Lincoln and Lawrence H. Mamiya have persuasively pointed to the influence of African religions and to the strong oral tradition in the African-American community as contributing to this phenomenon.[9] And, we would suggest, the independence, the can-do attitude that manifested itself in Nanny Burroughs and in Mary McLeod Bethune also showed up among preaching women, however much church and society tried to still their voices.

Almost certainly, women slaves preached in secret services in their homes or in the woods.[10] Volunteer black workers of both genders assisted white Methodist missionaries to slaves—black women naturally taking on this work because of the participation they had enjoyed in African religions.[11] From 1816 to 1849, though none was licensed or ordained, a number of African-American women were preaching more or less professionally—sometimes under the guise of ushers, elders, or deaconesses. Midweek prayer meetings and their own "prayer bands" offered them opportunities to testify and exhort.[12] Sophie Murray was described as the first evangelist of her African Methodist Episcopal (AME) church in Philadelphia. Elizabeth Cole converted many through her prayer meetings. Rachel Evans of New Jersey was "a preacheress of no ordinary ability." In Washington, D.C., Harriet Felson Taylor "distinguished herself as the First Female Exhorter and Local Preacher" of Union Bethel Church.[13] Though we know almost nothing else about these individuals, Jean Humez's intensive study has given us a composite portrait of nineteenth-century preaching women of the AME church: hardworking, intensely respectable, dissatisfied with marriage and family life, ambitious to better themselves but restricted by lack of opportunities for education and work.[14]

Freeborn African-American itinerant Zilpha Elaw (b. 1790) reported much acceptance and many invitations to preach from male clergy, even in the slaveholding states.

> [At a camp meeting] I began as it were involuntarily, or from an internal prompting, with a loud voice to exhort the people who yet were remaining near the preacher's stand; and in the presence of a more numerous assemblage of ministers than I had ever

seen together before; as if God had called forth witnesses from this day to my commission, and the qualifications He bestowed on me to preach his holy Gospel.

The ministers at her feet wept at her words, she records, and when she returned home and told the ministers there of her call to preach, they encouraged her, seeing no impropriety in it.[15]

Even more striking on the score of clerical acceptance is the history of African-American Jarena Lee (b. 1783).[16] When her visions persuaded her that God wanted her to preach, she approached Richard Allen, founder and bishop of the African Methodist Episcopal church. Allen disapproved, and she tried unsuccessfully to settle down as a minister's wife. Several years later, she was in church when the minister faltered and "seemed to have lost the spirit." She sprang up and took over, exhorting on his text, and comparing herself to Jonah, who had delayed in doing God's bidding. Her sermon persuaded Bishop Allen that she was called of God to preach. With his blessing Lee itinerated, covering many a weary mile, always preaching "Life and Liberty": in 1827 alone, she traveled 2,325 miles on foot and by wagon, ferryboat, and carriage, and delivered 178 sermons. She believed it better, she said, "to wear out than to rust out."[17] Rightly or wrongly, she described herself as "the first female preacher of the First African Methodist Episcopal Church." Apparently she based this claim on an agreement with the AME hierarchy that she would serve not as a licensed preacher but as an official traveling exhorter.

In the AME church exhorters were lowest in the preaching hierarchy; they were supposed to have permission before addressing individual congregations. They could lead Sunday School classes and prayer meetings, but in church services they usually spoke at the sufferance of the presiding minister and only in response to the biblical text selected for the day. Elaw and Lee of course went far beyond these limitations.[18]

The continuing vitality of Mother Ann Lee's teachings inspired African-American Rebecca Jackson (1795–1871).[19] Jackson was a free married woman, a seamstress, residing in Philadelphia, associated with the AME church through her pastor brother, with whom she and her husband lived and whose four children she tended. But neither then nor at any other time until she joined the Shakers did Jackson affiliate with any formal religious group, though she regularly attended weekly prayer groups of women.[20] In July 1835, the spiritual conversion so important in the Methodist tradition struck this visionary woman with a force that changed her life's course. Promising God to obey her inner voice, she thereafter invited mystic experiences by fasting during the first three days of each week and by depriving herself of sleep.

Women's praying bands had prepared her for this religious experience and perhaps inspired her to preach. Undoubtedly the Holiness movement so prominent in the Methodist tradition also helped to shape her conversion. This movement postulated two intense experiences of divine grace, the first "justification," in which the individual came to know that through the love of Christ her sins were forgiven and she was made just; the second "sanctification," which freed her from "intentional sin" (knowingly committed sin) and in that sense made her "perfect." A heady, empowering experience for anyone, and available to anyone, woman or man, black or white. To Jackson sanctification came during a neighborhood revival, a few months after her justification.

Jean M. Humez suggests that conversion experiences like Jackson's have enabled black women to control the anger and fear induced by racism. Once having carefully tested these experiences to assure that they were not of Satan but of God, they felt assured of divine protection against physical danger from both natural and human sources, inspired with the courage to speak before audiences not only gender-mixed but racially mixed.[21]

So transformed, Jackson now transformed her life. Though married, she felt that she must practice celibacy, for her body was no longer her own, but the vessel of the divine will. If she owned the earth, she said, she would willingly give it all away to become a single woman again.[22] She started a small weekly meeting to encourage family members to testify. In 1833 she defied the policy of the AME church, as well as other forms of Methodism, by beginning a preaching career. Breaking with both her husband and her pastor brother, for the rest of her life she lived and traveled with her friend and disciple Rebecca Perot.[23]

Jackson's itinerant ministry almost immediately attracted enthusiastic crowds. She also attracted hostility—not surprisingly, since she preached against the "carnality" of churches and their failure to teach "holy living," including celibacy. Without joining any church, she said, human beings could attain salvation through deliberate resistance to sin and reliance on divine grace.[24] She was accused of "chopping up the churches" and presuming to teach men, and three ministers threatened to excommunicate those who offered her their homes for her meetings. Some ministers felt she "ought not to live."[25] AME Bishop Morris Brown came to her defense: "If ever the Holy Ghost was in any place, it was in that meeting."[26] Nevertheless in 1837 she was accused of heresy. Church leaders refused her request for a formal interdenominational trial at her own home with a jury including five or six ministers who could read *and* some "mothers of the church"—laywomen whose conduct had won them authority as spiritual leaders.

In 1840 Jackson and Perot joined an interracial group of religious perfectionists near Albany, where she had been preaching. They led her to the Shakers, who were as impressed with her as she with them. So many things fitted: they agreed on celibacy, female leadership, and the importance of ecstatic, visionary communication with God. But by about 1850 living with the Shakers convinced Jackson of the desirability of founding a separate, predominantly black Shaker colony. Even though they admired and respected her as a prophet, the Shakers hesitated and eventually denied her permission. But in 1858 they changed their minds, granting her both their approval and their legal and financial backing. In Philadelphia, Jackson and Perot then established their predominantly African-American Shaker colony, which lasted for some forty years.

Even Quaker women ministers of the early nineteenth century felt the strictures that institutionalized religions were placing on women. Thanks in large part to the theology of its founder, the Society of Friends had escaped the pattern common among Christian denominations since their earliest days, whereby institutionalization has resulted in limiting women's roles. But now some Friends meetings were withdrawing from the world in favor of looking after the spiritual welfare of their own members. Elders grew more censorious, more authoritarian. The several schisms that beset the society during this period betrayed its aging by focusing on such issues as individual conscience versus institutional authority, paying clergy, and allowing women to preach.

On the last score one woman declared that a woman "ought to be better qualified to direct the spiritual life of her own sex than any belov'd disciple or even Jesus himself as a man or a brother."[27] Some male Quakers did not agree. British Evangelical Friend Joseph John Gurney touring the United States in 1837 "noted with some alarm that there were more women than men in the ministry, and he thought the balance ought to be rectified since 'the stronger sex' ought to fight the battles of the Lord, and not leave them to women 'whose physical weakness and delicacy have an obvious *tendency* to render them less fit for combat.'"[28] Quaker men like Gurney succeeded in silencing some women clergy, for example, Hannah Jenkins Barnard (1754?–1825), but not others, such as Lucretia Coffin Mott (1793–1880).

In 1800 Barnard, by then an experienced minister of at least seven years, was itinerating in England with her fellow American Elizabeth Coggeshall. Barnard's views provoked a charge of heresy from the London Yearly Meeting, which, after fourteen months of trials, censured her beliefs and sent her home. Doubtless Barnard's criticism of the Anglo-French war contributed to the unfavorable verdict, which faulted her asserting her right to think and believe independently and condemned her for "a caviling, contentious disposition of mind, disclaiming the authority of the monthly meeting."[29] In the trial that followed before her local meeting, Barnard defended herself spiritedly, circulating her opinions as a book and informing one of her examiners that he had no right to judge her without reading it. The meeting nevertheless disowned her, whereupon, said a commentator, she "betook herself of useful domestic pursuits."[30]

As a girl, Lucretia Mott heard Barnard's companion Elizabeth Coggeshall preach.[31] That occasion typified the experiences of her youth. A "birthright" Quaker (born into the faith), she was nurtured in the Quaker stronghold of Nantucket, where strong women with seagoing husbands managed families and finances on their own. Her father, a sea captain turned school superintendent and an ardent abolitionist, supported equal education for women. "I grew up," she said, "so thoroughly imbued with women's rights that it was the most important question of my life from a very early day."[32] Known as a spitfire early in her life, she matured into a feminist self-confident not only about her abilities but also about her understanding of Quakerism.

Accordingly, her expectations and her career differed from those of most women of her time. Immensely energetic despite her shaky health, she was one of the first American women to "have it all." She read William Penn and Mary Wollstonecraft while she nursed her babies. Her mother a shopkeeper, she herself before her marriage a teacher, Mott took it for granted that she would earn money when necessity pressed. Her intense and expert domesticity within both her nuclear and her extended families protected her against the usual allegations of neglecting women's proper work. Even in a time of schism her family history helped her to confront Quaker disapproval with relative impunity. But most of all her serenity enabled her to speak up for her convictions: she remained calm in the face of rioters and threats to burn down her house.

In 1811 she married James Mott, a quiet, intelligent man, with whom she had six children. He not only respected her abilities and shared her beliefs but also publicly supported her. When Lucretia preached against the use of slave products, James took the financial risk of boycotting them in his business. When Lucretia criticized a well-known minister in a public meeting, the gentleman turned questioningly to James, who said mildly, "If she thinks thee wrong, thee had better think it over again."[33]

In 1818 she began her ministry, which the Quakers officially recorded in 1821. She itinerated (sometimes without a chaperone), organized, and repeatedly served as clerk of the Philadelphia women's yearly meeting, though whenever she had a new baby she confined her ministry to near home.

Her career as a minister involved her in secular causes. She grew so accustomed to speaking in Quaker meetings against slavery that at the 1833 Philadelphia anti-slavery convention, to which only six women were invited, to her own surprise she spoke. She organized a local female antislavery society, which soon moved into protesting publicly and petitioning the government. She took her oldest daughter with her to the 1837 first national women's antislavery convention in New York, attended by both black and white women. Yes, she there insisted, the Grimké sisters were right to lecture against slavery, even before an audience of men.[34] She was undeterred by Quaker allegations that she was substituting good causes for true religion and an attack from Quaker minister George White, who said he would rather be a slave than an abolitionist. In 1840 the Motts attended the World Anti-Slavery Convention in London, where Lucretia failed to win permission for women to participate—but the women watched and listened. And there she and Elizabeth Cady Stanton met, took counsel, and agreed to form an organization to promote women's rights. From this world convention Mott emerged as a major figure in both abolition and women's rights.

By now she was mixing itinerating and reform work, for she understood religion and these causes to be intertwined. Opposition she confronted in plenty, both from mobs and from Quaker authorities. Quaker minister Rachel Barker preached against her at the Philadelphia Yearly Meeting for more than an hour—and Mott preached back for another. Someone tampered with her carriage; inns refused her service. But she spoke against slavery both at Quaker meetings and before the state legislatures of Delaware, New Jersey, and Pennsylvania. The House of Representatives refused to hear her, but in 1843 she preached in a Unitarian church to an audience that included forty congressmen. After October 1843, the Quakers frequently denied her a hearing and would no longer issue her traveling "minutes" approving her trips, but Mott continued her travels and her ministry.

Her religion liberalized. She knew every word of the Bible; she thought deeply and independently; and she learned from experience. In 1848 at an antislavery convention, she voiced her belief in many messiahs, of whom Jesus was one. The next year she told medical students:

> I confess to you, my friends, that I am a worshipper after the way called heresy, a believer after the manner many deem infidel. While at the same time my faith is firm in the blessed, the eternal doctrine preached by Jesus and by every child of God since the creation of the world, especially the great truth that God is the teacher of his people himself; the doctrine that Jesus most emphatically taught, that the kingdom is with man, that there is his sacred and divine temple.

Religion, she held, must not be constricted by the forms of the past, for orthodoxy and bigotry shut people off from their own inner light. Worship for her consisted in seeking and obeying the divine will, speaking from the inspiration that came from the love and reason implanted by God within her. She denounced "King and Priest Craft"; asserted that "Protestantism was only a modification, not a thorough reform of superstition"; and advocated "religion based on faith in the perfectability of men and patterned after Christ's example of doing good." By 1857 she was preaching against monopolies and urging a search for the causes of poverty. She eventually persuaded the Free Religious Association, a group of Christians and Jews dedicated to religious reform, that they should interest themselves not in the "scientific study of theology" but in the scientific study of the religious nature of human beings.[35]

Though she boggled at demanding woman suffrage, Mott's understanding of women's rights implied women's participation in public affairs. She advised Quakers working among Native Americans to consult the squaws before making changes in their society—an idea that her listeners regarded as facetious.

Mott's intellect, her position in Quaker society, her outspokenness, and her legendary hospitality won her many friends. Her roster of guests included John Quincy Adams, the political economist Harriet Martineau, the schoolmistress Prudence Crandall (martyred for teaching black women), William Lloyd Garrison, the astronomer Maria Mitchell, and the evangelist Sojourner Truth.

Mott planned to retire at sixty, but she could not. At seventy-six she preached of her faith in the progress of humanitarian concerns, chaired sessions of the Equal Rights Association, and helped to found Swarthmore College. At seventy-seven she undertook to speak in all the black churches of Philadelphia. In her eighties she did consent to cut down on trips to conventions, but she continued to chair the Philadelphia peace society. The spitfire reemerged, and she turned into a difficult, feisty old lady. "I'm a much over-rated woman," she said. "It's humiliating."[36] She wouldn't stick with the diet prescribed for her queasy stomach; she wouldn't use an umbrella; she insisted on traveling alone. If Eleanor Roosevelt had a spiritual foremother, surely it was Lucretia Mott.

Yet throughout their active lives Rebecca Jackson, Hannah Barnard, Lucretia Mott, and their sister clergywomen in all denominations suffered the slings and arrows shot from the bows of those who opposed women's full participation in religious life. They had to flout the restrictions of conservatism, brought on by economic shifts, the emergence of the "ideals" of Separate Spheres and True Womanhood, and above all the institutionalization of churches induced by denominational hardening of the arteries.

☙ Spinning Forward: Disestablishment, Denominational Shifts, and Prayer Bands

But equally strong currents, some of them woman-made, were impelling clergywomen forward.

Eighteenth-century trends toward the feminization of religion did not abate in the nineteenth. Women's proportional representation in church membership continued to grow, swelled in part by the revivals of the Second Great Awakening, which attracted more women than men. Women who had been converted at revivals proselytized among their women friends, further strengthening the feminine majority. At their school Catharine Beecher and Harriet Beecher (Stowe) actively encouraged proselytizing among their students, who even after graduation wrote to check on each other's religious health. Biographer Joan Hedrick comments: "If this peer outreach system had the virtue of impressing the evangelical character of religion upon neophytes, it also had obvious implications for *women* as ministers of the word. In the [Beechers'] Hartford Female Seminary every woman was a potential Christian and lay minister. The most radical aspect of this system—which in effect takes Protestantism to its logical completion—was that it undermined male clerical authority."[37]

As the disestablishment of the churches (1777–1833) sapped clergymen's authority, security, and status, they turned for support to the women who constituted most of their congregations.[38] No longer able to rely on state-supported funding, the clergy had to depend on the goodwill of the laity. What's more, the separation of church and state cut them off from political power. In the bustling new young republic of the United States, the stress on business acumen and accomplishment was also undermining ministerial power and status. On matters where earlier they could forbid and denounce, now they had to persuade. In fact, patriarchy generally wasn't what it used to be. The economy and culture that sent men out of the home strengthened women's power within it. Churches themselves had rattled the bars by telling women that indeed they ought to obey their husbands/fathers *except* in matters of duty to God and church. When conscience pricked, saying no to one's minister was surely no harder than saying no to one's father or husband.

As the nation divided on the question of slavery, Christian women found themselves at odds with ministers. Just such a conflict involved those southern gentlewomen Sarah and Angelina Grimké in a confrontation with male clergy not only about slavery but also about the inextricably intertwined issue of women's rights.[39] When as a matter of conscience these formerly slave-owning women publicly lectured against slavery, the Congregational ministers of Massachusetts in 1837 denounced the behavior of women "who so far forget themselves as to itinerate in the character of public lecturers and teachers" and predicted their downfall "in shame and dishonor into the dust." Thirty-nine students and faculty of Andover Theological Seminary followed suit by pontificating that "the public lectures of females we have discountenanced and condemned as improper and unwise."[40]

Male clergy could read the handwriting on the wall. They could do little to protect themselves against disestablishment and economic shifts. But some of them perceived putting down unruly women as a moral imperative and a necessary defense of their own prerogatives and their own views. Thus, from the outset of the nineteenth-century struggle for woman's rights, a sizable number of clergymen aligned themselves against it.

While ministerial moral authority waned, that of laywomen waxed, and the idea of themselves becoming ministers entered the heads of more women.[41] Women found a way to participate in theological controversy through their novels.[42] That barometer of public sentiment, the popular literature of the day manifested attitudes unthinkable for an Anne Hutchinson. The Quaker heroine of Eliza B. Lee's 1848 novel *Naomi* daringly defied pastoral advice: "I must live by my faith," she said, "not that of my church." In her 1854 book *Bertha and Lily* Elizabeth Oakes Smith told the story of a young woman who first exercised her freedom of choice by opting for a liberal minister rather than an orthodox one and wound up by herself becoming pastor of an independent congregation.[43]

Precisely. Questioning of churchly authority on the grounds of individual conscience or direct communication with divinity has always been the bedrock of women's demands for equality as clergy. Whenever or wherever churches make individuals responsible for their own moral welfare by insisting not that they merely follow regulations but that they themselves distinguish right from wrong, good from evil, sooner or later some members will defy the rules of that institution.

Churches themselves were changing, as a new theology emerging from nineteenth-century liberalism argued not only the possibility but the necessity of making an egalitarian heaven on earth by social reform. By its original nature, the argument ran, Christianity embodied the idea of the spiritual equality of all believers. History had corrupted that nature; its effects must be corrected and spiritual equality restored—a spiritual equality that might include the extension of ordination to women.[44]

Other internal phenomena and choices were inadvertently softening if not crumbling church prohibitions against women clergy. Churches were asking more from their women members, whether in raising money, offering testimony, or teaching Sunday School. From performing "ministerial" duties to demanding official validation was one short step for individual women, one giant step for womankind.

Denominations split, with one group accepting and the other refusing women preachers: in 1815, for instance, whereas most Baptist churches excluded women from their pulpits, Free Will Baptists licensed Clarissa H. Danforth to preach.[45] Other disaffected Protestants founded new sects that at least in their early days welcomed the leadership of women. In the Christian Church, for instance, Nancy Grove Cram (1776–1816) ministered to the Oneida Native Americans, held revivals, and organized a church. Abigail Roberts (b. 1791), one of Cram's converts, itinerated as a gospel preacher.[46]

Noted women preachers appeared in some older churches, such as the Universalists. Sally Barnes Dunn (1783–1858) of Maine was said to excel her clergyman father in clarity and logic. Maria Cook (1779–1835), usually considered the first woman to preach in Universalist pulpits, began holding religious meetings in Pennsylvania about 1810. Universalist societies showered her with invitations, and she was tendered an informal letter of fellowship—which she eventually destroyed because she doubted the sincerity with which it had been offered. A clergyman, ascribing her popularity to the novelty of hearing a woman speak in public, commented: "Difficult as many found it, to reconcile the ministry of Miss Cook, with their ideas of duty and propriety . . . they still accord her their sympathy and their hospitality."[47] But others so violently opposed her preaching that her friends feared lest it be made grounds for an accusation of insanity. In fact, her arrest as a vagrant in Cooperstown, New York, ended her brief career.[48]

In 1832 the national Presbyterian assembly officially approved pious women's meetings for conversation and prayer—just the sort of meetings that got Anne Hutchinson into so much trouble, the sort from which Rebecca Jackson launched her preaching career. One thing led to another, and the next thing they knew in 1836 the Presbyterians were having to deal with allegations of "a Female preaching in the Congregation of Pittsburgh, with the consent & authority of the [local] Session."[49]

J. Gordon Melton credits the Primitive Methodists with a visit from "the first female licensed preacher in America," the British Ruth Watkins.[50] Other Methodists discovered the potential of women's meetings in the life and work of the evangelist "Elizabeth," an African-American we know only from her own story.[51]

This narrative was one of the spiritual autobiographies common in the period; they must be used with care. Illiteracy forced some authors to rely on the services of another person, the extent of whose intervention it is difficult to judge. The autobiographies tended to conform to a blueprint, laying out a pattern of conviction of sinfulness and unworthiness, visions, and conversion. Typically they paid little attention to facts that their authors considered irrelevant to their spiritual development or to converting others. Marilyn Richardson remarks that they had little interest in describing their lives before conversion except as negative moral object lessons.[52] They defined "truth" in spiritual rather than objective terms. The rigid form that they early developed governed the perceptions of many a convert about what happened to her spiritually, and thus the perceptions of many a subsequent author. Reading a series of these autobiographies can be a numbing experience; however, Elizabeth's auctorial voice is poetic and occasionally witty.

Born in slavery in 1766, Elizabeth reportedly lived to be 101, writing her autobiography at ninety-seven. When at eleven she was sent away from her Methodist parents, her mother told her that she had "nobody in the wide world to look to but God." So when an overseer whipped her, she turned to God: "I mourned sore like a dove and chattered forth my sorrow, moaning in the corners of the field, and under the fences."[53] Her sufferings and her fears of dying "unsaved" brought on an elaborate vision of hell and heaven, the conviction that she was forgiven, and the belief that she must call people to repent. For a year she lived joyfully, communing with God daily, but then stopped—a kind of backsliding common in spiritual autobiographies. Being sold to a stranger jolted her into resuming her prayers, and she enjoyed new visions of where she was to preach. At about the age of thirty she was set free by a Presbyterian master who did not believe in life enslavement.

At forty-two she knew that the time had come for her to preach. How could she, when her near illiteracy kept her from understanding the scriptures? God sent her to a widow who lived in one of the worst streets in Baltimore, in whose home she held a prayer meeting with her African-American sisters, to whom she preached. When a watchman interrupted with complaints about the noise they were making, she told him that a good racket was better than a bad. Why was he molesting her and her sisters for praising God? The watchman backed off, apologized, and wished them success, but the less generous elders of their church forbade their assemblies. Elizabeth was not afraid and would continue, but her sisters grew cold.

Rejected by the elders, hunted down wherever she arranged a meeting, she felt "despised on account of this gracious calling, and was looked upon as a speckled bird by the ministers to whom I looked for instruction, and to whom I resorted every opportunity for the same; but when I would converse with them, some would cry out, 'You are an enthusiast,' and others said, 'the Discipline did not allow of any such division of the work,' until I began to think I surely must be wrong." But "I did not faint under discouragement but pressed on."[54]

She did indeed, until she was ninety, traveling at the dictate of the Spirit, preaching to whites as well as blacks, arguing theology with white ministers, establishing a school in Michigan for colored orphans. When officials in Virginia threatened her with imprisonment, asking her whether she was ordained, she answered, "Not by the commission of men's hands: if the Lord has ordained me, I need nothing better."[55]

❧ Spinning Forward: The Missionary Movement _____

If women's prayer meetings now and then spawned a preacher, women's missionary societies, which began to form at least as early as 1800, tapped women's energies both as volunteers and as professionals. As volunteers women found public roles, made acceptable by the association with religion. Here too they learned to pray aloud, to conduct meetings, to take group decisions, and to raise and eventually manage money.[56] Although originally these societies raised money solely for men to disburse in the support of male missionaries, reports from the mission field soon convinced church boards of the need of sending women. While it was obvious that in foreign lands as in the United States women's religious attitudes often determined the religiosity of their families, in many countries taboos shut native women off from male missionaries.[57] What's more, the boards came to feel, single male missionaries ran into trouble.

At first Americans, reeling at the idea of sending single women into alien cultures and untamed frontiers, thought to solve these problems through missionary wives, and dedicated young women began to think about saving the world by marrying missionaries.

> Sarah Huntington of Norwich began her missionary career in 1827 by trekking through the snow to near-by Mohegan Indian homes. She helped them build a church and served as their teacher before she married the Reverend Eli Smith in 1833. It was a choice she made deliberately in order to fulfill her dream of becoming a foreign missionary. They went to Syria in 1833 where Sarah Huntington Smith, before she died a year later, established the first school for young women in the Middle East.[58]

A few years earlier, twenty-two-year-old Ann Judson and eighteen-year-old Harriet Newall had similar goals in mind when in 1812 they married missionaries and sailed off in the first contingent destined for the Orient. Harriet died the next year. The Judsons, narrowly escaping deportation from India, where they had first landed, went to Rangoon, burying their first child at sea. In remote areas of Burma they labored unavailingly, waiting four years for their first convert, and in nine years persuading only seventeen others to give up Buddhism for Christianity. Another child died. Adoniram Judson was imprisoned on suspicion of spying. Ann staggered along, eking out a living as best she could, following her husband from one prison to another, nursing a third child through smallpox, enduring one illness after another. She died of tropical fever at thirty-six.[59]

Other idealistic young women married—sometimes men they barely knew—in order to serve as "home missionaries." Eager to win the west for Protestant Christianity, Congregationalists and Presbyterians sent their forces to the Oregon Territory. Narcissa Prentiss Whitman (1808–1847), Eliza Hart Spalding (1807–1851), and four other missionaries in 1836 became the first white American women to cross the Continental Divide.[60] The journey west was a prolonged nightmare. Poor pregnant Mary Walker, afflicted with diarrhea and fears about her marriage, wondering whether she would survive hardships and childbirth, rode sidesaddle for up to forty-five miles a day. This prodigal "cried to think how comfortable father's hogs were." Whitman's missionary career was a disaster: Native Americans massacred her and her husband, but not before she herself had become thoroughly disaffected with life among them. She pathetically wrote her sister of her disappointment with the coworkers who "think it not good to have too many meetings, too many prayers, and that it is wrong and unseemly for a woman to pray where there are men . . . ; and now how do you think I have lived with such folks right in my kitchen for the whole winter?"[61] Spalding proved more effective, winning the affection and respect of Native Americans, learning their language, and teaching the women among them—but tuberculosis killed her.

Published in 1829, Ann Judson's account of her ordeal stirred many a young woman to emulate her—but not necessarily by marrying a missionary. By this time missionary boards had learned that the combined burdens of early-nineteenth-century childbearing and housekeeping in a primitive setting often prevented missionary wives from working as effectively as they had hoped. Yet the need for full-time women was plain. Warily, in 1815 the American Board of Commissioners for Foreign Missions sent Charlotte White, a widow—who married a fellow missionary before she reached Burma. Never-married women soon followed, though the churches continued to have qualms about them. In 1834 the Methodists commissioned their first single woman missionary, Sophronia Farrington, for service in Liberia.[62]

This breakthrough into a new field of professional religious service for women was remarkable. First, in an era when even respectable married women needed male escorts when they traveled, for a single woman to go to a foreign country or to a remote area in North America to live and work, even in the company of other missionaries, was outré conduct. Contemporaries had thought Ann Judson's accompanying her husband "wild and romantic in the extreme."[63] Families often rebuffed women's decisions to serve far from home and "civilization"; sometimes they disowned their daughters. Ministers fiercely opposed women's assumption of missionary duties.[64]

Second, the women who went knew quite well the hardships and the dangers they faced. Ann Judson on her voyage to Calcutta wrote, "We conversed much on death and the probability of our finding an early grave. The subject was solemn and affecting, yet secretly pleasing and consoling."[65] Perhaps the theology that held out assurances of heaven as the reward of martyrdom overcame the fears of the women who aspired to emulate Judson. At any rate, her widely circulated account of her own sufferings apparently stimulated rather than daunted young women just beginning to contemplate the possibility of a life of service to the church—though they would not have put it in these words: a career.

Certainly missionary work resolved a dilemma for religious women whose denominations afforded them no other opportunity for service of the breadth that they craved. It also offered women opportunities for independence and power they could not possibly hope for elsewhere. Although they were almost always designated "assistant missionaries" under the authority of males, circumstances frequently necessitated that single women function alone or with another American woman at some remote station, almost incommunicado, and only occasionally visited by their supervisors. Much of the time they planned their own work, developed their own indigenous personnel, and handled independently whatever crises arose. "Women freely preached, evangelized, planted churches, trained nationals, established schools, and conducted humanitarian work. Their lack of clerical ordination had little effect on their ministries, and they were far out of reach of critics back home."[66] Ironically, the opening of missionary work to women may have delayed the approval of women's ordination in mainline Protestant churches, as the daring, devoted women who might otherwise have demanded it found adventure and empowerment overseas.

Like overseas missionaries, women home missionaries often did the work of ordained clergy, conducting services and baptizing. Although few, including themselves, thought of them in these terms, in fact they could not do the work assigned them by either divinity or mission boards without functioning as clergy.

✑ Spinning Forward: Theological Shifts _____

New theologies were contributing to the gradual shifts of power within churches from the male clergy to women, and to women's hopes of ordination. These new interpretations acknowledged the growing influence of women by softening the image of Christ, emphasizing his gentleness and self-sacrifice, portraying him as closer to the ideal of True Womanhood and presumably more acceptable to women.[67] Presbyterians, Methodists, and Baptists, the most rapidly growing denominations, taught the equality of women *in the eyes of God,* even while they continued to believe that God wanted women confined to home and church.

Widespread millennialism intensified religious feelings and imbued Christians with a sense of urgency.[68] Time's winged chariot, they believed, was even then overtaking them. The millennium was at hand—a final thousand years at either the beginning or the end of which Christ would come to earth. The optimism this belief spawned in many Christians infected even people who read their Bibles less literally, enabling Lucretia Mott in her old age to express faith in the progress of humanitarianism. Proponents of women's rights saw the increase of attention to their cause as a sign of the approaching millennium. Even after the disappointment of the thousands of followers of William Miller, who vainly waited for Christ's second coming in 1844, many Americans continued to anticipate the end of the earth, bringing paradise for the saved and damnation for the rest. High time, they thought, for Christians to save as many souls as possible. High time for them to effect as many reforms as possible. Millennial theology worked in favor of women preachers:

Joel had predicted that in the "last days" women would prophesy as well as men, so in some circles women's preaching heralded the second coming.

Charles G. Finney (1792-1875), the prophet of the Second Great Awakening and the messiah of the nineteenth-century revival movement, by 1827 was insisting on the necessity of women's public testimony in "promiscuous assemblies" (before men as well as women). His associate Theodore Dwight Weld and Weld's wife, Angelina Grimké, further liberalized Finney's acceptance of women's religious rights. So too Finney's second wife, Elizabeth Ford Atkinson, famed for her ministry to women at ladies' meetings; and his Oberlin students Antoinette Brown, Lucy Stone, and Sallie Holley, whose 1851 graduation speech upheld women's right to vote and preach. Finney often told stories of women initiating revivals, such as the New Jersey woman whose minister refused to hold one: she hired a carpenter to build seats, invited people to her house, and lo, instant revival.[69] "Each one," he preached, "male or female, of every age, and in any position in life whatsoever, should make it a business to save souls." To which Sarah Grimké added: "The business of men and women, who are ORDAINED OF GOD to preach the unsearchable riches of Christ to a lost and perishing world, is to lead souls to Christ, and not to Pastors for instruction."[70]

The revivals conducted by Finney and his many ardent followers—indeed all the revivals of the Second Great Awakening—also encouraged women to speak where they had been silent.[71] At Cane Ridge, the scene of the famous meeting at the beginning of the nineteenth century that ignited revivalism, a seven-year-old girl perched on a man's shoulders exhausted herself in speaking.[72]

Revivals were at the active center of American religious life, not on its fringes. Harold Raser writes of the "select group of American revivalists and social reformers who dominated American religious life on the eve of the Civil War and who 'seemed to their contemporaries the most distinguished spiritual leaders of the age.'"[73] Revival converts came from all classes; among thousands of others, they included most women's rights leaders, like Elizabeth Cady Stanton, Paulina Wright Davis, Mary Rice Livermore, and Lucy Stone.[74] Much as she disliked revivals, Frances Wright testified to their importance in early-nineteenth-century American life when she wrote:

> By the sudden combination of the clergy of three orthodox sects, a *revival*, as such scenes of distraction are wont to be styled, was opened in houses, churches, and even on the Ohio River. The victims of this odious experiment on human credulity and nervous weakness, were invariably women. Helpless age was made a public spectacle, innocent youth driven to raving insanity, mothers and daughters carried lifeless from the presence of the ghostly expounders of damnation; all ranks shared the contagion, until the despair of Calvin's hell itself seemed to have fallen upon every heart and discord to have taken possession of every mansion.[75]

Revivals frequently took the form of week-long camp meetings with multiple services. Families came, pitched their tents, cooked their meals outdoors, and visited with friends and new acquaintances. Often blacks and whites mingled, and black as well as white ministers preached to the interracial assemblies. Attendants watched and participated in dramatic repentances and conversions, in the shouting and dancing of religious ecstasies, and in joyous celebrations with gospel hymns and lively folk music.[76]

Zilpha Elaw tells us about these camp meetings. Thousands assembled in the open air, families arriving in wagons with their own tents, seats, provisions, and servants.

> A large circular inclosure of brushwood is formed; immediately inside of which the tents are pitched, and the space in the centre is appropriated to the worship of God, the minister's stand being on one side, and generally on a somewhat rising ground. It is a scaffold constructed of boards, and surrounded with a fence of rails. In the space before the platform, seats are placed sufficient to seat four or five thousand persons; and at night the woods are illuminated; there are generally four large mounds of earth constructed, and on them large piles of pine knots are collected and ignited, which make a wonderful blaze and burn a long time; there are also candles and lamps hung about in the trees, together with a light in every tent, and the minister's stand is brilliantly lighted up; so that the illumination attendant upon a camp-meeting, is a magnificently solemn scene. The worship commences in the morning before sunrise; the watchmen proceed round the inclosure, blowing with trumpets to awaken every inhabitant of this City of the Lord; then proceed again round the camp, to summon the inmates of every tent to their family devotions; after which they partake of breakfast, and are again summoned by sound of trumpet to public prayer meeting at the altar which is placed in front of the preaching stand. . . . at the close of the prayer meeting the grove is teeming with life and activity; the numberless private conferences, the salutations of old friends again meeting in the flesh, the earnest inquiries of sinners, the pressing exhortations of anxious saints, the concourse of pedestrians, the arrival of horses and carriages of all descriptions render the scene portentously interesting and intensely surprising. At ten o'clock, the trumpets sound again to summon the people to public worship; the seats are all speedily filled and as perfect a silence reigns throughout the place as in a Church or Chapel; presently the high praises of God sound melodiously from this consecrated spot. . . . At the conclusion of the service, the people repair to their tents or other rendezvous to dinner; at the termination of which prayers are offered up, and hymns are sung in the tents, and in the different groups scattered over the ground; and many precious souls enter into the liberty of God's dear children. At two o'clock, a public prayer-meeting commences at the stand, and is continued till three, when the ministers preach again to the people. At six o'clock in the evening, the public services commence again as before; and at the hour of ten, the trumpet is blown as a signal for all to retire to rest; and those who are unprovided with lodgings, leave the ground. On the last morning of the camp-meeting, which is continued for a week, a solemn love feast is held; after which, all the tents are struck and everything put in readiness for departure; the ministers finally form themselves in procession and march round the encampment, the people falling into rank and following them. At length the ministers turn aside from the rank, stand still, and commence singing a solemn farewell hymn; and as the different ranks of the people march by, they shake hands with their pastors, take an affectionate farewell of them, and pass on in procession, until the last or rear rank have taken their adieu.[77]

Antebellum revivals and revival camp meetings, argues R. Laurence Moore, may have been the first large-scale popular entertainments in the United States, the rock concerts of their day. Campsites featured concession stands selling gingerbread, lemonade, and in the early days liquor. Inevitably they attracted hangers-on—drunks, gamblers, pickpockets, lechers, and people losing control in "unseemly riot."[78]

These revivals not only gave itinerant women evangelists a chance to preach but also accustomed laywomen to praying, testifying, teaching, and exhorting before men as well as women, sometimes, as with Zilpha Elaw, setting their feet on the primrose path toward full-time ministry. As Margaret Lamberts Bendroth remarks, "In the heat of revival fervor, nineteenth-century evangelists cared little for social conventions or ecclesiastical rules against women preachers: all stood equal at the foot of the Cross. The populist appeal and the millennial urgency of their message simply overshadowed secondary matters of social conduct."[79]

✑ Spinning Forward: The First Women Lecturers _____

The history of America's first women lecturers and the history of clergywomen intersect in their defiance of the ban on women's speaking in public, particularly before men. Early clergywomen broke ground for the first secular lecturers, and the popularity of those lecturers smoothed the way for succeeding clergywomen.

In the early nineteenth century secular assaults against the taboo exceeded in vigor those of women within the churches. The colorful reformer and "moral observer" Frances Wright (1795–1852) waged not merely a battle but a war.[80] The Scots-born Wright in the course of her adventurous life was allied now with the Marquis de Lafayette, now with Robert Owen, skewered by newspapers as "The Great Red Harlot of Infidelity" and "Priestess of Beelzebub," and hero-worshiped by the young Walt Whitman. Fascinated by the United States of America, she moved from romantic adulation of it as a place where "women are assuming their places as thinking beings" to regarding the country as "the most decidedly anarchal and supremely corrupt of any on the face of the globe."[81] She established a reputation through her books, particularly her Views of Society and Manners in America (1821). In 1828, at a time when, as her friend Frances Trollope observed, most American ladies were "guarded by a sevenfold shield of habitual insignificance," Wright broke precedent by lecturing to audiences of both women and men.[82] Her appearances on the lecture platform—the first by a woman—brought on a critical storm and numerous physical attacks, which, however, did not deter audiences from attending her lectures throughout the Midwest and East. Her subject? An attack on clergymen (Wright believed they led their churches in a fight for the status quo against social reform) and a plan to restore the United States to its original grand design through education. The next year, having bought a New York City church and turned it into a "Hall of Science," she lectured there against capital punishment and for equal education for women, legal rights for married women, liberal divorce laws, and birth control. Still later she raised her voice in political campaigns.

In 1832 Maria Miller Stewart (1803–1879) daringly became the first African-American to lecture publicly. Her style was biblical, her motivation to serve God, and her content exhortations to free blacks to educate themselves and sue for their rights. Like Wright, she had no easy time; even black men pelted her with tomatoes and criticism.[83]

The rather frequent traces of women who turned to lecturing to support themselves and further their chosen causes in the ensuing years suggest that a considerable portion of the public soon reconciled themselves to the idea of women's public speaking, even to the point of paying to hear them.[84] For instance, in 1848 Ella Gibson (b. 1821) gave up teaching school and began traveling throughout New England as a temperance lecturer. Gibson went on to marry the Rev. John Hobart and to succeed him as chaplain of the First Wisconsin Heavy Artillery in the Civil War—the only woman accepted as a chaplain until the 1970s.[85] The men of the First Wisconsin elected her unanimously and their colonel confirmed her, but the governor and the Secretary of War refused to recognize her election, despite her ordination by the Religio-Philosophical Society of St. Charles, Illinois. She served anyway. According to some sources, Congress in 1869 finally granted her the full pay of $1,200, though she had trouble collecting it and never did get the pension that she claimed as her due for disability from service-connected malaria.

Nonetheless, the Grimké sisters encountered disapproval when in the late 1840s they began to lecture to "promiscuous" (mixed-gender) audiences. Sarah (1792–1873) and Angelina (1805–1879) parted company with their slaveholding South Carolina family to enlist in the cause of abolition. Sarah for a while felt called to be a Quaker minister, but Quaker authorities first discouraged and then "silenced" her. Angelina, having in 1836 published a dramatic abolitionist *Appeal to the Christian Women of the South,* was appointed by the American Anti-Slavery Society to talk with small groups of women—an activity in which she was well practiced through her ecumenical women's prayer meetings.

When, predictably, these meetings outgrew parlors, some churches afforded her space—provided that only women attend. Encouraged by the interest of men who wanted to hear a southern slaveholder's daughter talk against slavery and tiring of charades, Angelina in 1837 addressed a mixed audience and even publicly debated with men, whereupon the Massachusetts Congregational ministerial association took it upon themselves to denounce her in a public "Pastoral Letter." The ministers set the parameters of women's religious duties and privileges:

> We appreciate the unostentatious prayers and efforts of woman in advancing the cause of religion at home and abroad; in Sabbath-schools; in leading religious inquirers to the pastors for instruction; and in all such associated effort as becomes the modesty of her sex . . . but regret the mistaken conduct of those who encourage females to bear an obtrusive and ostentatious part in measures of reform, and countenance any of that sex

who so far forget themselves as to itinerate in the character of public lecturers and teachers.[86]

Both sisters responded. Angelina published a series of letters in William Lloyd Garrison's *Liberator* insisting on both a woman's right to speak and her right to participate in formulating the laws that govern her. Sarah entitled her pamphlet *Letters on the Equality of the Sexes and the Condition of Women.* The two went on to lecture triumphantly in Boston before audiences of thousands. In Philadelphia, Angelina gave what turned out to be her last lecture for many years while bricks and stones crashed through the windows from an angry mob outside, who, after the lecture, burned down the hall.

Quaker women ministers and independent women itinerants had helped prepare the way for Frances Wright, Maria Miller Stewart, and the Grimké sisters as speakers before audiences of both women and men. In turn Wright, Stewart, the Grimkés, Lucy Stone, and Anna Dickinson accustomed the public to women's speaking as it were from on high, with dignity and authority.

✑ Spinning Forward: The Holiness Movement

But of all the religious and secular crosscurrents in the early nineteenth century that energized or enfeebled women's emergence as clergy, none was stronger than the holiness movement produced by Methodism and revivalism.[87] This is not surprising, for the movement emphasized the Holy Spirit, promoting an understanding of God as immanent in human beings. Given the doctrinaire stance of many denominations, women were forced to claim the right to preach and pastor *not* on the apostolic succession (the descent of priests from the apostles) or on commission by churches *but* on the inspiration of the Holy Spirit.

Almost all women who made such a claim recognized the dangers of this approach, if only by fearing that their call came from Satan rather than from divinity. Hannah Whitall Smith (1832–1911), herself a "wonderfully successful" Quaker minister, illustrated these hazards by describing the way that in 1834 a revival "attacked a young woman named Lucinia Umphreville, who lived in the village of Manlius [in upstate New York], and she felt called upon to begin to preach. Her chief concern was the subject of sex, and she believed that everything connected with it was unrelievedly wicked." Under her leadership young women began to reject marriage, instituting instead "spiritual marriage," of which the main signs were holy kisses exchanged without arousing passion. Not only did Umphreville encourage extensive experimentation in the search for spiritual partners but she also advocated that "married people should separate to unite with their true spiritual partners. . . . The spiritual husbands and wives, it was said, carried their tests far beyond the limits of spiritual kissing; and, so long as they were able to persuade themselves that they did not feel the ordinary human passions, their conduct appeared to themselves highly commendable." At Brimfield, Massachusetts, the same doctrine induced young women to practice bundling and running naked through the countryside.

Whitall Smith summed up dryly:

> In giving themselves up to the guidance of the voice of interior impressions only, without regard to the other voices by which God speaks, Christians enter upon a pathway of the utmost danger. Nothing is more unreliable than these interior impressions taken alone, and, what is worse, nothing is more contagious. When an earnest Christian, who is seeking to know the guidance of the Lord, hears of another Christian being guided in a certain direction, it is ten to one that he will have the same guidance.[88]

Nonetheless, the discrimination that barred women from the pulpits of most churches forced them into reliance on inspiration—which could range all the way from Lucretia Mott's dependence on the reason and love implanted in her by divinity to the shenanigans of Lucinia Umphreville.

Holiness adherents documented the leadership of women in primitive Christianity before the development of male hierarchies and sought to restore women to their initial places. Most of the churches that developed out of the holiness movement recognized women preachers. Accordingly many women found the holiness movement congenial to their situation and inspiration. Jean Humez remarks that in African-American churches "the woman preacher was a believer in holiness and asserted her right to preach largely on the grounds of spiritual inspiration rather than on educational credentials or formal ordination."[89] In black churches preaching women were among the most ardent defenders of revivalistic spiritual and ecstatic experiences, whereas the male church hierarchies emphasized a more rational approach. The women defended the concepts of holiness and perfection against African Methodist Episcopal ministers.

These concepts postulated an activist two-step conversion, first by justification (forgiveness for past sins) and then by sanctification (freedom from future intentional sin). She who would be holy must actively seek sanctification, not merely passively await it, putting her all on the altar, surrendering her will completely to the divine will, if necessary sacrificing material goods and human relationships. Then she must publicly testify to her spiritual experience.

Sanctification brought with it a high optimism about the virtue that both individuals and society could achieve—a spirit that accorded well with millennial ideas. Within the churches women expressed this optimism in the missionary and Sunday School movements; outside the churches in the antislavery, temperance, and woman's rights movements.

In the development of the holiness movement, which later in the nineteenth century would produce new holiness sects and denominations, Phoebe Worrall Palmer (1807–1874) played at least as significant a part as Charles Finney.[90] She began her ministry quietly enough: her sister Sarah Lankford (b. 1806) instigated women's meetings in their joint household, which she eventually persuaded Phoebe Palmer to lead.[91] Later thousands flocked to hear Palmer and learn from her; thousands, including many clergymen, attributed their conversions to her. In the process she broadened acceptance of women who perform ministerial duties—de facto clergywomen—and moved them several steps closer to ordination. Unlike Frances Wright, Palmer was no flouter of custom; unlike Sarah and Angelina Grimké, she was no rebel against her upbringing. Palmer—whether consciously or unconsciously—went along to get along. She never sought ordination for herself. Instead she skillfully used her status as a married lady and a preacher's wife to deflect criticism from her own activities.

This eye-lowering maneuver has of course protected many professional women, including clergy. Hannah Reeves, who began itinerating in the United States as a newly married woman in 1831 after ten years' experience in England, used it. As George Brown, her 1870 biographer, explains:

> To remove all objections out of the way, as far as possible, it may be well to remember that this lady preacher, whose life and labors are portrayed in this volume, did not ambitiously aspire to the high places of the Church, or seek any position that would give her ruling authority or dominion over men. She never sought ordination, or the right to administer the sacraments, or to have a seat in the Quarterly or Annual Conferences, where she could in debate contend with men, and vote against their measures and interests. Here it was, as she thought, that St. Paul did not allow a woman to speak in public, and here she did not desire to have a voice or vote. Her only wish, claim, or desire was to be a teacher of the Christian religion, a preacher of the gospel; leaving all official ecclesiastical matters to the male portion of the Church.

In time a Methodist Protestant conference rewarded Reeves's modesty by "appointing a committee to wait on her, and ascertain her wishes in relation to her connection with the itinerancy, whether she desired to be considered effective, and take an appointment or not. . . . She thanked them and the Conference for this mark of respect and courtesy, and with a playful smile replied, declining the kind proposal," because she and her husband might be appointed to different circuits, "and you know, sirs, that would never do. All I desire is the concurrence of the Conference for me to labor and do all the good I can in connection with my husband." This reply so delighted the committee's Brother Springere that he said to Brother Shinn: "Did not I tell you that she was a woman of too much good sense to accept such a proposition?"[92]

The relationship between clergywomen and their husbands makes an interesting study—one that marital partners are still working out in the late twentieth century. Historically, Quaker women ministers seem to have had the best of it—perhaps because their denomination's approval of their ministries outweighed any dissatisfaction their husbands may have felt. But the husband of Public Friend Hannah Whitall Smith, who with her in 1874 in England led a series of revivalistic holiness conferences within the interdenominational Higher Life movement, brought on a scandal that forced them to leave the country. As Helen Lefkowitz Horowitz writes, "Public accusations flew in England that in his religious ecstasies Robert had laid his hands on prayerful female bodies. . . . Robert had been read out of the English holiness meetings and the aristocratic homes that had once thrilled to his words." Or was the accusation only a rumor spread by enemies who clashed with Robert Smith on doctrinal matters? As her mother explained to Hannah Smith's young niece, M. Carey Thomas, "Aunt Hannah has had some trouble about some very disagreeable things which have been in some of the papers about Uncle Robert. A young lady who came to him for spiritual help complained of impropriety in his conduct and conversation, though at the time she did not manifest the slightest displeasure, which was very remarkable if there was any real ground of complaint."[93]

In other denominations the records turn up many dissatisfied husbands who felt they were not getting their due and certainly not what they had bargained for: their wives' devotion to divinely imposed duty turned attention away from the husbands' ease and entertainment. Yes, often their wives obeyed them in every respect that did not interfere with the obligations imposed by the Holy Spirit, but those obligations were all-consuming—and could even include celibacy. Some husbands converted; others deserted. Quite a number of clergywomen of whom we have records ended up alone, whether by willful act (their own or their husbands') or by natural causes. Indeed, Phoebe Palmer's concept of "entire consecration" could require a woman seeking sanctification to "give up" to God her spouse and family because these attachments might distract her from God-imposed "religious duties."[94]

If Palmer was not one to defy her society and found protection against criticism in her married state, neither was she indifferent to the progress of other women. Throughout her own ministry she defended the right of women to preach and pastor. "And now, my dear sister," she wrote in *Faith and Its Effects,* "do not be startled, when I tell you that you have been *ordained* for a great work. Not by the imposition of mor[t]al hands, or a call from man. No, Christ, the great Head of the church, hath chosen you, 'and ordained you, that ye should go and bring forth fruit.'"[95]

Moreover, in her book *The Promise of the Father* (1859), she drew together arguments on women's ministry from the Bible, history, logic, and practical experience. There she attacked the attitude of the church as "most grievous in the sight of her Lord, who . . . would fain have every possible agency employed in teaching the gospel to every creature." She compared the church to "a sort of potter's field, where the gifts of woman, as so many strangers, are buried."[96] Palmer occupied much of this book with accounts of women's successful ministry both in primitive Christianity and in her own time—accounts that she regards as convincing proof that the women are doing what God wants. She sugarcoats her argument with moderation, arguing neither for ordination nor for woman suffrage; she makes it more palatable still by endorsing that tenet of True Womanhood, the moral superiority of women, citing Adam Clarke's staggering calculation that the influence of one woman is equal to that of seven and one-half men.[97]

Books of this sort adducing arguments on the propriety of women's preaching and pastoring have been published regularly (and repetitiously) from about the twelfth century on, and continue to be published today by such eminent scholars as Rosemary Radford Ruether as well as by more untutored authors. Saying anything new on the subject, pro or con, is rather like trying to be original on the abortion issue. The chance that such arguments, no matter how soundly based or effectively presented, will persuade the opposition is about as good as the chance that women's high performance will persuade their opponents that they belong in nontraditional jobs like the clergy. But Palmer's book had behind it the weight of her considerable reputation. The churches spawned by the holiness movement that she midwifed and nurtured asserted as central the right of *all* believers touched by the Holy Spirit to minister and preach.

Palmer's own devotional life began in the home of her Methodist parents in New York City. In 1827 she married a man similarly raised in a pious home; both Phoebe and Walter had been converted at thirteen, though Phoebe worried because her conversion was not a powerful experience. When three of their six children died, the Palmers did not curse God and die, but interpreted this then all-too-ordinary tragedy as a sign of God's displeasure with the conduct of their own lives and dedicated themselves anew to his service. Phoebe's sister Sarah Lankford, who with her husband lived with the Palmers, headed two women's prayer meetings, which in 1835 combined and began to meet in the Palmer-Lankford home. Phoebe went on expanding her religious horizons, teaching a young woman's Bible class, filling in for her husband when he had to miss his male or mixed classes, and finally, against tradition, teaching a mixed class of her own. In 1840 the Lankfords moved, and Phoebe reluctantly but fatefully took over the leadership of Sarah's Tuesday Meeting for the Promotion of Holiness, by that time attended by men as well as women, people from other denominations as well as Methodists.

Once again a women's prayer meeting/Bible study group channeled a gifted woman into religious leadership. Palmer led the Tuesday meeting for thirty-four years. It grew to as many as two hundred people, including pastors, missionaries, editors, college professors, and Methodist bishops, eager to learn from Palmer about entire sanctification. Her fame spread and she received invitations to speak first within New York City, then throughout the country, and eventually in England. For the first twenty years or so of her evangelistic career, she apparently traveled without her husband and children. In 1845 she published a widely read spiritual autobiography, *The Way of Holiness.* She also extended her labors to social welfare, notably in founding the Five Points Mission in New York City.

About the mid-1850s, as demands on her grew, her husband began to share more in her activities; the couple spent about half of each year attending camp meetings and conducting revivals. In 1857–1858, she was at the center of the so-called Prayer Meeting Revival, a largely urban, interdenominational, laity-led phenomenon that offered workers noontime meetings at city churches. The Palmers spent the years 1859 to 1863 conducting revivals in the British Isles. Although more and more frequently from the 1840s into the 1860s Phoebe Palmer headlined large protracted interdenominational revivals, when she thought it politic she used small groups that she called "class meetings" or "social religious gathers" to avoid the appearance of usurping man's place. She denied that she was preaching, but, as Harold Raser notes,

> In the church or hall meeting [of the Prayer Meeting Revival], however, Palmer was the preacher of the hour, doing all the things a Finney would do; occupying the pulpit, taking a text, presenting an exhortation calculated to persuade hearers to repent and turn to God or seek to more fully enter the 'say of holiness' (always replete with stories and illustrations), issuing an 'invitation' to the anxious to pray and be prayed for, and praying with and instructing those who responded to the invitation.[98]

Later in the 1860s, with attacks on revivalism mounting from Unitarians and Universalists, Palmer narrowed her focus, concentrating on the Tuesday meeting and editing the monthly paper *The Guide to Christian Perfection.*

In sum, although she always spoke of herself as a laywoman, for years she devoted her considerable talents, her energies, and her full-time efforts to performing ministerial duties. She converted thousands and promoted into a major force the theology she preached and to which she was recognized as the expert witness. From her preachings and the "Palmerites" who followed her came the new holiness sects of the later nineteenth century, churches within which many women preached and pastored with full official credentials.

☙ The Position of Early-Nineteenth-Century Clergywomen _____

It's impressive to add up the work of the early-nineteenth-century women evangelists and revivalists, the Sunday School movement, the missionary movement, women's importance in the holiness movement, the emergence of African-American preaching women (in the face of the immense disadvantages and dangers under which they labored in the antebellum era), and all the other forces and achievements propelling women's leadership in religion. But we must rein in runaway enthusiasm. Except in the Society of Friends, the numbers of women credentialed by their denominations as preachers and pastors may even have decreased in this period. For the early nineteenth century shrank and limited the scope of what women could respectably do. Woe to the women who defied the strictures of True Womanhood and the doctrine of Separate Spheres. United Brethren itinerant Lydia Sexton was contemptuously called a "crowing hen," for only roosters should make noise.[99] Even the circumspect Phoebe Palmer was cut by criticism in religious journals and mutterings from clergymen that she would be better off at home washing dishes.

Mavericks there would always be—like Salome Lincoln (1807–1841), who in 1829 led a strike against a wage cut at the New England mill where she worked, then took to journeying throughout New England, spreading the word that in the eyes of the Lord all are equal, and that women as well as men have the right to speak.[100] Or like the eccentric evangelist Harriet Livermore (1788–1868), self-dubbed the "Pilgrim Stranger," who even wangled an invitation to preach before Congress not just once but several times.[101]

Livermore was at once a thoroughgoing eccentric and a daughter of her times, often carrying to extremes the beliefs general around her. The granddaughter of a United States senator and the daughter of a congressman, until her early twenties she lived a fairly conventional, privileged life. But when her fiance at the insistence of his family broke off their engagement because of her "wild and irregular" disposition, she perceived this rejection as a divine judgment upon her, abandoned hopes of "sublunary bliss," and initiated a search for a satisfactory religious creed. Born an Episcopalian, she sampled the Congregational, Quaker, and Baptist faiths, then concluded that she was meant to be a "solitary eclectic." She spent the proceeds of her books on itinerating as an evangelist throughout New England and the Middle States. In Kansas the authorities defeated her efforts to convert Indians, whom she took to be the lost tribes of Israel.

The poor driven woman then focused on premillennialism, journeying some five times to Jerusalem to await Christ's second coming there. Livermore died impoverished, still thinking of herself as a "gazing stock" to inspire other women to a sense of their obligation to a Christianity that needed their services. In religious ardor, in her self-reliance in interpreting the Bible, in dedicating herself to the public role of evangelist, in her enthusiastic attempts to save souls, and in her millennialism, her life held a mirror, however distorting, up to her era and the role of women in it.

Despite the many traditional and biblical brakes on their progress, up until the mid-nineteenth century, clergywomen probably kept even with if not outran women in most other professions. Not, however, with those teaching the three Rs. By the 1830s women had begun to replace men in teaching at the lower levels, so that by mid-century women were approaching a quarter of all teachers. Catharine Beecher opened a training school for them in 1830. But in the halls of higher education, which women entered as students only in 1833, women faculty had penetrated only in such exceptional institutions as Oberlin College and Mary Lyon's Mt. Holyoke. Though women did almost all nursing of the sick, they had not yet begun to professionalize that work. Midwives and women practitioners of herbal medicine did a lot of doctoring of both women and men, but only in 1835 did the sisters Harriot Kezia and Sarah Hunt manage to gain access to enough education to be called (by some) the first formally trained female medical practitioners in the United States (they studied in Boston with a British couple), and only in 1849 did Elizabeth Blackwell become the first woman to earn a medical degree from an American institution. Although Sarah Grimké as a young woman cherished the dream of becoming a lawyer, and although it was common practice to prepare for the law by reading or by studying with an established attorney, no woman had yet been admitted to any American bar.[102]

Clergywomen may have been ahead of the curve in women's progress, even though most preaching women still functioned independently or within minority denominations like the Quakers, and even though none had yet been ordained in a mainline denomination. By any absolute standard, however, clergywomen, like other professional women, weren't doing all that well. Ministers and laymen were by no means ready to leave the ramparts unmanned.

But in 1848 women in Seneca Falls at the first American women's rights convention in their Declaration of Rights and Sentiments included among their grievances women's exclusion from ministry, man having "usurped the prerogative of Jehovah himself, claiming it as his right to assign for her a sphere of action, when that belongs to her conscience and to her God."[103]

Though this accusation caught the attention and the breath of many clergymen, it came naturally to the framers of the Declaration, among them Lucretia Mott, her sister Martha Coffin Wright, and Elizabeth Cady Stanton. As we know, Mott had a long history of following her own inner light regardless of Quaker authorities. Wright was to comment in 1872, "As to the teachings of the pulpit or the Bible, they come only from fallible mortals like ourselves, & their opinion is worth just as much as yours or mine . . . *less* if it seems less rational."[104] Stanton, early rejecting the Calvinism of her Presbyterian upbringing, in 1895 was to publish *The Woman's Bible,* reinterpreting scriptural passages derogatory to women. By 1848 all three of them had exhausted their stores of deference toward authority *qua* authority. While other women exhibited considerably more patience, more deference, and less audacity, the Seneca Falls convention sounded the note of the future.

And in 1850, though because she was a woman her professors refused her a diploma and a license to preach, Antoinette Brown successfully completed the three-year course of study at Oberlin theological seminary. Unawares, the Protestant churches were slouching toward the ordination of women.

Notes

1. Quoted by Celia Morris Eckhardt in *Fanny Wright: Rebel in America* (Cambridge, Mass.: Harvard Univ. Press, 1984), p. 170.

2. Dorothy C. Bass, "Their Prodigious Influence: Women, Religion and Reform in Antebellum America," in *Women of Spirit: Female Leadership in the Jewish and Christian Traditions,* ed. Rosemary Ruether and Eleanor McLaughlin (New York: Simon & Schuster, 1979), p. 281. Bass persuasively argues (p. 288) that women reformers spun out of the control of clergymen, thinking "less about containing the disorderly individualism of a democracy than about encouraging its attacks on stifling institutions."

3. Lois A. Boyd and R. Douglas Brackenridge, *Presbyterian Women in America: Two Centuries of a Quest for Status* (Westport, Conn.: Greenwood, 1983), p. 176. See also Ruth A. Tucker and Walter Liefeld, *Daughters of the Church: Women and Ministry from New Testament Times to the Present* (Grand Rapids, Mich.: Zondervan, Academie Books, 1987), p. 155, who note that soon after the 1816 formation of the interdenominational Female Union for the Promotion of Sabbath Schools men formed their own Sunday School Union and made the women's organization their auxiliary.

4. *Second to None: A Documentary History of American Women,* ed. Ruth Barnes Moyni-

han, Cynthia Russett, and Laurie Crumpacker (Lincoln: Univ. of Nebraska Press, 1993), 1:264. Susan Hill Lindley notes that in 1793 African-American Catherine Ferguson had opened a Sabbath school for poor children in New York City ("*You Have Stept Out of Your Place": A History of Women and Religion in America* [Louisville, Ky.: Westminster John Knox, 1996], p. 183).

5. Nancy Hardesty, *Your Daughters Shall Prophesy: Revivalism and Feminism in the Age of Finney* (New York: Carlson, 1991), p. 120.

6. Joan M. Jensen, *Loosening the Bonds: Mid-Atlantic Farm Women, 1750–1850* (New Haven, Conn.: Yale Univ. Press, 1986), p. 146.

7. This argument is advanced by Susan Juster in *Disorderly Women: Sexual Politics and Evangelicalism in Revolutionary New England* (Ithaca, N.Y.: Cornell Univ. Press, 1994).

8. Edwin Scott Gaustad, *A Religious History of America,* rev. ed. (New York: Harper & Row, 1990), p. 140.

9. Eric Lincoln and Lawrence H. Mamiya, *The Black Church in the African American Experience* (Durham, N.C.: Duke Univ. Press, 1990), pp. 276–77.

10. Lincoln and Mamiya, *Black Church,* p. 279. See also Toni Morrison, *Beloved* (New York: Penguin Plume, 1988), p. 177: Baby Sugg's "authority in the pulpit, her dance in the Clearing, her powerful Call (she didn't deliver sermons or preach—insisting she was too ignorant for that—she *called* and the hearing heard). . . ."

11. Harry V. Richardson, *Dark Salvation: The Story of Methodism as It Developed Among Blacks in America* (Garden City, N.Y.: Doubleday, Anchor, 1976), p. 175.

12. Jensen, *Lossening the Bonds,* p. 146. See also Jean M. Humez, "'My Spirit Eye': Some Functions of Spiritual and Visionary Experience in the Lives of Five Black Women Preachers, 1810–1880," in *Women and the Structure of Society,* ed. Barbara J. Harris and JoAnn K. McNamara (Durham, N.C.: Duke Univ. Press, 1984), p. 6.

13. Jualynne Dodson, "Nineteenth-Century A.M.E. Preaching Women," in *Women in New Worlds: Historical Perspectives on the Wesleyan Tradition,* ed. Hilah F. Thomas and Rosemary Skinner Keller (Nashville, Tenn.: Abingdon, 1981), pp. 276–89.

14. Humez, "My Spirit Eye," pp. 129–43.

15. *Memoirs of the Life, Religious Experience, Ministerial Travels and Labours of Mrs. Zilpha Elaw* (London, 1846), reprinted in *Sisters of the Spirit: Three Black Women's Autobiographies of the Nineteenth Century,* ed. William L. Andrews (Bloomington: Indiana Univ. Press, 1986), pp. 82–83.

16. Jarena Lee, *The Life and Religious Experience of Jarena Lee, A Coloured Lady, Giving an Account of Her Call to Preach the Gospel* (Philadelphia: The Author, 1836), reprinted in *Early Negro Writing, 1760–1837,* ed. Dorothy Porter (Boston: Beacon, 1971).

17. *Black Women in Nineteenth Century American Life: Their Words, Their Thoughts, Their Feelings,* ed. Bert James Loewenberg and Ruth Bogin (University Park: Pennsylvania State Univ. Press, 1976), pp. 135–36.

18. Richardson, "Foreword" to *Sisters of the Spirit,* ed. Andrews, p. 14.

19. The best source on Jackson is *Gifts of Power: The Writings of Rebecca Jackson, Black Visionary, Shaker Eldress,* ed. Jean Memahon Humez (Amherst: Univ. of Massachusetts Press, 1981). Humez suggests parallels between Jackson's career and that of Ann Lee.

20. Nelle Y. McKay, "Nineteenth-Century Black Women's Spiritual Autobiographies: Religious Faith and Self-Empowerment," in *Interpreting Women's Lives: Feminist Theory and Personal Narratives,* ed. Personal Narratives Group (Bloomington: Indiana Univ. Press, 1989), p. 148.

21. Humez, "My Spirit Eye," pp. 129–43.

22. McKay, "Nineteenth-Century Black Women's Spiritual Autobiographies," p. 148.

23. For a discussion of the possibility of sexuality in this relationship, see Humez, "My Spirit Eye," p. 9, text and note.

24. McKay, "Nineteenth-Century Black Women's Spiritual Autobiographies," p. 149.

25. Humez, "My Spirit Eye," p. 139.

26. Ibid., p. 21.

27. Nancy A. Hewitt, "The Fragmentation of Friends: The Consequences for Quaker Women in Antebellum America," in *Witnesses for Change: Quaker Women Over Three Centuries,* ed. Elisabeth Potts Brown and Susan Mosher Stuard (New Brunswick, N.J.: Rutgers Univ. Press, 1989), p. 100. Here Hewitt examines the possibility that these debates actually strengthened women's hands.

28. Margaret Hope Bacon, *Mothers of Feminism: The Story of Quaker Women in America* (San Francisco: Harper & Row, 1986), p. 95.

29. *Notable American Women: A Biographical Dictionary,* ed. Edward T. James, Janet Wilson James, and Paul S. Boyer, 3 vols. (Cambridge, Mass.: Belknap Press of Harvard Univ. Press, 1971), 1:89.

30. Jensen, *Loosening the Bonds,* p. 124.

31. The standard biography is Margaret Hope Bacon's *Valiant Friend: The Life of Lucretia Mott* (New York: Walker, 1980).

32. Otelia Cromwell, *Lucretia Mott* (Cambridge, Mass.: Harvard Univ. Press, 1958), p. 125.

33. Bacon, *Valiant Friend,* p. 111.

34. Mott perfectly understood the implications for women's rights of this stand, quoting a third party as speculating that perhaps "the unfettering of the female intellect from the thralldom of prejudice would prove of even more value than the original object of the anti-slavery movement" (Bacon, *Valiant Friend,* p. 75).

35. Ibid., pp. 119–22 passim, 158, 167, 197.

36. Ibid., p. 207.

37. Joan D. Hedrick, *Harriet Beecher Stowe: A Life* (New York: Oxford Univ. Press, 1994), p. 39. Diaries and letters of the period attest to women's concern for each other's spiritual state. Women dying of tuberculosis consoled each other in conversations and letters by appeals to religion and the afterlife. See, for example, Paul C. Nagel, *The Adams Women: Abigail and Louisa Adams, Their Sisters and Daughters* (New York: Oxford Univ. Press, 1987), p. 86.

38. In 1775 nine of the colonies had "established" churches; churches which the colonial governments required citizens to attend and maintain, and against which dissenters such as Methodists or Baptists were allowed only limited powers to compete. The American Revolution brought disestablishment, beginning in 1777 in New York and ending in 1833, when the Congregationalists ceased to receive state support in Massachusetts (Ann Douglas, *The Feminization of American Culture* [New York: Knopf, 1978], p. 23).

39. Even as liberal a minister and as dedicated an abolitionist as Theodore Weld, whom Angelina Grimké later married, boggled at her outspokenness on woman's rights, fearing that the issue might start a hare that would divert the chase from slavery. The Grimké sisters argued cogently that "[I]f we surrender the right to *speak* to the public this year, we must surrender the right to petition the next year and the right to *write* the year after and so on. What *then* can *woman* do for the slave when she is herself under the feet of man and shamed into

silence?" (Gerda Lerner, *The Grimké Sisters from South Carolina: Pioneers for Woman's Rights and Abolition* [New York: Schocken Books, 1967], p. 201).

The Rev. Mr. Samuel May, however, arguing on *theological* rather than on Weld's *pragmatic* grounds, defended the Grimkés' right to speak: "I have never heard from other lips, male or female, such eloquence as that of her [Angelina's] closing appeal. The experience of that week dispelled my Pauline prejudice. I could not believe, that God gave them such talents as they evinced to be buried in a napkin" (ibid., p. 197).

40. Ibid., pp. 189–90. Note that these events occurred eleven years before the Seneca Falls Declaration.

41. On this subject, see Hardesty, *Your Daughters Shall Prophesy;* Douglas, *Feminization of American Culture;* and Barbara Welter, *Dimity Convictions: The American Woman in the Nineteenth Century* (Athens: Ohio Univ. Press, 1976). Hedrick notes that between 1830 and 1860, the power to shape public opinion passed from ministers to the periodical press, in which women writers were publishing (*Harriet Beecher Stowe,* p. 348).

42. Elaine Showalter, *A Literature of Their Own: British Women Novelists from Bronte to Lessing* (Princeton: Princeton Univ. Press, 1977), p. 144.

43. Douglas, *Feminization of American Culture,* pp. 107–8. See also Hedrick's insightful discussion of Harriet Beecher Stowe's *The Minister's Wooing* in *Harriet Beecher Stowe,* pp. 279–85.

44. Rosemary Ruether and Eleanor McLaughlin, "Introduction," in *Women of Spirit: Female Leadership in the Jewish and Christian Traditions,* ed. Rosemary Ruether and Eleanor McLaughlin (New York: Simon & Schuster, 1979), p. 25.

45. Jeanette Hassey, *No Time for Silence: Evangelical Women in Public Ministry Around the Turn of the Century* (Grand Rapids, Mich.: Academie Books, 1986), pp. 56, 64.

46. Among other early ministers (not ordained) of the Christian Church were Ann Rexford, Sarah Hedges, and Sally Thompson (Barbara A. Withers, *Women of Faith and Our History* [Philadelphia: United Church Press, 1987], pp. 12–13).

47. *Historical Sketches and Incidents, Illustrative of the Establishment and Progress of Universalism in the State of New York* (1843), quoted in Catherine F. Hitchings, *Universalist and Unitarian Women Ministers,* 2d ed. (Boston: The Unitarian Universalist Historical Society, 1985), p. 3.

48. Russell E. Miller, *The Larger Hope* (Boston: Unitarian Universalist Association, 1979) 1:547.

49. Boyd and Brackenridge, *Presbyterian Women in America,* p. 94.

50. Gordon Melton, "Emma Curtis Hopkins: A Feminist of the 1880s and Mother of New Thought," in *Women's Leadership in Marginal Religions: Explorations Outside the Mainstream,* ed. Catherine Wessinger (Urbana: Univ. of Illinois Press, 1993), p. 90.

51. *Elizabeth: A Colored Minister of the Gospel, Born in Slavery* (Philadelphia Tract Ass'n of Friends, 1889). For the context of Elizabeth's work, see also *Black Women in Nineteenth Century American Life,* ed. Loewenberg and Bogin; and Humez, "My Spirit Eye," pp. 129–43.

Nelle Y. McKay notes that these spiritual autobiographies typically focus on religious convictions, response to a call, and the consciousness of authority derived from the author's own service. The first of these from a black woman appeared in 1810. Black women's narratives in particular, McKay says, delineate women's participation in ideological conflicts within religious communities, with the women insisting on the validity of ecstatic experience and the rights of women to be clergy ("Nineteenth-Century Black Women's Spiritual Autobiographies," p. 142).

52. Richardson, "Foreword," to *Sisters of the Spirit,* ed. Andrews, p. 14.

53. Loewenberg and Bogin, in *Black Women in Nineteenth Century American Life,* p. 128.

54. Ibid., pp. 132–33.

55. Ibid., p. 127.

56. Withers, *Women of Faith,* p. 14. Elaine Magalis notes the founding of the Boston Female Society for Missionary Purposes by Mary Webb in 1800 (*Conduct Becoming to a Woman: Bolted Doors and Burgeoning Missions* [n.p.: Women's Division, Board of Global Ministries, The United Methodist Church, n.d.], p. 8).

57. Barbara Welter suggests that a second reason for recruiting women into mission fields was that this work did not attract enough men because it did not offer the kind of centrally located church authority that men could acquire in the United States ("She Hath Done What She Could: Protestant Women's Missionary Careers in Nineteenth-Century America," in *Women in American Religion,* ed. Janet Wilson James [Philadelphia: Univ. of Pennsylvania Press, 1980], pp. 111–27).

58. Ruth Barnes Moynihan, "Coming of Age: Four Centuries of Connecticut Women and their Choices," *The Connecticut Historical Society Bulletin* 53 (Winter/Spring 1988): 64.

59. Accounts of Ann's life can be found in *Notable American Women,* 2:295–300. Elaine Magalis's *Conduct Becoming to a Woman* also provides interesting details of Ann's life.

60. On both Spalding and Whitman, see *First White Women Over the Rockies: Diaries, Letters, and Biographical Sketches of the Six Women of the Oregon Mission Who Made the Overland Journey in 1836 and 1838,* ed. Clifford Merrill Drury, 3 vols. (Glendale, Calif.: Arthur H. Clark, 1963–1966).

61. *First White Women Over the Rockies,* 2:91; 1:134. Their diaries indicate the power of the vocation that propelled these women westward. Whitman and Walker had each applied as a single woman to be a missionary, only to be turned down.

62. Magalis, *Conduct Becoming to a Woman,* p. 18. Catherine B. Allen notes that even in the 1870s Baptists had not yet warmed "to the idea of single women missionaries" (*The New Lottie Moon Story* [Nashville, Tenn: Broadman Press, 1980], p. 58).

63. James D. Knowles, *Memoir of Mrs. Ann H. Judson, Late Missionary to Burma. Including a Hist. of the Am. Baptist Mission in the Burman Empire* (1829), p. 36, quoted in *Notable American Women,* 2:296.

64. Douglas, *Feminization of American Culture,* p. 111.

65. *Notable American Women,* 2:296.

66. Tucker and Liefeld, *Daughters of the Church,* p. 291.

67. "Christ became a female symbol, not unlike the Virgin Mary in Catholicism. [Women] were God's viceregents in the home. Not even the minister had such spritual authority over the young" (William G. McLoughlin, *Revivals, Awakenings, and Reform: An Essay on Religion and Social Change in America, 1607–1977* [Chicago: Univ. of Chicago Press, 1978], pp. 120–21).

68. Douglas notes that, before the Civil War, "millennial speculation was particularly intense in America; many could not help associating the birth of this new nation with more general and religious possibilities of regeneration" (*Feminization of American Culture,* pp. 220–21). Millenarians divided into two camps: premillenarians, mostly among the less educated and more evangelical sects, who believed that Christ would come to earth at the start of the millennium—the thousand years of an earthly golden age, during which the devil would be powerless (as mystically projected in Revelation 20); and the postmillenarians, who held that Christ would not come until its end. Both confused the millennial period with a heavenly

afterlife. Millennial expectations were by no means confined to the naïve, but affected the thinking of such people as Harriet Beecher Stowe, who perceived the Civil War as the Armageddon preceding the millennium.

69. Hardesty, *Your Daughters Shall Prophesy*, p. 97.

70. Ibid., pp. 100–101.

71. Even Catharine Beecher, a conservative on woman's rights, felt called to conduct a revival. So did Mary Lyon, both before and after she founded Mt. Holyoke College.

72. R. Laurence Moore, *Selling God: American Religion in the Marketplace of Culture* (New York: Oxford, 1994), p. 46.

73. Harold Raser, *Phoebe Palmer: Her Life and Thought* (Lewiston, N.Y.: Edwin Mellen Press, 1987), p. 10.

74. Hardesty, *Women Called to Witness*, p. 61.

75. Frances Wright, "Preface," *Course of Popular Lectures*, quoted by Eckhardt, *Fanny Wright*, pp. 170–71.

76. See, for instance, Mechal Sobel, *Trabelin' On: The Slave Journey to an Afro-Baptist Faith* (Westport, Conn.: Greenwood, 1979), p. 98; and Catharine Cleveland, *The Great Revival in the West, 1797–1905* (Gloucester, Mass.: Peter Smith, 1916, 1959).

77. *Memoirs of the Life, Religious Experience, Ministerial Travels and Labours of Mrs. Zilpha Elaw* (London, 1846), reprinted in *Sisters of the Spirit*, pp. 65–66.

78. Moore, *Selling God*, pp. 44–49.

79. Margaret Lamberts Bendroth, *Fundamentalism & Gender, 1875 to the Present* (New Haven, Conn.: Yale Univ. Press, 1993), p. 14.

80. See Celia Morris, *Fanny Wright: Rebel in America* (Cambridge, Mass.: Harvard Univ. Press, 1984); A. J. G. Perkins and Theresa Wolfson, *Frances Wright: Free Enquirer: The Study of a Temperament* (Philadelphia: Porcupine, 1972); and Margaret Lane, *Frances Wright and the "Great Experiment"* (Totowa, N.J.: Manchester Univ. Press, 1972).

81. Frances Wright, *Views of Society and Manners in America* (1821), p. 218, quoted in *Notable American Women*, 3:676, and by Eckhardt, *Fanny Wright*, p. 283. See also Elizabeth Frost-Knappman, *Women's Progress in America* (Denver: ABC-Clio, 1994), p. 344.

82. Frances Trollope, *Domestic Manners of the Americans* (1832), p. 72, quoted in *Notable American Women*, 3:678.

83 *Black Women in America*, ed. Kim Marie Vaz (Thousand Oaks, Calif.: Sage, 1995), p. 264.

84. By mid-century, some lecturers commanded up to $400 in cities, $250 in towns (*Black Women in America*, ed. Vaz, pp. 263–64).

85. DeRobigne Mortimer Bennett, "Ella E. Gibson," in *The World's Sages, Infidels, and Thinkers* (n.p., n.d.); William J. Dickman, "Equal Rights at Battery Rodgers," in *Military Affairs* (Manhattan, Kan.: MA/AH Pub., 1980); Kenneth W. Duckett, *30th Star* (December 1956). These fugitive sources on Ella Gibson Hobart are contradictory, but military historians seem to agree that she did indeed serve for a time as a chaplain. We owe our knowledge about her to Renee Klish, archivist at the Army Chaplains' School.

86. *The Liberator*, Boston, Mass., Aug. 11, 1837, quoted in *Second to None*, ed. Moynihan et al., 1:252. Theological students were among the men who publicly condemned the Grimkés. In Athens, Ohio, a professor responded quite differently when some of his students "being skeptical in their opinions, declared that 'no woman could entertain them for an hour upon the subject of Christianity.'" He took them to hear Protestant Methodist Hannah Reeves (1800–1868) preach—at 6 A.M. "The time came, and the students, with the multi-

tude, were there. The students took the middle of the church, in front of the pulpit, so as to have a full view of the lady preacher. They used their opera glasses, and looked at her in rather a quizzical style. But all this did not daunt her in the least. She remained calm and self-possessed, in full view of the fact that her performance that day was to undergo no little criticism by the students. She was most graciously assisted in praying and preaching, and during the sermon those students listened with profound attention, and scarcely blinked an eye" (George Brown, *The Lady Preacher: or, The Life and Labors of Mrs. Hannah Reeves* [1870; reprint, New York: Garland, 1987], p. 225).

87. Among other helpful sources on the holiness movement and its significance for women clergy, see Susan Cunningham Stanley, "Alma White: Holiness Preacher with a Feminist Message" (Ph.D. dissertation, Iliff School of Theology, Univ. of Denver, 1987); Elisabeth Schüssler Fiorenza, *In Memory of Her: A Feminist Theological Reconstruction of Christian Origins* (New York: Crossroad, 1983), pp. 184–88; and Donald W. Dayton and Lucille Sider Dayton, "'Your Daughters Shall Prophesy': Feminism in the Holiness Movement," *Methodist History* 14 (January 1976): 67–92.

88. Hannah Whitall Smith, *Religious Fanaticism*, ed. Ray Strachey (London: Faber & Gwyer, 1928), pp. 55, 158.

89. Humez, "My Spirit Eye," p. 130.

90. For Phoebe Palmer, see Charles Edward White, *The Beauty of Holiness: Phoebe Palmer as Theologian, Revivalist, Feminist, and Humanitarian* (Grand Rapids, Mich.: Zondervan, 1986); and Raser, *Phoebe Palmer.* See also Delbert R. Rose, *A Theology of Christian Experience: Interpreting the Historic Wesleyan Message* (Minneapolis: Bethany Fellowship, 1965); Charles E. Jones, *Perfectionist Persuasion: The Holiness Movement and American Methodism, 1867–1936* (Metuchen, N.J.: Scarecrow, 1974); and Melvin Easterday Dieter, *The Holiness Revival of the Nineteenth Century* (Metuchen, N.J.: Scarecrow, 1980).

91. For information on Lankford, see John A. Roche, *The Life of Mrs. Sarah A. Lankford Palmer, Who for Sixty Years was the Able Teacher of Entire Holiness* (New York: George Hughes, 1898)—confusing as it is: after the deaths of her own husband and her sister, Lankford married Phoebe's widower, and Roche tends to call both sisters Mrs. Palmer.

92. Brown, *Lady Preacher*, pp. 12, 138.

93. Helen Lefkowitz Horowitz, *The Power and Passion of M. Carey Thomas* (New York: Alfred A. Knopf, 1994), pp. 64–65. Nevertheless Hannah Whitall Smith was another of those remarkable nineteenth-century women who successfully combined her private and public lives. She had seven children, including the writer Logan Pearsall Smith, a daughter who married the art critic Bernard Berenson, and another daughter who married Bertrand Russell; Hannah Whitall Smith also foster-parented two of her grandchildren. She acted as mentor and confidante for her niece M. Carey Thomas and was highly instrumental in Thomas's appointment as president of Bryn Mawr. Besides preaching to both whites and African-Americans, Smith wrote several books, the best known of which was *The Christian's Secret of a Happy Life* (1875).

94. Raser, *Phoebe Palmer*, p. 368.

95. Hardesty, *Women Called to Witness*, pp. 94–95.

96. Quoted by Raser, *Phoebe Palmer*, p. 204; and by Hardesty, *Women Called to Witness*, p. 250.

97. Raser, *Phoebe Palmer*, pp. 366–67.

98. Raser, *Phoebe Palmer*, pp. 115–16.

99. Magalis, *Conduct Becoming to a Woman*, p. 111.

100. For Lincoln's interesting story, see Almond H. Davis, *The Female Preacher: or, Memoir of Salome Lincoln* (1843; reprint, New York: Arno Press, 1972).

101. Magalis, *Conduct Becoming to a Woman*, p. 135. See also *Notable American Women*, 2:409–10.

102. Robert F. Riegel, *American Feminists* (1963), p. 26, quoted in *Notable American Women*, 3:684.

103. Hardesty, *Your Daughters Shall Prophesy*, p. 104.

104. Riegel, *American Feminists* (1963), p. 26, quoted in *Notable American Women*, 3:684.

Evangeline Booth, daughter of the founders of the Salvation Army in charge of Army activities in the United States, is shown in 1906 acting in "Rags," a dramatization of her message. *Courtesy of Salvation Army National Archives and Research Center.*

Emma Booth-Tucker, another daughter of William and Catherine Booth, and her husband Frederick Booth-Tucker visit a Salvation Army farm colony in Amity, Colorado, ca. 1902. Emma is seated second from the left, her husband second from the right. *Courtesy of Salvation Army, Western Territorial Museum.*

Myrtle Fillmore, co-founder of the Unity Church (an early spinoff of Christian Science) in her office c. 1898. *Courtesy of Unity School of Christianity, Unity Village, Missouri.*

Juliann Jane Tillman, an African Methodist Episcopalian, preaching, 1844. *Courtesy of Library of Congress.*

Marion Murdoch, the first woman to receive a bachelor of divinity degree from Meadville Theological School and a key member of the Iowa Sisterhood. *Courtesy of Unitarian-Universalist Association Archives, bMS 1446, Andover-Harvard Theological Library, Harvard Divinity School.*

Quaker minister Lucretia Mott. *Courtesy of Library of Congress Collection.*

A moment at the 1986 Fresno Conference of the Evangelical Women's Caucus (now the Evangelical and Ecumenical Women's Caucus). The conference theme was "Free Indeed . . . Empowered for Action." *Photograph by Joanne Ross Feldmeth.*

The young Antoinette Brown. *Courtesy of Oberlin College Archives, Oberlin, Ohio.*

Jarena Lee, antebellum black preacher and exhorter. *Courtesy of Library of Congress Collection.*

Anna Howard Shaw, ordained minister, physician, and renowned suffragist. *Courtesy of National Archives.*

A Methodist camp meeting, probably in 1836. *Courtesy of Methodist Collection, Drew University Library.*

3

Ordination for the Few
1853–1900 🍃

The Mainline Churches: Early Ordinations _____

To trace the history of clergywomen in the latter half of the nineteenth century is to follow a thousand threads that only occasionally get woven into swatches of cloth. In the mainline churches sustained group efforts to secure authorization for clergywomen were notably lacking. The minds of most churchwomen focused elsewhere, and even those clergywomen who most keenly felt the need of an official stamp of approval seldom sought the support of their lay sisters.

Accordingly, from 1850 onward, clergywomen's progress in winning hierarchical recognition crept at a pace slower than might have been expected, given their head start from colonial days among Quakers and to a lesser extent among Methodists. In the latter half of the nineteenth century, clergywomen of these denominations fell behind women physicians in winning acceptance. But all this cannot tarnish the imagination, persistence, and sheer hardihood of women like Antoinette Brown Blackwell, Olympia Brown, and Anna Howard Shaw, women who insisted that their mainline Protestant churches recognize their vocation through the ceremony of ordination.

Everyone—not least the United States government— struggles with the definition of "clergy," particularly the question of whether only the ordained are clergy. The Selective Service Act of 1940 defined the "regular minister" (whom it exempted from the draft) as "a man [sic] who customarily preaches and teaches the principles of religion of a recognized church, religious cult, or religious organization of which he is a member, without having been formally ordained as a minister of religion; and who is recognized by such church, sect, or organization as a minister."[1] In *Hull v. Stalter* (1945) the U.S. Court of Appeals said:

> One may preach or teach from the pulpit, from the curbstone, in the fields, or at the residential fronts. . . . To be a "regular minister" of religion the translation of religious principles into the lives of his fellows must be the dominating factor in his own life, and

must have that continuity of purpose and action that renders other purposes and actions relatively unimportant.

But the court allowed the clergy the possibility of secular employment.[2]

Clearly the Congress and the court could not use ordination as a defining characteristic of the clergy. The term itself causes problems. As Sara Maitland notes, "The word 'ordained' would not in fact be accepted by many of the Protestant denominations whose theology of ministerial leadership does not accept the concept."[3] Some denominations deny that any human agency can pronounce women or men qualified for the clergy; they believe that only God can call people to that service. At the other end of the scale churches like the Orthodox Christian vest in their bishops the sole power to ordain. Other denominations range on the misty flats in between these two extreme positions.[4]

What's more, standards for ordination vary widely. Some denominations ordain for life; others only for a period of active service or for a specific task. Many denominations ordain people at different ranks and with different rights and responsibilities: for instance, an ordained elder may not be empowered to pastor a congregation or to bless the Eucharist. Some denominations require graduate degrees, psychological evaluations, and approval by a committee of clergy and laity; some authorize a single official to ordain whom he or she will. The Universal Life Church, a California-based sect, ordains in response to a postcard request. Disciples of Christ pastor Elaine Lawless compares ordination in that denomination with getting a union card: "There's nothing that an ordained person, Disciples person, can do that a layperson can't do, including communion, because the movement started with people who were fed up with clergy and skeptical of clergy."[5] Jehovah's Witnesses, who have no paid local clergy, consider all members ministers, and all, women included, are required to "publish" (preach) door-to-door.[6]

Nonetheless, the flaming angels of ordination and excommunication have historically guarded the doors of the clergy against women. Refusal of ordination, the official seal of approval on her vocation, may damage a woman psychologically, professionally, and materially. Psychologically, a woman who considers herself called by God to the priesthood or ministry counts herself rejected and cast out by the denomination she has always thought hers when it denies her ordination.

Professionally, in many denominations employment in the pastorate depends on ordination. The United States military will appoint only chaplains recommended by their denominations, and almost all denominations recommend only those whom they have ordained. "It's really important as a woman chaplain to be ordained," a Navy lieutenant-commander chaplain told us.

Many denominations that will not ordain women for civilian pastors will give a special ordination to be on active duty. Those denominations will let their women go to war but they won't let them stay at home and pastor. Because there are approximately a thousand Navy chaplains on active duty and maybe at the most 50 or 60 are women at any given time—if you as a woman aren't fully ordained, it's like you're a second-class minister: the slang term is being a "throw-away woman."

Materially, ordination confers perquisites. In the nineteenth and early twentieth centuries, ordination entitled the recipient to a railroad discount—no small matter to evangelists and revivalists who often traveled thousands of miles a year. For a long time it brought clergy discounts from department stores and free service from doctors.[7] In a few denominations, notably the Methodist, it confers job security, for every ordinand is guaranteed employment. In the 1990s the Internal Revenue Service allows even retired ordained clergy deductions for their housing expenses. Ordination has always cast a certain aura of respectability, and it still provides some legal immunity. Sara Maitland cites a 1976 (negative) instance:

> Maria Cueto and Raisa Nemikin, two social workers employed by the National Episcopal Church Center to minister to Hispanic Americans, laid claim to the privilege of "ministers of religion" not to answer a Grand Jury on matters that they had learned in confidence. The judge ruled that the priest–penitent relationship could not exist as they were not ordained. Although unsupported by the Episcopal Bishops both women went to prison rather than breach confidentiality.[8]

While the lack of ordination has not fully protected pulpits and pastorates against women, it has denied would-be clergy the affirmation of their vocations; it has denied laywomen the pastoring of people like themselves; and it has denied religious institutions a clergy representative of the full range of human experience. Women couldn't help but know that churches and synagogues used ordination as a means of protecting the quality of their clergy; denying it to women as a class implied all too clearly women's spiritual inferiority.[9]

By the middle of the nineteenth century it was already becoming clear that without ordination clergywomen weren't going to get far in the mainline Protestant churches. Among themselves they could recognize as valid the vocation of the nonordained: as the Rev. Madeline Southard, President of the International Association of Women Preachers, commented in 1923, "Some think we should admit [to our organization] only those who are ordained. But this would defeat one of our purposes in organizing. There are several denominations represented in our membership that give no recognition whatever to women as preachers, yet individual members are preaching with power. We want to encourage these women, not shut them out."[10] But within the churches the progress of the nonordained was blocked.

Those women who first claimed the right to ordination supported and were nurtured by the two major movements that engaged the energies and attention of advanced women—woman's rights and temperance. Both of these movements originated in part because of men's refusal to let women speak in the causes of temperance and abolition; both movements at least at first understood themselves as promoting religious values. Women's Christian Temperance Union president Frances Willard and temperance hatchet woman Carrie Nation saw their work as Christian ministry. And both movements afforded women experiences helpful in the pulpit: Mary Lathrap first publicly spoke by reciting a temperance poem and eventually gained a license as a Methodist preacher.[11]

For ordination, Antoinette Brown (1825–1921) had to force seminary doors.[12] She could not have chosen doors more likely to open to women than those of Oberlin's Theological Department, but even so she faced daunting difficulties. When the liberal founders of Oberlin College established its Ladies' Department in 1833, they intended simply to create a more civilized environment for the all-important male students. In her undergraduate years there Brown sensibly kept quiet about her clerical ambitions; when in 1847 she sought seminary admission, she rocked Oberlin. Everyone worked her over—the faculty, the trustees, and the Ladies' Board of faculty wives, including the first Mrs. Charles Finney. They saw her persistence in apocalyptic terms, predicting irreparable moral harm to family and community.

The seminary faculty, who had the real say-so on her admission, didn't know what to do. On the one hand, they didn't want her; on the other, they felt uncomfortable about denying anyone, even a woman, a chance to learn more about religion. Apparently they had still to discover that if one intends to say yes, one might better do it graciously. Refusing to face up to their own ambivalence and to Brown's real ambition to occupy a pulpit, they didn't say yes and they didn't say no. They let her attend classes but treated her shabbily. She was not, they said, an officially enrolled student; some of them refused to call on her in class; they denied her a student's license to preach. They did publish in the *Oberlin Quarterly Review* her exegesis of St. Paul's "Let your women keep silence in the churches." But when in 1850 Brown and her fellow student Lettice Smith successfully completed the theological course, the faculty would not grant them the diplomas they had earned.[13]

Brown did not press for ordination from Oberlin, both because she knew of the opposition within the Oberlin community and because she preferred ordination from her own parish: "[I had] an instinctive desire to be ordained in my own church, and a belief that I could one day in the future be ordained by my own denomination which was then the Orthodox Congregational."[14] By 1853, though, perhaps having developed a keener sense of the advantages of ordination in seeking a church, she went back to Oberlin looking for help—in vain. As she wrote to Lucy Stone:

> I am not ordained yet either, so you may rejoice, and welcome, but what a milksop you must take me for if I can be manufactured over into a "would-be-but-can't priest" by so simple a ceremony as ordination. It is well that certain grave divines should have drawn back just in time for they were on the very brink of the fatal fall over the great wall of custom. A little more and I should have been a man-acknowledged minister, but somebody happened to think that though a woman might preach she ought not to administer the sacraments etc. Others thought this, and so they joined hands, and turning around walked backwards together, and I took up my bundle and walked home.[15]

To support herself while she looked for a church, Brown turned not to teaching, in which she was experienced, but to the lecture platform. As a step toward the ministry, Brown had carefully trained herself as a public speaker, and she spent the next few years speaking on woman's rights, temperance, and abolition, preaching when and where she could. Now and then a minister, usually a Unitarian, invited her to fill his pulpit. But most clergymen opposed her, as when in 1853 they outshouted her efforts to speak at the World's Temperance Convention, or when some clergy-man, like the Baptist Elder Coons of South Butler, New York, ostentatiously left the congregation when she rose to preach. She must have been impressive, though, for in 1853 Horace Greeley and Charles Dana offered her one thousand dollars a year and board and room to preach Sunday evenings in Metropolitan Hall in New York City. She refused, partly because she lacked confidence in her own qualifications, partly because she still cherished the hope of preaching and pastoring in her own congregation.

Events and inclination conspired to involve Brown ever more deeply in the bur-geoning woman's movement. As an Oberlin undergraduate she had confided her professional ambition to her classmate Lucy Stone. On the lecture platform she toured for temperance with Susan B. Anthony and Amelia Bloomer. Within the woman's movement, she carved out her own niche. As her *Oberlin Quarterly Review* essay indicates, she had early joined the succession of women who have believed that if only they could prove biblical authority for the ministry of women, the gates to the clergy would be opened unto them. That conviction developed into her mission. For years her research on that score eased the consciences of conventional women who felt that if this scholar and theologian could endorse woman's rights, then nice women could join up.[16] But her closest friends among the suffragists, Lucy Stone and Susan B. Anthony, sympathized neither with this effort nor with Brown's desire for ordination, since they regarded the church hierarchy as corrupt.

Brown's faithfulness to her call to the pastorate, her willingness to endure rejec-tion and dislike, and perhaps her widening acquaintance among liberals finally earned her a church. In 1853 she received and accepted a call to the First Congre-gational Church in Butler and Savannah, Wayne County, New York. This tiny con-gregation had been having trouble in finding a minister, partly, no doubt, because they paid only three hundred dollars a year; in the recent past they had employed an African-American clergyman, an unusual step even for an abolitionist congregation. They and Brown began her pastorate with high hopes, and in a few months the board voted to ordain her.

In the Congregational system of governance, the right to ordain belonged to the individual congregations. Brown's parish ordained her despite the protest of the Congregational General Conference, and despite difficulties in finding clergymen for the laying on of hands.[17] The church members said, though, that they would feel better if Gerrit Smith came and talked to them, for "we are standing all alone so, we need a little countenance in the matter." Smith demurred. A wealthy reformer and an abolitionist congressman who described himself as "a self-appointed minister who built the church [building] and gave religious instruction to friends and neigh-bors," he questioned the need for ordination, but Brown argued that it would advance the cause of woman's rights. She asked the Rev. Luther Lee, a liberal aboli-tionist Methodist from Syracuse and an old friend from the temperance movement, to preach the ordination sermon; he too hesitated, for he shared Smith's views, but in the end he assented.[18]

So on September 15, 1853, Antoinette Brown was ordained. George Caudee, farmer, of South Butler spoke for the congregation: "This church does not believe in the necessity of ordination as a qualification to preach the gospel. Why then have an ordination? The church needs instruction, and it is well for both pastor and people to be reminded of their duties. So it is today we have invited a few friends to be with us to recognize the relationship between pastor and people." Luther Lee concurred: "We have not come together to confer the right to preach the gospel. If Antoinette Brown has not this right already, God-given by her capability, then we cannot communicate it."[19] But the momentous significance of the first ordination of a woman by a congregation of a recognized denomination was well understood in clerical circles and among those who endorsed women's rights, such as the physician Herriot Hunt, who came from Boston to attend.[20]

Inevitably a storm of criticism followed, as violent as the rainstorm that had raged during the ordination. Clearly, to be ordained at all Brown had had to pressure her friends by an appeal to the cause of women. Legally her congregation was certainly within its rights to ordain her, but an aura of irregularity clouded the ceremony. Two years later when Brown asked Lee for a certificate of ordination he refused, saying that he himself had not ordained her, but only preached her ordination sermon: "I thought at the time there was a want of formality, and raised the question how you was to obtain your certificate, and was replied to that a certificate would be of no use."[21]

Auspicious as their relationship seemed at the time of the ordination, Brown and her congregation were ill-suited. In contrast to her dour Calvinistic parishioners, she had always insisted on a God of love. Her differences with her congregation shook her confidence in her ability to pastor and brought on a crisis in her own faith. She could not, she found, threaten a dying youngster with hellfire and brimstone, though his mother begged her to. In the summer of 1854 Brown and the congregation agreed to part. She wanted to continue preaching, she told both Gerrit Smith and Horace Greeley, but she did not want another parish. "I can never preach to a regular established church again, let them be ever so reformatory," she wrote Smith, "for I cannot breathe there freely." And to Greeley: "Of course I can never again be the *pastor of a church;* but must be *a preacher for the people.* . . . My present religion is a free one—all its truths are revelations from Nature's God to the soul; and one must be outside of all sectarian pressure to speak it freely."[22] After a few months of recuperation at her family's farm, she went to work in the slums of New York, under Greeley's patronage: she wrote about her observations for his *New York Tribune* and spoke and preached through invitations he arranged for her.

The experience in South Butler had both shocked and traumatized Brown. Although she continued to preach intermittently and at times professed to be looking for another pulpit, in effect she spent the next twenty years reconsidering her own faith, clarifying its tenets in her own mind, principally by writing books on metaphysical subjects. She took her own advice to the aspiring minister Olympia Brown: "Do not unite with any church organization unless you see your own way quite clear. . . . I know how sorely you will need every help; but first and surest of all you need to stand upright in your own convictions—not in any other persons [sic]."[23]

In 1856 Antoinette Brown married into the remarkable Blackwell family. Her new sisters-in-law, the physicians Elizabeth and Emily Blackwell, pioneered women's medical education in the United States. Brown's husband, Sam, and his brother, who married Lucy Stone, both approved their wives' feminist principles. Both men repudiated the egregious property laws that gave a husband sole control of his children, custody of his wife's person, sole ownership of her personal possessions and real estate, and absolute right to all her earnings. Even during the years when she was bearing seven children (five of whom, all daughters, survived infancy), Antoinette Brown Blackwell with her husband's support managed to protect three hours a day for "brain work," writing articles for the suffragist *Woman's Journal,* occasionally preaching and lecturing, and writing books on the theories of Darwin and Spencer, as well as a novel and a book of poems.

In 1875 Antoinette Blackwell arrived at a point where at last she could again associate herself with a specific church. She joined the Unitarians and requested recognition as a Unitarian minister. It was accorded in 1878, but with a caveat: "You are of course aware of the feeling that exists in many of our established churches in regard to the propriety of women appearing in the pulpit. I do not understand that the Committee share this feeling. I simply refer to it to remind you that no word of ours will remove any such difficulty or indeed touch upon any other matter than that referred to us, viz. the antecedents of the person applying."[24] The committee was quite right: Blackwell's search for a pastorate proved futile, though she advertised in the *Woman's Journal* and elsewhere.[25] So she continued to freelance as a lecturer and preacher.

Throughout her mature life Blackwell worked for woman's rights when and where she could, whether cooperating with Susan B. Anthony's efforts to found a Free Church where all would be welcome, acting as vice president of Julia Ward Howe's Association for the Advancement of Women, supporting Lucy Stone's presidency of the American Woman Suffrage Association, helping the astronomer Maria Mitchell steer young women into scientific studies, mentoring aspiring young clergywomen, or herself ordaining two young women ministers. Always, though, she thought of herself and wanted to be known more as a minister than as a reformer or a scientist. In her old age she finally rounded out her clerical career. Living in Elizabeth, New Jersey, she helped to found a Unitarian church, at whose services she officiated. When they decided to build, she donated land. The clergyman whom they called as a pastor graciously asked her to serve as their minister emeritus. In that status she remained for thirteen years, preaching her last sermon at ninety.[26]

Olympia Brown (1835–1926), the first woman ordained by a denomination (rather than an individual congregation), directly profited from Blackwell's pioneering.[27] Olympia Brown attended Mt. Holyoke Seminary and Antioch College, whose president, Horace Mann, was worrying lest his "great experiment" in coeducation lead women into the professions. There at Antioch she heard Blackwell preach: in her autobiography she remembered, "It was the first time I had heard a woman preach, and the sense of the victory lifted me up." So after graduating, Brown sought admission to various theological schools; only President Fisher of St. Lawrence would admit her as a regular student—even though it had been a commonplace at St. Lawrence "first, that women could not preach; second, that they would not preach; third, that if they did nobody would listen to them, and fourth, that, however much people might like to hear them, they never could be pastors of [Universalist] societies."[28] Although Fisher didn't approve of women ministers, he figuratively washed his hands and left the decision to Brown and "the Great Head of the Church."

Of her experience at St. Lawrence, Brown wrote that she left "with every feeling outraged and my nervous system permanently shattered, through the persecutions which I had endured at that institution inflicted solely because I, a woman, was seeking a chance to do the work to which the Lord had called me."[29] She also left with another problem: the seminary refused to ordain her because she was a woman. She appealed to the Northern Universalist Association meeting at Malone, New York—probably in fear and trembling, since Dr. Fisher had hinted that he would oppose her there. But with the backing of the parish at Heuvelton, New York, which invited her to become its minister, she carried the day. Fisher graciously bowed to the will of the meeting and participated in Brown's ordination on June 25, 1863.

Until 1887 Brown served Universalist churches in Weymouth, Massachusetts; Bridgeport, Connecticut; and Racine, Wisconsin, successively. Her husband, John Henry Willis, whom she married in 1873, moved with her from Bridgeport to Racine, shifting his business from groceryman to newspaper publisher. On the principles of Lucy Stone and with her husband's assent, Brown kept her own name. They had two children, a girl and a boy.

Early in her career Brown began her support for woman suffrage. In 1866 at a suffrage convention she met Susan B. Anthony, Lucy Stone, and Elizabeth Cady Stanton, and joined the American Equal Rights Association as a charter member. Her churches must have been both liberal and understanding, for she spent a great deal of time on women's issues, in 1867 traveling from July to October trying to get the vote for women in Kansas. In Racine she not only presided over the state woman suffrage association but also sued election officials, unsuccessfully, for not letting her vote in a municipal election; the statute that empowered women to vote in "any election pertaining to school matters," she argued, must mean that they could vote in all state and local matters, since all pertained to school matters in one way or another. Finally, after more than twenty years of ministry Brown resigned to concentrate on suffrage, rising to a vice presidency in the National Woman Suffrage Association and then to the presidency of the Federal Suffrage Association.[30] As an old lady she joined Alice Paul's radical Congressional Union, picketing in front of the White House and publicly burning President Wilson's speeches.

Unlike President Fisher of St. Lawrence, who when he couldn't beat Brown joined her, his diehard wife at Brown's ordination predicted, "You will see now the consequence of this. Next year there will be fifteen women in the class, and then women will flock to the ministry."[31] Mrs. Fisher, gloomy as Cassandra, lacked her prophetic powers. By 1868, five years after Brown's ordination, there were only four Universalist women ministers, including Brown.[32]

But during the rest of the nineteenth century other women not only followed Brown at St. Lawrence but also stormed the barricades at other seminaries. Meadville Theological School in Pennsylvania admitted women in 1868, granting its first degree to a woman, Marmora Devoe Moody, in 1873. Sometimes women had to be devious: the Rev. Ms. Barnard, for instance, ordained at the age of thirty-seven in 1897, had to find a seminary in the Boston area. The class schedule at Tufts would not allow her to earn her living at the same time. Harvard Divinity School would admit a woman for just one course, for which she would have to pay more than men paid for the whole theological program. She finally cobbled together a schedule which included one New Testament course at the Boston University School of Theology and tutoring from Harvard's William Reed—an arrangement that he and Dean Reccord of Harvard Divinity School referred to as the "Chelsea Divinity School."[33] Similarly, Mary Lydia Leggett Cooke combined study at Monticello Seminary, a summer session at Cornell, and one year (1887) at Harvard as a special student, "one of the first women to study in this institution."[34] Some women studied privately or took special reading courses with clergymen or clergywomen (like Olympia Brown). Some who could afford it went to England. Augusta Jane Chapin (1836–1905), the second Universalist woman ordained and later the first woman awarded the honorary degree of Doctor of Divinity, forewent seminary because she was too busy preaching.[35]

Ryder at Lombard University, Galesburg, Illinois; Tufts in Massachusetts; and Boston University theological seminaries, as well as the Pacific School of Religion in Berkeley, California, all show up as having granted degrees to women before 1900. Hartford in 1889 adopted a resolution to admit women, but limited their number to two a year, gave them no financial support, and required a statement that they did not expect to enter the ministry. In sum, in the last half of the nineteenth century determined women could get theological educations, one way or another, but the situation was still difficult enough that ordained women like Phoebe Hanaford and Marion Murdoch put out lists of theological seminaries that admitted women.

When or whether a school accepted women depended largely on the denomination. In 1904 the Christian Church (Disciples of Christ) still approached the possibility on tiptoe. That year the president of their College of the Bible in Kentucky accepted Gustine Codurson, who wanted to be a foreign missionary, into his class in sacred history—conditionally:

> If she sit on the back seat, next to the door; and if at the close of each session—when I nod my head to her, she arises at once and leaves the room before I dismiss my class—also if on days when I decide our text is questionable and she finds a note written by me on her desk—she quietly withdraws, before the class begins—yes—if—she always arrives—after the men students are all seated and we have started well in the lesson—and if—she speaks to none of the men students.

But he took even this tentative action only because he felt sure "that by the time [women] study the Scriptures with us they will learn that women are not to be preachers."[36]

Even when they won admission to seminaries, women seldom enjoyed the financial support afforded many male theological students, often by women's church organizations. Take Anna Howard Shaw (1847–1919).[37] Thanks to a feckless father and a somewhat incompetent mother, Shaw's childhood inured her to hardship. When she was twelve her father claimed 360 acres of Michigan land, on which, nine miles from the nearest settlement, he built a floorless log cabin with uncovered openings for doors and windows. There he sent his wife, his twenty-year-old son, and his four youngest children, while he remained in Massachusetts, occasionally sending money and boxes of books. Mrs. Shaw had a nervous breakdown, the older son got sick and went back home, and Anna and a younger brother somehow learned to hack a living out of the wilderness. The experience inspired Anna with disdain for men and a resolution to succeed in their world; she began preaching sermons to her nearest neighbors, the trees. She eked out her schooling in a frontier schoolhouse; when she was fifteen she began teaching.

In Big Rapids, where she moved after the Civil War, for the first time she heard a woman preach. The Rev. Marianna Thompson, a Universalist, encouraged Shaw's aspirations, and so did her high school principal, Lucy Foot, a Methodist, whose help enabled Shaw in 1871 to get a Methodist license to preach.[38] Since her Unitarian family, upset by her conversion to Methodism, would contribute toward her education only if she would abandon thoughts of a ministerial career, she earned her own way through a couple of undergraduate years by preaching and temperance lecturing.

In 1876 she enrolled in the divinity school at Boston University, dooming herself to penury, earning what she could by "pulpit supply" (filling in for ministers who could not preach on a given Sunday). Her male colleagues got free rent, inexpensive board, and an allowance of two dollars a week. She got nothing. So she ate what she could scrounge—mostly milk and crackers. Sometimes she felt too weak to climb the stairs. But she was a survivor. Finally women from a foreign missionary society gave her a small stipend, which she supplemented by an interim ministry in a nearby town.

Her classmates and professors did not make her life easier. Shortly before graduation, disturbed because the seminary was getting a reputation for turning out ambitious and worldly students, a professor asked for volunteers willing to do whatever the church wanted, no questions asked. Five students stood, including Shaw.

Splendid, the professor said. The four men would be ordained immediately and sent to South America. And Shaw could go along, to teach. "I tell you I was bitter . . . ," she wrote years later. "I almost came to think that the whole thing was a lie and that the church was a lie and Christianity a lie. I came very near unbelief then, unbelief in the goodness of God himself. I was so furiously angry, so scornful, I could hardly endure it."[39]

When she entered seminary she had the promise of the Bishop of the New England Conference of the Methodist Episcopal church to ordain her, but he died before she graduated, and the new bishop opposed women ministers. Shaw graduated first in her class; Anna Oliver was second. Both women had parishes but without ordination could not perform weddings or baptisms. The new bishop advised them both to get out of the church. Shaw agreed.

> But Miss O. said she wouldn't, that she was going to be ordained, that she was going to stay in and fight the church. And she did. She was a curious woman and had a hard time, but she was smart. But of course she had no chance really. She thought she was big enough to fight the church and she bought a church of her own in [Brooklyn] and called it 13th Methodist, or something of that sort. Well, of course she had no right to do that and it made them very angry. She went on struggling with them for a time, but she couldn't hold out and finally she had to sell the church. They had a great quarrel over the money. I don't know which was right, but I suppose she thought she had a right to the money and she kept it.[40]

Shaw took the more pragmatic course of applying to another denomination, whose standards for ordination she had already surpassed; as Rev. Ada C. Bowles commented, "Miss Shaw thought she would have her hands full in fighting the world, the flesh and the church, so she 'got out' and went into the Protestant Methodist church."[41] All the same, the Protestant Methodists spent two days discussing her character. Did she believe St. Paul? they asked. Yes. Then she would obey her husband? She danced around them. In her case, she said, the point was moot, since she had no husband. But, if they really believed that a wife should obey her husband, then they must ordain her, for some day she might have a husband who ordered her to preach; if she were ordained, she could obey him, and if he ordered her not to preach, she could stop. "Well," she wrote:

> of course that made them terribly mad, and there was one old chap I remember, a small thin windy little man who got frightfully angry and went walking up and down the aisle flapping his arms in his agitation with his hands under his coattails. . . . Oh, they asked me all sorts of questions of that sort, but I had the best of them, for they were not educated people at all, and of course I was straight from studying the Bible in Hebrew and knew a great deal about it. And then of course I'd taken special pains with that part of the subject [women's ordination] and knew all about it.

Bested theologically, the committee retreated to practical grounds.

> Well, then they were afraid a woman minister wouldn't do because so many of the difficulties that ministers had to settle were matrimonial difficulties, but I said there were

not likely to be so many matrimonial difficulties with a woman minister, and of course that made them mad. And then I said if there were, a woman was just as good to settle them as a man, especially as it was generally the woman who had to complain and she would often go to another woman sooner than to a man. . . . Then they were very much afraid they would have to support me [financially] and said there was no use ordaining me because no church would have me if it could pay a salary.

Don't worry, she reassured them. She already had a church, two in fact; indeed she would promise never to ask them for a church; if she could not get one on her own, she would do something else (an unusual assertion in the Methodist system of governance, where pastors are usually assigned by the hierarchy). A sympathetic committeeman remarked that his colleagues needn't worry: Shaw already earned a bigger salary than two of the cavilers earned together. Maybe, he said, she should worry about having to support them.[42]

In the end in 1880 they did indeed ordain her, the first woman so accredited in their denomination, and Shaw went about her business in her two parishes. Despite her humor, though, the whole brouhaha had bruised her; her church work did not challenge her abilities; and she looked around for other ways in which she could serve women. Continuing her pastoral duties, she enrolled at Boston University as a medical student, graduating with her M.D. in 1886. By then, though, she had decided that above all else women needed the vote, so she resigned from her pulpits to work for the Massachusetts Woman Suffrage Association and for the Franchise Department of the Women's Christian Temperance Union. For the rest of her life she devoted her intelligence, energies, passion, and impressive oratorical talent to woman suffrage. Her powers were lost to the church that had disdained them.

Later, as a famed, much-sought-after speaker, she described her attendance as a newly ordained minister at the all-important yearly conference that governs the affairs of the Methodist church. A set of young male ministers harassed her, questioning her right to make motions, laughing, jeering. At the end of the conference she rose to speak:

[I] said that I had attended to the business of the conference all week and had done my best to be helpful, but that there was a crowd of young men present who had persistently insulted me all the week and questioned my right to be a member of the conference and that in consequence I would never attend another conference or help them in any way until I received a formal apology. And I never have. Every year they write and beg me to come and preach the conference sermon or something, and I always refuse. One time, a few years ago, I wrote and told them why I refused and of course they'd forgotten all about it, and so the next time they sent an apology. But I don't go because I am too heterodox and I haven't any sympathy with it anymore. One time, a few years ago, they wrote to say they were going to drop me from their lists because I never came. And I replied that just as soon as they got ready to drop me they were at liberty to do it. They haven't yet. But I don't care. I'd be glad if they would, for I don't believe in the churches at all as I did.

From the vantage point of age and achievement, she summed up: "So that's how

I was ordained. It wasn't very glorious. It was rather like sneaking into the ministry by the back door. But if they won't open the front door to you, what else can you do? . . . And there's a good deal of fun to be got out of it if you can keep from being bitter and angry."[43]

Although the proximate cause to abandon their pulpits differed from Antoinette Brown Blackwell to Olympia Brown to Anna Howard Shaw, the same thinking underlay the decision of each—a recognition of the need for women's rights before women could serve the church to their full capacity. Gerda Lerner has remarked that by their time Jewish and Christian women had engaged in more than one thousand years of feminist Bible criticism and religious re-visioning, "a search among Jewish and Christian women for connection to the Divine," necessitated by the "dethroning of the goddesses" in ancient times. In all those years women's search for feminist consciousness had focused on religion, as they struggled to find a central place for women within it.[44] Now in the latter half of the nineteenth century these feminist Christians shifted their energies away from religion toward political solutions for their situation.

Blackwell, Brown, and Shaw were only three of the women in their time who walked the rocky road to ordination only to find their ministries severely limited by the stubborn and sulky resistance of their churches. As institutions these churches had approved women's ordination, but the people of those churches, particularly the clergy, gave less than wholehearted support to ordained women.

Olympia Brown compiled a longer, more substantial *ministerial* career than either Shaw or Blackwell, perhaps in part because she was working within the more favorable climate of Universalism. Universalists and Unitarians, tiny denominations, attracted a better-educated, more liberal membership than the Congregationalists and Methodists. But their male clergy could seldom bring themselves to allow women to play on an even field. This ambivalence evidences itself repeatedly in the nineteenth-century history of Unitarian clergywomen.

The Unitarians ordained their first woman, Celia Burleigh (1826–1875), in 1871. At her ordination Julia Ward Howe delivered the charge to the congregation and read a letter from the Rev. Henry Ward Beecher: "There are elements of the Gospel which a woman's nature ought to bring out far more successfully than a man can. We have no adequate expression yet for sympathy, for mercy, for pity, for love in the sermons of men. It is these very elements that our civilization and our popularity need."[45]

In this period some churches were beginning to understand their need for women clergy. Not just because laywomen could not always easily approach clergymen for relief from their guilt-ridden religious scruples or for help with their problems, but also because, as Burleigh herself remarked, "in the work of the Christian ministry it is not good for man to be alone. . . . Both men and women are needed for the work." In Victorian America the idea of the church's need for clergywomen also could be translated as congruent with the ideals of True Womanhood and the Separate Spheres. Burleigh again:

Nor is this work of the ministry a new work for woman. It is the work which she has always been doing. . . . God who gave into her hands the training of little children, the guardianship of the erring, the care of the sick and dying—set her apart as a consoler, inspirer. In the work of the ministry she will be carrying into a broader field the priestly office which she has always exercised in the family.[46]

Mainline Churches: Support Systems for Clergywomen

Olympia Brown had already voiced the church's need for clergywomen in 1868 at the ordination of Universalist Phoebe Ann Coffin Hanaford (1829–1921):

As a woman, you stand in some sense as a representative; as one of the earliest to assume the high office of preacher. . . . Young women will look to you for instruction and guidance—for that sympathy which they have not found in the ministry in the years that are past. . . . And my prayer is, that you will have opportunity to lead some of the young women of your parish to consecrate themselves to the work of the ministry. I would that you might lead them up, to be sharers with us in this work.[47]

Hanaford, a cousin of Lucretia Mott, did exactly that. A successful writer, as a young married woman she eked out the family income with the money she earned from her fourteen books. Raised a Quaker on the island of Nantucket, where, she wrote, "more women preachers there were than men," she converted first to the Baptist faith, and then to Universalism.[48] By 1865 she had begun to fulfill her childhood ambition to preach. Ordained in 1868, she apparently left her husband in 1870 to pastor the First Universalist Church in New Haven, sometimes serving as chaplain of the Connecticut legislature. In 1877 she moved to Jersey City, where in 1880 her congregation split over the issue of woman's rights, the cause next to Hanaford's heart, forcing her to preach for the next seven years in a public hall. After another stint in New Haven, she resigned her ministry in 1891 but continued her ardent support of woman suffrage and other women's issues.

What's particularly interesting in the history of these and other early Universalist and Unitarian women ministers is their concerted effort to recruit and mentor other clergywomen. We have found no record of such an effort in any other denomination, though some individual clergywomen did their best for other women. Nowhere does this effort manifest itself more plainly or to more effect than in the Unitarians' Iowa Sisterhood, of whom we know much, thanks to Cynthia Grant Tucker and Catherine F. Hitchings.

According to Hitchings, the Sisterhood was an offshoot of the "Women's Ministerial Conference, organized by Julia Ward Howe in 1875 as part of the rising women's rights movement."[49] This network of women flourished during the 1880s and 1890s on the frontier, where not many clergymen were eager to go, and where the parishioners were more flexible, more adventurous, and less traditionally minded than in longer-settled areas. These women clergy evolved styles of ministry different from those of clergymen, emphasizing church families, conceptualizing the church as a home, and thus allying their churches with the traditional woman's sphere. The liberals who constituted their congregations welcomed the warmth, reassurance, and comfort of this approach, for they had to endure not only the hardships of the frontier but also ostracism and sometimes persecution from their more orthodox neighbors. So churches pastored by the Sisterhood thrived.

The Sisterhood was birthed by Mary Augusta Safford (1851–1927) and her childhood friend Eleanor Gordon (1852–1942). Safford's father was a radical who argued for biblical fallibility, abolition, and the Darwinian theory; as a child she played at preaching. Gordon came from a family whose members debated passionately the different theologies that each supported. In their twenties these idealistic young women promised each other to spend their lives together in service to the world.[50] Prevented from taking college degrees by family responsibilities and poverty, they taught and tried to educate themselves. In 1879 they organized their first church in Hamilton, Iowa, with the staunch support of the Unitarian western secretary, Jenkin Lloyd Jones. It flourished, and Jones sent them next to Humboldt, Iowa, populated by independent-minded liberal dissenters. There in 1880 Safford was ordained.

Safford's and Gordon's lives in Humboldt were physically hard. They rented a second-floor flat of five rooms, to and from which they had to carry fuel, water, garbage, and ashes. Although clergymen usually would not take churches for less than eighty dollars a month, Gordon earned only half that, and Safford fractionally more than half. They also took on another church in Algona, twenty-eight miles away.

Just as their mothers had assumed the responsibility for teaching their daughters domestic skills, so Safford and Gordon undertook to train spiritual daughters in this new form of woman's work, the clergy. They took into their flat four teenage students at the local normal school who helped them as parish assistants and teaching aides. They spotted nine-year-old Mary Collson (1871–1953), encouraged her ministerial ambitions and helped her out with loans for her education. When Ida Hultin (1858–1938), a twenty-six-year-old Michigan lay preacher, arrived on the scene to assist Safford and take over the church at Algona, she joined in this recruiting and mentoring effort. When in 1885 Safford and Gordon moved to a new pulpit 125 miles farther west, they turned over their Humboldt ministry to sisters whom they had been grooming, Marion and Amelia Murdoch.

The Murdochs' father was a judge and legislator, their mother a freethinking liberal who encouraged her five daughters toward futures of service to society. Marion (1850–1943) as a young woman taught for several years, then at thirty-two entered Meadville Theological School as one of three women in a student body of twenty. At Humboldt she emulated Safford's conduct of her pastorate, clearing the debt, starting a new building program, and growing the membership. Harriet Beecher Stowe, Emerson, Victor Hugo, and William Gladstone spoke in her church. She herself preached most often on reform issues. And she recruited women clergy, copastored with women clergy, and tried to smooth their paths. At the Chicago World's Fair of 1893, she outlined career possibilities open to women, citing the ministry as one of the most appropriate, particularly since social work had become an integral part of the job. In 1890 she left Humboldt to work in Kalamazoo, Michigan, with Caroline Bartlett (1858–1935); in 1893 she moved on to Cleveland to serve with Florence Buck (1860–1925).

Bartlett and Buck were two more of the high-achieving women in the now well-established network of Unitarian clergywomen centered at Humboldt. Bartlett had consciously prepared for the ministry via journalism, covering murders, fires, and Native American uprisings, packing a pistol on her late-night assignments, working her way up to city editor in Oshkosh, Wisconsin. Journalism, she believed, sought to better society by raising public opinion, and taught her to write efficient prose, work rapidly amid confusion, and differentiate between reality and myth. Like many other members of the Sisterhood, she combined idealism with high administrative skills. During her pastorate at Kalamazoo her church organized the first kindergarten in the city, later incorporated into the public school system.

The members of the Sisterhood working the fertile Iowa religious soil a century ago would fit in well at the Re-Imagining Conferences of the 1990s. They involved the laity in the worship services, evolving a system of lay preaching, often by reading the sermons of famous clergy. Treating their congregations as a family, the pastors reminded them of their financial responsibilities to pay for and maintain the family (church) home. They insisted on the responsibility of their members to develop their own theology; their Unity Club searched for God, defined as "the power that makes for righteousness," where they could: in philosophy, in Darwinian theory, in biblical criticism, in temperance lectures. If the words of the hymns didn't fit their beliefs, they changed the words. Their philanthropic club adopted various charities in a primitive form of social action. "Lengthen the cord and strengthen the stakes," preached Safford and Gordon, setting an example by exchanging pulpits with other clergy and working in the state Unitarian association.

Above all the pastors of the Iowa Sisterhood challenged the received wisdom about women's role in the church. Hooting at the patriarchal churches' traditional reduction of women to the drudgery of serving church suppers and cleaning up afterwards, Marie Jenney Howe (1870–1921) speculated that no more than one in a hundred women really liked sewing as much as the typical clergyman seemed to think. Instead the clergywomen offered laywomen opportunities for self-affirmation rather than self-denial. They started groups in their churches that ensured consideration of women's perspectives and encouraged these groups to affiliate with the State Federations of Women's Clubs.

In this transformation they tactfully linked the ideology of the home with their own feminist visions.[51] They constantly paralleled church and home, instituting the practice of house christenings that marked parishioners' homes as "holy spaces." Analogously, the clergywomen saw to it that the twenty church buildings they and their parishes erected and paid for were homelike, hospitable, and designed for the needs of the church family. Often they thought of their own relationship to their parishes as one of motherhood. For instance, Florence Buck told a meeting of the Woman's Ministerial Conference about being "asked 'very diffidently' if she would conduct the funeral services of an honest and upright man who had died of drink, owing to an inherited tendency." His friends had expected, said Buck "to have [the funeral in the undertaker's rooms . . . but we had it in my own church. It was packed with people of all sorts, who had been interested in him; and the Bartenders' Union were there in a body. . . . It was an opportunity that I would not have given up to preach to the President and Senate of the United States. Next day . . . they said, 'We expected she'd wallop us to hell; but she talked to us like a mother.'"[52]

The Iowa Sisterhood recruited women ministers partly because its mentors were feminists interested in opening up the world for women. But necessity also played its part. Eliza Wilkes, a missionary whose interests lay in starting new church groups, was so often disappointed by the male seminarians sent from the East to keep the new churches going that she began looking for women in their stead. "A course at Harvard," she remarked, "is not sufficient antidote for a lifetime in Orthodoxy. You cannot plant 'eastern Unitarian churches' in this soil."[53]

So in the 1880s and in the 1890s not only in Iowa but also in Michigan, Minnesota, Nebraska, the Dakotas, and Ohio these Unitarian women ministers and their churches grew and flourished together. They were always a small group. Clergywomen were still so scarce on the ground that a railroad conductor questioned Caroline Bartlett's right to carry a clergy pass. But to their own parishioners their presence came to seem both natural and right. The first time Bartlett exchanged pulpits with a man, a child in her church cried, "Look, mama! There's a *man* up there in the pulpit." Anna Howard Shaw described the Iowa Sisterhood's work as "Women preaching back into the church the [lay]men who had been preached out of it by men."

But to the eastern establishment of the Unitarian church, the presence of the midwestern clergywomen was neither natural nor right: they saw the women more as a necessary evil, filling pulpits that men did not want in places men did not choose to live for salaries men would not accept. When a young newly ordained clergyman did venture westward, he often found the expectations of him incompatible with the life of study and contemplation that he had anticipated. The energetic, experienced clergywomen of the Sisterhood, comfortable on their own home grounds, were apt to show their disgust with his vaporings.

The clergywomen tended to ally themselves with church radicals, since conservatives would generally exclude them from leadership. Cracks opened between them and Unitarian headquarters in Boston. Highly qualified contemporary clergywomen whom we have interviewed have described the lack of respect and appreciation for their efforts displayed by their denominational hierarchies when they serve poor, struggling churches. In the 1880s and 1890s the Unitarian establishment showed the same indifference to the extraordinary achievements of the Iowa Sisterhood. The accomplishments of an Eleanor Gordon, who built a church from twenty-six members to almost two hundred in the first eighteen months of one pastorate, counted for little to them beside those of a clergyman in a large eastern church.

Inevitably the clergywomen, even those who worked in pairs, struggled with loneliness and feelings of inadequacy. Often their families as well as the overwhelmingly orthodox trinitarian townspeople among whom they lived disapproved of their career choices. Despite Safford's rise to the presidency of the Iowa Unitarian Association, few clergymen of other denominations welcomed them, and there were just not enough women in ministry overall for any substantial community. In 1892, two years after the United States census counted 101,640 Protestant clergy, Julia Ward Howe's Woman's Ministerial Conference comprised fewer than seventy ordained women (not counting Quakers): fifteen Methodists and Congregationalists combined, sixteen Unitarians, and thirty-two Universalists.

The differences between the Iowa Sisterhood and the eastern establishment were aggravated by intellectual and theological disagreements between the liberal midwestern and the conservative eastern Unitarian clergy, disagreements that eventually manifested themselves in church politics and financial disputes. Some hierarchy officials harassed the clergywomen in petty ways, refusing to send them enough church literature and standing them up on speaking dates. Some played not just hardball but dirty ball, as when Samuel Eliot suggested to Caroline Bartlett that she apply for a position in a church he knew to be closing. The women, struggling along on meager salaries, got tired of subsidizing by their labor pioneer work that young men with advantages refused.

Moreover, at the tag end of the nineteenth century, the Unitarian church was experiencing difficulties and losing status and members, especially in the often overchurched small towns of the Midwest. Clergymen worried about the emasculation of Christianity, just as the country generally was turning toward Theodore Roosevelt's rough-riding philosophy. What with one thing and another, many of the Sisterhood clergywomen had to wonder whether they couldn't find better things to do with their talents and energies.

Of course they could, expecially since many of them already had skills in another line of work: Eleanor Gordon for many years taught school; Lydia Jenkins also practiced as a physician.[54] Some of the talented, hardworking clergywomen transferred into the woman suffrage movement, others into social work, and still others into one form or another of municipal housekeeping. Some sought solutions to social problems through teaching and research. Celia Parker Woolley resigned from her Chicago church when after two years of her preaching against gambling her parishioners proposed to raise the money for her salary by card parties. She and her husband then moved to the edge of Chicago's black belt to found and run a settlement house, the Frederick Douglass Center. Late in the nineteenth century Caroline Bartlett became interested in urban sanitation, combining practical experience in it with brief study at the University of Chicago. Her expertise and the municipal "sanitary survey" she developed came into such demand across the nation that she finally had to impose a fee for her services, but she consistently refused to spend more than two months a year away from home—and the two children she and her husband adopted when she was fifty-five.[55]

✑ Clergywomen in Other Denominations

At the end of the nineteenth century prospects in the mainline churches could hardly hearten women who aspired to the clergy. Even the Quakers had wavered in their commitment to women Public Friends, as controversies about the nature of the ministry accompanied and provoked schisms among them. Though Quaker women still itinerated and acted as missionaries at home and abroad, some Quaker meetings had begun to professionalize the ministry: they began to pay pastors and coordinating secretaries, and for these positions they almost always hired men.[56]

Nonetheless, other denominations feared the influence of Quaker clergywomen, to the point of forbidding their own members to listen to them. When Quaker Sarah F. Smiley was invited to preach in one Presbyterian church a presbyter reprimanded the pastor for inviting her; in another the women of the congregation protested, preventing her from preaching there again. And in 1874 Presbyterian laity erected a special platform for her to speak from, so as to keep their pulpit pristine and uncontaminated by the presence of a woman.[57] Quaker Amanda Way in 1871 was actually licensed as a local preacher by the Methodist Episcopal church, but they came to themselves in 1880 and withdrew her license. She then returned to the Friends, serving as minister of the Monthly Meeting in Whittier, California.[58]

Among the Quaker clergywomen of the time the best known was Elizabeth Leslie Rous Comstock (1815–1891). Inspired by the example of the British Elizabeth Fry, Comstock combined itinerating across the nation with public work ranging from woman's rights to resettling African-Americans in Kansas. She focused particularly on prison reform and the urban poor. In an early form of lobbying she often arranged to speak before legislative bodies to promote her causes and to meet privately with governors and presidents. Her interview with President Lincoln, it was said, developed into a Quaker prayer meeting in which he participated.[59]

As nineteenth-century Congregationalists, Universalists, and Unitarians gingerly experimented with women's ordination, here and there other small spinoff denominations began halfheartedly to credential women. In 1887 Louisa Woosley, who had first felt the call to the ministry in 1874, gained acceptance by the Nolin Presbytery of the Cumberland Presbyterian Church as a candidate for the ministry; in 1888 she was licensed to preach and to keep all the funds she raised; and in 1889 she was ordained. Heated objections put many Presbyterian commissioners "in the uncomfortable position of supporting female ordination in order to protect the right of individual presbyteries to ordain."[60] Woosley went right on preaching and pastoring, but few women followed in her footsteps. In 1893 the denomination did appoint Edith Livingston Peake a lay evangelist, a post apparently resorted to by small, poor, rural churches that could find no "real minister."[61]

For a short period it looked as though the Methodist Episcopal church might be edging toward women's ordination. For instance, local Methodist authorities in 1868 awarded evangelist Maggie (Margaret Ann Newton) Van Cott (1830–1914) an exhorter's license and the next year a local preacher's license, making her the first American woman that church licensed to preach and allegedly "the only licensed female preacher in the State of New York."[62]

By that time this New York City widow had already made a success of the drugstore she inherited from her husband, selling remedies such as "frog-in-the-throat lozenges."[63] She had already experienced a shouting conversion, made converts at Phoebe Palmer's Five Points mission, and led a series of revival meetings in upstate New York—after many ladylike protests that "it is the work of the gentlemen to preach." She had also endured criticism, hearing folks whisper, "They say that she is a bad woman from New York, Or . . . that Col. R—'thinks it an abominable shame, and declares the Methodist Church will never get over the disgrace of allowing a woman in the pulpit. And if *she* should put her foot in the Presbyterian Church [of which he was a member], he would soon show her the door and put her out.'"[64]

But the Methodist church as a denomination refused to accept Van Cott's exhorter's license. By that time her many conversions had given her the courage to counter, "Don't it? Well, God allows it. I received my commission from him, brother. . . . I think what God owns and blesses, man has no right to condemn." After all, during the previous year she had preached 335 hour-long sermons; attended ninety-one class meetings and sixty-nine prayer meetings; united five hundred probationers with the Methodist church; and traveled three thousand miles. She had saved many souls from the "whirlpool of intemperance" or from infidelity, bringing them "from darkness into light."[65] For all this she received from the churches she visited $735.35.

Contemporary reports on her, whether effusive or condemnatory, agreed that Van Cott was an impressive figure. "Queenly and majestic," weighing in at over two hundred pounds, she dressed elegantly, "with faultless taste—rich, yet with becoming simplicity." Her face was "sweet and winning." One reporter described her elocution as "natural and florid, and her sentences uttered in a bass tone voice." Another complained that "She has a voice of great power, but of no compass. She expends about four times as much vocal energy as is necessary. . . . [Her discourse is] characterized by a very offensive familiarity."[66] Whatever Van Cott's style, the *New York Times* went to the crux of the matter when it reported on May 17, 1869, that one Rev. Dr. Ferris had asked a meeting of Methodist ministers "whether it was well for the official board of a church in this city to invite her into their pulpit? If this woman preached, crowds would throng to hear her from curiosity, and congregations would be drawn away from their own proper churches."[67]

None of Van Cott's accomplishments won over the denomination to women's ordination. In 1880, when Anna Oliver and Anna Howard Shaw sought ordination, the Methodist Episcopal church responded by rescinding all licenses to preach granted to women. Van Cott went her way unperturbed.

The Free Will Baptists, after balking at women's ordination at their General Conference of 1883, in 1886 resolved "that intelligent, godly women who are so situated as to devote their time to the work of the ministry, and desire to be ordained, should receive such indorsement and authority as ordination involves, provided there are no objections to such indorsement other than the matter of sex." That year they implemented their resolution by fully ordaining Anna Bartlett.[68]

In 1892, when she was "about 40," the ordination of Amelia Adelaide Frost was described as "the first ordination of a woman in New England to the Orthodox Congregational ministry." Frost, having taught for seven years, had married a budding minister and attended lectures at Andover theological seminary with him. After three years in the parish ministry the couple undertook missionary work in the West, where the terrifying experience of being lost in a North Dakota blizzard brought on the husband "nervous prostration" so severe that he never recovered fully. His wife began to read his sermons, then to preach in his place, then to assume responsibility as interim minister, meanwhile meeting near penury by taking in boarders. With delighted relief, the pair landed at a Congregational church in Littleton, Massachusetts, where the congregation, knowing that the husband could not physically carry out his duties, ordained Amelia Frost as associate minister. A woman journalist for the Leominster *Enterprise* bitingly reported the examination Frost underwent: "Before her, rows of clergymen, determined to prove her fitness (some of them bore the look of hoping to prove her unfitness) by the strictest tests." The "ordeal by questioning" provoked "more than one clergyman" to say "that it was sharper than any to which he had ever heard a man subjected." But Frost won their smiles and hearts when asked "Why did you preach at first?" by answering, "To please my husband."[69]

If women's ordinations in white churches were few and far between, in African-American churches even less pressure for women's ordination seems to have been exerted. A number of reasons help to account for this difference. Obviously black women were otherwise occupied with the jarring transition from slavery to freedom. Preaching developed as the primary upwardly mobile occupation for black men, teaching for educated black women. Concerned for their menfolk in a society that demeaned them, black women have historically hesitated to "usurp" traditionally male functions. The other roles that women played within the black churches afforded them considerable influence and esteem. And throughout American history black women have been more likely than white women to evangelize independently and to start up their own churches rather than to seek ordination in the churches of their upbringing.

Like its white ancestor, the early mainline African Methodist Episcopal (AME) church, established in 1816, did not ordain clergywomen, though many AME women preached unlicensed and their unremitting pressure by 1900 had opened to women the post of evangelist.[70] In 1894 Julia Foote (b. 1823), whose record flickers in and out of history, became the first woman ordained deacon in the African Methodist Episcopal Zion (AMEZ) church, and in 1900 its second ordained woman elder. But all this happened only after a lifetime of effort.

Foote, converted at fifteen and sanctified at seventeen, ran into her sailor husband's opposition soon after her marriage when she began to preach sanctification to the members of her Boston AMEZ church. Even when he threatened to send her back to her parents, neither he nor her minister could quell her call to preach. "Though my gifts were but small," she said, "I could not be shaken by what man might think or say." With her husband "it was difficult for me to mark the exact line between disapprobation and Christian forbearance and patient love." But she was consoled by reading in her Bible that "thy Maker is thine husband." She had to preach, she felt, for extended visions and angelic messengers told her over and over, "You are lost unless you obey God's righteous commands."[71]

So after her church expelled her, she evangelized at home, then in hired halls, and from 1845 on in itinerancy. Some ministers invited her to preach in their churches; some fought her bitterly. In 1849 Ann M. Johnson began traveling with her, assisting at services by singing, praying, and testifying. On their travels they experienced discrimination and danger because of their race: they were forced to sit up on a boat deck all night because no cabins were available to them; they were delayed because on trains they were not permitted to ride in coaches if any white passenger objected; in Baltimore their bodies were searched for marks of whippings in an endeavor to prove them runaway slaves. In 1851 we lose sight of Foote; throat troubles may have silenced her for a long period, but in 1869 she evidently resumed her preaching, now alone, for Johnson had died in the 1850s. Eventually Foote became a missionary for the AMEZ church, that work in time leading to her ordination as deacon and then elder. Foote's long experience in African-American churches so buffeted her that in her autobiography she wrote, "Dear sisters, who are in the evangelistic work now, you may think you have hard times; but let me tell you, I feel that the lion and lamb are lying down together, as compared with the state of things twenty-five or thirty years ago."[72]

At least one clergywoman experimented with a new kind of ministry, as a prison chaplain. In the 1850s the United Brethren had compromised on the question of ordaining women by giving Lydia Sexton (b. 1799) "recommendations" as a "pulpit speaker." Despite the many converts she made, bitter experience led her to write, "Quite a number of the people would rather go to a ball than to meeting; yet they would go to hear a woman preach. As soon, however, as the hammer of God's word bruised their flinty hearts, oh! how they would cry out against woman-preaching. 'I don't see why people let women go around preaching and setting children all in an uproar when they know that some people—and a good many, too, will be fools enough to go and hear them.'" Yet Sexton encouraged other women to enter the ministry, praying for one woman, "May God give her the victory over the man-fearing or man-pleasing spirit." And for another potential clergywoman she mourned, "What a pity that such talents should be buried in a napkin."[73]

In 1870 Sexton was appointed chaplain of Kansas State Prison at Leavenworth. Prison authorities did not welcome her. Why, they asked, should prisons have chaplains at all? And why such an outlandish phenomenon as a woman chaplain? It must be illegal. A prison conference in Cincinnati that year debated the question, "Is it right for women to labor in penitentiaries for the reformation of men, and to what extent?" Called on to respond, Sexton rephrased the question to "Is it right for a woman to do good?" But she herself perceived the ironies of the situation: "To preach to a congregation dressed in such strange uniform and guarded with guns, was a circumstance hard to reconcile with the gospel of peace which I was preaching." Concluding that she must make a virtue of necessity, she went on with her work, distributing tracts, teaching the three Rs along with the Bible, preaching, and giving communion. She had some successes, baptizing twenty-four. Some of the men, she claimed, began studying for the ministry. In her old age Sexton was often cited as the oldest woman preacher in America: she was still pastoring in Seattle, Washington, at ninety-three.[74]

✑ The Holiness and Pentecostal Churches

The holiness churches were a different kettle of believers. During the latter years of the nineteenth century and well into the twentieth, evangelical sects proliferated. The holiness movement in which Phoebe Palmer had worked parented many of them. This group within the Methodist church had at first innocuously formed interdenominational associations that sponsored camp meetings, but its members had gone on to threaten the Methodist establishment by organizing interdenominational missions and then independent churches. Between 1893 and 1907, the movement generated at least twenty-five holiness sects in the United States.[75] Pentecostalism, which insisted on speaking in tongues as a sign of conversion, added its current to the spate of new churches.

In the freshness of the world to which they believed themselves reborn, some of these new denominations recognized women as equal in the eyes of God, as long as they remained submissive in their families. But they still believed in the natural inferiority of women, and they still limited women's opportunities. Indeed, most churches were experiencing fears about the feminization of religion; fundamentalist men shared with mainline men the effort to masculinize religion—they just went about it differently. As Betty DeBerg argues, while mainline clergymen advocating reform and a social gospel tried to claim a place in the masculine political world, fundamentalists "tried to remasculinize the church with aggressive language and militant posturing."[76]

But for a time clergywomen flourished in some holiness and pentecostal churches. Max Weber has commented that the religion of the "disprivileged classes, in contrast to the aristocratic cults of the martial nobles, is characterized by the tendency to allot equality to women,"[77] and by and large these were churches of the "disprivileged" classes. Pragmatically, they didn't have enough clergymen to go around, and their theology allowed for the validity of women's call to ministry. Among themselves these churches differed heatedly on some theological points and in their approval of practices such as speaking in tongues, but they were as one in emphasizing sanctification resulting from direct interaction between the Holy Spirit and the human soul.[78] Even if the soul was in a female body.

In their beginnings, a call from God was the litmus test for clergy. Studying the primitive Christianity of the first centuries after Christ, holiness churches found stories of women spreading the gospel as missionaries and sponsors of church houses and tried to restore their women communicants to the status of those early days. Even more importantly, they acknowledged the validity of the experience of the Holy Spirit in women like Rachel Peterson, who testified: "The Lord tells us not to be man-pleasers, but to fear God." Sarah Smith (b. 1822) said, "When God sanctified me he took all the shrink and fear of men and devils out of me." So fortified, at the age of sixty-one Smith told her husband, "I am done cooking for farming," announcing her intention to evangelize. He finished eating breakfast, walked out, came back, asked when she was leaving, and said, "I will get you some money."[79] He "sold a cow, gave her the money and his blessing, and agreed to get the housework done some other way."[80]

The Church of God's Nora Siens Hunter (b. 1873) ministered from the Floating Bethel, a gospel houseboat built on a flatboat, where workers advertised meetings by putting notices in bottles and throwing them into the Ohio River. Mary Cole (b. 1853) tore up her Methodist membership letter when her church refused to acknowledge her call to the ministry; she then resorted to the Church of God. Cole put up with a lot. Her meetings were plagued with hurled eggs, fumes from the red peppers someone put on a stove, even gunshots, and the spread of a rumor that she was one of the James boys, disguised as a woman. But she survived to win many a camp meeting race to the pulpit, where the person who got there first was the person who preached.[81]

African-American women also pioneered for the Church of God. Jane Williams about 1886 started a congregation in Charleston, South Carolina, that became the denominational headquarters in the South. Prayer warrior and evangelist Mary Frambo, born a slave, helped to found a Church of God in Atlanta and pastored a storefront church in Chicago. Mother Priscilla Wimbish and her husband saved campgrounds in Pennsylvania from foreclosure by selling their own home.[82]

As Cheryl Townsend Gilkes has taught us, African-American Sanctified churches in the holiness and pentecostal traditions have differed in their perceptions of women from the black Baptists and Methodists who broke away from mainline white denominations.[83] By and large, women within them succeeded better than their Baptist and Methodist sisters (white or black) in winning ordination, to the extent that some women left the Baptists and Methodists to exercise their calling in a Sanctified church. Even those Sanctified denominations that barred women from their male hierarchy permitted them official roles in an *almost* autonomous female system of church goverment *and* understood such women's roles as evangelists and deaconesses as ministry. This parallel structure, Gilkes notes, was "closer to the dual sex political systems characteristic of some West African societies than to the patriarchal episcopal politics of European origin." Distinctions between women teachers and men preachers blurred: "In some denominations, [women] evangelists not only could have charge of churches but also, as in the case of Pentecostal Assemblies of the World, could serve communion and perform marriages. In some instances, the difference between women's and men's credentials was merely internal; for all practical and legal purposes, women evangelists were clergy."[84]

Controversies over gender issues nonetheless arose within Sanctified churches. Denominations that ordained women as elders and pastors did not want women bishops; some refused to ordain women at as early an age as men; some termed what men did preaching, what women did teaching. In the Church of God in Christ women developed their own standards for examining and promoting evangelists, more stringent than the men's, requiring candidates for licenses to preach successfully at revivals in seven states.[85] In the Church of the Living God, Christian Workers For Fellowship (C.W.F.F.) women pastored congregations and evangelist wives copastored with their husbands, but men usually won ordination soon after their call, while women had first to serve as missionaries and evangelists for as long as twenty years.[86] Sometimes denominational controversies over women's functions provoked schisms. And beyond a doubt, many women chose instead of the ministry community service and reform, "sublimated paths to ministry."[87]

Of all African-American holiness "preacher women" of the late nineteenth century, evangelist Amanda Berry Smith (1837–1915) achieved the most fame. Her powerful preaching and her singing won her repute not only in the United States but also in Europe and Africa. Although she often spoke of herself as a washerwoman, Frances Willard called her "the African Sybil, the Christian Saint." In her autobiography Smith wrote that until she was sanctified she always feared whites "because they were white, and were there, and I was black, and here!" After sanctification, "the great mountain had become a mole-hill." But, she commented realistically, "Some people don't get enough of the blessing to take prejudice out of them, even after they are sanctified."[88] Believing herself ordained by God, she never sought institutional ordination, but refraining availed her nothing: clergymen blamed her anyway for what they supposed her to believe.

Holiness churches, whether black or white, accounted for most of the increase in the numbers of women clergy during the nineteenth century. The holiness movement was to reach new numbers and new heights in the twentieth century. But of all the holiness churches, none has affected American life so significantly and in such distinctive ways as the Salvation Army. Most of the American laity and some American clergy think of the Salvation Army solely in terms of Christmas kettles; pickup trucks for the flotsam and jetsam of our households; and soup, soap, and salvation for homeless men. Conditioned by the stage, we talk of Salvation Army lassies like Shaw's Major Barbara or Miss Sarah Brown of *Guys and Dolls.* We're off the mark. The Salvation Army is a major Protestant denomination that ordains (commissions) more women clergy than any other.[89]

The Army was founded in Great Britain in 1865 by William and Catherine Booth. Catherine, who had already defended Phoebe Palmer in *Female Ministry,*[90] saw to the unequivocal reading of clause 14 of the Foundation Deed: "Nothing shall authorize the Conference to take any course whereby the right of females to be employed as evangelists or class leaders shall be impeded or destroyed or which shall render females ineligible for any office or deny to them the right to speak and vote at all or any official meetings of which they may be members."

Unofficially the Army invaded the United States in 1879, when seventeen-year-old immigrant Lt. Eliza Shirley and her parents held a service, announcing that "Two Hallelujah Females"—Eliza and her mother—would sing and speak for God.[91] Their streetcorner meeting drew jeers and mud balls, and no one showed up in the hall they had hired. Undeterred, they continued to proselyte, and in 1880 the Booths sent seven women, headed by ten-year Army veteran Capt. Emma Westbrook, and under the leadership of Commissioner George Scott Railton, to take charge of the mission work—the Army's first overseas crusade. Why so many women? For one thing, in England the Booths' fledgling Army was attracting a lot of women. For another, Railton and Catherine Booth wanted to ensure the advancement of women within the Army. Finally, Railton assumed that the women would marry in the States, thereby making the Army indigenously American. As one officer emphatically told us, "A lot of people will tell you the founders of the Salvation Army [in the United States] were George Scott Railton and seven ladies. Well, don't you believe it. Number one, Eliza Shirley did it, and I've always been ticked off that we don't know what the seven ladies' names are."

From the outset, thanks to necessity, a pragmatic approach to the Army's mission, and Catherine Booth, the Salvation Army held out to competent women the same appeal and rewards as the secular military service extends today: women got responsibility and power, and they got it young. Absent from the Army's records are the dithering and debate over whether women could/should preach and pastor so rife elsewhere in Christianity and in Judaism. William Booth was a practical man, focused on winning the world for Christ, not arguing doctrine—a characteristic that saved him from the circumlocutions about women preachers and forced retreats of, say, a John Wesley. Catherine Booth's intelligent sensitivity to women's issues kept her husband from the patriarchal assumptions into which he as a man of his times might otherwise have fallen. So in 1880 Captain Westbrook was at once put in charge of New York #1 on Seventh Avenue in Manhattan, where "she preached the gospel and collared roughnecks," and the rest of the missionary platoon marched on to new fields.[92]

Salvation Army women soldiers (laity, church members) and officers (clergy) went right on in the forefront of the work to establish new outposts in America, using the Army's strategy of responding to needs. In 1887 in Brooklyn four home-sick Scandinavian laundresses—Salvation Army soldiers—began holding Swedish services after the regular Sunday services, an undertaking that eventually developed into several new Army corps. Capt. Emma J. Brown sent plainclothes soldiers she called "Slum Sisters" to help the poor in any way they could; when asked why, they spoke of Christ. During the Spanish-American War Brigadier Alice Lewis and another woman officer ministered to troops assembling at Tampa and Key West to invade Cuba.[93]

In these early days Salvationists faced physical assaults. In Brooklyn bricks thrown at short range struck Capt. Mary Powell in the head. In Portland, Maine, a chunk of ice knocked a young woman officer unconscious and permanently deaf-ened her. Fortunately, by the mid–1890s the Salvation Army had conquered suffi-ciently that these attacks ceased.[94]

Despite the many leadership posts that from the outset the Salvation Army has offered women, they have not of course enjoyed equality of opportunity or reward within it. Its orthodox Wesleyan theology notwithstanding, the Army has always been too much in and of the society and the times to escape the general societal prejudices and practices, some of which have been hardened, if not engraved in stone, by Salvation Army regulations. In at least one sense, these regulations invade the private lives of its officers even more than those of the United States military affect its members: Salvation Army officers may marry only each other. This requirement raises surprisingly few objections: usually it is simply accepted unques-tioningly.

One officer told us about her engagement and marriage:

I really didn't think I would be a married person, because as everywhere else we women [in the Salvation Army] outnumber the men by a great deal. [My future hus-band] had been sent to train in the finance department, and my mother worked there in the headquarters. She and another lady who had known me said, "Wait until you meet our Alice." So really all I had to do was go home and pick him up. During our courtship we only saw each other five or six times before we were engaged, which was a giant leap of—faith. By this time I was on the training college staff; the training princi-pal called me in and said, "We're hoping not to change the staff in the middle of a ses-sion next year, and we noticed this young man coming up to see you. What are your intentions?" I said, "I'm going to marry him." That's when I knew that it was the right thing. He hadn't asked. I just knew. I said, "Don't tell anybody, because he doesn't know it yet." So I ran upstairs and called him on the phone. In our marriage ceremony we promise to be a continual comrade in the salvation war. I called him and said, "I have found the continual comrade for you." He said, "Oh, really? Who is that?" And I said, "Me." He went speechless. He said, "I'll call you back." He called my mother, and she said, "You probably ought to get her back on the phone." So we were engaged. We were married the following November. Thirty-four years now.

Our next question took the officer by surprise: would she have considered marrying him had he not been in the Salvation Army? "Why, I don't know," she said. "You see, our most common bond is the Army. It's our whole life. I personally don't think it could work otherwise. It's such a commitment. If you're a corps officer, you're on duty twenty-four hours a day."

Even structurally the Army is built on the assumption that husband and wife are one, and that one is the husband. True enough, both married partners are officers, for the Army expects both husband and wife to do its work, though it allows some flexibility when the family has young children. Until the 1990s the wife was addressed and expected to sign herself as "Mrs. Major John Doe," to avoid the problem of having two Major Does in one office. Until the 1990s, both partners held the same rank, *even if it was lower than the one she had earned* as a single woman, since at marriage the wife took the husband's rank. (Now both hold the higher of the ranks earned: a lieutenant husband marrying a captain wife becomes a captain.) Even in the mid-1990s, for the work of both, one check is made out, to the husband. The husband alone has a social security account, a practice with devastating results for the wife in case of a divorce, when both must at least temporarily leave the Army: she may be left late in her working life with no social security credits to her account at all.

What's more, the wife's work assignment has almost always been governed by her husband's. In the corps—that part of the Army that runs its missions and churches (rather than its rescue work or stores or administration)—the couple's on-site autonomy allows them to divide up the work as they see fit. Even so, until late in the twentieth century, the Army has typically assigned couples primarily on the basis of the husband's qualifications. Outside the corps, the wife's options have been much more limited. The Army has assigned the husband on the basis of his qualifications and abilities, and the wife has willy-nilly performed whatever duties had evolved for the wife of the man who had formerly held her husband's job. At best these duties have often been far afield from the wife's experience, abilities, or interests; at worst they have felt like made work.

Single women have had other problems, primarily in that not all assignments were open to them. Partly this is a matter of a sort of glass ceiling, though twice in its history women have held the Army's top spot. Partly the practice simply duplicates that in other denominations, by which clergywomen are most often sent to small churches, poor churches, or moribund churches.

For the most part Salvation Army women have accepted these handicaps uncomplainingly. A cheerful lot, they understand themselves to be under orders in the service of a cause that they value and to which they have committed their lives. Usually they do not know how long an assignment will last or where they will next be sent. When they transfer, usually on short notice, they move into Army-owned quarters furnished down to the last dishtowel, sometimes tastefully, sometimes not. The situation simplifies their moves, but must harrow the souls of those among them with strong nesting instincts. In any case a historic shift in headquarters practice, at least in some corps, suggests that news of transfers has not always occasioned rejoicing: at one time the Scandinavian corps read out the new appointments at a festive occasion, but eventually, to avoid "disturbing the joy," they sent the orders by mail, then took off on vacation.[95]

But Salvation Army women are accepted; they hold the Army's commission; they are sure of a job and a pension; and their uniforms announce who they are and how far they have risen within the Army's ranks. Moreover, they can look forward to "promotion to glory." As one of them told us, "I have this absolute belief that God called me into the Army, that he fitted me for the task that was there, that there was no place in the Salvation Army I could serve where God could not use me. Therefore, if I was frustrated because I had ambition, I was not frustrated in God's plan for my life."

Logic would suggest that a nineteenth-century phenomenon closely related to millennialism, the founding of religiously based utopian communities, would contribute to the acceptance of clergywomen, but not so. Most of these communities, from Bronson Alcott's Fruitlands to Joseph Smith's Mormon colony, were male dominated; the outstanding exception, the Sanctified Sisters (a.k.a. the Woman's Commonwealth), exercised no perceptible influence on the history of clergywomen. Even when a group elevated a woman to religious leadership, attitudes toward women remained unchanged. Look, for example, at the Amana Inspirationists, about whom reporter Charles Nordhoff wrote, "The [female] sex, I believe, is not highly esteemed by these people, who think it dangerous to the Christian's peace of Mind."[96] They recognized Barbara Heinemann Landmann as a *Werkzeuge* or incarnate vehicle of Holy Spirit and obeyed her adjurations, no matter how unreasonable, but they demeaned women generally.

✒ The Position of Clergywomen at the Turn of the Century _____

Although mainline churches were indeed the first not to credential but formally to ordain women, it remained for the holiness churches to ordain them in significant numbers. In these churches *for a time* the theological concept that all believers stand equal before God outweighed the strictures of St. Paul against noisy women and the second-class position of women in the general society.

By and large, in the late nineteenth century Universalism and Unitarianism provided as nurturing an environment for clergywomen as could be found in any mainline denomination except the Society of Friends. Other established clergywomen as well as those in the Iowa Sisterhood did their best to attract other women to the profession they loved, Effie McCollum Jones in 1910 even going so far as to say that she had encountered no antagonism and could always easily find a parish. Some Universalist and Unitarian clergymen tried to recruit and mentor promising women, spoke out in their favor, and loaned them their pulpits. Longtime Universalist pastor George S. Weaver endorsed clergywomen in irrefutable terms: "Whether they do better or worse, a church that has stood the failures and blunders of a man ministry as long as the Christian church, need not fear the experiment of a few woman preachers."[97]

What's more, all clergywomen, but especially Unitarians, had the devoted support of Julia Ward Howe (1819–1910), famed since 1862 for writing "The Battle Hymn of the Republic." Howe herself from the nursery had clerical aspirations. As her daughters wrote, "Our mother was never ordained; it is doubtful whether she ever contemplated such a step; but she felt herself consecrated to the work; wherever she was asked to preach, she went as if on wings, feeling this call more sacred than any other. She preached in all parts of the country, from Maine to California, from Minnesota to Louisiana."[98] She appointed herself an admiring guardian angel for Unitarian clergywomen, turning up at their ordinations, entertaining them in her home, going to hear them preach, trying to relieve their sense of isolation by a twenty-year struggle (1873–1893) to put on a sound footing the Woman's Ministerial Conference, originally called the Woman's Church. She saw it as linked to the cause of woman suffrage and, her daughters said, valued it even above the Association for the Advancement of Women, over which she presided for twenty-five years. Howe wrote:

> The new liberties of utterance which the discussion of woman suffrage had brought us seemed at this time not only to invite, but to urge upon us a participation in the advocacy of the most vital interests both of the individual and of the community. With some of us, this advocacy naturally took the form of preaching. Pulpits were offered us on all sides, and the charm of novelty lent itself to such merit and power as Nature had vouchsafed us. I am so much of a natural churchwoman, I might say an ecclesiast, that I at once began to dream of a church of true womanhood.

Her words were gentle, but her ideas accord with late-twentieth-century feminist theology.

> I felt how much the masculine administration of religious doctrine had overridden us women, and I felt how partial and one-sided a view of these matters had been inculcated by men, and handed down by man-revering mothers. Now, I thought, we have got hold of what is really wanting in the Church universal. We need to have the womanly side of religion represented. Without this representation, we shall not have the fulness of human thought for the things that most deeply concern it.[99]

Howe was not alone in such hopes. Frances Willard (1839–1898) worked to support clergywomen and even teetered on the brink of becoming one: she actually worked for a few months in 1877 with the evangelist Dwight L. Moody. That same year Elizabeth Oakes Prince Smith (1806–1893), woman's rights advocate and author of dime novels, pastored an independent church in upper New York state for about a year.[100] Clergywomen themselves seized on every sighting of another as cause for good cheer. In an 1890 letter Anna Howard Shaw described herself as "almost in the seventh heaven when we all three [clergywomen] ascended the pulpit" of Mila F. Tupper's Methodist church in Grand Rapids, Michigan. Universalist minister Emma Bailey boasted of the Woman's Ministerial Conference at the Columbian Exposition of 1893, where "We heard fifteen women preachers give their experience."[101]

Others shared Bailey's optimism. A newspaperman interviewed a group of women delegates denied seating at the 1892 Methodist conference; he reported that one woman "had divulged that there is a movement among the women of the church for 'ordination' outside the church authorities," noting that "about 200 women are studying Greek and otherwise preparing in scripture study" to be ready for such an event.[102] An 1890s clipping evidently from a Unitarian or Universalist publication proclaimed:

> Wherever the work of women in the ministry is known, there is a demand for their services. Women ministers are constantly appealed to to secure women to fill places vacated by them, and to fill other pulpits where women have never preached. "Send us a woman," is the cry from dozens of parishes we have visited. One member of this committee has spoken for a Congregational, a Methodist, and a [?] society; and each in turn asked, through its officers, with much earnestness, "Could we, by any possibility, secure a woman to take charge of our church?" The liberal churches of the West seem always ready and eager to hear a woman from the pulpit. It is not too much to say that, if fifty more women were ready for the work, places could be secured for them.[103]

Maybe so, but testimony from women who responded to the call indicates that they had to slog through dispiriting conditions. Ella Elizabeth Bartlett (d. 1931), for instance, a Universalist home missionary ordained in 1878, wrote of her work in New York state: "Geneva, Farmerville, Fulton, were dormant or dead. Fulton preferred to stay dead. Farmerville lived a year. Geneva for quite a number of years." She earned only a minimal salary, sometimes only enough to cover her train fare. At the end of her life she bitterly summed up her career, describing herself as "just a commonplace nobody who has done what she could to promote the faith called Universalism and had so little success that it is not worth mentioning."[104]

Ruth Tucker and Walter Liefeld believe that in 1888 women pastors in mainline denominations probably numbered only about twenty. This figure may well be low; Elizabeth Cazden notes that the 1880 census listed 165 women ministers with parish jobs, of whom thirty-three were Unitarian-Universalists. That figure, however, probably included spiritualists. In any case the number of clergywomen was strikingly low.[105] At century's end a woman's ordination was still a marvel. About

1899, a laywoman reminisced about having heard Olympia Brown twenty-five years earlier: "She was the first woman preacher I ever saw; she has remained the only one." Given that clergywomen had been at large in North America for more than two hundred years, given that the 1900 census enumerated 7,399 women physicians and surgeons, one has to ask what was holding women back in the clergy?

✍ Channeling Women Away from Ordination: Missionaries and Deaconesses

Instead of credentialing clergywomen, churches continued to steer women into missionary work, both overseas and in North America. Presbyterian Sue McBeth (d. 1895), for instance, spent a lifetime as a fully accredited missionary in service to the Nez Perce tribe in the Northwest, where she trained native male ministers.[106] After abolition, in an effort focused primarily on secular education, mission boards and societies sent women teachers, both black and white, to work among the newly freed slaves. These missionaries endured not only hardship and suspicion, but obloquy; some denominations warned them that if they undertook such work they could never after its completion live in the South. Baptist Joanna P. Moore had spoken to a black person only once in her life when in 1863 as a twenty-year-old she went to work on a Mississippi River island. There in the face of active opposition from whites she established a home for the aged, a number of mini-libraries, and several schools, which she then turned over for operation to African-Americans she had trained.[107]

The missionaries to the former slaves encountered opposition also from black men. African-American Virginia Broughton, a freeborn teacher educated at Fisk University, spent most of her adult life in mission to black communities, especially to their women and children. Commissioned in 1882 by the Bible and Normal Institute, she organized Bible Bands of women to study the scriptures and morally influence home and family. Along the way she had to deal with black clergymen and laymen, "as if," Broughton said, "there was some cause of alarm for the safety of their own positions of power and honor. . . . we were given a good shaking and thrashing, and for a season the work seemed to stand still." One brother said, "I would rather take a rail and flail the life out of a woman than to hear her speak in the church." Another fulminated that he would throw Broughton out the window, men locked church doors against the Bible Bands' meetings, and one husband drew a gun on his wife and threatened to kill her if she attended her Band.[108]

Churches were also experimenting with a new profession into which to divert aspiring clergywomen. Perhaps casting an envious eye at the useful and uncomplaining Roman Catholic nuns, Protestant clergy in several denominations came up with the idea that women could be deaconesses, who would nurse, teach, and assist clergymen with tasks like parish calling or record keeping. After 1850, when Lutheran Katherine Louise Martin became the first American deaconess, several other Protestant churches established that office.[109] Lutherans usually have employed their deaconesses in social service. So have the Mennonites and Evangelicals. Episcopal deaconesses, however, have served mostly in parishes, although some functioned with considerable independence as de facto home missionaries, in Appalachia, on Indian reservations, and in rural ghettos and urban slums. Methodist deaconesses could serve the church or any of its agencies in any capacity not requiring full clergy rights, from teacher to pastor's assistant—or supply pastor.

Although as with women missionaries some clergymen feared that deaconesses might invade the pulpit, many others welcomed them.[110] In fact, Catherine M. Prelinger suggests, the development of the deaconess order helped clergymen to professionalize the modern ministry, for the deaconesses could do the work that clergymen had abandoned or did not want to do, leaving the men free to pursue scholarship.[111] On the other hand, as the founding clergy had hoped, the deaconesses greatly extended the range of social services sponsored by churches, well beyond what clergy were trained or could be expected to do, enabling churches to serve society in accordance with the social gospel developing in the late nineteenth century. Even after churches stopped recruiting deaconesses, their influence lingered and remains today, notably in the support services that churches offer the aged and the poor.

Deaconesses were often trained at the new Bible schools that originated in the United States in the 1880s, along with Sunday School teachers and superintendents, settlement workers, Bible teachers, evangelists, church visitors and church secretaries, YWCA workers, missionaries, church musicians, evangelists, and even pastors—what Virginia Brereton calls "God's Army."[112] Designed for fast, practical training, these schools usually took their students as they were and planned courses to meet their immediate needs, often operating on a high-school level. They concentrated on a thorough knowledge of the Bible and on practical evangelistic skills. They required their students to do fieldwork and brought in as speakers activists such as "Mother" Whittemore, who in 1890 had founded the Door of Hope, the New York City mission to rescue "fallen" women. Students were usually in their early or mid-twenties, or even older. Sometimes the schools were (and are) denominationally sponsored, such as the Baptist Missionary Training School founded in 1881 in Chicago; more often they were ecumenical or at least unaffiliated. In their emphasis on practical and applied skills these Bible schools breathed the air of their times, when many turned away from classical education toward the social sciences and technology, which students learned in new normal schools, vocational schools, and professional schools of one kind and another.[113]

Women participated in their founding, as with Moody Bible Institute: Emma Dryer, quondam principal of the Illinois State Normal University, with Dwight Moody's encouragement conducted a program in Chicago in the 1870s and early 1880s that trained women as Bible teachers and city missionaries. Obviously the Bible schools appealed to women, whom most theological seminaries refused to enroll, and for whom these schools met a felt need. Even in coeducational institutions, women usually predominated both in the student body and on the faculty. Faculty women were commonly graduates of normal schools or of Bible schools, often of the schools in which they taught. Some of them combined teaching with "lives as active evangelists, revivalists, missionary leaders, and even preachers."[114] Certainly Bible school women did not have to face the harrowing experiences that Antoinette Brown underwent in theological seminary at Oberlin or Olympia Brown at St. Lawrence. The schools provided a nurturing culture for women desiring careers in religion. Yet once they had ensured their own survival, even some of these schools treated women as second-class citizens, barring them from ministerial courses and limiting their enrollment.[115]

Inevitably, though, some of their alumnae became preachers. The Bible schools often included women in homiletics classes, along with the male ministerial students. At the Missionary Training Institute, for example, women sometimes took Greek and were required to practice preaching in church, along with the men. In the Institute's 1888 graduation, a prize for excellence in "Homiletic Exercises" went to a woman. The Boston Bible School, conducted by Advent Christians, permitted women to take pastoral courses in preparation for ordination along with the men students. Pioneering "Girl Evangelists" from the Northwestern Bible Institute started Sunday Schools, preached, and pastored churches in northern Minnesota.[116] Such practices did not necessarily mean that school leaders sanctioned the entry of women into the ordained ministry, but intentionally or not, the schools in fact enabled "determined (sometimes 'Spirit-led') women to assume unconventional leadership roles in the church."[117]

Particularly notable among the Bible schools, especially in relation to the deaconess movement, is the Chicago Training School founded by Lucy Rider Meyer (1849-1922), who became known as the "Archbishop of Deaconesses."[118] Meyer, a nineteenth-century female equivalent of the Renaissance man, did it all: teaching in a southern freedmen's school, studying at Oberlin and at MIT, earning an M.D. from the Woman's Medical College of Chicago, teaching chemistry, birthing and mothering a son, lecturing, and writing a science textbook and a novel—as well as pioneering in Methodist urban social work and shaping the Methodist deaconess movement.

In 1885 she and her husband, at severe personal sacrifice and risk, started their school to train women for careers in religion, particularly as missionaries. They raised the money themselves, living in the school even as they built it. They ate the dozens of sandwiches left over when they gave a party for sponsors and nobody came. For the most part he was the businessman and she the idea woman, though she dreamed up such money-raising ploys as a nickel crusade (if every Methodist woman would give five cents . . .), the chain letter (just send a dime and write three of your friends), and sacrifice for Jesus (give the money you save to the Training School). Slow and chancy as it must have seemed to them, and frequently as wife and husband disagreed over policy, their project evolved at an astonishing pace. As the fieldwork they laid out for their students deepened their understanding of the needs of the urban poor, they spun off a number of philanthropic institutions designed to meet these needs. In 1887 they opened the first "deaconess home" in the United States, and in 1888 the General Conference of the Methodist Episcopal church approved the office of deaconess.

From the handful of young women with whom they started, enrollment in the school peaked in 1910 at more than two hundred. In 1917 when they resigned, the Meyers had trained some five thousand students. By then the school had six buildings and assets of half a million dollars. All told the Meyers and their students were credited with founding some forty philanthropic institutions.

Despite the dedicated service and notable achievements of American deaconesses, the concept never really caught on in the United States as it did in Europe. Though of course in their heyday—say from 1875 to 1930—deaconesses far outnumbered clergywomen, the group failed to thrive over the long run.

Perhaps the founding came at the wrong time and in the wrong place. Protestant laity, intensely suspicious of Roman Catholics, thought they sniffed latent Catholicism when deaconesses wore distinctive dress. Doubtless many women attracted to church service preferred the more dramatic role of missionary. Maybe women just thought the position neither fish nor fowl. In Protestant churches generally deaconesses have not taken perpetual vows and could leave if and when they wished. Some have lived in communities; others have lived independently, receiving their expenses plus a small stipend and the promise of care in their old age. They have usually worked under supervision, whether of a local pastor or some other authority—in marked contrast to the many Roman Catholic sisters who carry enormous responsibilities. Until the latter part of the twentieth century, when they were long since a disappearing breed, most churches denied deaconesses even the powers or semiclerical status invested in (mostly male) deacons.

In any case a tinge of artificiality always marked the mobilization of deaconesses. At least in America it was less a naturally occurring movement than an imposition. Except in the Methodist Episcopal church, the impulse for it came primarily from male clergy. In contrast, women missionaries wanted into the action and struggled for a place in a profession originally created and reserved for men. Professions meant for men carry status; professions meant for women do not.

The concept of deaconesses was built on the ideal of True Womanhood, and the duties assigned them were usually those traditionally allotted to women. But in the latter part of the nineteenth century, when clergy were recruiting deaconesses, that ideal was fading. It carried within it the seeds of its own destruction, for it assumed an absurd and absolute distinction between the public and the private spheres. Once society had thrust upon True Women the responsibility for the well-being and morality of their families, the women soon discovered that they could not raise healthy children in unsanitary cities or in a society that required children to work long hours in factories; they could not raise morally responsible children in an immoral culture; they could not keep their husbands sober and free from venereal disease in the midst of saloons and brothels. This recognition brought True Women out of their houses into clubs that undertook to mitigate or abolish the evils they identified. The same recognition swelled the ranks of the Women's Christian Temperance Union and the woman suffrage movement: more women wanted the vote so that they could rid society of some evil than for any other reason. The New Woman was being birthed from the forehead of the enlightened (and disillusioned) True Woman.

The New Woman was coming into her own by the 1890s. She usually had more formal education than her mother. She expected to earn her own living, at least until she married, *if* she married. She insisted on the right to live and breathe as a separate human being. "I bet I never finish on any ole gravestone as 'also Rheta, wife of the above,'" boasted the young Rheta Childe Dorr.[119] The New Woman's admirers praised her healthy attractiveness, her independence, her strong-mindedness, and her zest for living. Bemoaning her loss of a proper spirit of self-sacrifice, her detractors accused her of egotism, selfishness, self-assertion, and "too much dirty, nasty independence."[120] A career as deaconess would have appealed to her much less than a career as clergywoman.

But the New Woman was much less likely than her mother to be a churchwoman of any sort. As Margaret Deland remarked, "She will do settlement work; she won't go to church."[121] The ideal of a career of service still appealed to her. But any New Woman could see that their experiences in the church had led Antoinette Brown Blackwell, Olympia Brown, Anna Howard Shaw, and many members of the Iowa Sisterhood to opt out of the clergy into other careers.[122]

✑ The Separation of Feminists and Clergywomen

During the latter part of the nineteenth century, the leaders of the woman's movement, particularly the younger ones, moved away from the churches. Up until this point, as we have seen, clergywomen had been on the cutting edge of the woman's movement, and women's leaders like Frances Willard had piously and staunchly supported the churches. Indeed, both Willard and hatchet woman Carrie Nation considered their temperance work to be a Christian ministry. Women who moved into public activism through the temperance movement went on into other spheres of ministry, such as Michigander Mary Lathrap, who began by reciting a temperance poem and wound up as a licensed Methodist preacher.[123] Sarepta M. Irish Henry, a worker for the Women's Christian Temperance Union and an opponent of ordination for women, held daily temperance meetings in a vacant factory. These meetings, which in the revival mode featured singing, praying, reading the Bible, and testifying, won so many converts that local clergymen took them over—and attendance fell off. Despite her convictions, by 1877 Henry found herself preaching three times a day. She took her problem to God, was called to the ministry, and became a national evangelist.[124]

Equally, many clergywomen had staunchly supported woman's rights; their sermons sometimes reflected their views on that issue. Lydia Sexton, for instance, in a sermon on temperance said:

> The noble white man sometimes expresses great alarm at the prospect of women being allowed the right to vote. This is most natural. The political parties are run in the whisky interest, and they know that if women were allowed to vote the occupation of the rum-seller would be at an end in a few months, or years at most. Until then we shall hold our man-voting population responsible for these gross wrongs and licensed vices that now curse our land.[125]

But during the course of the nineteenth century, as women widened their sights to include reform, as they shifted their public work from charity to antislavery and temperance, they came up against society, their male pastors, and their institutional churches. When women asked their ministers to announce benevolent society meetings, the men lauded them, but when they sent notices of antislavery meetings some pastors accused them of seeking "undue publicity" and told them they "had better stay at home."[126] Barbara Leslie Epstein sees the Woman's Crusade of 1873–1875, the forerunner of the women's temperance movement of 1880–1900, as the first step toward the secularization of what had been a church-centered women's culture.[127] Donald Meyer speaks of the Women's Christian Temperance Union as not only the first autonomous mass women's organization in the world but also the first direct challenge in modern history by a mass of women to a mass of men: "In America, religion was a realm for rich creative endeavor for women, for feminists at once a challenge and a trap."[128]

Several feminists entertained the idea of starting churches of their own. In 1858 Antoinette Brown Blackwell wanted to use a bequest to found a free church where she could "preach woman's rights with the gospel." In 1859 Susan B. Anthony went so far toward establishing such a church as to sponsor a series of Sunday evening services in Rochester, New York, with Blackwell one of a series of preachers. In 1877 Frances Willard began to discuss a possible church union open to all who would subscribe to the Apostles' Creed and pledge social purity and abstinence from liquor; in 1888 she called publicly for both laywomen's representation in church assemblies and women's ordination, saying that otherwise "it will be our solemn duty to raise once more the cry, 'Here I stand, I can do no other,' and step out into the larger liberty of a religious movement, where majorities and not minorities, determine the fitness of women as delegates, and where the laying on of hands in consecration, as was undoubtedly done in the early church, shall be decreed on a basis of 'gifts, graces and usefulness,' irregardless [sic] of sex."[129]

By century's end Stanton's *Woman's Bible* and Matilda Joslyn Gage's (d. 1898) *Woman, Church, and State* (1893); the shift away from their churches of clergy-women like Antoinette Blackwell, Olympia Brown, and Anna Howard Shaw; and the several feminists' proposals for a woman's church evidenced their dissatisfaction with the churches as institutions. Stanton wrote Antoinette Blackwell that she had two reasons for undertaking the *Woman's Bible*: "First, because as long as the religion of the country teaches women's subjection her status is necessarily degraded in the state. . . . 2nd There is no way in which we could get wide spread agitation on the whole question of woman's true position as in opening a vigorous attack on the church."[130]

Often, though by no means always, those women who continued to support the churches devoted themselves to church societies and temperance work, particularly in small-town America. More liberal and radical women, richer and more highly educated women, particularly in the growing cities, were more apt to choose labor reform or politics or municipal housekeeping or women's clubs or woman suffrage, or to carve out careers in one of the new helping professions, such as social work. Sometimes church doctrine clashed with the principles of the woman's rights movement. For instance, the very branch of the Society of Friends that emphasized the *spiritual* equality of the genders and whose women itinerated into the twentieth century denied women equality in the temporal world, even objecting to higher education for women.[131]

Notes

1. Quoted by Barbara Grizzuti Harrison in *Visions of Glory: A History and a Memory of Jehovah's Witnesses* (New York: Simon & Schuster, 1978), p. 202.

2. Ibid., p. 204.

3. Sara Maitland, *A Map of the New Country: Women and Christianity* (London: Routledge & Kegan Paul, 1983), p. 203.

4. Ibid., p. 85.

5. Elaine J. Lawless, *Holy Women, Wholly Women: Sharing Ministries of Wholeness Through Life Stories and Reciprocal Ethnography* (Philadelphia: Univ. of Pennsylvania Press, 1993), p. 38.

6. Lee R. Cooper, "'Publish' or Perish: Jehovah's Witness," in *Religious Movements in Contemporary America,* ed. Irving I. Zaretsky and Mark P. Leone (Princeton: Princeton Univ. Press, 1974), p. 714. As attorney Hayden Covington argued in a court case: "Each of Jehovah's witnesses is a minister. If he [*sic*] is not a preacher he is not one of Jehovah's witnesses" (Harrison, *Visions,* p. 202).

7. An Episcopalian priest told us about going to buy a coat in Waterbury, Connecticut, a city with lots of Roman Catholics, and being offered a discount. She explained that she was not buying it for the church but for herself, but the clerk insisted: "We always give discounts to people like you." She said, "There's no other people like me."

8. Maitland, *Map,* p. 3.

9. Religious theorists and institutions eager to emphasize the equality of all believers still struggle with the problem of how to ensure integrity and expertise without ordination. See Wendy Hunter Roberts, "In Her Name: Toward a Feminist Thealogy of Pagan Ritual," in *Women at Worship: Interpretations of North American Diversity,* ed. Marjorie Procter-Smith and Janet R. Walton (Louisville, Ky.: Westminster/John Knox Press, 1993), p. 139.

10. Madeline Southard, in *Woman's Pulpit* 1 (April 1923).

11. Ruth A. Tucker and Walter Liefeld, *Daughters of the Church: Women and Ministry*

from New Testament Times to the Present (Grand Rapids, Mich.: Zondervan, Academie Books, 1987), p. 273.

12. On Brown, see Elizabeth Cazden, *Antoinette Brown Blackwell: A Biography* (Old Westbury, N.Y.: Feminist Press, 1983); Susan Phinney Conrad, *Perish the Thought: Intellectual Women in Romantic America, 1830–1860* (New York: Oxford Univ. Press, 1976); Elinor Rice Hays, *Those Extraordinary Blackwells: The Story of a Journey to a Better World* (New York: Harcourt, Brace & World, 1967); Laura N. Kerr, *Lady in the Pulpit* (New York: Woman's Press, 1951); and *Reclaiming the Past, Landmarks of Women's History,* ed. Page Putnam Miller (Bloomington: Indiana Univ. Press, 1992).

13. Smith was engaged to marry a minister; her projected role as minister's wife sufficiently explained her interest in studying theology and spared her some of the slings and arrows directed at Brown.

14. Cazden, *Antoinette Brown Blackwell,* p. 51.

15. Ibid., p. 73.

16. On Brown and the woman rights movement, see Conrad, *Perish the Thought;* and Nancy Hardesty, *Women Called to Witness: Evangelical Feminism in the Nineteenth Century* (Nashville, Tenn.: Abingdon, 1984), pp. 84–85.

17. Catherine F. Hitchings, *Universalist and Unitarian Women Ministers,* 2d ed. (Boston: The Unitarian Universalist Historical Society, 1985), p. 155.

18. Cazden, *Antoinette Brown Blackwell,* pp. 77–78.

19. Kerr, *Lady in the Pulpit,* p. 199.

20. In 1859, having after her twenty-five years in medicine become quite wealthy, Hunt (1805–1875) became a missionary preacher in New England (Russell E. Miller, *The Larger Hope* [Boston: Unitarian Universalist Ass'n, 1979], 1: 550).

21. Cazden, *Antoinette Brown Blackwell,* p. 84.

22. Ibid., pp. 94–95.

23. Ibid., p. 190.

24. Cazden, *Antoinette Brown Blackwell,* p. 182.

25. Cazden notes that Antoinette years later told her niece Alice Stone Blackwell that the church at Brooklyn, Connecticut, had offered her a job, which she refused, but church records show that from 1877 to 1881, the relevant period, their pulpit was occupied by Rev. Caroline R. Jones (*Antoinette Brown Blackwell,* pp. 193–94).

26. Regina A. Coll writes in *Christianity and Feminism in Conversation* (Mystic, Conn.: Twenty-Third Publications, 1994), p. 71: "Antoinette Brown, the first woman ordained in the United States, gave up the ministry after being convinced by the 'scientific' argument." As authority, Coll cites Barbara Ehrenreich and Deirdre English, *For Her Own Good: 150 Years of the Experts' Advice to Women* (New York: Doubleday, 1978), pp. 128–30. As Cazden makes clear, Blackwell courteously examined this argument as advanced by Edward Hammond Clarke, agreeing that women and men have different abilities and may exhibit their intelligence differently, but heartily disagreeing with his central theory (that women's studying would incapacitate them for childbearing) and insisting on the necessity of encouraging women to undertake intellectual work (*Antoinette Brown Blackwell,* pp. 170–77). And, of course, Blackwell never "gave up the ministry" in the sense that most readers will understand the phrase.

27. On Olympia Brown, see her autobiography, edited and completed by her daughter, in the 1963 *Annual Journal of the Universalist Historical Society;* Charlotte Cote, *Olympia Brown: The Battle for Equality* (Racine, Wis.: Mother Courage, 1988); and Hitchings, *Universalist and Unitarian Women Ministers.*

28. Hitchings, *Universalist and Unitarian Women Ministers,* p. 4.

29. Miller, *Larger Hope,* 1:552.

30. In her retirement Brown continued to encourage other women who wanted to be clergywomen: "While she was state lecturer for the Wisconsin Woman Suffrage Association, 1892–1894, Nellie Mann Opdale studied for the Universalist ministry under Olympia Brown" (Hitchings, *Universalist and Unitarian Woman Ministers,* p. 112).

31. Ibid., p. 31.

32. Tucker and Liefeld, *Daughters of the Church,* p. 58, citing H. K. Carroll, *Religious Forces of the United States* (New York, 1893), p. 392. In 1870 Unitarians had only five clergywomen; by 1890, Universalists and Unitarians together had ordained only about seventy, of whom far fewer actually were serving in full-time, paid pastorates.

33. Hitchings, *Universalist and Unitarian Women Ministers,* p. 19.

34. Ibid., p. 51.

35. Ibid., p. 43.

36. Lorraine Lollis, *The Shape of Adam's Rib* (St. Louis: Bethany, 1970), p. 20, quoting from Gustine Codurson Weaver, letter, Transylvania University Library.

37. On Shaw, see her autobiographical *The Story of a Pioneer* (1915; reprint, Cleveland, Oh.: Pilgrim Press, 1994); and "My Ordination," ed. Nancy N. Bahmueller, *Methodist History* 14 (Oct 1975–July 1976): 125–31. See also Wil A. Linkugel and Martha Solomon, *Anna Howard Shaw: Suffrage Orator and Social Reformer* (New York: Greenwood, 1991); and Elaine Magalis, *Conduct Becoming to a Woman: Bolted Doors and Burgeoning Missions* (n.p.: Women's Division, Board of Global Ministries, The United Methodist Church, n.d.).

38. Hitchings shows Thompson's name as Folsom.

39. Shaw, "My Ordination," pp. 125–31; quotation p. 127. The original of this document is at the Schlesinger Library.

40. Ibid., p. 128. This evidence contradicts the assertion in *Notable American Women,* 3:275, that Shaw was the only woman in her class.

41. Newspaper clipping in scrapbook of Helen D. Lyman. The evidence of paper and date is confusing: the clipping may be from a Boston paper of Nov. 13, 1909, or from the *Union Signal* of September 1889. Helen D. Lyman papers, Schlesinger Library, A-33, Box 2, Folder 3.

42. Shaw, "My Ordination," p. 129.

43. Ibid., pp. 130–31.

44. Gerda Lerner, *The Creation of Feminist Consciousness: From the Middle Ages to Eighteen-Seventy* (New York: Oxford Univ. Press, 1993), p. vii.

45. Hitchings, *Universalist and Unitarian Women Ministers,* p. 38.

46. Ibid., p. 39.

47. Ibid., pp. 79–80.

48. *The Woman's Journal,* Dec. 27, 1890, Helen D. Lyman Papers, A-33, Box 2, Folder 3, p. 27, Schlesinger Library, Cambridge, Massachusetts.

49. Hitchings, *Universalist and Unitarian Women Ministers,* p. 108. Howe, who frequently preached in Universalist and Unitarian pulpits, held annual gatherings of women ministers in her home, beginning in 1873. The best source on the Iowa Sisterhood is Cynthia Grant Tucker, *Prophetic Sisterhood: Liberal Women Ministers of the Frontier, 1880–1930* (Boston: Beacon Press, 1990). Also useful is Tucker's *Healer in Harm's Way: Mary Collson, A Clergywoman in Christian Science* (Lexington: Univ. of Tennessee Press, 1994). Tucker does not mention Howe in connection with the Sisterhood.

50. ". . . these women frankly regarded the deep emotional bonding of females as the most

sustaining of any relationships. . . . the governing mode of relationship or dynamic seems to have been a professional domesticity that they themselves thought of as more 'sisterly' than 'romantic,' more suggestive of the shared vocation than the 'Boston marriage'" (Tucker, *Prophetic Sisterhood,* pp. 81–82).

51. See Tucker, *Prophetic Sisterhood,* p. 97.

52. Laura E. Richards and Maud Howe Elliot, with Florence Howe Hall, *Julia Ward Howe, 1819–1910* (Boston and New York: Houghton Mifflin, 1916), 1:391.

53. Tucker, *Prophetic Sisterhood,* p. 47.

54. Miller, *Larger Hope,* 1:549.

55. Dorothy and Carl J. Schneider, *American Women in the Progressive Era, 1900–1920* (New York: Facts on File, 1993), p. 103.

56. Margaret Hope Bacon, *Mothers of Feminism: The Story of Quaker Women in America* (San Francisco: Harper & Row, 1986), p. 97.

57. Lois A. Boyd and R. Douglas Brackenridge, *Presbyterian Women in America: Two Centuries of a Quest for Status* (Westport, Conn.: Greenwood, 1983), p. 99.

58. Margaret Hope Bacon, *As The Way Opens: The Story of Quaker Women in America* (Richmond, Ind.: Friends United Press, 1980), p. 62.

59. *Notable American Women: A Biographical Dictionary,* ed. Edward T. James, Janet Wilson James, and Paul S. Boyer, 3 vols. (Cambridge, Mass.: Belknap Press of Harvard Univ. Press, 1971), 1:369–70.

60. Boyd and Brackenridge, *Presbyterian Women,* p. 116.

61. Ibid., p. 112.

62. *New York Tribune* (April 13, 1869), quoted by John Onesimus Foster, *Life and Labors of Mrs. Maggie Newton Van Cott, the First Lady Licensed to Preach in the Methodist Episcopal Church in the United States . . . with an introduction by Reverend Gilbert Haven and Reverend David Sherman* (Cincinnati, Oh.: Hitchcock and Walden, for the author, 1872), p. 318. Maggie Van Cott's *The Harvest and the Reaper: Reminiscences of Revival Work of Mrs. Maggie N. Van Cott* (New York: N. Tibbals, 1876) is a slightly revised and enlarged version of the Foster work, on which Van Cott collaborated.

63. Magalis, *Conduct Becoming to a Woman,* p. 113.

64. Foster, *Life,* pp. 152, 167.

65. Ibid., pp. 219, 257, 262.

66. *The Methodist* (April 14, 1869), quoted by Foster, *Life,* p. 321.

67. Foster, *Life,* p. 326.

68. *Union Signal,* Mar. 12, 1892, Helen D. Lyman papers, A-33, Box 2, Folder 3, Schlesinger Library, Cambridge, Mass.

69. Helen D. Lyman papers, A-33, Box 2, Folder 3, pp. 21 and 31, Schlesinger Library, Cambridge, Mass.

70. Jualynne Dodson, "Nineteenth-Century A.M.E. Preaching Women," in *Women in New Worlds: Historical Perspectives on the Wesleyan Tradition,* ed. Hilah F. Thomas and Rosemary Skinner Keller (Nashville, Tenn.: Abingdon, 1981), pp. 276–89, describes in detail the struggles within the AME church over credentialing women.

71. Julia A. J. Foote, *A Brand Plucked from the Fire: An Autobiographical Sketch* (1879), reprinted in *Sisters of the Spirit: Three Black Women's Autobiographies of the Nineteenth Century,* ed. William L. Andrews (Bloomington: Indiana Univ. Press, 1986), pp. 189, 197, 202.

72. Ibid., p. 214.

73. Magalis, *Conduct Becoming to a Woman,* p. 111; *Autobiography of Lydia Sexton: The*

Story of Her Life Through a Period of over Seventy-Two Years, From 1799 to 1872 (1882; reprint, New York: Garland, 1987), pp. 522, 580; Nancy Hardesty, *Your Daughters Shall Prophesy: Revivalism and Feminism in the Age of Finney* (New York: Carlson, 1991), p. 92.

Bacon notes the concerns of Quaker clergywomen for prisoners and prison reform. "The traveling Quaker women ministers, such as Elizabeth Comstock, Lucretia Mott, and Sarah Smith, routinely visited asylums as well as prisons." Mary Waln Wistar (b. 1786), a recorded minister in a Philadelphia Monthly Meeting, pioneered women's prison reform in America (Bacon, *Mothers of Feminism,* pp. 144, 139ff.). But Sexton's autobiography suggests that her struggles as a prison chaplain were to protect her own turf: she had all she could do to keep her authority over her work and justify her presence.

74. Sexton, *Autobiography,* pp. 628, 646–47; and an undated newspaper clipping from *The Call,* Helen D. Lyman papers, A–33, Box 2, Folder 3, p. 60, Schlesinger Library, Cambridge, Mass.

75. Susan Cunningham Stanley, "Alma White: Holiness Preacher with a Feminist Message" (Ph.D. dissertation, Iliff School of Theology, Univ. of Denver, 1987), p. 79.

76. Betty A. DeBerg, *Ungodly Woman: Gender and the First Wave of American Fundamentalism* (Minneapolis: Fortress, 1990), p. 152.

77. Max Weber, *The Sociology of Religion* (Boston: Beacon, 1963), p. 104.

78. Stanley valiantly attempts to distinguish holiness churches from fundamentalist churches ("Alma White," pp. 210–11; see also pp. 247–49). Holiness churches, she says, are more oriented to ethics and spiritual life than to a defense of doctrinal orthodoxy. Holiness churches emphasize the Holy Spirit and promote an understanding of God as immanent in human beings, not transcendent. The holiness approach rests on the individual religious experience, thus challenging the rationalism of fundamentalism. Holiness religions operate inductively and pragmatically instead of relying solely on deduction from old principles. Holiness believers accept free will, rejecting the fundamentalist concept of predestination. Most holiness groups have supported women preachers, while most fundamentalist groups have opposed them. Holiness churches neither practice nor believe in glossolalia (speaking in tongues); pentecostal churches do.

79. Susie Stanley, "Women Evangelists in the Church of God at the Beginning of the Twentieth Century," in *Called to Minister . . . Empowered to Serve: Women in Ministry and Missions in the Church of God Reformation Movement,* ed. Juanita Leonard (Anderson, Ind.: Warner Press, 1989), p. 44, citing Sarah Smith, *Life Sketches of Mother Sarah Smith* (Anderson, Ind.: Gospel Trumpet Co., 1902), pp. 260, 33.

80. Barry L. Callen, *She Came Preaching: The Life and Ministry of Lillie S. McCutcheon* (Anderson, Ind.: Warner Press, 1992), p. 158.

81. Stanley, "Women," pp. 50, 48.

82. Alice J. Dise, "Black Women in Ministry in the Church of God," in *Called to Minister,* ed. Leonard, p. 59.

83. See Gilkes' articles "'Together and in Harness': Women's Traditions in the Sanctified Church," *Signs* 10 (Summer 1985): 678–99; and "The Roles of Church and Community Mothers: Ambivalent American Sexism or Fragmented African Familyhood?" in *Journal of Feminist Studies in Religion* 2 (Spring 1986): 41–59.

84. Gilkes, "Together and in Harness," pp. 682–83, 692, 688. Mechal Sobel has also commented on the prominent role in revivals taken by African-American women in continuity with the West African tradition in which so many women had been mediums (*Trabelin' On: The Slave Journey to an Afro-Baptist Faith* [Westport, Conn.: Greenwood, 1979], p. 233).

85. Gilkes, "Together and in Harness," p. 686.

86. Gilkes, "Church and Community Mothers," pp. 53–54.

87. C. Eric Lincoln and Lawrence Mamiya, *The Black Church in the African American Experience* (Durham, N.C.: Duke Univ. Press, 1990), p. 281.

88. Amanda Smith, *An Autobiography: The Story of the Lord's Dealings with Mrs. Amanda Smith, the Colored Evangelist; Containing an Account of her Life Work of Faith, and her Travels in America, England, Ireland, Scotland, India and Africa, as an Independent Missionary* (Chicago, 1893), p. 226. See also *Black Women in Nineteenth Century American Life: Their Words, Their Thoughts, Their Feelings,* ed. Bert James Loewenberg and Ruth Bogin (University Park: Pennsylvania State Univ. Press, 1976).

89. Edward H. McKinley, *Marching to Glory: The History of the Salvation Army in the United States of America, 1880–1980* (San Francisco: Harper & Row, 1980), p. 213.

90. Catherine Booth, *Female Ministry: Or, Woman's Right to Preach the Gospel* (1859; reprint, New York: Salvation Army, 1975).

91. But see Edward G. Carey, "The Army's First Overseas Pioneers," in *Pioneering Salvationists: An Anthology of Selected Articles by Salvationist Authors, Past and Present, on the Pioneering Exploits of Salvationists the World Over,* comp. John D. Waldron (New York: Salvation Army, 1987).

92. McKinley, *Marching,* p. 17.

93. Ibid., pp. 47, 55, and 67.

94. Ibid., pp. 62–65, passim.

95. William A. Johnson, *O Boundless Salvation: The Story of the Scandinavian Salvation Army in the United States* (New York: Salvation Army, 1988), p. 8.

96. *In Our Own Voices: Four Centuries of American Women's Religious Writing,* ed. Rosemary Skinner Keller and Rosemary Radford Ruether (San Francisco: HarperSanFrancisco, 1995), p. 371.

97. Hitchings, *Universalist and Unitarian Women Ministers,* p. 558.

98. Richards and Elliott, *Julia Ward Howe,* 1:391.

99. Ibid., 1:390.

100. Mary Alice Wyman, *Two American Pioneers: Seba Smith and Elizabeth Oakes Smith* (New York: Columbia Univ. Press, 1927), p. 226. See also *The Autobiography of Elizabeth Oakes Smith,* ed. Mary Alice Wyman (Lewiston, Me., 1924).

101. Emma Bailey, *Happy Day; or, The Confessions of a Woman Minister* (New York: European Pub. Co., 1901; reproduced on microfilm New Haven, Conn.: Research Publications, 1976, History of Women, #5031), p. 370.

102. Peggy Pascoe, *Relations of Rescue: The Search for Female Moral Authority in the American West, 1874–1939* (New York: Oxford Univ. Press, 1990), p. 45, citing the *Daily Nebraska State Journal,* May 7, 1892.

103. Helen D. Lyman papers, A-33, Box 2, Folder 3, Schlesinger Library, Cambridge, Massachusetts. This optimism was widespread: for example, Marie Hoffendahl Jenney wrote in the *Meadville (Penn.) Portfolio:* "Prejudice against clergywomen is almost extinct. There are still occasional whispers of a whirlpool ahead in the mist, but too many women have steered beyond for us to believe in it as a seething reality" (Helen D. Lyman papers, A-33, Box 2, Folder 3).

104. Hitchings, *Universalist and Unitarian Women Ministers,* pp. 22–23.

105. Tucker and Liefeld, *Daughters of the Church,* p. 279. Maybe. Note that these are women actively occupying pulpits. More had been ordained. Cazden writes: "By 1880 close to 200 women had been formally recognized as ministers, and many held full-time parish jobs" (*Antoinette Brown Blackwell,* p. 192), but she gives no source and she does not distinguish between mainline denominations and others. Conflicting contemporary reports reduce to despair the historian's hopes of getting an accurate figure. *The Woman's Journal* of Octo-

ber 26, 1895, reported 350 Quaker clergywomen; 54 Universalists; 24 Unitarians; 20 Congregationalists, with the note "Ordination of women exceptional, and possible under Congregational system"; 7 Protestant Methodists, with the same note; 20 Free Baptists; and 3 Christians—with a request for additions and corrections. Virginia Brereton and Christa Klein say that by 1900 there were fewer than forty Congregational women ministers ("American Women in Ministry: A History of Protestant Beginning Points," in *Women in American Religion,* ed. Janet Wilson James [Philadelphia: Univ. of Pennsylvania Press, 1980], p. 183). Around the turn of the century, according to another report, "the Quakers have 350 women ministers; the Universalists have 35 in their last year book; the Unitarians have 16, chiefly in the West; the Congregationalists have ordained six; the Lutheran and Free Baptists have increasing numbers. . . ." This source demonstrates the frustrations awaiting the historian who tries to get any kind of reliable count of the numbers of clergywomen before the 1950s. The relevant clipping is pasted in Helen Lyman's scrapbook, but we cannot determine whether it came from a Boston paper of Nov. 13, 1909, or from the *Union Signal* of September 1889 (Helen D. Lyman papers, A-33, Box 2, Folder 3, Schlesinger Library, Cambridge, Mass.). Another unidentified and undated clipping (which other evidence suggests to be around 1899) claims 720 clergywomen, of whom 350 were Friends, 47 Universalists, 16 ordained Unitarians and "a large number who preach more or less regularly," and 6 or 8 Congregationalists. Who were the other 300 or so? And the *Universalist Register* for 1899 lists 79 women ministers, though apparently a significant percentage were not active (Helen D. Lyman papers, A-33, Box 2, Folder 3, p. 33).

106. Susan Hill Lindley, *"You Have Stept Out of Your Place": A History of Women and Religion in America* (Louisville, Ky.: Westminster John Knox, 1996), p. 161.

107. Eleanor Hull, *Women Who Carried the Good News: The History of the Woman's American Baptist Home Missionary Society* (Valley Forge: Judson, 1975), p. 22.

108. V. W. Broughton, *Twenty Year's Experience of a Missionary, in Spiritual Narratives* (1907; reprint, New York: Oxford Univ. Press, 1988), pp. 35, 37.

109. Elizabeth Meredith Lee, *As Among the Methodists: Deaconesses Yesterday, Today, and Tomorrow* (New York: Woman's Division of Christian Service, Board of Missions, Methodist Church, 1963), p. 3. The date and identity of the first American deaconess are disputed, the situation confused by some early abortive efforts to establish such an order.

110. In 1920 the threat of deaconesses becoming clergywomen seemed about to materialize when the Lambeth Conference of Anglican bishops from all over the world declared deaconesses fully ordained clergy within holy orders, a statement that they withdrew in 1930 (Alice Bozarth-Campbell, *Womanpriest: A Personal Odyssey* [New York: Paulist Press, 1978], p. 108).

111. Catherine M. Prelinger, "Ordained Women in the Episcopal Church: Their Impact on the Work and Structure of the Clergy" in *Episcopal Women: Gender, Spirituality, and Commitment in an American Mainline Denomination,* ed. Catherine M. Prelinger (New York: Oxford Univ. Press, 1992), p. 290.

112. Virginia Lieson Brereton, *Training God's Army: The American Bible School, 1880–1940* (Bloomington: Indiana Univ. Press, 1990).

113. The founders of the Quaker training school perceived a different need and met a different purpose. By the end of the nineteenth century, the transformation of many Quaker meetings to Friends churches "was creating a demand for trained pastors with some knowledge of the Quaker background. Both these needs were met in 1892 when Walter and Emma Brown Malone, a Quaker couple from Cleveland, Ohio, opened the Friends Bible Institute and Training School, later renamed Malone College, for Bible study and the training of ministers and missionaries. Emma Malone had grown up in a Canadian Quaker family and was

accustomed to women playing an equal role with men. She was a recorded minister, and she and Walter shared the pastoral responsibilities of the First Friends Church in Cleveland, as well as the founding and administration of the school. . . . Her influence helped to keep the concept of the equality of women strong in the evangelical wing of the society" (Bacon, *Mothers of Feminism,* pp. 178–79). In the twentieth century Bible schools have become predominantly associated with fundamentalist churches.

114. Brereton, *Training,* p. 130.

115. Margaret L. Bendroth, *Fundamentalism and Gender: 1875 to the Present* (New Haven, Conn.: Yale Univ. Press, 1994), p. 27.

116. Ibid., p. 27.

117. Brereton, *Training,* p. 130.

118. Isabelle Horton's *High Adventure: Life of Lucy Rider Meyer* (New York: Methodist Book Concern, 1928) requires the reader to wade through sentimental balderdash, but Horton had access to excellent sources, especially in her interviews with members of Meyer's family.

119. Rheta Childe Dorr, *A Woman of Fifty* (1924; New York: Arno Press, 1980), p. 5. For a discussion of the New Woman, see Schneider and Schneider, *American Women,* pp. 16–17.

120. Martha Farnsworth, *Plains Woman: The Diary of Martha Farnsworth, 1882–1922,* ed. Marlene Springer and Haskell Springer (Bloomington: Indiana Univ. Press, 1988), p. 145.

121. Margaret Deland, "Change in the Feminine Ideal," *Atlantic Monthly* 105 (March 1910): 291.

122. Phoebe Hanaford forthrightly described her experience: "I have left my pastorate in New Haven. The men in the congregation opposed me and they asked for my resignation. . . . I do not think that I will continue my work in the church because of the treatment accorded women ministers" (Cote, *Olympia Brown,* p. 122).

123. Tucker and Liefeld, *Daughters of the Church,* p. 273.

124. On Henry's life, see Hassey, *No Time for Silence,* chapter 7; and Mary Henry Rossiter, *My Mother's Life—The Evolution of a Recluse* (Chicago: Revell, 1900), reproduced in History of Women: Microfilm Collection (New Haven, Conn.: Research Publications, 1976–79), Reel 597, #4723.

125. Sexton, *Autobiography,* p. 318.

126. Hardesty, *Your Daughters Shall Prophesy,* p. 123.

127. Barbara Leslie Epstein, *The Politics of Domesticity: Women, Evangelism, and Temperance in Nineteenth-Century America* (Middletown, Conn.: Wesleyan Univ. Press, 1981), p. 116.

128. Donald Meyer, *Sex and Power: The Rise of Women in America, Russia, Sweden, and Italy* (Middletown, Conn.: Wesleyan Univ. Press, 1987), p. 329.

129. Hardesty, *Your Daughters Shall Prophesy,* p. 100. On Willard's proposal for a separate church, see Tucker and Liefeld, *Daughters of the Church,* p. 281.

130. Cazden, *Antoinette Brown Blackwell,* p. 228. Middle-of-the-road suffragists of course did not want to be tarred with the brush of heterodoxy and accordingly wished to dissociate themselves from the views of Stanton and Gage (see Lindley, *"You Have Stept Out of Your Place,"* pp. 288–92).

131. Bacon, *Mothers of Feminism,* pp. 96–97.

4

Evangelism and New Thought for the Many 1850–1900 🍂

THE FEW WOMEN WHO ACHIEVED ordination in the latter half of the nineteenth century were, of course, not the only clergywomen of their time. As in the past, many women did not wait for men's permission to preach and pastor: some functioned independently, and a startling number founded new churches. They operated, as it were, without benefit of clergy.

Their numbers were swelled by home missionaries, particularly as women began to outnumber men in the mission field. "Women [missionaries] freely preached, evangelized, planted churches, trained nationals, established schools, and conducted humanitarian work," write Ruth A. Tucker and Walter Liefeld. "Their lack of clerical ordination had little effect on their ministries, and they were far out of reach of critics back home."[1] Emancipation sent northern women south to educate former slaves—women like Sarah Dickey of the United Brethren, who though ostracized, threatened, and shot at by the Ku Klux Klan built a "Mt. Holyoke" in Mississippi for young black women and established a community where African-Americans could build their own homes. In 1894 the United Brethren granted her full clergy rights.[2] Home missionaries also served Native Americans, Spanish Americans, and Asians on the west coast, as well as the multitudes of immigrants of European ancestry swarming into the United States through New York.

Another group consisted of clergywomen and para-clergywomen, like W.C.T.U. and Y.W.C.A. professionals, who worked outside the church, their religion fueling their passion for reform. Dedicated to the ideal of human perfectibility, Sojourner Truth (1797–1883) and her sort turned their considerable energies to creating the kingdom of God on earth—or at least to achieving the best of all possible worlds, in which women as well as men, blacks as well as whites, enjoyed opportunities and privileges as a matter of natural right.

A third group of clergywomen, more or less closely allied with the holiness movement, turned away from modernism and shifting concepts of women and their place in the world, back toward a literal reading of the Bible and a patriarchal tradition of

102

family and societal organization. Clergywomen of this group, like Maria Woodworth-Etter, based their claim to preach and pastor almost solely on the inspiration of the Holy Spirit.

A fourth group epitomized the nineteenth-century fascination with the interactions between science and religion, body and spirit. Mary Baker Eddy and the women of the New Thought movement incorporated this fascination into a plethora of new religious foundations.

✒ Reform and Evangelism

Sojourner Truth, one of the reformers, accurately described herself when she said to Lyman Beecher, "You dear lamb! The Lord bless you. I love preachers. I'm a kind of preacher myself."[3] Born into slavery as Isabella Baumfree and emancipated by New York law in 1827, Truth spent her life until 1843 in hard domestic labor, suffering cruelty, deceit, and deprivation. In her girlhood a vision converted her to Christianity, whose rudiments her mother had taught her. Clearly a woman of remarkable intelligence and courage, she picked up when and where she could a knowledge of the Bible, helped by the extraordinary memory that sometimes accompanies reliance on the ear rather than the eye, for she never learned to read. She also acquired respect for the rule of law, for twice she won lawsuits, once to recover a son sold away from her into slavery, and once on her own behalf against slander.

At forty-six, she later told Harriet Beecher Stowe:

> I left the house of bondage, I left everything behind. I wa'n't goin' to keep nothin' of Egypt on me, an' so I went to the Lord an' asked him to give me a new name. And the Lord gave me Sojourner, because I was to travel up an' down the land, showin' the people their sins, an' bein' a sign unto them. Afterward I told the Lord I wanted another name, 'cause everybody else had two names, and the Lord gave me Truth, because I was to declare the truth to the people. . . . I journeys round to camp-meetin's, an' wherever folks is, an' I sets up my banner ["Proclaim liberty throughout all the land unto all the inhabitants thereof"], an' then I sings, an' then folks always comes up round me, an' then I preaches to 'em, I tells 'em about Jesus, an' I tells 'em about the sins of this people.[4]

What she preached frequently had to do with the rights of African-Americans and women. Like Anna Howard Shaw, Sojourner Truth learned to use her Christianity as the base of her passionate work for social reform, for as she said, "Religion without humanity is poor human stuff."[5] Repeatedly she told the story of her conversion, always beginning "Chillun, I talks to God, and God talks to me."[6] She walked through Connecticut and Long Island preaching where she could, frequently at camp meetings, doing domestic work when need be, and gradually building a reputation as a charismatic speaker.

Footsore and weary, she came to rest at the Northampton Association of Education and Industry, a Utopian community at Florence, Massachusetts, where the members lived in a "factory boarding house" and manufactured silk. No clergy existed, and men and women of many different viewpoints spoke at will. Under these conditions Truth flourished. She lived there for three years, doing her part by taking charge of the laundry. She met the abolitionists William Lloyd Garrison, Frederick Douglass, Wendell Phillips, and Sam Hill, impressing them and her fellow colonists with her speaking ability and quick wit. Douglass at first ignored her, because, he said, she struck him as "a genuine specimen of the uncultured Negro." But after one of his paeans to education Truth silenced him by remarking, "You read, but God himself talks to me."[7]

When the Northampton Association broke up in 1850, Truth took to the road again, this time on the abolitionist circuit. To support herself she sold her autobiography, dictated in Northampton to Olive Gilbert. An invitation to represent the state of Massachusetts at the first woman's rights convention persuaded her to add woman's rights to her causes, for, as Jacqueline Bernard remarks, to Truth's mind abolitionism and woman's rights and religion were all intertwined.

Though in time she bought modest homes first in Northampton and later in Battle Creek, Michigan, Truth spent almost all the second half of her life itinerating in one cause or another. After the Civil War she devoted much of her energy to resettling freed slaves in Kansas. When she described the abolitionists commanding black troops and the women gone south to care for slaves escaping through the lines as "appointed to God," she might equally well have been describing herself.[8]

Sojourner Truth labored in the liberal spirit of Lucretia Mott and Anna Howard Shaw, devoted to social reform and deeply conscious of the plight of women in their lack of civil rights and of suffrage. Maria Woodworth-Etter (1844–1924) belonged to that more conservative group of clergywomen who thought of themselves as apart from the world and concerned themselves far less with its well-being than with glory in the world to come. She thought of women's status in terms of equality in the eyes of God and of women's right to preach and pastor as authorized by scripture and by the inspiration of the Holy Spirit.

Brought up in the Disciples church, she was converted at thirteen and immediately felt herself called to preach—but how? The Disciples did not endorse women's preaching. She married a farmer, with whom she endured the deaths of five of their six children—an experience that almost deranged him. Through it all she remained convinced of her call to ministry, a call frequently reiterated in visions, so when in 1879 she underwent a second conversion at a revival meeting, she launched evangelistic meetings of her own. According to her books, she succeeded immediately: in a year and a half in the vicinity of her home she held nine revivals; founded two churches, one of which started with seventy members; organized a Sunday School of about one hundred; and preached in twenty-two meetinghouses and four schoolhouses, delivering two hundred sermons—for eight different denominations.[9] Her growing reputation brought an invitation to itinerate from the United Brethren, who credentialed Woodworth's husband as an exhorter (even though apparently he did not preach) and the couple set off, she to preach and he to put up tents and sell food, literature, and her photograph.

The secular press often reported Woodworth-Etter's colorful ministry as the activities of a con woman, and its reporters did not spare her husband. On August 21, 1885, the Wabash *Weekly Courier* wrote: "The husband of the evangelist is of a thrifty turn, and while the meetings are in progress he and two assistants operate a peanut, candy and lemonade stand within sixty feet of the pulpit. The other day, as men and women were shouting and going into trances, old Woodworth sat beside an ice cream freezer and cranked it unconcernedly." Several years of this division of labor disillusioned Woodworth, who variously described his wife's mission as a "trance business," "a great money-making scheme," and "a damned fraud."[10] Though she believed firmly in the marriage relationship, the preacher divorced her husband in 1890 on charges of infidelity and threatening her with a pistol. The poor rascal promptly married a sixteen-year-old, only to die soon thereafter—they say of typhoid.

(Other women evangelists enjoyed much happier relations with their husbands. African-American Emma J. Ray [b. 1859], for instance, who worked on the west coast, wrote: "The people that came to the meetings, in their testimonies, would frequently say, 'Sister Ray's Mission,' as they always found me there and Brother Ray out working. I did not feel that it was fair, because Brother Ray made it possible for me to get out to the day meetings to work with the children, by going out and making the means of our living. . . . I would oftimes say, 'I'm preaching the gospel and he is working to pay expenses,' which was a real truth."[11])

Despite her husband's accusations, there can be little doubt of Woodworth-Etter's effectiveness on the revival platform. Reportedly she attracted enormous crowds, mostly urban, blue-collar people—sometimes, it was said, as many as twenty-five thousand. Rather than preaching of God's forgiving love, she literally scared the hell out of her thousands of converts, firmly believing that if she failed, her listeners were doomed. Her meetings were noisy, for she thought that true conversion manifested itself physically, in shouting and/or falling into trances. "The devil is mad/And I am glad./Oh my soul!/Praise the Lord! Glory to God!" chanted her congregations. She herself frequently went into trances, to the joy of the press: "Cataleptic Revival," "Rigid Religion," "She Knocks 'Em Cold at Hartford City," and "Woodworth's Wand, Most Mysteriously Moving Masses Making Wicked Wildly Weep, Wretched Weirdly Wail." "Once started on the subject of religion," said the *Indianapolis Times* on May 12, 1885, "she can get in as many words to the hour, and as many hours to the day, as the most accomplished lightning-rod agent that ever plied his calling."[12]

In 1884 the Indiana Eldership of the Churches of God licensed her to preach and appointed her evangelist. Twenty years later they demanded the return of her credentials. Meantime she enjoyed success not only in conversions and healing but also in establishing new churches and reviving dead ones, and in recruiting ministers, including several women.[13] She evoked extravagant praise, as "the greatest woman evangelist in the history of the Christian church," and criticism and skepticism to match.

Perhaps she owed both praise and criticism to her flamboyance, which flared up in Oakland, California, in 1889. That revival, in the biggest tent any revivalist had ever used, went badly from the start. (The history of revivalists is starred with boasts of having the biggest tent ever.) A male revivalist who had formerly supported her defected, though her well-known sister revivalist Carrie Judd Montgomery came to her defense.[14] It rained constantly. Ministers of the gospel attacked her rhetorically; hoodlums attacked her tent physically, putting explosives into the heating stoves. The wind tore the tent apart, and the owner of the lot on which the tent was pitched evicted her. Mentally disturbed people and drunks came and insisted on staying, raising accusations in the press that Woodworth-Etter had driven them insane. When the police deputized some of her followers, their overzealous efforts to keep the peace provoked riots. She discovered her husband's infidelity and he jumped revival. All in all, she was having a really bad week.

She didn't improve matters when in January 1890, she warned that on April 14 an earthquake and tidal wave would destroy the cities of Alameda, Oakland, and San Francisco. The black evangelist Mrs. Simmons seconded her, and other prophets, some of them her converts, joined in. A lot of people believed them, sold their furniture and their houses, quit their jobs, and made for the hills. Whether because of the press brouhaha or for her own reasons, four days before the touted catastrophe Woodworth-Etter left the area for St. Louis.

This fiasco scarcely embarrassed her. Instead she positioned herself to catch the great wave of pentecostalism at the turn of the century. At first skeptical of speaking in tongues, she soon realized that her earlier mystical experience included just that manifestation: she had been a sort of Joan the Baptist of the pentecostal movement. Though she flickered out of view for several years, from 1912 to 1918 Woodworth-Etter drew larger crowds than any other pentecostal evangelist.[15]

✍ Spiritualism and Faith Healing

Woodworth-Etter's trances and mysticism fitted right in with the nineteenth-century fascination with spiritualism. Spiritualism held out the hope of communication with the dead, usually through women mediums. At the time a large proportion of the populace believed or at least professed to believe in direct communication with God and in immortality for human beings, a consensus that held the door open for credulity about talking with the dead. What with the high death rate, particularly among babies, many people yearned to talk with their beloved dead. As Ruth Bordin writes of Frances Willard, president of the Women's Christian Temperance Union, "She truly believed in an unseen world, a world of the spirit in touch with the everyday world and a very real heaven where she would again live happily with those she had lost on earth."[16]

By mid-century spiritualists—as well as an assortment of more or less reputable mesmerists, healers, mediums, and phrenologists—were flourishing, and con men and true believers alike were selling all sorts of magical devices from magnetic fluids to electric healing machines. The opportunities for financial gain and/or notoriety did not escape notice. Among the many who seized the day were the teen-age Fox sisters, Ann Leah, Margaret, and Catherine, who claimed to receive messages from the dead by spirit rappings. Even Margaret's confession forty years later that she and Kate had begun the rappings to fool their mother, a confession complete with demonstration of their techniques, failed to dissuade some of their followers, who felt their faith vindicated when Margaret Fox later recanted her confession. Among some New Agers and in certain quarters of the twentieth-century women's movement, spiritualism still finds favor, in part because of its female leadership and support for women's rights.

In 1865 spiritualists held a grand convention in Chicago, claiming three million adherents. However reliable that estimate, all sorts of people dabbled in the movement. From 1837 to 1844 the Shakers had been caught up in it. The Beechers tried it out, Isabella Beecher Hooker to the point that in 1876 she was persuaded that within a year she would become the head of a matriarchal government of the United States and the world.[17] Her sister Harriet Beecher Stowe toyed with both spiritualism and mesmerism.[18] The skeptical seemed to confirm even as they denied: M. Carey Thomas's Quaker father, James, "especially mistrusted spiritualism, for Satan is loose, as well as 'evil spirits capable of transformation into what may seem angels of light.'"[19]

Through the agency of Helena Petrovna Hahn Blavatsky (1831–1891), spiritualism gave birth to theosophy.[20] This Russian, who emigrated to the United States in 1873, sought to grasp the unity of life by joining with science the "realities" discoverable through spiritualism. Challenging both the religion and the science of her time, Blavatsky claimed the authority of male spirits who revealed to her the secrets of ancient religions and cultures. Though some of her contemporaries considered her a fascinating fraud, others found empowerment in Blavatsky's own example and her insistence on the ability of human beings to discover fundamental truths through communication with spirits. Women such as Katharine Tingley (1847–1929), who built a theosophical community in California, have figured prominently in the history of the Theosophical Society, and feminist spirituality at the end of the twentieth century continues to draw on its teachings. Despite its female founder, its many strong women leaders, and its interest in the feminine principle, theosophy has spawned its antifeminists, notably Charles W. Leadbeater, who in 1920 argued against ordaining women on the grounds that "the forces now arranged for distribution through the priesthood would not work efficiently through a feminine body."[21]

In its origins spiritualism had been connected with faith healing, another strand of the popular culture of the day. Little wonder that people seized on whatever cure offered itself, for doctors could do little to help them. Indeed, patients could count themselves lucky if they survived physicians' ministrations. Many agreed with physician Oliver Wendell Holmes that were all materia medica to be thrown into the sea, only the fish would suffer. So in the water cure people drank gallons and wrapped themselves in wet sheets. Others relied on magnetism or electrical shocks, altered their diets, doggedly counted the number of times they chewed their food, moved to a different climate, and if they were male treated their tuberculosis by signing on for an ocean voyage as able-bodied seamen.

In the absence of effective medical care, faith healing flourished. Biblical reports of Christ's miraculous cures reinforced consciousness of the effect of mind and body on each other. In the mid-nineteenth century as with many New Agers in the twentieth century, spiritual and physical well-being interlocked as the ultimate good. As R. Laurence Moore suggests, new religions were virtually marketed as a quest for health. Mesmerism claimed to benefit both body and spirit. Sylvester Graham, of graham cracker fame, founded a Christian Health Movement. And in these healing religions, women shone, reclaiming the roles of healers that men had usurped in orthodox medicine.[22]

Two elements in Ellen Gould Harmon White's (1827–1915) makeup particularly mark her as a woman of her time: her visionary capability and her proclivity for health fads.[23] They may well be related to each other. A woman who sometimes weighed less than eighty pounds and was unable to speak above a whisper might indeed have been more likely to see the unseeable than someone who enjoyed more vigorous health. In any case, both her visions and the force with which others either rejected or embraced them belonged to an age when spiritualism flourished.

White either was or was not a clergywoman. She did or did not co-found the Seventh-Day Adventist Church. She was or was not a prophet. Adventists differ vigorously on these scores. But she certainly itinerated. She certainly participated in many of the activities that led to the organization of the Seventh-Day Adventists. And she certainly described her visions to others, many of whom accepted them as prophecies—as the Seventh-Day Adventist Church today still officially accepts them.

White stands out as a compendium of her times, whose experiences epitomized her period. In adolescence she went through the usual religious crises, including a camp-meeting conversion in Maine, baptism by immersion, being disfellowshipped by her Methodist church, and ultimately a conviction that Christ would soon return to earth. As a millennialist, she strove to bring the world to a state of perfection suitable for the second coming of Christ. A mystic, she laid claim to some two thousand visions. Besieged by illnesses throughout her life, she nonetheless managed to publish fifty-four books, numberless pamphlets, and forty-six hundred articles, as well as organize, preach, prophesy, lay the foundations of the extensive Seventh-Day Adventist educational system, and bear four sons. A health enthusiast, she flitted from cure to cure, lending her latest favorite the authority of religious dicta. From the beginning of her professional life, controversy swirled around her. Every conceivable accusation was leveled against her, from plagiarism to bearing an illegitimate baby named Jesus.

After the world's failure to end as Miller had foreseen, eighteen-year-old Ellen Gould Harmon went among the discouraged Millerites urging them to regroup, reassuring them by her visions that Christ would indeed come soon, though she wisely refrained from naming a date. Visions also told her to celebrate the Sabbath on Saturday. In 1847 she married Adventist preacher James Springer White, and the two dedicated themselves to the Adventist cause, eventually becoming a rallying point for scattered groups of believers. In 1863 they helped to form a General Council of Seventh-Day Adventists. Ellen White's visions and biblical interpretations shaped their theology.

In this environment, accident- and sickness-prone Ellen White behaved like many others, only much more so. Like other Adventists, when she ailed she relied primarily on prayer, though later in her life she consulted physicians. She believed that Christians owed a duty to God to care for their bodies. By and large her prescriptions for that made sense: stay away from medicine; be temperate; don't drink alcohol or beverages with caffeine; exercise; get lots of sunshine; don't eat meat or dairy products. For ten years she struggled to change women's dress to a short skirt over pants, but with other like-minded women of her day she at last concluded that dress reform was "an injury to truth." With her husband and their protégé Dr. John Harvey Kellogg she established at Battle Creek, Michigan, the Western Health Reform Institute, later the Battle Creek Sanitarium. White was a good advertisement for her own regimen, for after a decade's stint of evangelizing in Australia, she spent a vigorous old age writing voluminously, extending the string of Adventist sanitaria and reorganizing the denomination. She died at eighty-eight.

White thought Mary Baker Eddy (1821–1910) little more than a spiritualist. But, as Ronald L. Numbers has pointed out, the two women had much in common:

> Both women were born in New England in the 1820s. As children they both experienced debilitating illnesses, which curtailed their formal schooling; and as young women they suffered from uncontrollable spells that left them unconscious for frighteningly long periods of time. They both sought cures in grahamism and hydropathy. Early in 1863 Mrs. White found hers through Dr. Jackson's essay on diphtheria, but just six months earlier Mrs. Eddy had left a New Hampshire water cure in disappointment. Abandoning hydropathy for the mind cure of Phineas P. Quimby, she did for Quimbyism what Ellen White did for health reform: she made a religion out of it. Both she and Mrs. White claimed divine inspiration, and both succeeded in establishing distinctive churches.[24]

But Mary Baker Eddy was a dictator.[25] She dictated the structure of the Church of Christ, Scientist. She dictated its theology. She dictated its governance. She chose and ruthlessly defrocked its personnel. She told communicants what they might read and what they must believe: her words filled their ears. No matter what she did, no one said her nay. All her life she had known how to get her own way, and she institutionalized that power within her denomination.

Getting to the truth about Mrs. Eddy is like trying to discover whether there was a conspiracy to assassinate President Kennedy. Mark Twain describes her as "a shining drop of quicksilver which you put your finger on and it isn't there."²⁶ She presented herself at times as the female equivalent of Jesus Christ, at others as the modern incarnation of the Virgin Mary—birthing Christian Science and her book *Science and Health* rather than a divine son. In her church she assumed the position of pope—or perhaps more accurately, of St. Peter. She was so frequently transfigured, so many critics have had at her, so many true believers have passionately defended her, and so many people have propagated myths about her that the true Mrs. Eddy probably never will stand up. One sympathizes with her biographers Willa Cather and Georgine Milmine when they write: "The record of these wandering, vagarious years from 1864 to 1870 is far from being satisfactory biography; the number of houses in which she lived, her quarrels and eccentricities, by no means tell us the one thing which is of real importance: what, all this time, was going on in Mrs. Glover's [Eddy's] own consciousness."²⁷ The facts are there, but the woman is not.

Certainly she was no ordinary woman. After all, most women do not engage in repeated litigation, do not accuse enemies of killing their husbands long-distance, do not engage followers in vigils to ward off evil influences and control the weather, do not arrange railroad journeys with one train ahead and one behind to protect the cars in which they ride, and do raise their own children. On the other hand, ordinary women do not achieve what Eddy achieved.

Before she found her vocation, she had endured a long invalidism and two frustrating marital experiences. The orthodox medicine of the day, homeopathy, the Graham diet, and hydropathy all failed to cure her various illnesses. Her first husband, a contractor, died in 1844 a few months after their wedding, leaving her pregnant and ill. She did not rally to care for her son, who was raised by friends; he grew up largely apart from her, after age eleven almost as a stranger to her; as an adult he joined in an unsuccessful suit to have her declared incompetent. In 1853 she embarked on a disastrous second marriage, this time to an itinerant dentist. They never managed to dwell together in peace, and twenty years later they divorced.

Meantime in 1862 Mary Baker Glover Patterson met a man who for a time succeeded in making her well and happy, one Phineas Parkhurst Quimby, a clockmaker turned mesmerist who had developed a "science of health" that at least once he called "Christian science." Quimby denounced both doctors and ministers. He believed that he had rediscovered the method by which Christ and his apostles had healed the sick naturally. The mind caused illness; the mind could cure illness, even at a distance, through telepathic magnetism. It worked for Mrs. Patterson (Eddy), who began to sing his praises and study his ideas, bearing out his theory that women by virtue of their greater share of "pure love" are better equipped to teach spiritual science.

Quimby's death in 1866 plunged her into grief and a nine-year period of developing the theories that she would eventually fashion into the orthodoxy of her church. Mind is all; matter is nothing. Human beings are spiritual, not material. God is all-good, all-powerful, and omnipresent, so that no room exists in the universe for evil. Illness is error. Death is error. Sin is error. Well-being and prosperity evidence right thinking. But a force that she called "Malicious Animal Magnetism" rampages through the world, threatening the bodies and minds of true believers. For these tenets she acknowledged no debt to Quimby, instead writing in *Science and Health:*

> In the year 1866, I discovered the Science of Metaphysical healing, and named it Christian Science. God had been graciously fitting me, during many years for the reception of a final revelation of the absolute Principle of Scientific Mind-healing. . . . No human pen or tongue taught me the Science contained in this book . . . and neither tongue nor pen can overthrow it.

This revelation was connected with a spill on the ice Eddy took on February 1, 1866. The attending physician recorded it as having caused a nervous "disturbance" and complaints of back and neck pain, which he treated with minute amounts of morphine; he thought that she had returned to normal in a couple of weeks. But the contemporary *Lynn Reporter* account said that her internal injuries were "of a very serious nature, including spasms and intense suffering"[28] and the approved Christian Science report in 1907 transfigured the accident into the cause of a spiritual experience in which "all pain evanesced into bliss, all discord in her physical body melted into harmony, all sorrow was translated into rapture." Eddy "recognized this state as her rightful condition as a child of God" and arose, miraculously cured.[29]

In the years from 1866 to 1875, she not only developed her creed but also discovered her own strengths. Beginning to teach, she discovered her charisma. She aimed not at education but at training. She wanted not students of independent mind but disciples who would follow her unquestioningly. She won them. Whatever she may have lacked in clarity of thought and verbal skills, according to her students she could impart "a certain spiritual or emotional exaltation . . . so strong that it was like the birth of a new understanding and seemed to open to them a new heaven and a new earth."[30] Quite literally she made many of her students her disciples, to do her bidding and to preach her gospel. Their admiration for her as an inspired teacher outlived even disillusionment with her as a person.

For instance, Augusta E. Stetson operated for years as "Mrs. Eddy's most attractive and effective field lieutenant." The First Church of Christ, Scientist, which Stetson founded in New York City, prospered to the point that Eddy began to perceive both it and Stetson as threats. Stetson flourished on her own as healer, teacher, administrator, and money raiser, but when Eddy spoke, she obeyed without complaint. When Eddy decreed that her denomination would substitute readers for pastors, Stetson stepped down to the position of reader.[31] When Eddy announced that Christian Science healers must not defile church buildings with their offices, Stetson moved her own offices and those of all other healers out of the New York church. When Eddy ruled against the overflow and branch services Stetson had instituted to handle the crowds she attracted, Stetson canceled them. When Stetson's own church praised her as "the vessel of the Father-Mother God and as the manifestation of Truth, the 'bread of Heaven and the water of Life,'" Stetson tactfully transferred this adulation to Eddy. Nothing availed. Eddy saw to it that the Mother Church in Boston forced Stetson's resignation from the church she had founded.[32] It was not nice, nor was it safe, to rival Mother Eddy.

The mother/child metaphor was the way that Eddy most frequently represented her relationship with her students and followers. She thought it her duty to be a kind of scourge of God, keeping them spiritually pure by correcting them harshly when they erred—in modern terms, exercising "tough love." Her critics saw her as a woman happy with her "children" only so long as they did not threaten her own power, and given to stirring up jealousies and backbiting among them.

Eddy came to understand her own mission not only as teaching her doctrines but also as organizing those who believed them. She alone could discern the truth; she alone must protect the truth, keeping it unsullied from false interpretation—interpretation, that is, by anyone else. For this purpose she must build a church so constituted that she as its head could keep absolute control over it, its doctrines, and its operations.

For this task she employed both her charisma and her genius as a strategist. Unfortunately for her and for her followers, she was as weak a tactician as she was powerful a strategist. But she could not keep her hands off micromanagement.

"In business disputes," write Cather and Milmine, "Mrs. Eddy had always one argument which none of her associates could hope to equal: she would draw up her shoulders, look her opponent in the eye, and say, very slowly, 'God has directed me in this matter. Have you anything further to say?'"[33] She subjected her closest, most dedicated, most talented followers to temper tantrums and accusations of disloyalty and corruption of truth; many of them sooner or later found this conduct unbearable. Her list of enemies grew daily. What's more, she handed them a weapon before which she herself trembled: Malicious Mesmerism or Malicious Animal Magnetism (MAM). This force, she believed, was so strong that it killed her third husband, so concentrated that it permeated houses she owned, forcing her to move out. To contend with it she required the daily spiritual services of a group of disciples and instituted an unending series of lawsuits.

Nonetheless, the good news of health and prosperity that she preached and her charisma and strategic abilities triumphed. Despite herself Eddy managed not only to found but to preserve and control a new denomination. In 1875 eight of her students united as "the Christian Scientists," undertaking to pay her to speak to them every Sunday. Four years later the group obtained a charter as a church. In her lifetime she was to reorganize that church almost as thoroughly as she revised *Science and Health,* which went through 382 editions.

Always, however, she centered the religion on healing, happiness, and health. Moral reform presumably followed automatically on the acceptance of Christian Science doctrine. In the classes that for most of her professional life were her chief support, she talked most about healing. There she trained her students in the doctrines that enabled them to hang out their shingles and earn their livings as practitioners. All her students took her three-week basic course; some of them went on to her "normal" course, a review of the basic course. At her Massachusetts Metaphysical College, for a time the curriculum consisted of three courses offering in all twenty-four lectures: twelve lessons constituted the Collegiate Course in Christian Science Metaphysical Healing; six more made up the normal course; and six more the Course in Metaphysical Obstetrics. To qualify for them the students must enjoy good health and be of good character.

The self-confidence these practitioners then displayed again testifies to Eddy's charisma. For instance, many practitioners did not hesitate to take sole responsibility as midwives. In 1888 tragedy struck when Mrs. Abby Corner officiated at her own daughter's lying-in; mother and baby died. Corner was indicted, tried, and finally acquitted on the grounds that her daughter had hemorrhaged so massively that no one could have saved her. Eddy repudiated Corner, her own student, and instituted a course in obstetrics, a course that concentrated on defending the patient against Malicious Animal Magnetism and "denying" such "errors" as premature birth, abnormal presentation, and hemorrhage. Later, Eddy brought in an obstetrician to coteach this course.[34]

For Eddy could and did learn and change, another of her strengths that helps to account for the rapid growth of her church. Over the years she grew shrewder and more astute. She learned to submit her writing to others for revision that often amounted to rewriting. In her later years, with a facility for delegating responsibility while retaining power that King Lear would have envied, she even handed over details of administration to others, withdrawing into a remoteness that enhanced her status and deepened that magical charisma.

The Church of Christ, Scientist, grew phenomenally. Consider the difficulties. Its appeal was limited primarily to white folks, many of them well-off. Its claims to mind cures by a variety of practitioners made it vulnerable to disillusion and scandal. Internal dissension and schisms repeatedly tore it apart and drastically reduced its numbers. Clergymen and physicians fearing Mrs. Eddy's invasions of their territory attacked her frequently, sometimes viciously, badmouthing her as the "Lydia Pinkham of the soul."[35] Judges did not always sympathize with practitioners' pleas that they were not practicing medicine but rather were conducting a religious exercise. Yet the April 1883 issue of the *Journal of Christian Science* contains the advertisements of fourteen authorized healers, whose numbers two years later increased to forty-three, and four years later, in 1887, to 110. What's more, by 1887 nineteen Christian Science institutes and academies advertised schools that were constantly preparing more practitioners.

Despite an unusually rapid turnover within its rolls, at her death Eddy left a financially sound, tightly structured denomination with an affluent membership of some one hundred thousand in more than six hundred churches. She had established a respected newspaper, the *Christian Science Monitor.* Her personal estate of some two and a half million dollars she left mostly to the denomination. It was governed by a dozen people she had handpicked. She had done all that any mortal, even such a one as she, could do to ensure doctrinal purity and continuity.

In more than one way Mary Baker Eddy influenced the progress of clergywomen. Theologically she insisted that humankind "reflected the Principle of male and female, and was the likeness of 'Us,' the compound Principle that made man." God, she believed, has no gender but embraces the masculine, feminine, and neuter. Indeed, she said: "We have not as much authority in science, for calling God masculine as feminine, the latter being the last, therefore the highest idea given of him. . . . Woman was a higher idea of God than man, insomuch as she was the final one in the scale of being; but because our beliefs reverse every position of Truth, we name supreme being masculine instead of feminine."[36]

Practically, as Jean McDonald has observed, though Mrs. Eddy did not authorize an ordained clergy (except herself), she did offer women more opportunities in leadership than any mainline church of her day, particularly older women previously untrained to support themselves. Though the highest positions in her denomination's hierarchy usually went to men, most full-time practitioners were women, who she insisted should be well paid. Moreover, willy-nilly she gave a start to many women, some of whom then went on to officiate as clergy in the New Thought movement.

Others preached their own versions of Christian Science. Eddy had done her level best to prevent them. In the days of the Christian Science Association, which she abolished around the turn of the century, members were forbidden to read any literature on mind cure apart from hers. No two association members were allowed to discuss Christian Science without inviting the participation of all members. If they wished to leave the association without reason, they were to be considered guilty of immorality for having broken their oaths.[37] One way or another, though, during and after the life of the Association, many of Eddy's disciples struck off on their own.

Take Josephine Curtis Woodbury, long one of Eddy's foremost healers and teachers, a writer for the *Journal,* a lecturer who had itinerated widely, organized classes and church societies, and conducted a Christian Science academy. She had her own charisma, and she took on Mrs. Eddy in Boston, on her own stamping grounds. The dramatic Mrs. Woodbury hired a hall in which to conduct Sunday services, sometimes lecturing, sometimes preaching, sometimes reading poetry. If she couldn't be there, her daughter Gwendolyn took her place. Like clashed with like, as Eddy and Woodbury accused each other of exercising Malicious Animal Magnetism. About 1899 Woodbury sued Eddy for criminal libel—and lost.[38]

But Eddy did not always win. Some of the disciples whom she expelled (sometimes after they had quit in disgust) founded and ran their own brands of Christian Science or started new sects based on similar principles.

◈ New Thought

The New Thought movement, nominally Christian, tried to incorporate the best of all religions. "Its central message was a metaphysical power of positive thinking which identified the divine Spirit with an immanent power in each person."[39] It descended from Quimby, through the Eddy line. In 1883 Eddy's students could read in the newspapers the accusations of plagiarizing from Quimby leveled against Eddy by Julius Dresser, who had studied with Quimby at the same time as Eddy. Some of these students then turned to books by Warren F. Evans, yet another Quimby patient, which set forth the basic principles of mental healing without denying the existence of either illness or matter. Now and then a student was moved to criticize.

Ursula Newell Gestefeld (1845–1921), once a trusted follower, sinned against Eddy by writing *Ursula Newell Gestefeld's Statement of Christian Science,* an exposition of Eddy's theories that Cather and Milmine praise as admirably clear and logical. Eddy on the other hand regarded it as an infringement of her own prerogatives and cast Gestefeld into outer darkness. Gestefeld responded in kind with a pamphlet called *Jesuitism in Christian Science* and went on to found the Church of the New Thought and the College of the Science of Being.

Consider Emma Curtis Hopkins (1853–1925), whom Eddy after Hopkins's defection dubbed a "Mind-Quack," but whom New Thought circles honored as the "Teacher of Teachers."[40] She took Eddy's course in 1883 and soon entered the inner circle, working as assistant editor and then editor of the *Journal.* After the usual difficulties Hopkins moved to Chicago about 1886 and set up in her home the Christian Science Theological Seminary, lectured, and published her own magazine, the *Christian Metaphysician.* She and her "Spiritual Science" prospered as she lectured all over the country. *Her* followers in turn founded their own societies, and so the New Thought movement pyramided.

Hopkins differed from Eddy. A mystic, she developed a more complex theology, a theology that gave women greater importance. Within the Trinity, she believed, the Holy Ghost represented the mother principle (also correlated with the Jewish concept of Shekinah, the indwelling presence of God). She divided history into three eras: the first, that of God the Father; the second, that of Jesus Christ marked by a struggle against oppression; and the third, that of the Holy Spirit, whose hour she believed had recently struck, as was evidenced by women's increasing activity.[41]

More importantly for the history of clergywomen, Hopkins sought to give women leadership roles. Eddy's students ordained Eddy; Hopkins ordained Hopkins's students. Claiming for herself the position of bishop and thereby the right to ordain, on January 10, 1889, she ordained twenty-two ministers. She also helped them find employment and establish themselves as full-fledged clergy—right down to insisting on their right to a clerical discount on railroad tickets. They were, Hopkins believed, the spokeswomen of the new era of the Holy Spirit, the divine Mother. In effect, Hopkins legitimated women's leadership in New Thought, undergirding it with her theology, actualizing it with recruiting, training, ordaining, and mentoring women.[42]

Hopkins's contribution to the position of clergywomen was compounded by the prominence and accomplishments of her students. As J. Gordon Melton has pointed out, with very few exceptions (i.e., several other former Eddy students who later affiliated with the movement), all of the early leaders of New Thought were either her students or her students' students. Her most important students included Myrtle and Charles Fillmore (founders, Unity); H. Emilie Cady (Unity); Kate Bingham and Nellie Van Anderson (teachers of the founders of Divine Science in Colorado); Annie Militz (Home of Truth); Melinda Cramer (founder, Divine Science), Clara Stocker (teacher of the founder of the Church of Truth); and Ernest Holmes (founder, Church of Religious Science). These leaders in turn taught Nona Brooks and Fannie James (founders, Divine Science, Colorado); and Lambert Grier (founder, Church of Truth).[43]

Accordingly, it was Hopkins's far-flung influence that largely determined the distinctly feminine composition of New Thought's clergy in its early years, at least up until about 1910.

Since New Thought societies were, so to speak, by-blows of Christian Science, claiming a kind of illegitimate descent from it by way of the defecting disciples, it is hardly surprising that they exhibited in differing degrees many of its characteristics. The Unity church, for example, founded by Myrtle Page Fillmore (1845–1931) and Charles Fillmore, proclaimed the gospel of health and prosperity.[44] As often happened in New Thought, the Unity movement originated in a healing: in this instance, Myrtle Fillmore's healing from tuberculosis began when she went to hear one of Emma Hopkins's students. The Fillmores went on to study with Hopkins herself. Eager to share their good news with others, they began teaching and publishing.

They did not intend to found a church, but, as Charles Braden remarks, the tightly structured organization that has emerged looks very much like a church.[45] They require their ministers to attend their own training school. Central authority, including that of maintaining doctrinal purity, is in the hands of their ministerial association.

In the late 1880s and 1890s, though, the Fillmores set out simply to share their discoveries with others. They started a series of publications and developed in Missouri the Unity School of Christianity. They liked to describe their teachings as "practical Christianity," borrowings of the "best from all religions, that is the reason we are called Unity. . . . Unity is not a sect, not a separation of people into an exclusive group of know-it-alls. Unity is the Truth that is taught in all religions, simplified and systemized so that anyone can understand and apply. Students of Unity do not find it necessary to sever their church affiliations. The church needs the vitalization that this renaissance of primitive Christianity gives it."[46]

In time the Fillmores realized that they had to institutionalize. About 1891 to extend Myrtle Fillmore's much-sought-after counseling to more people, they established the Society of Silent Unity, under whose auspices Kansas City Unity disciples gathered to pray, meditate on her writings, and, as Myrtle Fillmore wrote, "meet in silent soul communion every night at 10 o'clock all those who are in trouble, sickness, or poverty, and who sincerely desire the help of the God Father. Whoever will may join this society, the only requirement being that members shall sit in a quiet, retired place, if possible, at the hour of 10 o'clock every night, and hold in silent thought, for not less than fifteen minutes, the words that shall be given each month by the editor of this department."[47] Pleas from the lonely and desperate poured in, asking for the spiritual help that the Kansas City disciples offered on a twenty-four-hour basis.

With their accepting, eclectic leanings, the Fillmores did not like to tell people what to teach, but what were they to do when in the name of Unity people held seances, cast horoscopes, told fortunes, read palms, and practiced numerology? They could see no solution but to make rules, and so institutionalization took its inevitable course. The Unity Society of Practical Christianity was incorporated July 29, 1903.

The Fillmores' protests that their society was not a church or a new denomination point up characteristics of New Thought groups. Although they varied in degree of orthodoxy, most of them identified themselves as Christian. Often their founders, eager to tell others about their own experiences of healing, began by thinking of themselves as teachers. This understanding of their mission left their status as clergy in doubt; ordination when and if it occurred could be a casual affair.

Thus it was with Divine Science.[48] Two women, Melinda Cramer of San Francisco and Nona Brooks of Pueblo, Colorado, founded this group. Both had been healed about 1885. Several years later when they discovered that they were heading groups based on startlingly similar principles, they merged their movements. As part of their educational enterprise, they conducted meditations on weekday mornings and vespers on Sunday evening. When in 1899 their followers requested a Sunday morning service, they decided that such an innovation would require the services of clergy. So Cramer ordained the Rev. Nona L. Brooks, who thereafter served as both minister of the church and president of the Divine Science College. Graduates of the college formed new centers around the country; Divine Science grew into one of the largest New Thought organizations; and the movement still survives.

This amalgam of educational and religious identities presaged the New Age groups that have proliferated at the end of the twentieth century, but it also harked back to an old concept in both Judaism and Christianity whereby clergy are understood primarily as teachers. The happy-go-lucky approach of some New Thought groups toward ordination is telling. Clearly, to some extent it reflects the confusion about whether the ordinand was a teacher or a clergymember. But it also suggests an indifference to or even a repudiation of institutionalization, hierarchy, and authority. Women predominated in New Thought as in no other religious movement of the time. Here they could freely claim and themselves authenticate a call from God.

Far from the crest but still riding the wave of New Thought were women such as Carrie Judd Montgomery and Jennie Smith. Smith, known as the railroad evangelist, for years functioned as a professional invalid bearing her illness in saintly patience, traveling by baggage car on her bed of pain from one religious revival or camp meeting to another, selling accounts of her own life; eventually she underwent a miraculous healing, which she related in yet another book.[49] Montgomery in *her* books sentimentally recounts her own healing and those of innumerable "precious" others, somewhat straining credulity by insisting that she was pioneering with divine healing.[50]

✑ What Went Wrong

New Thought was hardly the only place where standards of ordination were loose. In the late nineteenth century in many occupations professionalization was just beginning. Even in old professions such as medicine and law, standards were still evolving; a hundred years later those nineteenth-century standards seem undemanding. In religion the situation was chaotic, as it remains.

Setting standards for ordination, after all, presents unique difficulties. Whatever their other considerations, ordaining bodies must in the end determine mystical qualifications: Has the candidate a true vocation? From one denomination to another and even within denominations, standards for ordination varied with theology, the age of the denomination and its corresponding degree of institutionalization, and church polity—whether standards were set by individual congregations or by the whole denomination. Would-be clergywomen faced difficulties in meeting the educational standards of the more stringent mainline denominations, simply because many theological seminaries would not admit them. In most of those denominations they could not meet the mystical standards at all, since those churches flatly refused to believe that God ever calls any woman to the ministry.

What all this amounted to in practice was that fifty years after Antoinette Brown's ordination the mainline churches were ordaining no women or just a handful. No significant group pressure was being brought to bear on them to ordain women, by church laywomen or by secular women's reform advocates or by clergywomen themselves.

Laywomen had their hands full with their own problems. They were fighting hard for their laity rights. Methodist women wanted a voice in church governance: in the 1890s the Methodist General Conference was still refusing to seat as a delegate Frances Willard, president of the large and powerful Women's Christian Temperance Union and the most widely known and respected Methodist laywoman of her day.[51] Elsewhere women's missionary societies battled to keep control of their own funds. Secular groups working on reform generally did not address professional issues. When they thought about working women, they were apt to think in terms of sweatshops or wages and hours.

Why is there no evidence of ordained clergywomen moving on their own? True enough, their numbers were tiny and they were divided among several denominations, each separately governed; many ordained clergywomen belonged to denominations where individual congregations chose their own clergy; and mainline clergy-women seldom communicated with those in holiness churches. On the other hand, contrast what Elizabeth and Emily Blackwell did in opening doors in medicine for women to what their sister-in-law, Antoinette Brown (Blackwell), did not do in opening doors for women in the ministry. Against the odds the Blackwells enabled women to get medical training and practical experience and even provided them with jobs.

No one, of course, can criticize Brown for not working the miracles that the Blackwells wrought; it's remarkable enough that she managed to get trained and ordained. Moreover she contributed notably to the advancement of women both through her suffrage work and through her work in the Association for the Advancement of Women. Her disillusioning experience with her first parish may have made her hesitate to involve others. Her choosing to marry (while the Blackwell sisters remained single) forced her to divert a lot of her energies elsewhere. And temperamentally she was not a politician, not an organization woman.

Most probably, Antoinette Brown and other clergywomen ordained in the nineteenth century simply chose the wrong strategy. Brown spent much effort on attempts to establish a scriptural basis for woman's equality. As many a woman has discovered after her, logic, reason, and the accumulation of evidence seldom win the day on this front. The Iowa Sisterhood also erred strategically when they reasoned that proving women competent to do the job and providing women a support group would level the playing field. The eastern Unitarian establishment remained unmoved.

The holiness churches, a younger cohort, were ordaining more women. As far as the record shows, no one in them foresaw how women's chances would dwindle as these churches aged and institutionalized, so no one was trying to guard against that contingency. The New Thought movement was ad-libbing, sometimes bizarrely; but among them, holiness clergywomen, New Thought clergywomen, women founders, and women who simply preached and pastored without waiting for a laying on of hands were keeping alive the concept of women in the clergy while many mainline churches were still wandering in the wilderness or puzzling about how to cross the Red Sea.

Nineteenth-century clergywomen had asked little of the mainline churches—only a tiny place in the sun. Few went so far as Frances Willard, who made an early attack on sexist language, complaining that "preachers almost never refer to the women of their audiences, but tell about 'men' and what 'a man' was and is and ought to be," calling this a "one-eyed way of looking at an audience."[52]

But outside the mainline churches, women had wrought far more basic changes in religion: theological changes, changes in ideas of gender roles and gender relationships. Among others, Mother Ann Lee, Jemima Wilkinson, and Mary Baker Eddy had claimed a central place for women in religion, insisting that the deity could not be understood as simply masculine.

Notes _____

1. Ruth A. Tucker and Walter Liefeld, *Daughters of the Church: Women and Ministry from New Testament Times to the Present* (Grand Rapids, Mich.: Zondervan, Academie Books, 1987), p. 291. Some women missionaries were ordained ministers (Elaine Magalis, *Conduct Becoming to a Woman: Bolted Doors and Burgeoning Missions* [n.p.: Women's Division, Board of Global Ministries, The United Methodist Church, n.d.], p. 118).

2. Magalis, *Conduct Becoming to a Woman*, pp. 83–84, 118.

3. Arthur Huff Fauset, *Sojourner Truth: God's Faithful Pilgrim* (New York: Russell & Russell, 1938, 1971), p. 111. All of the biographies of Truth are based on her own *Narrative of Sojourner Truth*, ed. Olive Gilbert (1878; reprint, New York: Arno Press, 1968). Among the best are Jacqueline Bernard, *Journey Toward Freedom: The Story of Sojourner Truth* (New York: Feminist Press, 1967); and Hertha Pauli, *Her Name Was Sojourner Truth* (New York: Appleton-Century-Crofts, 1962), both of which have benefited by extensive research on Truth's environment.

4. Joan D. Hedrick, *Harriet Beecher Stowe: A Life* (New York: Oxford Univ. Press, 1994), p. 270. Pauli notes that Truth's speech in her youth was reported as grammatical, though her first language may have been Dutch, and speculates that Truth may have found folksy black speech effective on the platform (*Her Name*, p. 6). Truth herself objected that Stowe had laid it on thick.

5. Bernard, *Journey*, p. 143.

6. Pauli, *Her Name*, p. 3.

7. Ibid., pp. 153–54.

8. Ibid., p. 109.

9. Wayne E. Warner, *The Woman Evangelist: The Life and Times of Charismatic Evangelist Maria B. Woodworth-Etter* (Metuchen, N.J.: Scarecrow, 1986), p. 15. Woodworth-Etter herself published a slew of books, mostly autobiographical.

10. Ibid., p. 133.

11. Emma J. Ray, *Twice Sold, Once Ransomed: Autobiography of Mr. and Mrs. L. P. Ray* (1926; reprint, Freeport, N.Y.: Books for Libraries Press, 1971), p. 122.

12. Warner, *Woman Evangelist*, pp. 43–44, 52, 25.

13. In 1885 at Alexandria, Indiana, a Mrs. Sarah A. Dilts was raised from her invalid's bed as Woodworth-Etter prayed for her in a buggy some distance away. Mrs. Dilts went into ministry as an evangelist and was still preaching in 1921. Two converts of hers, Sister Elizabeth Sisson and Zelma Argue, both became evangelists (Warner, *Woman Evangelist*, pp. 147, 148, 170).

14. Montgomery conducted a faith-healing ministry in Buffalo under the aegis of the Christian and Missionary Alliance, a group founded in 1887, open to women in ministry.

15. Warner, *Woman Evangelist*, p. 27.

16. Ruth Bordin, *Frances Willard: A Biography* (Chapel Hill: Univ. of North Carolina Press, 1986), p. 157.

17. Elizabeth Frost-Knappman, *The ABC-Clio Companion to Women's Progress in America* (Santa Barbara, Calif.: ABC-Clio, 1994), p. 153.

18. Hedrick, *Harriet Beecher Stowe*, p. 346. About 1868 Stowe believed that there were four to five million spiritualists in the United States; she sought to appeal to that market by endowing one of her central characters with spiritualist abilities.

19. Helen Lefkowitz Horowitz, *The Power and Passion of M. Carey Thomas* (New York: Alfred A. Knopf, 1994), p. 41.

20. On Blavatsky and other women theosophists, see Robert Ellwood and Catherine Wessinger, "The Feminism of 'Universal Brotherhood': Women in the Theosophical Movement," in *Women's Leadership in Marginal Religions: Explorations Outside the Mainstream,* ed. Catherine Wessinger (Urbana: Univ. of Illinois Press, 1993). See also K. Paul Johnson, *Madame Blavatsky and the Myth of the Great White Lodge* (Albany: State Univ. of New York Press, 1995); and Peter Washington, *Madame Blavatsky's Baboon* (New York: Schocken, 1995).

21. Quoted by Mary Farrell Bednarowski in "Widening the Banks of the Mainstream: Women Constructing Theologies," in *Women's Leadership,* ed. Wessinger, p. 224.

22. R. Laurence Moore, *Selling God: American Religion in the Marketplace of Culture* (New York: Oxford Univ. Press, 1994), pp. 140–42. Moore also notes that Lydia Pinkham, she of the vegetable compound of high alcoholic content, was a committed spiritualist.

23. For White's life and work, see Ronald L. Numbers, *Prophetess of Health: A Study of Ellen G. White* (New York: Harper & Row, 1976); and Roy E. Graham, *Ellen G. White, Co-Founder of the Seventh-day Adventist Church* (New York: Peter Lang, 1985).

24. Numbers, *Prophetess,* p. 201.

25. Mary Baker Eddy has attracted the attention of many feminist scholars as a study of a woman's seizing and holding authority. See, for example, Jean A. McDonald, "Mary Baker Eddy and the Nineteenth-Century 'Public' Woman," *Journal of Feminist Studies in Religion* 2 (Spring 1986): 89–111.

26. *Christian Science,* in *The Writings of Mark Twain* (New York: Harper, 1907) 25:211.

27. Willa Cather and Georgine Milmine, *The Life of Mary Baker G. Eddy and the History of Christian Science* (1909; reprint, Lincoln: Univ. of Nebraska Press, 1993), p. 131. The difficulty of presenting a fair and balanced interpretation of Mrs. Eddy is suggested by the length of the section devoted to her in *Notable American Women,* some ten pages—more, we think, than to any other woman. Sydney E. Ahlstrom there makes a gallant attempt to condense and balance the multitudinous details of her life and work and offers invaluable information about the publications on Eddy up to 1971. Julius Silberger, Jr., in the introduction to his book *Mary Baker Eddy: An Interpretive Biography of the Founder of Christian Science* (Boston: Little, Brown, 1980) also surveys the literature helpfully, as well as providing a psychiatrist's insights into Mrs. Eddy's character. See also Louise A. Smith, *Mary Baker Eddy* (New York: Chelsea House, 1991); Robert David Thomas, *"With Bleeding Footsteps": Mary Baker Eddy's Path to Religious Leadership* (New York: Alfred A. Knopf, 1994); and Lyman P. Powell, *Mary Baker Eddy: A Life Size Portrait* (Boston: Christian Science Pub. Soc., 1991).

28. Thomas, *"With Bleeding Footsteps,"* p. 114.

29. Silberger (*Mary Baker Eddy,* p. 97), quoting a report composed by Sibyl Wilbur with Eddy's "acquiescence and encouragement."

30. Cather and Milmine, *Life,* p. 156.

31. In 1895 the bylaws of The Mother Church were amended to read: "I, Mary Baker Eddy, ordain the BIBLE, and SCIENCE AND HEALTH WITH KEY TO THE SCRIPTURES, Pastor over The Mother Church,—The First Church of Christ, Scientist, in Boston, Mass.—and they will continue to preach for this Church and the world." At this point, writes Silberger, "the pastors of all other Christian Science churches withdrew from their positions and ensured the adoption of similar ordinances in their own churches. . . . The reader was not a leader and could not be president of a church. Readers were forbidden to make remarks explanatory of the lesson-sermon, nor were they permitted, during their term of readership, to give any lectures at all" (*Mary Baker Eddy,* pp. 204, 210).

32. Silberger, *Mary Baker Eddy,* pp. 232ff.

33. Cather and Milmine, *Life,* p. 395.

34. Cather and Milmine, *Life,* p. 353. Silberger identifies this "obstetrician" as "'Dr.' Charles J. Eastman . . . whose practice consisted primarily in performing abortions" (*Mary Baker Eddy,* p. 142).

35. McDonald, "Mary Baker Eddy," p. 101.

36. Cather and Milmine, *Life,* pp. 187–88.

37. Ibid., p. 349.

38. Ibid., pp. 428–40. Thomas analyzes the bizarre story of the Eddy–Woodbury relationship at length (*"With Bleeding Footsteps,"* pp. 245–59).

39. Rosemary R. Ruether, "Radical Victorians," in *Women and Religion in America,* ed. Rosemary R. Ruether and Rosemary S. Keller (San Francisco: Harper & Row, 1986) 3:8.

40. For information on Hopkins, see J. Gordon Melton, "Emma Curtis Hopkins: A Feminist of the 1880s and Mother of New Thought," in *Women's Leadership,* ed. Wessinger.

41. Ibid., p. 94.

42. Ibid., pp. 93, 98. Melton credits Hopkins with being the first woman to hold the office of bishop in the United States.

43. Ibid., p. 96.

44. On the Unity movement, see Charles S. Braden, *Spirits in Rebellion: The Rise and Development of New Thought* (Dallas: Southern Methodist University Press, 1963); Dell deChant, "Myrtle Fillmore and Her Daughters: An Observation and Analysis of the Role of Women in Unity," in *Women's Leadership,* ed. Wessinger; and James D. Freeman, *The Story of Unity* (Lee's Summit, Mo.: Unity School of Christianity, 1954).

45. Braden, *Spirits,* p. 54.

46. Freeman, *Story of Unity,* p. 61.

47. Ibid., p. 81.

48. Braden, *Spirits,* pp. 264ff.

49. See, for example, *Incidents and Experiences of a Railroad Evangelist* (Washington, D.C.: n.p., 1920); and *Ramblings in Beulah Land: A Continuation of Experiences in the Life of Jennie Smith* (Cincinnati, Oh.: By the Author, 1887).

50. Carrie F. Judd, *The Prayer of Faith* (1880; reprint, New York: Garland, 1985); and Carrie Judd Montgomery, *"Under His Wings," The Story of My Life* (1936; reprint, New York: Garland, 1985).

51. Bordin, *Frances Willard,* p. 167.

52. Donald W. Dayton and Lucille Sider Dayton, "'Your Daughters Shall Prophesy': Feminism in the Holiness Movement," *Methodist History* 14 (January 1976): 78.

"The Truest Fish Story Ever Told." Aimee Semple McPherson, evangelist and founder of the Foursquare Gospel Church, dramatizes the story of Jonah and the whale. *Courtesy of Heritage Department, International Church of the Foursquare Gospel.*

LEFT: Dr. Audrey Bronson, a contemporary clergywoman, founded and pastors the Church of the Open Door in Philadelphia. *Courtesy of Dr. Audrey Bronson.*

RIGHT: This active Salvation Army officer has a daughter who is also an officer. *From a private collection.*

Rabbinical students at Hebrew Union College, with Torah. *Courtesy of Richard Lobell.*

The entering class at Eden Theological Seminary, St. Louis, Missouri, 1992. *Courtesy of Eden Theological Seminary.*

"While the saints look on." *Courtesy of Eleanor Mill/Mill News Art Syndicate.*

LEFT: Reverend Lillian Daniel, associate minister at the UCC church in Cheshire, Connecticut, with members of the Masonic Order of Knights Templar after receiving an award to visit the Holy Land. The Knights Templar make these awards to young ministers near the beginning of their ministries. *Courtesy of the Reverend Wayne Sandau.*

RIGHT: Dr. Lillian (Lillie) McCutcheon followed in her mother's footsteps as church builder, evangelist, and minister of the Church of God (Anderson, Indiania). *From the collection of Dr. Lillian McCutcheon.*

Chaplain (Major) JoAnn Knight holding a communion service during a field exercise. *Courtesy of U.S. Army.*

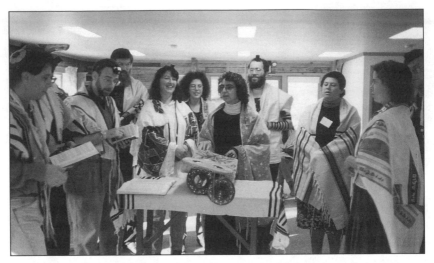

Rabbinical students of the Academy for Jewish Religion attending a retreat. *Courtesy of Academy for Jewish Religion, New York City.*

A moment in a service. *Photograph by Rick Hartford / The Hartford Courant.*

5

The Mixture as Before
1900–1960 🖎

What Didn't Happen for Mainline Clergywomen
—and What Did

AT FIRST GLANCE THE HISTORIAN of American clergywomen stares in astonishment at the first sixty years of the twentieth century and says, "Nothing happened." Nothing happened? In sixty years that saw the triumph of woman suffrage, the country's deepest depression, and its tragic involvement in two world wars and the Korean "peace-keeping mission"? In sixty years when church and synagogue membership surged? In sixty years when images of the American woman went through successive incarnations as the New Woman, the flapper, Rosie the Riveter, and a stay-at-home mom? In sixty years when women nationwide voted for the first time, were incorporated into the military services, and persistently edged into the workplace? Absurd.

After all, in the Progressive Era, encompassing the first two decades of the twentieth century, American women won major battles in the public sphere. On the labor front they fought through legislation protecting women in the workplace and almost eliminating children from it. They supported strikes and learned how to work in unions. On the temperance front, although they had yielded the vanguard to men, they saw the enactment of the Eighteenth Amendment prohibiting the manufacture, transportation, and sale of intoxicating beverages. Most impressive of all, with the passage and ratification of the Nineteenth Amendment they won the suffrage. Carrie Chapman Catt and Alice Paul led the dedicated women of the National American Woman Suffrage Association and the National Woman's Party to that final victory. Meanwhile, the numbers of employed women soared, feminizing whole segments of the workplace: clerical workers grew from 187,000 in 1900 to 1,421,000 in 1920.[1] Women professionalized nursing and social work and created such new vocations as physical and occupational therapy. In World War I the Navy and Marine Corps Reserves enlisted women as "yeomen" and twenty-five thousand

American civilian and military women, including more than ten thousand nurses, went overseas.[2]

Even in the era between the two world wars, the female labor force kept expanding—though mostly into dead-end jobs. Oddly enough, at least during the first part of the Great Depression (1929–1939) this tendency continued, as employers looking for cheaper labor turned to women. World War II called for all the workers of either gender that could be found. The country now solemnly told its married women and mothers, whom it had previously adjured to stay at home and raise children, that they had a patriotic duty to build airplanes and submarines. After the war, of course, with equal solemnity the country urged women back into the kitchen and consumerism, an argument that failed to arrest for long the steady movement of women into the workforce: it soon became clear to the housewife that to consume more the household needed more money to buy consumer goods, and even in the Dick-and-Jane era of the fifties more and more women went to paid work. Those women who did stay at home and many of the paid workers meanwhile contributed to the economy not only by keeping house and raising families but also by hours and hours of volunteer work, much of it supporting churches.

So surely it was absurd not to expect great days for clergywomen. Or was it? It's all too easy in looking back from the vantage point of half a century or more to overlook the human response, the emotions and uncertainties of the people who lived through these events, the emotions and uncertainties that were manifesting themselves particularly in religion.

At the turn of the twentieth century, industrialization and urbanization were shifting gender roles. The suffrage movement and the rapid entrance of young women into the workplace plainly demonstrated that many people were perforce thinking about what it means to be a woman and what it means to be a man. That necessity elated some but deeply frightened others, both men and women, who felt the earth tremble under their feet. They perceived both the New Woman of the Progressive Era and the post–World War I flapper as threats to the traditional relationships between men and women.

In religion these fears manifested themselves in splits—sometimes schisms— between fundamentalists and those who preached the social gospel, with the fundamentalists calling for a return to some dreamed-of golden age when women knew their place as subordinate to men. Anxieties about gender roles and the recurrent dread of the feminization of religion also evoked desperate efforts to "get men back into the churches" and spawned a theology of "muscular Christianity."[3] Churches moved to place men in positions of control, often by eroding the power of laywomen, denying women the power to vote in church governance, and depriving them of control over the moneys they raised in their missionary societies. In African-American churches these attitudes were exacerbated by urgings that women "step aside and let a man take over" on the grounds that otherwise it would "look bad for the race."[4]

Laywomen were kept so busy protecting themselves that they had little time or thought to expend on the issue of women's ordination. Some denominations even played off the few would-be clergywomen against the many laywomen. In 1929, for instance, the Presbyterian General Assembly voted to ordain women as elders (though not as pastors); such concessions, writes Margaret Lamberts Bendroth, mitigated laywomen's anger over losing their independent mission boards.[5] On the other hand, Sara Maitland suggests that deprivation of lay rights actually intensified demands for ordination, as "women who had previously had a separate channel [in the churches] for their energy and vocation now had to demand of the denominations themselves the right to serve and exercise ministry."[6]

Whether or not laywomen's possession of power improves the chances for women's ordination remains an open question. Barbara Brown Zikmund has noted that the empowerment of laywomen typically precedes women's ordination. Sometimes lay power has directly led to the decision to ordain, as when in 1953 Presbyterian ruling elder Lillian Hurt (Alexander), indignant because a friend's daughter had graduated from seminary but could not be a ministerial candidate because of her gender, asked the General Assembly to permit ordination; with the support of the Presbyterian Women's Organization the assembly passed the resolution, and in 1956 Margaret Towner was ordained.[7] But Cheryl Gilkes argues that the esteem and appreciation that laywomen enjoy in African-American Sanctified churches disinclines them to seek higher status.[8] Though the empowerment of laywomen may be a contributing and in some cases a necessary cause for women's ordination, it often is not a sufficient cause.

At the end of the twentieth century it is hard to comprehend, let alone to stomach, the emphasis that religious institutions, like the rest of society, were putting on male superiority and supremacy when the century began. Some clergywomen fought back: in 1922 the Rev. Madeline Southard (1877–1967) retorted, "Some brethren are very fearful that women preachers will feminize the church, apparently unaware that the masculine monopoly of the pulpit has already done that."[9] But all too often the masculine emphasis discouraged would-be clergywomen and undermined the confidence of those already ordained. In the 1940s, with fifteen years of successful ministry under her gown, Margaret Blair Johnstone still remembered the words spoken during her candidacy for ordination: "Wouldn't you always feel you were keeping from [the parishioners] the counsel of some consecrated, able man?"[10] Prathia Hall Wynn writes empathetically of the many black lay churchwomen from 1880 to 1920, whom she calls "secular evangelists":

> My own suspicion is that many of these women leaders felt as called to the ministry as I do today. Their speeches would easily qualify as sermons. But because of patriarchal suppression of even the thought of female Baptist clergy, they had to work out their call by marrying ministers and becoming involved in their husband's ministries, or by devoting themselves to the "women's work" of their denomination, as defined by men.[11]

The stupidities of World War I and the Treaty of Versailles induced disillusionment, a loss of faith in the perfectibility of humans, a questioning of the idea of progress. Society secularized, particularly among the young. The young women who in another era might have thought of entering the clergy had little use for religion; their idealism soured into cynicism by the useless slaughter and sacrifices of the war. As Patricia R. Hill writes, "Far too many young women of the middle and upper classes in postwar America found . . . that 'religion did not satisfy.'"[12] This disillusionment combined with the isolationism of the postwar period to shrivel interest in missions, both among laywomen and among those who might otherwise have become missionaries.

While the state of the nation always influences the conditions of life, in the years from 1914 to 1945 national emergencies affected individual lives with unusual force. Wars and depression not only disrupted private lives but controlled them, determining when, where, and whether people ate, slept, sheltered, and had babies. Most people had all they could handle just to keep their feet under them. Women of the 1990s may analyze changes in gender roles during World War II, but women of the 1930s and 1940s were far too worried about survival and too busy doing whatever needed to be done next to think in those terms. In many ways churches flourished as people turned to them for reassurance and memberships grew. But neither the leadership nor the laity had much time for or interest in women's ordination or employment opportunities in the churches. Even with the induction of thousands of women during World War II, the military blandly disregarded the efforts of ordained women to serve as chaplains. One clergywoman protested, "It doesn't seem possible that in a women's camp, the one position where a woman should excel has been given to a man. I waited to see what type man would be selected. It seemed to me he would have to be a combination of Dorothy Dix, the Voice of Experience, and Harry Emerson Fosdick." Instead the military installed in the Women's Auxiliary Army Corps "an Army Chaplain, who has spent the last 25 years with leathernecks, roughnecks, and horses," who reckoned that the problems of servicewomen would be about the same as those of any other army recruit.[13] The wonder is that in such times a few determined women, headed by women in the national offices of mainline denominations, had the energy and courage to persist in the demand for women's ordination.

The indifference to or at least distraction from these issues persisted from 1945 to 1960, as Americans drew deep breaths of relief and rejoiced in the liberty once again to go about their own affairs. American Jews, in shock, were still dealing with the horrors of the Holocaust and devoting passionate efforts to the creation of Israel. The United States and its religious institutions seemed more likely to congratulate themselves on the new, hard-earned status quo than to try to change it.

At any rate, in some senses it is true that in the first sixty years of the twentieth century, little happened for clergywomen. True certainly in that their numbers did not grow substantially in proportion to the population. The available statistics are pathetically shaky. Denominational records vary from incomplete to nonexistent; cross-denominational surveys were scarce and incomplete; and the census records indicate both shifting standards and bewilderment about how to separate professional clergywomen from lay preachers, preachers and pastors from healers and fortunetellers.

But the general trend is clear. Seventy-five years after Congregationalists had ordained Antoinette Brown, they had ordained a total of only one hundred women. Almost a hundred years after Unitarians had ordained Olympia Brown, their yearbook listed only six women, of whom five were retired.[14] In the twentieth century even Quaker women ministers declined in numbers and prominence. The increase of programmed meetings and some professionalization of the clergy may have contributed to this decline, but it seems also to be one more case of women's losing out as religions become institutionalized.

In 1949 the Federal Council of the Churches of Christ in America reported "little or no substantial increase in either the number of women ministers or, in most denominations at least, their use in the pastorate since 1940, in spite of the grave lack of ministers." In 1978, at least fifteen years into the second women's movement, the National Council of Churches in "the first comprehensive data on women clergy to be gathered in 27 years," revealed that "[ordained] women constitute only about four percent of all clergy." Of these, almost two-thirds were Pentecostal or in paramilitary religious organizations like the Salvation Army; only 17.4 percent were in mainline Protestant denominations. The survey's author, Constant H. Jacquet, reported that from 1930 to 1970 the percentage of women clergy had increased *less than one percent*.[15] In 1972 Georgia Harkness estimated that at the time fewer women were serving parishes than at the turn of the century, though the number of women with a theological education had increased.[16]

The journalist Inez Haynes Irwin in the 1930s enthused about women's breakthroughs in the other professions but wrote dismally of their status among the clergy. She told of a young woman college graduate who in 1926 wrote eighty-two theological schools asking whether they accepted women. Sixty replied. Of these, seventy percent would admit women—but forty-one said that either the seminary or its denomination opposed women's ordination. Almost all emphasized the prevailing opposition in churches. Twenty-five suggested other fields of Christian work.[17]

The case of Margaret Blair Johnstone illustrates the rarity of clergywomen in the first half of the twentieth century, the general ignorance of the history of clergywomen, and the inevitability that each clergywoman should consider herself a maverick and a pioneer. After a battle for a license to preach with a board whose male ministers felt sure she could use any talent she might have to the full as a pastor's assistant or a director of religious education, after being sent to keep a church from closing with the understanding that if she succeeded a man would replace her, she was ordained in 1937, almost eighty-five years after Antoinette Brown had been ordained in another Congregational church. At Johnstone's ordination Dr. Arthur Cushman McGiffert of the Chicago Theological Seminary told her congregation, "There is no proper certificate printed on which to record your minister's ordination. We are crossing out the words *him* and *he* and writing over them *her* and *she*. We cannot search for precedent for there *is* no precedent."[18]

Each clergywoman faced alone the attitude that as a woman she did not deserve a man's pay. Take Helen Adams of Urbana, Illinois. When during World War I her husband went off for chaplain's training, at his request his Universalist church appointed Mrs. Adams in his place at the same salary. But when he requested an extension of his leave, they lowered her salary.[19]

Many clergywomen had never heard another woman preach. Social controls on them were stringent, even discouraging their association with one another. "When I stated [in 1925] that I intended to go to the Assembly of Women Who Preach the Gospel," wrote Lucy T. Ayres, "some very dear friends of mine, women who were highly cultured and held important places in the religious world, implored me not to go. They accepted the fact that I was a minister, but insisted that, if I mingled with other women who preached, it would make me mannish, spoil me."[20]

All in all, in the years intervening between the ordinations of Antoinette Brown and Margaret Johnstone, the official climate for clergywomen in the mainline churches had warmed a little. But the numbers of clergywomen suggest that the thermostats still had to be turned up many degrees to raise the temperature above freezing. By 1960 most members of mainline churches had neither seen nor heard of a clergywoman in a pulpit, and their clergymen were still protesting the need to protect women from the rigors of the ministry.

Historian Susan Ware has pointed out that the "liberal feminism" of the 1920s and 1930s concentrated on individual achievement. "Even though individual female success stories were uplifting, they did little to inspire women collectively to mobilize for change. Furthermore, individualism as a basis for feminism failed to offer any challenge to the prevailing gender system. . . . individualism offered no way to achieve the goal of equality other than to act as if it had already been achieved."[21]

This emphasis on individual effort dominated the attitudes of clergywomen from their beginnings up until the 1960s and 1970s. Until then individual clergywomen spent their energies rolling the same Sisyphean rock up the same hill. They left the patriarchy of their religious institutions almost untouched. As Ware observes, "One of the most critical limits of individualism as a feminist strategy was the difficulty of institutionalizing success."[22] Julia Ward Howe in the late nineteenth century and the Rev. Madeline Southard in the 1920s did try to organize clergywomen, primarily to provide opportunities for fellowship among these isolated women. Both organizations remained small and exerted little influence, though Southard's International Association of Women Preachers claimed credit when the Methodist Episcopal Church granted women licenses to preach.[23]

What's more, in the absence after 1919 of an organized women's movement, with little public discussion of women's rights and problems, the high-achieving woman was tempted merely to concentrate on her own work and career with little thought about opportunities for other women. Consider Leila W. Anderson. She abandoned her intention to follow up her M.A. in church history with a doctorate for fear that people in the rural areas where she wanted to work might reject a woman so highly educated. Instead she took a bachelor of divinity, at the time the degree preparatory for the ministry. She did not aspire to ordination, but her first boss thought she could do a better job as an ordained minister. Pragmatically, she agreed, apparently without dealing with her own earlier qualms: as she writes, "I had no objection to the idea of ordination. . . . My mental block—and one which I then supposed everyone had—was a personal dislike for women in the pulpit, perhaps because the practice was foreign to the tradition in which I had been reared."[24] Ordained in the Congregational church, Anderson went on to create a challenging and adventurous career for herself as a "pilgrim circuit rider" in religious education who drove a station wagon equipped as both home and office to counsel churches on ways to improve their Christian training. Throughout her career she preached and worked as an interim minister, but in her autobiography she never mentions another clergywoman. The question of ordination for women and the problems of ordained women apparently did not exist for her.

The failure to thrive among women clergy as a group to some degree reflects what was going on in the country. The churches, like the workplace generally, were hiring more women, but as throughout the workplace most of them were on the lower levels—in the case of the churches, laywomen or paraprofessionals: stenographers, typists, bookkeepers, file clerks; camp counselors; pastoral assistants and secretaries; youth directors and music directors; missionaries and fieldworkers. The Great Depression of the 1930s set women professionals back in the church as it did in the economy as a whole; the general feeling that women ought not take "men's jobs," which crested then, left its mark for decades afterward. For instance, in the 1930s the percentage of college teachers who were women fell from 32.5 percent to 26.5 percent and continued to fall until the late 1950s. In the churches clergywomen fared no better. The General Superintendent of the Universalist Church reported in 1935 "a tremendous prejudice against women ministers. . . . at the present time, I find it is practically impossible to get any woman minister a hearing at any salary whatever." The Pacific School of Religion, Canton Theological School, the Tuckerman School in Boston, and other seminaries began to steer women away from the ministry into training courses for parish assistants.[25] In 1937 clergywoman Eleanor Gordon, responding to an appeal for clergymen, wrote in *Unitarian Horizons*:

> What disturbed me was that it was made so very plain that no woman need apply. . . .
> Since the [first] world war there has been a distinct trend in both the professional and industrial worlds . . . against woman's place in both. Positions of trust, authority, leadership, are being taken from her and given to men.[26]

But clergywomen had to meet the additional challenge of the religious debate over their right to be clergy, a debate still being waged in some quarters with as much ignorance, prejudice, and energy as if the past eight hundred years had not existed, whether in the tone of sweet reason of a C. S. Lewis or in the shouted imprecations of John Rice, author of *Bobbed Hair, Bossy Wives, and Women Preachers: Significant Questions for Honest Christian Women Settled by the Word of God.*[27]

In other ways, though, the impression that in the first part of the twentieth century nothing was happening with clergywomen is false. In the mainline denominations movement was tortoise-slow. Inch by inch they were liberalizing their positions. In 1897 Maud Nathan (1862–1946) lectured on "The Heart of Judaism," calling Jews to commit themselves to social justice—perhaps the first woman to give a speech in a synagogue in place of a sermon by a rabbi.[28] In 1903 the Jewish Theological Seminary admitted its first woman, Henrietta Szold, albeit on condition that she not use her knowledge to seek rabbinical ordination. In 1904 the Methodist Episcopal General Conference "gave" women laity rights. In 1907 the Free Methodist Church granted ordination to women as deacons but not as elders. In 1908 the Presbyterian Church opened the Philadelphia School for Christian Workers and the Presbyterian College of Christian Education, to train women for unordained careers in the church. Sometime after 1912, her district superintendent suggested to Baptist Isabel Crawford, a missionary to the Oklahoma Kiowa Indians, that she ask for ordination, a suggestion that she instantly repudiated: "It is bad enough to be called an old maid, but to be called a Reverend Old Maid would finish me in 24 hours!"[29] In 1919 M. Madeline Southard founded the Association of Women Preachers, later the Association of Women Ministers, which in 1922 began publication of the *Woman's Pulpit.* Its first issue reported the third annual conference of the association where the Rev. Lee Anna Starr, D.D., reminisced about the early opposition to clergywomen, telling "one amusing incident of the building of a special platform in a certain church where a woman was to speak lest she should defile the pulpit by speaking from it." In 1920 Harvard's theological seminary ceased to require from women students statements that they did not intend to enter the ministry. For some thirty-five years after her husband's death Tebilla Lichtenstein (1893–1973) led the Society of Jewish Science in New York City, an offshoot of Christian Science that he had formed.[30]

In 1935 the Episcopal church, as part of the international Anglican church, proclaimed that no theological reason for or against ordination of women exists but continued to close the priesthood to women. In 1939 Georgia Harkness (1891–1974) was appointed professor of applied theology at Garrett Biblical Institute, the first woman to teach in a major American theological seminary in a field other than Christian education; throughout her career she advocated for women's ordination, a voice crying in the wilderness. The same year Edith Elizabeth Lowry (1897–1970), the national director of interdenominational Protestant work among agricultural migrants, became the first woman to occupy the National Radio Pulpit. In 1943 its president, Sister Madeleva Wolff (1887–1964), saw to it that St. Mary's College in Notre Dame, Indiana, instituted the first Roman Catholic graduate program in theology open to women, qualifying women to teach religion at the college level. In 1948 Marilda Belva Spicer (b. 1894), a lay preacher in Nebraska, became the first clergywoman ordained by the African Methodist Episcopal church.[31]

In 1950 Mary Ely Lyman (1887–1975) became the first woman to hold a faculty chair at Union Theological Seminary, its dean of women, and an increasingly passionate advocate for the many women students then enrolling—most often in religious education programs. In 1955 Betty Robbins began her service as the first American woman cantor. In 1958 the Episcopal Theological Seminary in Cambridge, Massachusetts, became the first in its denomination to accept women. In the course of the 1950s the education of nuns undertaken in the Roman Catholic Sister Formation movement changed their outlook on society and transformed their perceptions of themselves and their duties.

And so it went, sometimes with a big step backward, as when in 1910 the Methodist Episcopal, South, General Conference denied women laity rights, joined together disparate woman's societies, and subsumed them into the general missionary organization, thereby depriving laywomen of much of their former power base. Or as when, in 1933, the Assembly of God, which had ordained women as evangelists and missionaries (though not as elders) since its 1914 founding, denied them the right to bury the dead, administer the ordinances of the church, and perform weddings; two years later the church restored those rights.[32]

Now and then a denomination took a giant step forward, as when in 1922 the Central Conference of American Rabbis resolved on complete equality between men and women, including ordination (though this declaration had only moral force). Or when in 1956 the United Methodists voted that henceforth women should have full clergy rights, after in 1919 having resumed awarding them local preachers' licenses, and in 1924 having begun to ordain them while still denying them rights to placement, pension, and a voice in the national church governance.[33]

All the while, of course, stalwart women were preaching and pastoring. They ran the gamut of personalities, and some of them must have been hard to bear. A layman years later wrote of an Iowa Methodist:

the Rev. E. W. Her husband, E., was a house painter and interior decorator. He was very well liked. The pastor was very conservative, somewhat to the right of Primitive Baptists. She didn't believe in eating in the church, or selling things at a bazaar, or telling jokes. She made me angrier than any pastor, or almost anyone else, ever did. At that time our Conference, and I believe South Dakota, were in a program with Rust College in Mississippi. Touring groups of singers came each summer. We (my family) had made plans to have them with us for the noon meal. The meal was ready at 12:00 o'clock, no guests. At 12:30, I went to town to the parsonage to inquire. She said, 'I just couldn't believe that anyone would take them into their homes. I sent them to the cafe.' . . . I went to the cafe and apologized, told them that we had hoped to have them. They, of course, recognized an old, and to them, familiar situation. They had been served and were eating, so I ordered a cup of coffee and sat with them while they ate, and paid the check.[34]

By mid-century Georgia Harkness had won a national reputation as a theologian.

Holding two master's degrees in religious education and a Ph.D. in philosophy from Boston University, she was ordained a local deacon in 1926 and a local elder in 1938. Her teaching ministry took her from Elmira College to Mount Holyoke to Garrett Biblical Institute in Illinois and eventually to the Pacific School of Religion in Berkeley, where she taught applied theology. Her own pioneering example in the academic ministry, her attack on the church as a "bastion of male dominance," and her 1948 debate with Karl Barth on women's religious leadership helped to change perceptions of clergywomen.

Yet these contemporary comments summarize the realities as perceived at mid-century by most of the population:

> When a young woman of our church leaves college halls today, she has an intelligent idea of every vocation, from aviation to brokerage, and may enter every one except the ministry. She may become a policeman or a judge, she may be a mayor or a senator, but she may not be ordained as a minister of the Gospel of Christ. . . . [Women] specialize in journalism and become editors; they specialize in education and become college presidents, but they may not, in the name of the Father, receive a child into the church nor administer the sacrament to the dying.[35]

❧ A New World for Mainline Clergywomen?

All these small increments added up to formal approval of ordination for women in more Christian denominations. In 1956 the United Methodists and the Presbyterian Church of the U.S.A. joined the short roster of major mainline churches recognizing and affirming the vocation of women clergy, notably the Congregationalists, the Unitarians and Universalists, and the Quakers.

The process among Presbyterians illustrates the way that during this period ordaining women gained approval almost negligently, as if it didn't really matter, blindsiding most of the membership while their attention was elsewhere.[36] Until 1900, with the usual exceptions for the sake of expedience, the ruling of the 1832 General Assembly was hardly challenged within the main body of Presbyterians: "To teach and exhort, or to lead in prayer, in public and promiscuous assemblies, is clearly forbidden to women in the Holy Oracles."[37] In the first two decades of the twentieth century the fight for woman suffrage brought on some discussion of ordaining women, but without effect.

In 1930, though, the General Assembly granted women ordination as elders. Nobody was saying much about ministerial ordination, but by World War II the camel had her nose in the tent, with a few Presbyterian women serving as stated supplies (qualified to fill in for regularly appointed clergy in their absence), lay preachers, and evangelists. In Olympia, Washington, for instance, Mary Jane Turner served a congregation of forty-four communicants. In Ohio, Lena L. Jennings served two congregations as interim pulpit supply; at her retirement her presbytery designated her "minister emeritus" and awarded her a small pension. In

Denver, Mrs. E. E. Smiley substituted for her husband at one of his churches while he presided at the other. The Rev. Hanna L. Almon, ordained by the Congregationalists, served various Presbyterian churches in Kansas and Missouri as their full-time pastor.

The manpower crunch of the war multiplied the exigencies that such women had been meeting. In 1943 the Cedar Rapids Presbytery broke ranks by ordaining Ellizabeth Brinton Clarke, who wanted to be an army chaplain for the Women's Auxiliary Army Corps, only to have the General Assembly quickly overrule. But by 1945 the General Assembly tried to meet the increasingly desperate shortage by the familiar method of creating a subspecies of clergy, in this case called missioners, who could teach and preach but not perform marriages, administer sacraments, or moderate sessions.

In 1956, without fanfare, the United Presbyterian Church U.S.A. (UPCUSA) began to ordain women.[38] Margaret Towner, the first of these, modestly predicted that "ordained women may prove the solution to the smaller churches' problem. A woman minister could help with pastoral duties and guide the education program too." Anyway, she thought, few women would seek pulpits.[39]

Twenty years later in the troubled 1970s, ordinand Walter Wynn Kenyon mounted a challenge to Presbyterian women's ordination by telling his presbytery that he believed that the Bible forbids it. The UPCUSA stood firm, refusing Kenyon ordination: "The UPCUSA," the Permanent Judicial Commission of the General Assembly ruled in 1974, "in obedience to Jesus Christ, under the authority of Scripture (and guided by its confession) has now developed its understanding of the equality of all people (both male and female) before God. It has expressed this understanding in the Book of Order with such clarity as to make the candidate's stated position a rejection of its government and discipline." In the opinion of the commission, Kenyon had "erroneously rejected the established law of the church that all humans are equal."[40] Inevitably Kenyon's argument found supporters, some of whom left UPCUSA to form new congregations in the Presbyterian Church in America, a group which in 1975 had split away from the Presbyterian Church in the U.S. over the issue of women's ordination.

These years also heard the first whispers of ordination for Jewish women. Rosemary R. Ruether and Rosemary S. Keller theorize that as long as American Jews were oppressed Jewish women conceded institutional leadership to Jewish men, but once the Jewish community was well established and accepted in this society, Jewish women began to challenge the patriarchalism of their institutions.[41]

At any rate the path of Jewish women to ordination has diverged from that of Protestants and Roman Catholics as the Jewish experience has diverged from the Christian. As Ann Braude has pointed out, Jewish women's understanding of women's economic function, their possession of their own rituals, and their leadership roles among women in the synagogue all help to account for the differences.[42] Jewish immigrants to the United States brought with them sharply differentiated gender roles, with males responsible for godliness and women for supporting males in all ways, often including earning the family living—an attitude encapsulated by the prayer of a Jewish woman who early each morning visited the synagogue: "Good Morning, God. I haven't much time to spend here; I must go home and feed Abraham, my son, so he will have strength to study your holy Torah. Good day, God."[43] The Jewish woman had her own prayer book and her own religious duties, less onerous than her husband's, to allow her the time necessary for her other responsibilities. She had her own rituals: attendance at the ritual bath (mikvah) of purification after menstruation, baking challah, observing dietary laws, lighting the Sabbath candles, and celebrating the New Moon ceremony (Rosh Chodesh). In the women's section of the synagogue, she could lead other women through the service. A woman with such a sharply defined place in the religion, subordinate though it was, was less apt than a Christian, some think, to feel that the religion shut her out, and correspondingly less apt to call for a change.

Many of the German Jews who immigrated to the United States between 1820 and 1880 brought with them the ideas of Reform Judaism, which in 1846 had made women theoretically the religious equals of laymen. In the United States Rabbi Isaac Meyer Wise implemented this theology by counting women in the minyan, allowing them to sit in the main body of the synagogue, giving them equal access to religious education, and advocating the ordination of women. Thereupon some women began situating their religious lives not mainly in the home but in the synagogue. Reform rabbis were now called upon to preach to women as well as men and to advise women's organizations. So why not a woman rabbi?

Once the Jewish population in this country had reached a critical mass, around the turn of the century, Judaism once again displayed its traditional ability to adapt to a new culture, and in many quarters questions were raised about the role of women in secular life and in religion. Henrietta Szold (1860–1945), the founder of Hadassah and the first woman ever to receive the honorary degree of Doctor of Hebrew Letters, recognized the traditionally assigned gender roles as a problem not just for women but also for Judaism: "The incorporation of women into the synagogue service and into the Jewish communal structure have been essential elements of the most successful movements in American Judaism."[44]

Nineteenth-century Jewish women participated actively in American reform movements. Ernestine Rose (1810–1892) had often brought the voice of common sense to the woman suffrage movement, as when she opposed Antoinette Brown's politically inept effort to base women's right to vote on biblical grounds. Clubwoman Hannah Solomon (1858–1942) organized for the 1893 World's Columbian Exposition the Jewish Women's Conference, which at her urging took permanent form as the National Council of Jewish Women. The council emphasized both duty to religion and duty to community. In the twentieth century the National Federation of Temple Sisterhoods (later known as the Women of Reform Judaism) periodically issued calls for women's ordination.

In synagogues as in churches the system that barred women from religious leadership functioned imperfectly, as need overcame prejudice and tradition. Very occasionally, here and there unordained women did the work of rabbis, leading services in small towns that could not support regular rabbis. In the far West Ray Frank (Litman) (1864–1948) preached in communities without ordained rabbis; often these towns then established their first congregations. After Frank had taken courses at Hebrew Union, a Chicago group wanted to install her as religious leader of a new community, but then as always she refused both the title of rabbi and permanent affiliation in favor of keeping her freedom to determine her own service to her faith.[45] At the World Columbian Exposition she asserted that Jewish women by their labors and accomplishments had earned the right to the pulpit, "even as nature created their sensitive beings to act as its finest interpreter."[46]

Other Jewish women functioned as synagogue presidents. Now and then a rebbetzin filled in for her husband during his illness or after his death. Thus, though unordained, Paula Ackerman succeeded her husband as rabbi of Beth Israel in Meridian, Mississippi, in 1950, and Beatrice Sanders succeeded her husband as president of Temple Aaron in Trinidad, Colorado, in 1952, and for more than two decades conducted its weekly and High Holiday services.[47]

The first Jewish seminaries to admit women, in the 1890s, were in the Reform tradition, Cincinnati's Hebrew Union College and New York's Jewish Institute of Religion.[48] In 1903 Henrietta Szold "integrated" the (Conservative) Jewish Theological Seminary, which, however, protected itself by demanding her promise that she would not try to enter the rabbinate. After 1909, the seminary directed women who wished advanced Jewish educations to its Teachers Institute. In 1941, Zionah Maximon wangled special permission to take classes in the rabbinical program, but without credit. Understandably, most women turned to seminaries in the more liberal Reform tradition, which had from time to time issued statements supporting women's equality within Judaism and had moved to improve women's status within Jewish law. From the 1890s on, a trickle of women studying for the rabbinate seeped into the Reform schools.

But even within Reform Judaism they hardly found unobstructed channels. Though Hebrew Union College had occasionally admitted women since its founding in 1875, in 1921 Martha Neumark, a student and daughter of a professor, brought matters to a head by agitating for women's ordination. In the ensuing debate Neumark's father argued:

> The entire question reduces itself to this: women are already doing most of the work that the ordained woman rabbi is expected to do. But they do it without preparation and without authority. I consider it a duty of the authorities to put an end to the prevailing anarchy by giving women a chance to acquire adequate education and an authoritative standing in all branches of religious work.

The faculty concluded that women could not "justly be denied the privilege of ordination." But the lay majority of the Board of Governors overruled both the faculty and its own two rabbi members.[49]

About the same time the new Jewish Institute of Religion (JIR) in New York confronted the same issues. Irma Lindheim had been enrolled as a special student with the enthusiastic support of the Institute's liberal founder, Rabbi Stephen Wise. She had on her side maturity, influence, wealth, and a record of public service. Deciding that she knew far too little about Judaism, this matron packed her four children off to her Long Island mansion, rented a studio apartment near the Institute, and settled down to study ten hours a day. So far, so good. But Lindheim's eventual request for standing as a rabbinical student raised the predictable flurry of questions: What about dormitory facilities? Would the presence of women keep the men from serious study? Wouldn't it be better to admit women only as auditors in extension courses? After all, the faculty had already dismissed as unsuitable for the rabbinate another student, Dora Askowith, who not only held a doctorate from Columbia but also had taught at Hunter. But in May 1923, the faculty unanimously recommended the acceptance of women on the same basis as men, incorporating in its charter the statement that it had been founded "to train, in liberal spirit, men and women for the Jewish ministry, research and community service." Lindheim never completed her program of study, but she and the JIR faculty among them had justified her belief that "if I prepared myself in accordance with the requirement of being a rabbi, the door would be opened for other women, should they wish and have the gift to minister to congregations."[50] Withal, Jewish woman's ordination had to wait another half century. When in 1929 Helen Levinthal completed the curriculum, daughter and granddaughter of prominent rabbis though she was, the faculty awarded her a master's in Hebrew Letters but not ordination.[51]

In an odd way the struggles for women's ordination during the first sixty years of the twentieth century were almost covert, subterranean. The denominational general assemblies or national conferences that voted on the issue saw only the tip of the iceberg. Among the laity in local congregations, few thought much about the matter. As Sara Maitland insightfully comments:

> the evolution towards ordination was gradual and in many of the denominations was finally approved without a massive consciousness-raising campaign which involved lay women and created a tight network of support and sisterly concern. Women tended to be admitted one by one more on their personal merits than as a point of theological principle.[52]

Contrast this quiet individual effort with the noisy group battle for woman suffrage. Carrie Chapman Catt and her famed winning plan required leaders of the National American Woman's Suffrage Association to dedicate almost all their waking hours to the cause. They publicized the issue in parades, barnstorming speeches across the countryside, and petitions bearing the signatures of thousands of women. Alice Paul's Woman's Party picketed the White House, publicly burned President Wilson's speeches, got arrested, and went on a hunger strike. In effect women shouted for suffrage but only murmured for ordination.

❧ *The Real World of Mainline Clergywomen* _____

As a result, denominational approval of women's ordination did not earn clergy-women a clear victory. Almost always ordained women were doomed to dead-end, subordinate positions. Churches might capitulate on women's ordination, but seldom did they take thought for the new clergywomen. As Sara Maitland comments, "All institutions with histories as long as Christianity's are accomplished in the art of co-opting dissident factions."[53] Many a newly ordained woman became merely a second-class minister, not in her performance but in the way her church treated her. Most clergywomen advisedly walked softly, but carried no stick at all, let alone a big one.

Frederica Mitchell (b. 1895) exemplifies one of the more fortunate of these women. The daughter of a Hartford Seminary professor, she topped off her education with courses there. Rejected as a missionary to China because of bad eyesight, she settled for work in religious education at her home church, living at home and caring for her aging parents. In 1930–1931 she took graduate courses at Union Theological and Columbia Teachers' College, then accepted a job away from home—only to be called back by parental illness. After both her parents died, a retired minister suggested that she "help out" a church until a minister could be found. Her top-notch work there won her a call to their pulpit, and in 1935 she was ordained. Henry Sloan Coffin preached her ordination sermon, commenting, "If you have to have a woman minister, take Frederica Mitchell."[54]

Mitchell was assisted by the kind of help most professional women only dream of. For a time her father's former secretary not only ran her house but also took over the leadership of the church school, typed, and did the Sunday bulletins. Later on a divorced friend with a master's in child psychology came to live with her and assumed the responsibility for Christian education and the nursery school. Mitchell herself rendered a lifetime of dedicated, principled, and highly competent service.

The tone of her biographer, Rosemary Coffin, speaks volumes about attitudes toward clergywomen during the period. Though Mitchell was usually the only woman at ministerial conferences, says Coffin, she was never made to feel uncomfortable, though another (presumably weaker) clergywoman fainted at one of these meetings. Mitchell, she says, sensitive to the low esteem in which clergywomen were held, was doubly pleased twice to be invited to other churches, though in both cases she declined. She served for a year as president of the board of New York State Congregational Churches and two terms on the National Council of Congregational Christian Churches Committee on Ministry, but "she was scared to speak up in the presence of very alert, knowledgeable and more experienced men." Mitchell never used women as trustees, deacons, ushers, or lay readers—perhaps, Coffin speculates, because she wanted men to feel needed, not as if they were having "their roles usurped by women."[55] She was courageous about going into homes where men resented her influence with their families, usually persuading the men to let her continue that ministry.

Compared to other clergywomen of the period, Mitchell was well-off. For some women ordination changed their situation hardly at all. When in 1956 the Presbyterians approved women's ordination, the newly anointed discovered few new opportunities. Wilmena Rowland found a few associate pastorates, but mostly jobs for directors of religious education; she wound up in the national church offices. Priscilla Chaplin finally did receive a pastoral call, but only after congregational rejections so blunt about not wanting a woman minister that she commented, "Some people seem to think I'm a cross between a public monument and a three-headed freak."[56]

Even among the Methodists, where the hierarchy assigns most ministers, getting ordained was one thing and getting a pastorate was another. It was pretty hard to gain congregational acceptance when the congregation was only dimly aware of the existence of clergywomen. In 1980 a study of United Methodist clergywomen reported:

> A small number [of women], now older, were ordained before 1968, some as "local deacons" or "local elders"; many of these served the church for a number of years in some full-time capacity; most in this group with little or no college training. . . . Those ordained before 1968 who have college degrees, many with graduate study including master's and doctoral degrees, have been serving the church as missionaries, deaconesses, directors of religious education, church or hospital visitors, or on college and seminary faculties.[57]

Careers like Margaret Henrichsen's were the exception, not the rule. After her husband's death, she inquired from a Methodist district superintendent in Maine whether she could take theological training by correspondence. He at once offered her a job: she wound up with not one, not two, but seven small country churches near Portland, Maine. Some of them she had to resurrect, but in each she held services every Sunday. She lived under rugged conditions; at first her parsonage had no water and was heated downstairs with wood stoves, with warmth theoretically rising upstairs through holes in the floors. On her rounds by day and by night she dodged forest fires and plowed through snowstorms. She was all things to all people. She concludes a story about carrying supplies to a dying man and his wife: "With these in one hand and the silver baptismal font and my service book in the other, I made my way back to the little house. First aid and food and religion all mixed up together! It is a good symbol of the life of a country pastor."[58] Meanwhile she studied at home, annually spending a week at Union Theological Seminary. Eventually she became a district superintendent.

Even more unusual was the career of Congregationalist Hilda Ives, who through force of personality earned fame, respect (testified to by four honorary degrees), and affection throughout New England. About 1918 as a young, rather well-off widow with small children and without training, she accepted an appointment to a small country church. "I was totally unprepared for the work," she later wrote. "An extra handicap existed because of the very definite prejudice in churches against women ministers—a prejudice that all women have to meet in their various professions."[59] The pastoral committee unanimously voted to refuse her, but they had no choice, since they contributed only $250 toward her salary, and the hierarchy, which paid the rest, insisted. On her arrival a deacon greeted her: "Ain't no use your coming here. This place is dead, just as dead as it can be. Every one they send us is wuss than the one before and the last one is always the wust of all." The church, she remarked, was indeed on a downhill path, having been served variously by old men needing money to supplement their pensions, sick men, young students, and now a woman—a woman, moreover, who had never preached, never prayed with and for a congregation, and never read scripture from a pulpit.

But reviving the church was the first step on a career path that she followed with verve and the exercise of whatever feminine wiles or display of independence she thought appropriate to the situation. "Why," she asked, "incur the dislike of any group of men by asking their advice, when you know you have decided to do what they will advise you against doing?" Or, she remarked on one of those occasions on which clergymen were explaining that their qualms about clergywomen arose from concern lest the women be placed in danger or hardship, "Let men be fearful, if they must, for ladies. But do not let women acquiesce in their unwarranted emotion and sense of protection." Or even more forthrightly: "Women ministers today are judged by many to be the lowest form of minister or to be no ecclesiastical form at all. Sad is the sin of male superiority in the church, declaring that the Holy Spirit of God is the prerogative of men for ordination into the ministry of Christ."[60]

No queen bee despite her success, Ives continued to speak out for clergywomen. She wrote in 1958:

> I am used now to being placed in unconsecrated parts of some churches. Sometimes I am placed behind a table in front of the altar rail, and I am not allowed to enter within the chancel. Sometimes I am asked to wear a hat when preaching, because I am a woman and must not enter the chancel of the church without a hat to cover my head. It isn't the hat I mind, though I cannot agree with the ideas that demand it. It is the tassel of the hat [her academic cap] that disturbs my religious thinking. I instinctively blow it aside out of my eye. That upsets my preaching technique.[61]

In the African Methodist Episcopal church Marilda Belva Spicer (b. 1894) earned her spurs differently.[62] After teaching in Kansas, Missouri, and Nebraska for some twenty years, Spicer felt called to the ministry. Licensed as an evangelist, she labored in Nebraska churches as a lay preacher for thirteen years. Ordained in 1948, she became the first woman so recognized in her denomination. She went on to earn a master's degree and a second bachelor's, this one in Christian education. In 1956, nearing retirement age, she requalified herself as a teacher and spent the next fourteen years teaching Native American children in South Dakota.

Native American Hazel Botone (b. 1898) followed a well-worn path to ordination, serving as a minister's wife for thirty-eight years and on her husband's death becoming successively a lay speaker, a local preacher, and an ordained minister in his Methodist church. "The most difficult thing I had to do was physical. It was the wood stoves. There was always no wood and especially when it rains. I had to take everything from here, cardboard boxes, gunny sacks, corn cobs wherever I could find 'em." Despite such difficulties, she not only kept her late husband's church going but brought back to life a nearby abandoned church. "Everybody respected me, you know," she reminisced. "It wasn't any different than my husband. And spiritually, to my way of thinking, it was like one lady said. 'I just love to hear you read the Bible. You tell us some Kiowa and then you sing a song that matches. It just makes me float in the air.'"[63]

As the careers of Henrichsen, Ives, Spicer, and Botone illustrate, highly competent women who through extraordinary ability and effort got themselves trained and ordained could hardly expect appointment to pastorates of large and prosperous churches. Most mainline clergywomen of the first half of the twentieth century could not manage to get *any* independent pastorate, but served instead in subordinate roles.

Or their churches shut them out of employment completely. Universalist Lottie Irene Earl (1865–1938), once an associate minister at a mission, after her 1925 ordination never found another pastorate that would pay enough for her to live on. Persistently searching year after year, she meanwhile supported herself by library work, as director of a community house and executive secretary for the Delaware Society for Social Hygiene. Even so, Earl may have thought herself a degree or two better off than Clara Helvie (1876–1969), who when she applied for ordination about 1917 "found that no woman had been ordained to the Unitarian ministry since Rowena Morse Mann in 1906."[64]

A good many would-be clergywomen, perhaps most of those who wanted full-time work, labored outside the churches. Some created their own ministries. Other women worked in parachurch organizations such as the Campus Crusade for Christ, the InterVarsity Christian Fellowship, Campus Life, the Navigators, the Child Evangelism Fellowship, and the Bible Club Movement, usually functioning as their own fund-raisers.

Once in a great while a woman beat out a new path to mainline ordination. Victoria Booth Demarest (b. 1890), granddaughter of Catherine and William Booth, sprang straight from the heart of the Salvation Army. Her mother, an Army officer, taught the children that they must not be "cumberers of the earth." Unless they planned to devote their lives to the service of others, she said, she would not spend a penny for their educations. Accordingly Victoria was saved at six and called to God's service at fourteen. She learned theology from her father and evangelism from her mother, whom she assisted in her work. Her parents' separation from the Army over disagreements about governance and doctrine when Victoria was twelve made little difference in their lives; her mother continued to evangelize. In 1913 Victoria came to the United States to organize Victory Clubs for young women willing to do anything for Christ: "A Victory girl never says I can't." Gifted in music, languages, and drama, clad for preaching in an Alice-blue gown with a little white collar and a silver cross, she must have made an appealing figure. Even Episcopalians, she wrote, invited her to conduct preaching missions in their churches.

In 1918 she married the widower Agnew Demarest, an organist and choirmaster with two little boys; the couple went on to have six more children. She could hardly have found a more supportive man, for herself and for clergywomen generally. As she wrote:

> Just as it was natural for me to be the leader in our evangelistic work, so it was natural for Agnew to be the follower. This did not take away from my femininity or from his masculinity. My dear husband knew well how mentally, physically, emotionally, and spiritually exhausting my work could be. He appreciated its value because he constantly witnessed its joyful results. Many times he told me that he felt it to be his calling to share in this ministry by relieving me as much as possible from avoidable stress and strain. He felt no hesitation about changing a baby, cooking a meal (he loved to cook), or attending to any chores I could not take care of. As for me, I was akin to my grandmother who wrote her parents, "Indeed, I feel quite at home on the platform, far more than I do in the kitchen!" My husband and I shared responsibilities, whether for the home, music, ministry, or the rearing of our children. That, to my mind, is a true marriage.[65]

Victoria Demarest's own insouciance probably helped. Babies never interfered with her ministry; while she preached she just propped them on pillows on the floor of the vestry, where, she reported, they gurgled happily. It was difficult, she admitted, to leave the children when they were small, but she exchanged daily letters with the volunteer helpers at home—a familiar comment in the annals of traveling clergywomen, whose disciples often enabled their traveling by looking after their families. She suffered the usual financial worries of the itinerant minister, relying mostly on "thank offerings" from grateful converts. It was, she wrote, "an uphill fight all the way." During the Great Depression the Demarests lost their family home and the children were scattered. She had to accept whatever invitations came her way, even if it meant preaching in an abandoned store. She underwent the usual hardships: "Through the years I have been train-wrecked, ship-wrecked, preached in a temperature of 110 in the shade and below zero in the winter, preached with blood-poisoning in my arm, preached as long as able before babies were born and as soon afterwards as I could. Numerous times I have risen from a sickbed to preach."[66] Like other clergywomen, she combatted prejudice, criticism, and opposition.

But among her champions stood an amazing number of male clergy in the leadership of their denominations. In 1931 the Federal Council of Churches engaged her to conduct union evangelistic campaigns in every borough of New York City, the only evangelist ever so honored. If Demarest's own reports are to be believed, she was offered ordination by three major mainline denominations: the Baptists, the Methodists, and the Congregationalists. The first two she turned down, because she did not want to be honored as an "exception" among women. But in 1949 she accepted ordination from the Congregationalists, though it was agreed that she would not take a pastorate, because she wished to continue her ecumenical evangelistic ministry. At her ordination service her husband played the organ and a prominent Presbyterian clergyman offered the ordination prayer.

But few women enjoy the advantages of Demarest's birthright as a Booth. Most aspirants to the ministry had to settle for less. Some did the work of pastors without recognition. In 1919, for instance, the Presbytery of Cleveland licensed Winifred Wirts Dague as an evangelist, but the next year the General Assembly denied her request for ordination. Nonetheless, she continued to serve a congregation in Ohio and to conduct revivals.[67] Rev. Azuba Jones of the Evangelical church was irregularly licensed by her own conference by virtue of "her long years of excellent service," even though that church did not license women.[68] And in 1923 Ruth Grimes Ewing, then a Baptist missionary, was reporting that at one time her father, her mother, her brother, and she each had a parish in the Methodist Episcopal Church.[69] Would-be African-American Methodist and Baptist clergywomen, during the years when those churches either refused to ordain women or ordained them with the greatest reluctance, often simply moved over to another black church: many of their Sanctified (holiness and pentecostal) churches did ordain women.

☙ Directors of Religious Education

Just as in the nineteenth century women who might otherwise have aspired to be clergywomen were diverted into the roles of missionaries or deaconesses, so in the twentieth century they were channeled into subordinate positions as directors or ministers of religious education. Margaret Blair Johnstone wrote of the pressures exerted on her as a Congregational seminarian to become a pastor's assistant or a director of religious education (DRE): "We are your friends," the male authorities advised her. "It is because we know so well the frustration awaiting any women in the ministry that we are urging you to enter related work. We are trying to protect you not only from heartbreak, but also ridicule. . . . And consider our obligation to protect the dignity of the profession."[70]

About 1900, a century after Joanna Graham Bethune had introduced Sunday Schools into the United States, a number of Protestant churches began to professionalize religious education by setting up positions for specialists in that area in local churches, appointing field representatives from national hierarchies to oversee local efforts and opening schools to train these workers.

The example of the Presbyterian church demonstrates the rapid growth of this innovation; they established the Presbyterian Training School in Baltimore in 1903, the Philadelphia School for Christian Workers in 1907, and the Presbyterian College of Christian Education in Chicago in 1908.[71] The tradition of women's carrying most of the responsibility for Sunday Schools manifested itself in the expectations for this new religious profession. All of these Presbyterian institutions built dormitories only for women.

In the spirit of the Progressive Era, professionalization and status demanded higher and higher standards and more and more education, whether for nurses or for social workers or for directors of religious education. By the 1920s some of the new religious training schools were offering the bachelor's degree in the field, and in that decade they broke into graduate study. That move brought the long-established seminaries scurrying into competition. Union Theological Seminary set up a joint program with Teachers' College at Columbia University. The incursion into DRE programs was a coup for the seminaries, for it brought them many women students without committing them to produce full-fledged clergywomen.

Though many women found great satisfaction in the job, the lot of the DRE was often not a happy one—particularly as a lifetime career. She earned little money, and she held a dead-end job. She had to take orders from the church pastor, who might or might not know anything about religious education, and might or might not allot her other pastoral duties. She had a modicum of status, but almost no power, and the laywomen who had been running the Sunday School often suspected her of encroaching on their territory. Henrietta Wilkinson commented on her service as DRE in two churches during the 1940s: "The minister of Christian education has no part of the organizational life of the church at any level."[72]

Sophia Fahs (1876–1966), a distinguished liberal authority on religious education, in 1923 registered at Union Theological Seminary for the bachelor of divinity program, then the program leading to ordination, explaining, "If I work as a director, I need to have the advantage of an equal standing with the pastor in the church. If I should take a little community church someday myself, then I could organize the church on a democratic basis and we could together work out an entirely new program of church activities in which preaching would be merely an occasional feature of the program." Although she was eventually ordained at the age of eighty-two, her vision of clerical equality was never fulfilled either for her personally or for other able and well-educated DREs.[73] Nonetheless the numbers of women DREs continued to grow during the 1940s and 1950s, dropping only in the 1960s when ordination became a possibility for more women *and* when churches began to replace women DREs with ordained men who could perform other pastoral functions or with nonprofessional women at lower pay, often on a part-time basis.

But some women found the position of DRE just their niche, like the famed conservative Presbyterian Henrietta Mears (1890–1963). An incident at the Taj Mahal affords insight into her temperament: when to demonstrate the monument's acoustics the Muslim guide shouted, "There is no God but Allah," Mears felt called upon to counter, "Jesus Christ, Son of God, is Lord over all."[74] She is credited with saving Sunday School lessons from "destructive and debilitating liberalism." Raised by a mother who bore the penalty for her children's wrongdoing by foregoing butter, Mears began teaching Sunday School at twelve and in college committed herself to a life of Christian service. After a few years of teaching high school, she accepted the position of DRE at the First Presbyterian Church of Hollywood, where she enjoyed enormous success. In 1929 in cooperation with educators in that congregation, she began writing materials for their church school and, at the urging of people from other churches, to publish them in a kitchen-table operation that grew into the Gospel Light Press. These carefully graded materials, designed to inculcate thorough biblical knowledge, exercised such great appeal that the press doubled or tripled its sales every year throughout the Great Depression.

Mears also worked creatively in her own church, multiplying Sunday School attendance year after year, starting teacher-training workshops, sending students to foreign countries to help missionaries, founding a camp conference center, and encouraging young people to commit to those religious professions she thought appropriate for them. She herself did not like to be perceived as a minister, believing that role reserved for men, but she adopted likely male ministerial candidates as her sons, furnishing them with clothes and mentoring them.

African-American Olivia Pearl Stokes built a career in both religious and secular education. A rarity as an ordained Baptist clergywoman, she further distinguished herself in 1952 as the first black woman to earn a doctorate in religious education. She worked for the Massachusetts Council of Churches as director of religious education, and for the National Council of Churches as associate director for urban education before moving into teacher education at the City University of New York, the executive directorship of the Greater Harlem Comprehensive Guidance Center, and teaching at New York University—not to mention writing children's books and serving as an interim pastor.[75]

ை Clergywomen in the Hierarchies

As Dr. Stokes's career illustrates, in the years from 1900 to 1960, the national offices of the mainline denominations also began to hire women, sometimes in positions of influence. The leadership of the more liberal of these churches tended to display more advanced attitudes toward women than the people they led. In 1949 the Information Service of the Department of Research and Education of the Federal Council of the Churches of Christ in America noted that "in civic life women are usually most active at the lowest rungs of the ladder but there are very few women in responsible policy-making positions. In the church, however, it seems that women are likely to be given first token representation on national boards and committees. Gradually, this is extended to local church committees and then to boards."

Many of the women the church hierarchies found for these positions blazed with ability. These were the women who year after year eroded the hierarchal resistance to women's ordination in several mainline denominations. Every Methodist clergywoman owes several debts to Mabel Madeline Southard.[76] This native Kansan taught to save enough money for seminary, then in 1915 integrated the all-male seminary class at Garrett. No respecter of the existing order, while she was a seminarian she established a congregation in Kansas, though rules forbade such an activity to women. Her denomination refused her a license, so she settled for lecturing on the Methodist circuit and at Chautauqua, counseling women infected with syphilis by their husbands, ministering to prostitutes, and acting as a decoy to expose white slavers.

But she had not abandoned the cause of women's ordination. In 1919 she earned a master's degree at Garrett, writing her thesis on "The Attitude of Jesus toward Women." That year she also founded the International Association of Women Preachers for clergywomen, whether ordained or qualified to be so but denied ordination by their churches. Seeking a famous woman to lead it, Southard turned to Anna Howard Shaw, but Shaw died before the organizational meeting could be held, so Southard reluctantly accepted the presidency. In 1920 Southard began lobbying for the licensing of women Methodist preachers, a cause in which she won a limited victory in 1924.

After several years as a lay evangelist, in 1928 Southard accepted a job with the Methodist church in the Philippines, where she got after Douglas MacArthur to do something about the United States Army's use of prostitutes. Then on to India, to work with E. Stanley Jones. In 1932 she returned Stateside to work with the International Association of Women Ministers, campaigning vigorously for full clergy rights for Methodist women.

In the early days of hierarchal effort to employ women, they were indeed tokens, but persistence right up to the end of the twentieth century has given a significant number of women considerable power in these church hierarchies, though opposition to them continues to surface from right-wing constituencies. Working with the movers and shakers has given these women a wider overview of their denominations and insight into decision making, so that at times they have been able to influence policy and the ways in which denominational funds are spent. They have come to know each other across denominational lines and to work together for common aims. Networking, supporting one another, and mentoring younger women, they have protected and enlarged lay and clerical rights for women.

Notes _____

1. Dorothy Schneider and Carl J. Schneider, *American Women in the Progressive Era, 1900–1920* (New York: Facts on File, 1993), p. 74.

2. Dorothy Schneider and Carl J. Schneider, *Into the Breach: American Women Overseas in World War I* (New York: Viking, 1991), Appendix A.

3. This effort ran the gamut of denominations. From 1910 to 1930 in the fundamentalist churches "Christianity and church ministry were recast as truly masculine pursuits; the ideal Christian as a warrior. . . . The Social Gospel theologians wanted the church and its male

ministers active again 'at the very center of society,' and they wanted women at home" (Betty A. DeBerg, *Ungodly Women: Gender and the First Wave of American Fundamentalism* [Minneapolis: Fortress, 1990], pp. 143, 151–52).

4. Jualyne E. Dodson and Cheryl Townsend Gilkes point to Booker T. Washington's influence on this score ("Something Within: Social Change and Collective Endurance in the Sacred World of Black Christian Women," in *Women and Religion in America*, ed. Rosemary R. Ruether and Rosemary S. Keller [San Francisco: Harper & Row, 1986], 3:88–89).

5. "The push for women elders in 1929 was engineered chiefly by denominational officials who hoped that the promise of broader equality would compensate women for the loss of organizational independence" (*Fundamentalism and Gender: 1875 to the Present* [New Haven, Conn.: Yale Univ. Press, 1994], p. 57).

6. Sara Maitland, *A Map of the New Country: Women and Christianity* (London: Routledge & Kegan Paul, 1983), p. 86.

7. Lois A. Boyd and R. Douglas Brackenridge, "Questions of Power and Status: American Presbyterian Women, 1870–1980," in *Triumph Over Silence: Women in Protestant History*, ed. Richard L. Greaves (Westport, Conn.: Greenwood, 1985), p. 220.

8. Miriam Therese Winter, Adair Lummis, and Allison Stokes, *Defecting in Place: Women Claiming Responsibility for Their Own Spiritual Lives* (New York: Crossroad, 1994), p. 149.

9. *Woman's Pulpit* (1922).

10. Margaret Blair Johnstone, *When God Says "No": Faith's Starting Point* (New York: Simon & Schuster, 1954), pp. 215–16.

11. Prathis Hall Wynn, "Called But Not Chosen," *The Women's Review of Books* (Sept. 1994).

12. Patricia R. Hill, *The World Their Household: The American Woman's Foreign Mission Movement and Cultural Transformation, 1870–1920* (Ann Arbor: Univ. of Michigan Press, 1985), p. 175.

13. *Woman's Pulpit* (July–Aug. 1942).

14. Susan Hill Lindley, *"You Have Stept Out of Your Place": A History of Women and Religion in America* (Louisville, Ky.: Westminster John Knox, 1996), p. 309.

15. In her thoughtful and provocative book Sara Maitland writes that the twentieth century saw "a rapid change and evolution among women's professional ministries in all the denominations." She adduces a number of facts in support of this generalization, many of which we have used to reach an opposite conclusion. She adds: "By 1927 there were 100 women ministers in the American Congregationalist church, as opposed to less than 40 in 1900" (*Map*, pp. 85, 87). Although it is true that this represents an increase of 150 percent in a little less than thirty years, that's only about two more ordinations of women in that denomination every year. We consider that a snail's pace, but we respect Maitland's more cheerful view.

16. Georgia Harkness, *Women in Church and Society: A Historical and Theological Inquiry* (Nashville, Tenn.: Abingdon, 1972), p. 131.

17. Inez Haynes Irwin, *Angels and Amazons: A Hundred Years of American Women* (1933; reprint, New York: Arno Press, 1974).

18. Johnstone, *When God Says "No,"* p. 75.

19. "The First Hundred Years of Religious Liberalism in Urbana-Champaign, Illinois," Universalist-Unitarian Church of Urbana-Champaign, 1959. The church ordained Helen Adams in 1918.

20. Lucy T. Ayres, in *Woman's Pulpit* (Jan.–Feb. 1948).

21. Susan Ware, *Still Missing: Amelia Earhart and the Search for Modern Feminism* (New York: W. W. Norton, 1993), p. 118.

22. Ibid., p. 139.

In a letter of June 16, 1923, to American clergywoman Euphemia Drysdale, English minister Constance M. Coltman says, "There may be more women ministers numerically in America but for most of them it seems to be just an individual vocation, while for us it is not only that, but also a movement of immense spiritual significance, the crown and consummation of feminism, and an avenue towards the fuller interpretation of the mind of Christ" (papers of Euphemia Drysdale, Schlesinger Library, Cambridge, Mass.).

23. *Woman's Pulpit* (April 1923).

24. Leila W. Anderson, *Pilgrim Circuit Rider,* in collaboration with Harriet Harmon Dexter (New York: Harper, 1960), p. 42.

25. Catherine F. Hitchings, *Universalist and Unitarian Women Ministers,* 2d ed. (Boston: Unitarian Universalist Historical Society, 1985), p. 6.

26. Quoted by Hitchings, *Universalist and Unitarian Women Ministers,* p. 74.

27. (Wheaton, Ill.: Sword of the Lord, 1941).

28. Elizabeth Frost-Knappman, *The ABC-Clio Companion to Women's Progress in America* (Santa Barbara, Calif.: ABC-Clio, 1994), p. 205.

29. Eleanor Hull, *Women Who Carried the Good News: The History of the Woman's American Baptist Home Missionary Society* (Valley Forge, Penn.: Judson, 1975), p. 24.

30. Ellen M. Umansky, "Spiritual Expressions: Jewish Women's Religious Lives in the Twentieth-Century United States," in *Jewish Women in Historical Perspective,* ed. Judith R. Baskin (Detroit: Wayne State Univ. Press, 1991), p. 282.

31. Marilyn Johnson, "Marilda Belva Spicer, Educator and Minister," in *Perspectives: Women in Nebraska History* (Lincoln: Nebraska Dept of Ed. and the Nebraska State Council for the Social Studies, June, 1984).

32. Margaret M. Poloma, *Assemblies of God at the Crossroads: Charisma and Institutional Dilemmas* (Knoxville: Univ. of Tennessee Press, 1989), p. 107.

33. Deborah (Luethje) Mariya has pieced together the story of Mrs. Remington of the Methodist Protestant Church in Iowa. Received into the itinerancy in 1897 and receiving her elder's orders in 1898, in 1907 she was serving a circuit at the lowest annual salary recorded, $125—only to be censured by a special committee who found her "in direct violation of the plain law of the church in her failure to report to the President the condition of her charge each quarter and abandoning the work without asking the President for a release," having gone to preach for another denomination. It turns out that poor Mrs. Remington was widowed in 1906 and broke her left leg in 1907 (paper presented to the North Central Jurisdictional Conference of the Commission on Archives and History of the United Methodist Church, July 7, 1987).

34. Ibid.

35. Victoria Booth Demarest, *God, Woman and Ministry* (St. Petersburg, Fla.: Sacred Arts Int'l and Valkyrie Press, 1978), p. 70.

36. For a detailed description of this process, see Lois A. Boyd and R. Douglas Brackenridge, *Presbyterian Women in America: Two Centuries of a Quest for Status* (Westport, Conn.: Greenwood, 1983).

37. Ibid., p. 94.

38. The Presbyterian Church, US (PCUS), a southern group, held out against ordaining women until 1964.

39. Boyd and Brackenridge, *Presbyterian Women,* p. 183. Towner lived to regret her prophecy.

40. *Women and Men in Ministry,* ed. Roberta Hestenes (Pasadena: Fuller Theological Sem., 1985), p. 150.

41. *Women and Religion in America,* ed. Ruether and Keller (San Francisco: Harper & Row, 1986) 3:xvi–xvii.

42. Ann Braude, "The Jewish Woman's Encounter with American Culture," in *Women and Religion,* ed. Ruether and Keller, vol. 1.

43. Elinor Lenz and Barbara Myerhoff, *The Feminization of America: How Women's Values Are Changing Our Public and Private Lives* (Los Angeles: Jeremy P. Tarcher, 1985), p. 143.

44. Ann D. Braude, "Jewish Women in the Twentieth Century: Building a Life in America," in *Women and Religion,* ed. Ruether and Keller, 3:131.

45. Reva Clar and William M. Kramer, "The Girl Rabbi of the Golden West: The Adventurous Life of Ray Frank in Nevada, California and the Northwest, *Western States Jewish History* 18 (1986).

46. Ray Frank Litman, "Women in the Synagogue," in *Women and Religion,* ed. Ruether and Keller, 1:187.

47. Pamela S. Nadell, "The Women Who Would Be Rabbis," in *Gender and Judaism: The Transformation of Tradition,* ed. T. M. Rudavsky (New York: New York Univ. Press, 1995), pp. 124–25, 135 n. 12.

48. For an overview of the entrance of women into Jewish theological seminaries, see Nadell, "Women Who Would Be Rabbis," in *Gender and Judaism,* ed. Rudavsky.

49. Braude, "Jewish Women in the Twentieth Century," in *Women and Religion,* ed. Ruether and Keller, 3:135, 163.

50. Nadell, "Women Who Would Be Rabbis," pp. 126–29. For Lindheim's story, see her *Parallel Quest: A Search of a Person and a People* (New York: Thomas Yoseloff, 1962).

51. Nadell, "Women Who Would Be Rabbis," p. 131.

52. Maitland, *Map,* p. 88. See also Bendroth, *Fundamentalism,* p. 56.

53. Maitland, *Map,* p. 104.

54. Rosemary H. Coffin, *A Ministry of Grace: An Account of the Life of the Reverend Frederica Mitchell* (Exeter, N.H.: Privately published by the author in association with the Phillips Exeter Academy Press, 1983), p. 22.

55. Ibid., p. 50, 53.

56. Boyd and Brackenridge, *Presbyterian Women,* p. 183.

57. Harry Hale, Jr., Morton King, and Doris Moreland Jones, *New Witnesses: United Methodist Clergywomen* (Nashville, Tenn.: Board of Higher Education and Ministry, The United Methodist Church, 1980), Summary of Main Findings, pp. 16–18.

58. Margaret Henrichsen, *Seven Steeples* (Boston: Houghton Mifflin, 1953), pp. 130–31. Information on Henrichsen's district superintendency is given by Georgia Harkness, *Women in Church and Society,* p. 134.

59. Hilda Ives, *All in One Day: Experiences and Insights* (Portland, Me.: Bond Wheelwright, 1955), p. 47.

60. Ibid., pp. 113, 114, 48.

61. Ibid., p. 47.

62. Johnson, "Marilda Belva Spicer."

63. Ch. 2, Document 11, in *Women and Religion,* ed. Ruether and Keller, 3:75.

64. Hitchings, *Universalist and Unitarian Women Ministers,* pp. 60–63, 84–85.

65. Demarest, *God, Woman and Ministry,* p. 23.

66. Ibid., p. 109.

67. Boyd and Brackenridge, *Presbyterian Women,* p. 262.

68. *Woman's Pulpit* (Dec. 1922).

69. *Woman's Pulpit* (April 1923).

70. Johnstone, *When God Says "No,"* p. 37.

71. For a history of the development of the directors of religious education in the Presbyterian church, see Boyd and Brackenridge, *Presbyterian Women*.

72. "Bridges," in *Voices of Experience: Lifestories of Clergywomen in the Presbyterian Church,* ed. Alice Brasfield and Elisabeth Lunz (Louisville, Ky.: Presbyterian Pub. House, 1991), p. 31.

73. Edith Hunter, *Sophia Lyon Fahs* (Boston: Beacon, 1966), pp. 130, 256.

74. Ethel M. Baldwin and David V. Benson, *Henrietta Mears and How She Did It* (Glendale, Calif.: Gospel Light, 1966), p. 3. See also *Dream Big! The Henrietta Mears Story,* ed. Earl Roe (Ventura, Calif.: Regal Books, 1990).

75. An interview with Dr. Stokes is held by the Black Women Oral History Project at the Schlesinger Library.

76. Information on Southard is from the *Woman's Pulpit* (Oct./Dec. 1994).

6

The Holiness and Pentecostal Churches 1900–1960 🖎

Dear brother, let the Lord manage the women. He can do it better than you, and you turn your batteries against the common enemy.
—A. B. Simpson, founder of The Christian and Missionary Alliance[1]

WHILE MOST OF THE MAINLINE CHURCHES in the first part of the twentieth century inched along the path of progress for clergywomen, those of the new pentecostal and holiness churches that at outset recognized women's claims to preach and pastor slowly followed the course of institutionalization that has historically limited opportunities for clergywomen.[2] Churches split over their status.

Frederik Franson of the Free Church movement pamphleteered for women's ordination: "the devil has succeeded in excluding nearly two-thirds of the number of Christians [i.e., women] from participation in the Lord's service through evangelism. The damage to God's cause is so great as to be indescribable."[3] At the turn of the century the Free Church Conference was sending ordained women home missionaries out on their own, usually two by two, relying on free-will offerings and encountering persecution and hardship. Some Free Churches called (employed) women pastors, and many depended on women evangelists to conduct revivals.[4] Founder Seth C. Rees of the Pilgrim Holiness Church encouraged clergywomen, including his wife, Hulda, the "Pentecostal Prophetess." The Church of the Nazarene included provision for women preachers in its 1894 constitution, and for a time one conference of this denomination in western Tennessee had only women clergy. In the Church of God, according to a 1902 publication, an astounding 25 percent of the church leaders were women.[5]

But often these women were not credited as "real" clergy: they might do to preach and evangelize but not to take over a pastorate. If a woman successfully organized a new congregation, sooner or later she might be expected to hand it over to a man. For instance, Frances Eastman founded the Church of God in Midland, Michigan, and pastored it without salary from 1911 to 1934. When Blaine Varner succeeded her, in the depths of the Great Depression, he was paid five dollars a week.[6] The Church of God's Nancy McClure Ford, the first black graduate of Johnson C. Smith University and its first female graduate with a divinity degree, said, "It was very hard when I came along for women to get into the ministry. Especially if you had any training and if you had a gift that men recognized, then you got in trouble. If I had a large crowd to hear me, then the pastor would not let me preach any more for a long time."[7] Mary Cole wearied of having to explain the scriptural teaching on women preachers at almost every meeting.[8] A clergywoman in the Church of God insightfully commented on the economic factor: "When the reformation movement of the Church of God was just originally starting, women would work without wages and men had to have wages to keep their children, so women were serving in many capacities. When I first started out, I worked for $12 a week, and my husband was my support."

Nonetheless the holiness and pentecostal denominations were offering women opportunities in the clergy they could find nowhere else. Santos Elizondo (1867–1941), possibly the first ordained Mexican woman, began her career among the Nazarenes by organizing a church in El Paso, then spent the rest of it as a missionary in Mexico.[9] African-American Emma Alberta Nelson Crosswhite (b. 1882) and her husband in gratitude for her healing from tuberculosis built an interracial Church of God fellowship, which she pastored for forty-seven years. In 1947 Ozie Garrett entered full-time ministry as an evangelist; in 1951 she went as the first Church of God home missionary to the deep South; in 1953 she accepted a call to pastor an all-white congregation in Columbus, Nebraska, where she was the only black person in town and the only woman pastor in the state.[10]

✑ Women Founders

The women who founded their own churches—and there were several—like Florence Crawford of the pentecostal Apostolic Faith church—fared better.[11] Surely no more ardent a feminist ever founded a church than Alma Bridwell White (1862–1946). She believed that the institutional Christian church of her day oppressed women but that the Bible offered a basis for liberating them. She wanted not just a room of her own but a church of her own—not a church exclusively for women but a church in which women would enjoy real equality. A quirky, contradictory woman who oxymoronically supported both the woman suffrage movement and the Ku Klux Klan, White dominated the theology and administration of her Pillar of Fire church. "A narrow mind may fail to grasp [women's equality]," she said, "and it may take other sledgehammer blows to release the public mind from the old traditions against equality of the sexes." Heavyset, standing five feet eight inches tall, of forceful demeanor, White was ready to deliver these blows. The Pillar of Fire church was not only the sole church but the sole organization, religious or secular, to endorse the equal rights amendment on its introduction by Alice Paul in 1923.[12]

Reared a Methodist, White was converted in true fundamentalist fashion at sixteen: "Suddenly, I lost consciousness and felt I was carried away to hell. Black demons were all about me in this awful place, and lost men and women were weeping and wailing and gnashing their teeth. Some of the latter had bodies like serpents and heads like human beings, and vice versa." God had called her to the ministry, she decided, resisting the advice of her spiritual mentor to marry a minister. But how could she serve, since Methodists did not ordain? They did at the time (from 1869 to 1880) license women preachers, but White didn't know it; she was not to hear Margaret Van Cott, so licensed, until years later, and then she disapproved of the train on Van Cott's skirt and her fashionably dressed hair. Nor apparently had White heard of any women evangelists, such as Julia Foote or Amanda Smith. She tried Methodist missionary work in Utah, but, she said, "Methodism in Salt Lake City had keenly disappointed me."[13]

So in 1887 she married a minister, Kent White, and they went to live in Colorado, where she added study at the University of Denver to her one year of college, sang in the choir, took in boarders, and bore two sons. It wasn't enough, and she went into a decline, suffering pangs about her inability to preach. Intermittently she bribed God to cure her sons of their childhood illnesses by promising to preach. Her sanctification in 1893 provided her salvation, for she believed that to retain it she must testify publicly. At once her health improved. That same year she began substituting for her husband in the pulpit. Encouraged by winning converts at a revival where others had failed, she preached there every night for a month. Invitations to preach elsewhere followed, and in 1894 she began holding independent services at a rented hall. Turning over housework and baby tending to relatives and later to followers, she conducted revivals with her husband and with her brother, traveling ever more widely, staying away from home for longer periods.

In 1895 the Whites undertook evangelistic work full time. In the course of this work Alma White came to know other women evangelists, notably African-American Rebecca Grant of the Free Methodists and holiness evangelist Mother Miranda Vorn Holz. The next year the Whites opened a mission in Denver, putting in charge Vorn Holz and Alma White's mother. By 1899 they had five missions, a missionary home, and a school to train gospel workers to staff their missions. But if their work prospered, their marriage did not, ostensibly because of theological disagreements.

White was also suffering troubled relations with the Methodist hierarchy, because of her gender, because of their accurate perception that they were losing control of independent evangelists, because emotional displays of old-fashioned revivalism like White's had passed out of fashion among them, and because of her association with the holiness movement.

Like many another reformer before and after, White believed that she was restoring Christianity to its primitive purity. She was at least as eager to dissociate herself from the Methodist hierarchy as they were to disown her, for she had come to believe that pastors of established denominations were wolves in sheep's clothing out to devour her lambs (converts), and that if her converts joined any of the existing denominations they would die spiritually. She had also tired of acting the "supplicant at the feet of the pastors of the churches" so that she could preach. She did not after all need the approval of men to preach; God had ordained her.[14]

Accordingly in 1901 she incorporated her interdenominational mission work as the Pentecostal Union. It was a misnomer, for the Union was really a holiness church in the Methodist tradition and not pentecostal. White neither practiced nor preached speaking in tongues and in time denounced it as "tongues sorcery," "satanic gibberish," and "demon worship."[15] The Union placed about forty mission pastors and evangelists under her supervision, and in 1902 White was ordained an elder of this new sect, along with another woman and three men. For the next several years she battled to maintain control, against another holiness association, against being labeled a pentecostal, and against her husband. Eventually she separated herself from them all. In 1909 she and her husband parted, probably for a variety of causes, including doctrinal disagreements, her complete inability to act the submissive wife, and their power struggle within the Pentecostal Union. In 1917 she changed its name to the Pillar of Fire. And in 1918 she triumphed as its first woman bishop.

White judged society unsatisfactory and arranged for her followers to withdraw from it. Their mission and hers was evangelism, and she carried it overseas, crossing the Atlantic more than fifty times. Members could live in Pillar of Fire communes, work for the Pillar of Fire, educate their children in its schools and college. White forbade them to frequent theaters, dances, and bars, and put them into uniforms: dark blue dresses with white crocheted collars for the women; black suits and black shirts with white ties for the men. She wouldn't even let them ride in automobiles until 1913, when she had her first ride and promptly bought one.

Yet how could White, a natural-born manager, keep her hands off a world so obviously badly mismanaged? In 1911 she decided to allow members to engage in political activity, and she herself came out for Warren Gamaliel Harding. Then in an even more idiosyncratic display she aligned herself with both the National Woman's Party (the radical wing of the suffrage movement) and the Ku Klux Klan, which she perceived as promoting the old-style religion, temperance, patriotism, and anti-Catholicism. Somehow she even convinced herself that the Klan advocated women's rights. Apparently she did not share their hatred of African-Americans and Jews, but otherwise she went flat out for them, drawing cartoons for their attacks on Roman Catholic Al Smith (governor of New York and presidential candidate), and accepting money from them.

In many ways White's career paralleled that of Mary Baker Eddy. Both enjoyed success, fame, and prosperity. White was as dictatorial toward the Pillar of Fire as Eddy was toward the Church of Christ, Scientist. But they appealed to different people and by different means. In Henry Adams's terms, Eddy played the virgin and White the dynamo.

Eddy spoke to the upper middle class in small groups in her college or in services held in stately churches. White shouted at as many plebeians as she could crowd into her tents, rejoicing in their "holy jumping," exhorting them in what one news-paper called a "staccato shriek." Another reported: "There never was a madder soul out of Bedlam. She began pianissimo and worked herself up into a torrent about Hell and damnation and brimstone." Eddy was no feminist, but White in her last sermon was still pleading for women in the ministry. In old age, when Eddy with-drew into the fastness of privacy, emerging only occasionally to receive the plaudits of the crowd or to issue an edict, White was traveling forty-five thousand miles a year, buying property, editing six Pillar of Fire journals, and preaching up to twenty-one sermons a week, five on Sunday, activities that she maintained until her death at the age of eighty-four.[16]

For all her industry, business acumen, and managerial powers, White succeeded in establishing only a sect, which by 1950 had a mere five thousand members. Her con-temporary Aimee Semple McPherson, whom she derogated as a "necromancer, familiar with the black arts," whose "words were the mutterings of a witch,"[17] founded a denomination that still is growing rapidly at the end of the twentieth century.

The life of Aimee Semple McPherson (1890–1944) demonstrates what happens when a born advertising genius and natural actress becomes a pentecostalist.[18] She must have felt like a child of destiny. Gifted with good looks, intelligence, fairly prosperous and adoring parents, and a merry heart, the infant Aimee was dedicated by her mother to the service of the Salvation Army, "for the Salvation of the world." She was to spend all her life in "Salvation War." When as a teenager she experi-enced religious doubts over the absence of modern miracles and the conflict between Darwinism and the Bible, along came handsome evangelist Robert Semple. She was converted in 1907; they were married in 1908; and the couple set off about the Lord's business. In their wedding ceremony, performed by a Salvation Army officer, each promised to help the other to "constant and entire self-sacrifice for the Salvation of the world," taking one another as a "continual Comrade in [the Salvation] War."[19]

Robert Semple was a student and disciple of Charles Parham, who about 1905 had founded pentecostalism. Pentecostalism identifies four major charismata, or gifts of the spirit: the power to speak in tongues, the power to interpret tongues, the power to prophesy, and the power to heal. Even before her conversion Aimee believed that she had experienced healing by faith, when at her request a Salvation Army officer had laid hands on her broken ankle. At her conversion she spoke in tongues. Traveling from town to town with her husband as he conducted revivals, she herself in 1909 in Chicago was ordained a Pentecostal minister. The next year the couple sailed for China. On the way in London Aimee Semple preached by invi-tation to fifteen thousand people, speaking by the inspiration of the Spirit for more than an hour—that is, she prophesied. In pentecostal terms, to the many gifts that Aimee had received at her birth were now joined the four major gifts of the spirit. Everything augured well for the young Semples.

But in China disaster struck. In a matter of months Robert Semple was dead of malaria and dysentery, and Aimee, eight months pregnant, was left to bury her husband and bear her daughter. As soon as she could, she returned to her parents' Canadian farm. In the years that followed she tried to carry on, evangelizing in Chicago, working for the Salvation Army in New York, but her daughter's sickliness frustrated these attempts. In 1912 she married accountant Harold McPherson and they went to live with his mother in Providence, Rhode Island. Aimee McPherson gave over about three years to tending her daughter and the son to whom she gave birth in 1913. But she suffered a postpartum depression in which she began to hear the voice of God calling her to preach. Officiating at night services in pentecostal churches failed to satisfy her call, and she fell ill. Rest and surgery could not cure her, but her 1915 decision to go back to work did.

Like Alma White, McPherson owed her freedom to preach and evangelize to someone else's willingness to help with the care of her children—in McPherson's case her mother, Minnie Kennedy. Minnie had meant it when she dedicated her daughter to God's service. So for most of McPherson's career Minnie did whatever her daughter had neither time nor inclination to do. When in 1915 Aimee returned to the farm, Minnie took over the children and packed Aimee off to a camp meeting. McPherson shifted into high gear, began a series of tent meetings, and telegraphed her husband to join her. In a few weeks he came, was converted, and joined her mission.

As Daniel Mark Epstein cogently observes, charismatic and premillennial religions appeal most to the dispossessed, who have reason to want things changed. In the two decades from 1890 to 1910 the population of the United States grew from sixty-three to ninety-two million, more than half the increase caused by immigration. At the same time the country was rapidly urbanizing. Ill at ease in their new settings, immigrants and migrants from country to city swelled the ranks of the disoriented and dispossessed. So in 1915 when McPherson hit the sawdust trail, for multitudes she was the right person with the right message at the right time.

For the next seven years McPherson gypsied throughout the United States, crisscrossing the country coast to coast six times, twice traveling it between New England and Florida. She and whoever traveled with her slept where they could—in a tent, on beaches, in her "Gospel Car," plastered with Bible verses. They ate whatever manna her followers provided. This hand-to-mouth, hobbledehoy existence did in her marriage; in 1919 each of the McPhersons sued the other for divorce.

The children adapted to their vagabond life; when they tired of wandering, McPherson helped them construct not a castle in the air but a house, the home she promised they would someday inhabit in California. Minnie Kennedy joined them on the road, exhibiting a flair for publicity, assuming the responsibilities of bookings and bookkeeping, putting her daughter before as many people as possible as often as possible. Some ministers welcomed McPherson into their pulpits; others feared her. Episcopalians called her the Witch of Endor.

During these years McPherson was developing the techniques that would make her successful. With little money for clothes, she bought a maid's uniform and a second-hand cape to wear when she spoke: with her red hair and her graceful beauty she looked much like a nurse on a war poster, suggesting at once both the virginal and the maternal. The healings with which her followers credited her enhanced the image: McPherson's own faith in Christ's power to heal apparently changed the lives of several thousand invalids.[20] The lame, the halt, and the blind flocked to her.

She welcomed one and all, black or white, rich or poor. She visited night clubs, restaurants, and brothels to invite people to her meetings. From a boxing ring she challenged each person in the audience to find the worst sinner in the city and bring him or her next evening, when she would "go into the ring for Jesus."[21] She enticed people with syncopated music, reassured them of God's love, and held their interest with stories, acting out the parables, herself playing the parts of both the wise and the foolish virgins. When she preached she asked questions and invited her listeners to respond with singing, shouting, and applause. She rejected the idea of sanctification with its accompanying moral perfection as undemocratic, snobbish, and divisive. She got along with all sorts of people, calling herself "Everybody's Sister." When young punks heckled her, she prayed for each of them. To keep in touch with her followers she began to publish a newsletter, *The Bridal Call.* Her happy, generous spirit permeated her services and her theology.

Her growing fame preceded her to California. In Los Angeles the already established pentecostal community heralded her, flocked to her services, and built their dream house for McPherson and her children. She outdrew P. T. Barnum or Teddy Roosevelt. Remarkably, she kept her head. Unlike Alma White, she led her people to accommodate the society rather than withdraw from it. She quelled the more ecstatic religious expressions of her pentecostal followers and downplayed the spectacular healings that attracted the crowds. "My meetings," she said, "are ninety-nine percent *soul*-saving and *one* percent healing."[22]

At this juncture the team of Aimee McPherson and Minnie Kennedy could not put a foot wrong. Kennedy did not haggle over money when she booked meetings, and McPherson made no emotional appeals for money when collection plates were passed; God, they believed, would provide. Secure in this faith, they undertook to build a cathedral in Los Angeles; in two years the Angelus Temple, thereafter the center of McPherson's activity, was built and paid for.

McPherson designed the temple as an interdenominational meeting place, just as she designed the Foursquare Gospel Association as an interdenominational organization, to evangelize people who would then return to their own churches. ("Foursquare" sometimes represented holiness, happiness, healing, and heaven. At other times it stood for "Jesus, the Only Saviour; Jesus, the Great Physician; Jesus, Baptise [*sic*] with the Holy Spirit; Jesus, the Coming Bridegroom, Lord and King."[23]) She intended her association to supplement and augment, not to displace existing churches and denominations. In a way, the Foursquare Gospel church was a denomination created despite its founder.

She continued to itinerate widely. In 1922 she extended her influence still farther with radio sermons. Drawn by publicity like a winning float in the Tournament of Roses parade and handbills strewn from airplanes, her congregations swelled and surged. Reporters loved her, and her fame fed on itself. In 1920 the YMCA, the pentecostal community, and the mainline churches of St. Louis joined together to sponsor her in revival meetings. They rented a coliseum with twelve thousand seats and standing room for more. Every day the crowds began to gather at 5:00 A.M. for the noon service; police estimated that each time four or five thousand had to be turned away. Police worked in shifts to keep people from being trampled or crushed, as the desperate fought just to touch the building in which McPherson would appear. The sponsors benefited, for converts at the revival added to local church membership.

Her 1922 handling of the Ku Klux Klan illustrates both her difference from Alma White and her adeptness in interacting with all kinds of people. When the Klan "kidnapped" her, presented her with a bouquet, and demanded a speech, she preached about men's responsibility for the young girls whom they betrayed, asked how many of them were in a position to cast the first stone, and told them, "So long as you stand for righteousness, and as defenders of the defenseless, I shall pray for you and ask you to pray for me."[24] When in their disguises Klansmen bullied their way into Angelus Temple during a service, displacing other people, she held up the example of an old African-American man shut out of the church, only to be joined by the Christ, also shut out. "You men who pride yourselves on patriotism," she told them, "you men who have pledged yourselves to make America free for white Christianity, listen to me! Ask yourselves how is it possible to pretend to worship one of the greatest Jews who ever lived, Jesus Christ, and then to despise all living Jews? . . . JUDGE NOT THAT YE BE NOT JUDGED!"[25]

In the Angelus Temple, McPherson perfected the techniques she had developed in her revival tents. Now, however, she had the support of teams of ministers, two orchestras, three bands, three choirs, six quartets, and twenty-four soloists. The Bible stories acted out at revivals were now transformed into dramatized sermons, complete with costumes, props, scenery, and professional lighting. For the music she mixed old hymns with pop music; sometimes she herself wrote religious lyrics for current tunes. In the temple services people could laugh, tap their toes, and rejoice. For all the grandeur of the building, folks felt at home.

Besides its immense sanctuary and an elaborate Sunday School, the temple housed an agency to find jobs for men released from prison; a commissary for the poor; nurseries; a prayer tower, where volunteers prayed around the clock in two-hour shifts for any who called in to ask for help; a night school for day laborers; a broadcasting studio; and a training school for radio announcers. Next door McPherson built quarters for the L.I.F.E. Bible College, which by 1926 was enrolling almost a thousand students. In the huge organization and multiple activities into which the Church of the Foursquare Gospel had expanded, McPherson worked feverishly, broadcasting, presiding at healing services where she sometimes stayed on her feet for eight hours at a time, teaching future evangelists, meeting reporters, writing operas and oratorios, and traveling widely in the United States and abroad. Her preaching schedule alone would stagger most clergy: every Thursday, Friday, and Saturday evening, twice on Wednesdays, three times on Sundays; often she had to repeat sermons on the same day for the crowds awaiting admission.[26]

To the jaded ears of the late twentieth century, all this sounds like a Jim-and-Tammy Bakker setup. Yet McPherson with her mother and children lived in a four-bedroom house so crowded with visitors and people seeking help that she often shared a bedroom with her mother, or retreated to the privacy of a hotel. In 1925, in her prime, she drew a salary of twenty-five dollars a week—though the church paid many of her expenses.

Yet she had come a long way from the small-town Canadian girl who had set off on her evangelistic mission with her new husband. The reporters who watched her every move, the managerial staff who ran the business affairs of the church, the pregnant unmarried girls and battered women who sought her help, the babies literally left on her doorstep, her students, and the thousands who begged for her prayers in the belief that she could heal them exerted enormous pressures on her. Rich and famous people sought her company. Inevitably, she changed. Since her followers had thought her perfect, they did not welcome the changes.

From 1926 on, things began to go awry. The team of Minnie Kennedy and Aimee McPherson that could do no wrong faltered, quarreled, and broke up. Sister Aimee made mistakes in choosing her associates. The complex organization of the Foursquare Gospel church spun out of control. Scandals, accusations of love affairs, schisms with the branch churches, financial disputes, and lawsuits dogged her, often as a result of her own bad judgment. She underwent nervous breakdowns and committed to a disastrous and short-lived third marriage.

What went wrong? True enough, in the 1920s and 1930s evangelists as a group were losing status. Epstein may well be right in theorizing that McPherson was trying to steer her people away from an isolationist fundamentalism toward the social gospel and the betterment of the society.[27]

Her mission had always been to advocate, not to criticize; to unite people, not to divide them. McPherson preached the availability of religious experience to all, not correctness of doctrine. If once again she was trying to lead her followers into closer association with contemporary society—this time to the society of the Roaring Twenties, and to win that society to Christian salvation, she did not achieve her purpose. Nor, one supposes, could anyone. It's also likely that as the years passed her own church and other holiness churches found it more difficult to accept the leadership of a woman. Yet it is impossible to ignore the erratic behavior and errors of judgment that scarred McPherson's career and reputation.

She still had her great moments. The satellite churches continued to grow. In the Great Depression her church fed, clothed, and sheltered thousands. The Angelus Temple asked no questions; a telephoned request would guarantee succor. In one month they fed eighty thousand people. In 1933–1934, McPherson launched another revival tour, traveling fifteen thousand miles, preaching 336 sermons to more than two million people. She was among the first to denounce Hitler and Mussolini and to defend Zionism.

In 1944 she fatally overdosed on sleeping pills; the jury ruled that she had not committed suicide. Her personal estate amounted to only ten thousand dollars. But the Church of the Foursquare Gospel now numbered 410 churches in North America, two hundred mission stations, a membership of twenty-nine thousand, and assets of 2.8 million dollars. Under the leadership of her son, Rolf McPherson, by 1993 the assets increased to almost 360 million dollars, its churches to 25,577 in seventy-four countries, and its membership to 1.7 million. It was among the fastest-growing churches in the world.

As for her influence on clergywomen, Aimee Semple McPherson left a mixed legacy. She had grown up in the Salvation Army, surrounded by its clergywomen. As a child she had heard Evangeline Booth preach. Her mother had served in the Army both before her marriage and in Aimee's maturity; as an adult McPherson herself had worked briefly for the Army. Throughout her life she knew other women evangelists, like Mary Craig, cofounder of the Glad Tidings Pentecostal Mission.[28] So she had no patience with disputes about women's ordination. "Oh, don't you ever tell me that a woman cannot be called to preach the Gospel!" she wrote. "If any man ever went through one-hundredth part of the hell on earth that I lived in, those months when out of God's will and work [not evangelizing], they would never say that again."[29]

McPherson herself ordained seventeen hundred ministers of both genders. In the Foursquare Gospel training school she taught, mentored, and inspired scores of young women evangelists. Some were already experienced when they enrolled, like Goldie Schmitt, who had been a child evangelist. Many of them worshipfully imitated McPherson's mannerisms and dress. McPherson also hired clergywomen to work with her. Evangelist Anna Britton conducted "aftermeetings" at Angelus Temple, for people inspired by the service who wanted more help. Harriet Jordan was dean of the training school. Lilian Yeomans traveled for the Four Square Association: a physician addicted to narcotics, she had been healed by an evangelist and lived the rest of her life testifying, teaching, praying for the sick, and writing about healing.[30]

But as time went on McPherson quarreled with many of her women associates—as indeed she quarreled with the men. In the early 1930s she employed Rheba Crawford, reputedly a spellbinder, to preach in her absence. The two were to alternate in the Temple and in the field. Almost as colorful a figure as McPherson, Crawford too was the child of Salvationists and herself a Salvation Army officer, known as the "Angel of Broadway," and the inspiration for Damon Runyon's Miss Sarah Brown, so popular that she was once arrested in New York City for blocking traffic with the crowd attracted by her preaching. She had resigned from the Salvation Army by request, married, divorced, been ordained a Congregational minister, married again, resigned her ministry, and served as the state social service director. Not surprisingly, McPherson and Crawford did not last long together.[31] But Minnie

Kennedy had held up McPherson's arms throughout most of her career, and McPherson's only daughter, Roberta, had been groomed since babyhood as her successor. Yet Sister Aimee fell out with them both.

Tellingly, during McPherson's lifetime the percentage of female pastors in Foursquare Gospel congregations declined. In 1927 eighteen of the Temple's fifty-five branch churches were pastored by single women; one by two women associate pastors; sixteen by married couples; nine by men; and one by a group of training school students. In 1944 when McPherson died, only seventy-three of the 446 branch churches had clergywomen. Although the Foursquare Gospel church had no regulations against women in positions of authority, at the Temple all the elders were men. Apparently McPherson thought of women's ordination and service as clergywomen as an accomplished fact, not as a cause. In the absence of her concern, her church followed the usual course of churches as they age and institutionalize, masculinizing the clergy.

✑ Black Holiness and Pentecostal Churches _____

For every Aimee Semple McPherson, there were scores, maybe hundreds of unsung women church founders. Some were white, but for cultural and historical reasons, the practice was much more common among the uncounted black women who "preached out" or "dug out" churches of their own.

An African-American pentecostal clergywoman told us:

> In the black community historically the pulpit has been the domain of the black male because the black male may not be able to make it too well in the corporate world but can be his man in the pulpit, and he doesn't want these women coming and taking that away. I think the black male feels that this has been the one place that they can be king, and please, black women, don't take this away from me. Yes, yes, some black women have listened. They bought into what the black men were saying. To me that's the old self-hatred. You have bought into the fact that you're not supposed to be in a certain place.

Perhaps partly as a result of this reluctance of black women to contest with black men, even at the end of the twentieth century only three African-American main-line denominations support the ordination of women: the African Methodist Episcopal church, the African Methodist Episcopal Zion church, and the Christian Methodist Episcopal Zion church. Black Baptists, like their white coreligionists, do not ban it, but their individual congregations rarely ordain women.

Black pentecostal and holiness churches have also had problems with accepting women as pastors, even though they honored them as religious leaders. Cheryl Townsend Gilkes writes: "In those denominations in which women were unable to become elders, pastors, and bishops, they assumed the roles of churchmothers, evangelists, missionaries, prayer bandleaders, deaconesses, and, most important 'teachers.' These alternatives were also available in those denominations in which women were eligible for all leadership roles. Where churchwomen were officially, 'the second sex,' they achieved quite powerful positions of influence and structural authority"—to the extent that some denominations spoke of a "double pulpit," one for men and one for women, and in its way the title "Mother" conferred as much honor as "Reverend."[32] (Still, as a black American Baptist clergywoman vigorously remarked to us, "When you introduce me as 'this great woman pastor,' you ain't over this thing, no matter how much you say you are. Every time you say that, you say 'Looka here, this is a woman, guys, this is not one of us.'")

The Church of God in Christ (COGIC), the largest black pentecostal denomination, at the end of the twentieth century still refuses women full ordination —though now and then a woman has slipped through the barrier. In 1976 Repsie Warren was ordained by COGIC's Bishop R. T. Jones, Sr. As Dr. Warren explained to us, "The bishop went against the tradition of the denomination. OK? He got in a little trouble. I was the first woman that he ordained. Not the last. I think he only ordained though about two more after that. Because he did get in trouble, but I was already ordained then, so he couldn't take it back! God meant that to be." Now and then in COGIC widows have "inherited" a church from their minister husbands, the right of clergy to pass on churches to family members being recognized in this and some other pentecostal churches. Even then women have sometimes confronted difficulties. An independent clergywoman told us about a COGIC church "where the husband died and left the church to the wife. OK. Now, the men tried to take the church away from her; they stood in the door and said, 'You're not coming in here.' Now they accept her as a pastor, but most of the time they call her 'Mother Somebody,' not 'Reverend' or 'Elder Somebody.'"

Rather than struggle for a place in the pulpits of existing churches, as Barbara Brown Zikmund writes:

> If they felt the call to preach, [African-American women] simply started their own independent Holiness or Pentecostal church. Although certain women have built up lasting congregations that attracted large numbers, most Black women pastors have been content to serve small independent storefront churches. Overall in American church history, in proportion to the population, there have probably been more Black women preachers and pastors than white women clergy.[33]

Indeed in the black holiness history there exists a long tradition of women starting their own churches. In it Elder Lucy Smith established the All Nations Pentecostal Church in Chicago in the 1930s, Bishop Ida Robinson the Mount Sinai Holy Church of Philadelphia in 1924, and more recently Dr. Barbara King the Hillside International Truth Center, and Rev. Johnnie Colemon the Christ Universal Temple in Chicago.[34]

African-American Mother Shannon during the 1930s and 1940s was pastoring her St. Anthony's Daniel Helping Hand Divine Chapel of the Spiritualist Church of the Southwest in New Orleans, a church in a cottage from which she dispensed religion and charity, borrowing extensively from the practices of her Italian Roman

Catholic neighbors.[35] In 1957 in Detroit African-American Mother Charleszetta Campbell Waddles (b. 1912), an ordained minister in a nondenominational church, founded the Perpetual Mission for Saving Souls of All Nations, which "reaches over 100,000 people a year, offering food, clothing, furniture, job training and placement, a variety of medical and legal services, and sponsoring low-cost housing."[36] Some of Waddles's imaginative and efficient techniques for helping poor people have been adopted by governmental agencies.

"This is the book *I*'m going to write," said African-American Dr. Audrey Bronson, who began her ministry in the 1940s, "about those people who mentored me in the city of Philadelphia."

> Most of the women had established their own churches, and most of them were pentecostal. I only knew one that was AMEZion and one that was AME. I knew these women as a teenager. That was the thing that let me know, hey, if you can do it I can too. As a matter of fact, as a little kid, around 7 or 8 years old, there was a woman in my hometown who had a church; that was back in 1941. I've always seen women preaching in the pulpit. My dad, when he pastored a church, he used to have women to come preach for him. When I would go out to preach later on Dad would go with me and sit in the pulpit with me.

After some twenty-five years as an ordained pentecostal evangelist, Bronson started her independent Sanctuary Church of the Open Door in Philadelphia in 1975 with twelve members meeting in her own home. Today the church boasts fifteen hundred members; in part of its half-block-long building it runs an elementary school with two hundred students. Established denominations have invited Bronson's church to join: "I've been courted by all of them to come into their organizations. Yes, and I just get a kick out of being courted. I'm never going." Indeed, though Bronson makes no such claim for it, her church shows some signs of becoming a denomination on its own. Ordained a bishop in 1994 by bishops from several different denominations who got together and proposed this ceremony to her, Bronson has herself ordained about twenty ministers: "So many of them," she says, "have gone out and had their own churches, and they wanted to stay with an organization like mine. I really didn't want that, but that's what's happening." She currently is training within her own church some six clergywomen and clergymen.

Bronson to be sure is unusual in her qualifications. The daughter of a preacher/school administrator and the sister of a college president, she herself taught college psychology for many years. She holds a master's degree in psychology and a doctorate in ministry. "If I hold any place in history of especially the black pentecostal woman," she told us, "it's that I might have been one of the first ones to get a formal education up to this point. I've often had people tell me that they like my combination of spiritual fervor with an education. The women prior to me maybe had the spiritual fervor but didn't have the education." In the latter part of the twentieth century many black women have followed the path that Bronson blazed, seeking the training to fulfill their vocations.[37]

A woman of boundless energy, Bronson not only pastors her church and runs her elementary school; she is also dean of the Philadelphia Urban Education Institute, which after considerable struggle has succeeded in instituting Afrocentric courses in the four primarily white theological seminaries in Philadelphia, with the goal of better preparing students to serve in the black community. "Let's face it," Bronson says, "racism is just so rampant, even in the church it is rampant. We had such a hard time, even in trying to get these courses into the seminaries. It was marathon hours trying to get them to understand what we were talking about."

Just as ardently as she opposes racism and strives to mitigate its force, so also with sexism.

> I feel very deeply that if we don't take the good news of the gospel, regardless of what vessel it comes through, to the people, they're going to take the bad news to us. So many drugs. And so many killings on the street. Why have you got to worry whether I'm a male or a female? When this guy puts a gun to your head you don't care whether he believes in women preachers or not. If I'm able to draw in maybe a man who comes to my church and gets regenerated and his life gets better, maybe that'll stop him from killing this black male preacher's wife. So I think we ought to come together around this issue. I've had many a male tell me, which I don't *appreciate,* you're the only woman I'll let in my pulpit because you don't get up there and fight. You just go ahead and preach. Well my answer to that is, if you don't put your women through such a hard thing, they could be like that too! I know lots of black male preachers in the Baptist churches in particular, they have been some of the main ones in the vanguard, out there fighting segregation and discrimination, but then they let it stop with them. They don't seem to see that they're doing the same thing to the female that the white man has done to them.

Like Bronson, other black women founders have served not just their churches but also their communities—or communities they adopted—served not only spiritual needs but others as well. Repsie Warren talks about her holistic ministry, meeting the physical, intellectual, emotional, social, and spiritual needs of her congregation—especially the black deaf. She integrated them into her own independent church for the deaf and hearing, where everybody signs at least a little, where the deaf are in the choirs—sometimes signing, sometimes singing. She set up a social service agency that procured federal, state, and city funding for training them and finding them jobs. She and her church reach out to the hearing members of their families, teaching them how to communicate with their deaf relatives.

✺ And All Those Others

Several girl-child evangelists emerged in the twentieth century. Madeline Southard, founder of the American Association of Women Ministers (AAWM), personally inspected Ora Stoddard of Miami, Oklahoma, terming her "the youngest woman preacher of whom we know" but to her relief finding that though Stoddard seemed more like seventeen than fourteen, "her happy wholesome devotion to

Christ makes a profound impression on both young and old. She has been licensed by the district conference of the Methodist Episcopal church. All will be glad to know that she has a wise and devoted mother."[38] In 1986 the AAWM turned up a still younger phenomenon, Darlene Alford of Kenosha, Wisconsin, an elder in the Old Way Holiness Pentecostal Churches of America, founded by her father; she was called to ministry at six, licensed at seven, and ordained at eight.[39]

Far more famous was Uldine Utley (b. 1912). Growing up in California, she aspired to become a stage dancer or a movie star. Conversion as a nine-year-old at a revival redirected her ambitions; she began trying to convert her schoolmates on the playground. At church services her testimonies to her visions and mystical experiences attracted invitations for her to speak elsewhere, and to be paid for it. Soon she was conducting revivals. Though, she said, she assumed that "only great big men" could preach, Jesus commissioned her.[40] Soon she was preaching every weekend and worrying about missing services when she was kept after school on Friday. With her family's backing she left the seventh grade for full-time, country-wide evangelism: Daddy took care of administrative detail; Mother did her laundry and saw to her meals; and a volunteer tutor oversaw her schoolwork. In her spare time the youngster edited her own magazine, *Petals from the Rose of Sharon.*

Of course most holiness and pentecostal clergywomen labored with less fanfare than White or McPherson or Utley. Despite the opposition that flashed back at them for daring to defy social expectations and norms, they centered their lives on their ministries. Take southerner Mary Lee Wasson Harris Cagle (1864–1955) of the Church of the Nazarene. Her mother told her she would rather have her go to her grave than preach. Rumor accused Cagle of abandoning her children and operating a brothel. But her work sustained her. She organized churches; she functioned as a district's evangelist to animate the religious life of its churches; she shared the job of her second husband (whom she described as "a good big-hearted cowboy, who was converted under [my] own ministry") as district superintendent, with never a sign of burnout. "I almost had to know that it was preach or hell before I would do it," she wrote, "and now when the time is nearing when I will have to quit, the thought of it nearly breaks my heart."[41]

One way and another numbers of clergywomen served in holiness and pentecostal churches in the early part of the twentieth century. Then, in the words of Margaret M. Poloma, "the ever present danger of an erosion of charisma" materialized in the 1920s and 1930s, as the churches moved from prophetic to priestly mode.[42] That is, no longer did the claim of a call from God suffice; the clergy professionalized and masculinized. For instance, the Assembly of God, founded in 1914 with its pulpits open to both genders, by 1917 was already distinguishing between "licensed" and "ordained" ministers, and women found it increasingly difficult to move up that ladder. So marked was the shift away from approval of clergywomen in the holiness churches that Nilah Meier-Youngman was seventeen years old before she discovered that her own mother, Lilliam Meier, had been ordained by the Church of God in 1929 when she completed her training at the Gospel

Trumpet Training School in Anderson, Indiana. "All those years she and father had worked as the first Church of God pioneer missionaries from the United States in Brazil and Argentina and this 'secret' [of her ordination] had never leaked out! Nobody had asked, I suspect, and mother, very aware of the male dominance in the church, had never shared this fascinating fact!"[43]

✑ Hard Times

So during the years that more mainline denominations were approving ordination for women, the numbers of clergywomen were dropping in many evangelical and pentecostal groups as those churches aged and consigned women into the outer darkness of the laity. These churches historically conceived of themselves as withdrawn from the society, critical of it, or wanting to reform it. Their insistence on biblical literalism and/or inerrancy and their primitivist desire to restore the society of early Christian times fed their traditional ideas about women's place. Many of them recoiled from the suffrage amendment and all that it represented, perceiving it as an attack on home and family.[44] In defense of their own patriarchal authority men attacked the clergywoman as a "female pulpiteeress," an "unscriptural monstrosity," and an "ecclesiastical freak."[45]

Given such deep-seated attitudes, not even the most apparently supportive men could be counted on to defend women's ordination. Robert Brown, for example, was converted by and soon married Marie Estelle Burgess Brown (1880–1971), founder of the Glad Tidings Tabernacle, the first pentecostal institution in Manhattan. For forty years the couple copastored the tabernacle, a ministry that she continued after his death in 1948. Yet he was responsible for many of the restrictions placed on women ministers by the Assembly of God in the twenties and thirties.[46]

Often during this period of rejection clergywomen got along by going along —that is, they repeatedly asserted that they did not want to invade male territory, often carefully not even calling themselves preachers; and they emphasized their traditional womanliness, their acceptance of "women's work" both in the home and in the church. Even at the end of the twentieth century Pastor Ruth Hatley likes to claim, "I've always said I've got more sermons over the ironing board and the dishpan than I ever did on my knees." Such women describe themselves as mothering their congregations. "The girl who wishes to be a [Pentecostal] pastor," wrote Elaine Lawless in 1988 "must also be a wife and mother, and she must extol the virtues of those capacities at every opportunity. She must declare her 'motherly' nature, exclaim her delight in being a wife and mother, her joy in her children, her home. And she must deny her sexuality as a possible temptress while at the same time she must acknowledge her inferior status as woman and submit herself to all men."[47]

A woman could win approval a bit more easily if she copastored with her husband, presenting herself as "Mrs. Preacher." For example, Grace Fuller broadcast with her husband Charles on the "Old Fashioned Revival Hour," reading and answering personal letters from listeners.[48]

✑ The Special Case of the Salvation Army _____

The Salvation Army historically and presently outshines all other holiness denominations in its openness to clergywomen. Indeed, the Army's liberalism in this respect evoked a horrified response from a fundamentalist who had expected "to find women preachers among the Unitarians and Universalists, for they care nothing for the Bible," but was disgusted to find them in the Salvation Army. "Oh well," he concluded, "it will only hasten the appearing of the antichrist. . . . As it was with the first woman, so shall it be with the woman at the close of the age, listening to the tempter."[49]

In America Evangeline Cory Booth (1865–1950) shaped the twentieth-century Salvation Army.[50] She was, of course, the daughter of founders William and Catherine Booth and reputedly her father's favorite. It never occurred to anyone, certainly not to Evangeline Booth, that she would not do the Army's work. From her childhood she and her six older sisters and brothers played at mock revivals, reenacted biblical scenes, and participated in mission work. When she was small her mother told her, "I want the world to be a better place because you, Eva, have lived in it."[51] Her very name reflected her parents' expectations for her.

At fifteen she donned the Army uniform. Like the military, the Salvation Army has always offered its women more responsibility at an earlier age than they can find in most jobs. Perhaps in this respect Evangeline was even "more equal" than others, as if General Booth were out to prove that he would not send other young women anywhere he would not send his daughter. At seventeen she was not only selling the *War Cry* on the London streets but also living with other Army women in the slums as a member of the Cellar, Gutter, and Garrett Brigade. There they acted as visiting practical nurses, counselors, and exemplars. At twenty she was taking charge of a training home for women, holding open-air meetings, and leading cadets in raids to halt child prostitution. When Army invasions of public houses provoked attacks on Salvationists by thugs hired by the liquor industry, Booth recruited bodyguards from gang leaders. When one Army woman was kicked insensible and another died of her injuries, Evangeline's father sent his daughter to the trouble spots.

Throughout her young womanhood Booth matured professionally as her responsibilities and powers grew. Her private, emotional life was another matter, for General Booth opposed her wish to marry one or another of the many men attracted to her, brandishing both Army discipline and a kind of moral blackmail. In one instance he forbade the proposed marriage to another officer on the dubious grounds that both were too valuable to the Army to be linked together; in another he reminded Evangeline that as a child she had committed her life to the poor, the wicked, and the helpless. To any Salvationist these would be powerful arguments. Evangeline bowed to the wishes of her general/father, but all her life she believed that she would have made a good wife and mother and took a special interest in children.

In 1904 the general ordered her to take charge of work in the United States. Already a national figure in Canada, where she had headed Army work since 1896, she had learned how to gain the support of the rich and powerful and how to influence national policy. There she had started the first Canadian parole system and instituted an Army immigration system that eventually brought into Canada more than a quarter of a million British. She also maneuvered skillfully in the increasingly troubled political situation within the Army itself, where several of her siblings rebelled against what they perceived as autocracy and defected from the Army.

The programs that Booth immediately instituted in the United States, like her school lunch program, not only met real needs but also chimed with the liberal mood of the Progressive Era, winning approval for the Army among people of influence from John Wanamaker to Theodore Roosevelt. Moreover, exercising her already well-developed flair for the dramatic, she cast her activities in a form irresistible to reporters and to a spectacle-hungry public. In 1909, for instance, she warmed the hearts of the millions in the temperance movement with her First Annual Boozers' Convention, promising to repeat it every year until the Eighteenth Amendment passed. On the first day of the convention, she advertised "Free Eats All Day." A fleet of 5th Avenue coaches cruised around picking up drunks and conveying them to the Salvation Army Memorial Hall. The afternoon parade featured a water wagon from the street cleaning department drawn by four horses and loaded with drunks, with Salvationists marching alongside them to catch them if they fell off the wagon. Floats depicted the miseries of the drunkard's life. A ragged, bloated man stumbled along chained to a ten-foot, walking papier-mache whiskey bottle, a thin, poorly-dressed woman, and ragged children trailing behind.

The same dramatic sense animated the meetings Booth conducted—which may well have inspired Aimee Semple McPherson's illustrated sermons. Music from a children's choir and a processional of officers in the costumes of all the nations in which the Salvation Army worked introduced "Miss Booth in Rags," a lecture on her service in the London slums, which ended with a plea for sinners to repent. Though such presentations were carefully rehearsed and staged, occasionally things went wrong. When a prop man explained that he hadn't found a lamb, so he had clipped a poodle to look like one, Booth sighed and said, "O.K. But one bark from that lamb and you've had it."[52] Booth also understood the effectiveness of audience participation. In those pre-Kleenex days, she had her audience give a "lily field salute" of upraised white handkerchiefs. So effectively did techniques like these attract crowds that in 1908 one journalist estimated that during the previous year eleven million people had heard Booth speak—in person, without benefit of radio or television.

Their work in World War I under Booth's leadership earned the American branch of the Salvation Army national recognition. In 1914, confronting the dilemma that Salvationists were fighting on both sides of the conflict, Booth tactfully announced an Old Linen Campaign, appealing for funds to hire the unemployed to roll bandages. When the United States entered the conflict in 1917, she placed her Army on a war-service basis, setting up railroad canteens and huts and hostels near military camps. "I want to send my Army to France," Booth told U.S. Army General Pershing. When he responded that he already had an army in France, she retorted, "But not *my* Army." She won her point, and thousands of servicemen and their families had cause to rejoice that she did. The Salvation Army distinguished itself among other relief agencies by never charging for its food, refusing to sell cigarettes, focusing on service to enlisted men, and welcoming all to its huts, regardless of color.

Booth herself chose the officers to serve overseas and personally charged each group. Of the married couple, four single women, and five single men in the first group she said:

> These officers are not going on any pleasure excursion; they are not going out of any sensational curiosity to see how things look, or test how it feels to be at the front. They go authorized by a specific commission, with their Commander's confidence that they are fitted to accomplish the specific work inscribed upon that commission. Anyone failing will be shot! It is quite enough for us to pay their expenses to be a success—we could not contemplate paying them to be a failure.

The Salvation Army officers understood their mission as a continuance of their work in the States: the women might spend much of their time frying doughnuts and baking pies, but they purposed always to save souls.[53]

Unlike Aimee Semple McPherson, who preferred to leave business arrangements to others, Booth as the head of the Salvation Army in the United States functioned expertly and joyfully both as spiritual leader and as executive. She understood financing and undertook money raising not as an onerous, embarrassing task but as an interesting challenge. Confronting empty coffers after the many expenses of World War I, she seized the opportunity to refashion the Army's mode of funding, which she thought was consuming too much of the officers' time. Henceforth, she decided, except for the Christmas kettle collections the Army would conduct just one campaign annually.

With her usual flair, she launched this nationwide Home Service Fund Campaign in 1919 by setting up a stove on the steps of the federal treasury building near Wall Street, frying a doughnut, and auctioning it off for five thousand dollars. Then she and Cornelius Vanderbilt led a parade up Broadway, holding between them a clothes basket into which spectators tossed cash and checks. Veterans' tributes to the Army's overseas work promoted the campaign. In cities Army cadets boarded buses with collection boxes; people in small towns collected in the country. To get the coins back into circulation, cadets for two days literally shoveled collected coins into borrowed counting machines. Nationally the campaign exceeded its goal by two million dollars.

A perfectionist, Booth lived and breathed for the Army. She kept a notepad by her bed for ideas that came to her in her insomniac hours. When she rode horseback, one of her several favorite sports, she might dictate or hum a tune she had composed for some harassed aide to note down while he rode beside her. She spent summers at a place on Lake George given her by admiring industrialists, but in the company of young women and men officers whom she invited to share camp life, sleeping in tents, eating at long tables. At night they played parlor games or music, with Booth on the harp.

She was, after all, the head of American operations in a paramilitary organization, expected to give orders, not to make requests. Inevitably such an obsessive worker was demanding and impatient with her fellow officers, expecting them to jump to it. She didn't put up with much guff: when a band conductor balked at playing the doxology without music, protesting that it was against regulations, she snapped, "I'm the regulation."[54] She loved military show—wearing tailor-made, silk-lined uniforms, and taking the salute at headquarters morning and evening.

But she excelled at building staff, especially encouraging creative people with original ideas. And she had a redeeming sense of humor. When an aide whom she had just fired said, "I'll go if that's the way you want it, Commander, but I'll tell you one thing: you're losing a good man," she laughed off the incident.[55]

Like everyone else, the Salvation Army suffered during the Great Depression. Officers took 10-percent cuts in their already small stipends, and the Army temporarily closed its training schools. But it maintained its spiritual programs and its charities. Journalist and novelist Adela Rogers St. John donned working clothes to do research for a series on unemployed women. "I picked the Salvation Army as the only charity organization I could recommend 100 percent," she noted. "[At the Salvation Army home for women I had a] room of my own. Clean bed. Few things I have experienced in the way of physical pleasure like the hot bath with *soap*, towels, and privacy after weeks without them. I don't know how they could love me, but they did. Like God. And the lassies [the women officers] had breakfast with me and cheered me on my way."[56]

In 1934 Evangeline Booth was elected the Salvation Army's first woman general. It had been a long road, and she might well have expected an earlier election. Catherine Booth, on her deathbed forty-four years earlier, had said, "I have been telling [Eva] that if she keeps on, and if she keeps single, she will one day be General of The Salvation Army."[57] When in 1929 Evangeline's brother Bramwell was forced into retirement, much against his will, the election of another man must have been a bitter pill for her to swallow. She had, after all, an international reputation; she had enormously strengthened and expanded the Army in the United States and enhanced its prestige; and more than once she had acted the peacemaker in incipient revolts against Bramwell Booth's authority. But like the good soldier she was, she loyally pledged her support to the new general. When he later sent her a telegram of reproof on another matter, she said, "Well, . . . you know if I can't take discipline, I can't discipline others. He's the General. I may not like this cable, but I've got to salute."[58] On her election Booth had but two years before the compulsory retirement age.

And what of the other women officers of the Salvation Army during the first sixty years of the twentieth century? Their image certainly improved both because of Booth's leadership and because of their own dedicated work. The two World Wars and the Great Depression familiarized many people with their work who would otherwise have known little or nothing of them. In 1930 Booth published a booklet, *Woman,* praising the service rendered by women officers:

> Many people think that the women of the Salvation Army are lassies who, in the main, spend their time and energies on waving the tambourine and shouting their "Hallelujahs." During the War, our girls achieved a reputation scarcely less embarrassing. It was supposed that their whole energies were devoted to serving out the doughnuts to the boys in the trenches and daily welcoming bombardment as a shortcut to glory. . . . But death and danger had not been the only trial of these women's faith. They had faced dirt, they had handled disease, they had not flinched before uttermost degradation, they had not been dismayed in the most awful defacements of God's image, imprinted on our race; there is no depth of misery, of despair, of iniquity that is concealed from the steady eyes of the women of the Salvation Army. The hospitals and homes for mothers, deserted by those who should have been at their side as partners in parenthood, the hotels for working women, the visitations of women in prisons, the bureaus of employment, the young women's residences, and the Home League in every corps for helping women to be better housewives, these are only some of the agencies which are conducted by the women officers of the Salvation Army.[59]

But within the Army the status of women officers and their opportunities slipped—just as in the holiness and pentecostal churches generally. As one of them told us, "It was Catherine and William who birthed the Army. He was a preacher and she was his brain. She understood tons of things. Catherine is the secret to the Salvation Army. Then, as we began to grow and develop—in the beginning they made women divisional commanders. Somehow, over the years, it became a man's world. In the 1950s, there was not one woman doing anything in administration. Nowhere." Nor did the appointment of a second woman general, Eva Burrows, do much for women.

The Army has always appealed mainly to working-class people, who fill the pews of its churches and from whom it draws most of its officers. For its personnel it has found competent and intelligent officers, whom it has trained almost entirely in its own schools. Rarely, at least until quite recently, has it sent its officers on to colleges and universities, except perhaps for technical training in the business skills necessary to administer its huge organization. Interested more in the practical application of Christianity than in doctrinal subtleties, it has emphasized a thorough knowledge of the Bible rather than academic theology.

Consequently, the Army's organization and personnel policies have tended to reflect traditional, working-class assumptions and values. From 1920 to 1960, when throughout society people attempting to improve conditions for women could barely make their voices heard in the wilderness, few Salvationists questioned the Army's increasingly patriarchal mode of operation. Additionally, all through this period clergywomen in general, inspired with the ideals of duty to God and service to humanity, were paying more attention to the text "Blessed are the meek" than to the parable of the talents or the adjuration not to hide one's light under a barrel—even though they were visibly not inheriting the earth. For Salvationists the imperative of obeying Army discipline stiffened this impulse.

In another era Booth might have done more for Army women. As it was, she worried about being perceived as a militant on women's issues. "No," she said in 1913, "I don't believe in militant women's suffrage. However, I am a suffragist—I made that known long ago. Men have not made such a good fist of it with the ballot that women would do any worse." And she admitted, "I've always been afraid to take too much notice of women officers because I am a woman and people would think I was giving all the favored jobs to women."[60]

❧ A Resurgence of Faith Healing

To look at American clergywomen over the three centuries from Mary Dyer to Kathryn Kuhlman is to marvel at the power of the church hierarchies that so effectively kept most women out of their pulpits and at the persistence of the women who nonetheless preached and pastored professionally. Among these women one phenomenon manifests itself again and again, in women as clashingly different as Mary Baker Eddy and Aimee Semple Mcpherson, or Alma White and Ellen White: all of these women suffered wretchedly bad health before they began to practice their vocations, and all of them were transformed into energetic high achievers afterwards. The phenomenon is not, we must remind ourselves, confined to would-be clergywomen, for it manifested itself also in Jane Addams and perhaps afflicted poor Alice James. Its first stage has been diagnosed as neurasthenia, or laid to sulky laziness or penis envy. Milton was nearer the mark when he wrote of "that one Talent which is death to hide." Whether we talk about a vocation or a talent, its frustration or the failure to follow or exercise it demonstrably results in misery that expresses itself not only spiritually and psychologically but also physically. All the possible arguments about women's ordination cannot change that law of human nature—regardless of gender.

Perhaps their own experience in physical illness in the days of their frustration gave such clergywomen a special interest in healing and encouraged them to associate physical with spiritual well-being. Or perhaps the popularization of Freudian theory embedded this association in the public mind, so that people believing themselves reborn spiritually also perceived themselves as restored to health physically. At any rate, Alma White and Aimee Semple McPherson were both famed and sought after for the healings that occurred during their services. Both attributed these to the power of the Holy Spirit, and McPherson worried a good bit that the sensationalism of the "miraculous" physical transformations would distract attention from the spiritual. Yet she found the insistent pleas for her personal touch and prayers hard to deny, and eventually the overwhelming numbers of sick and traumatized people seeking her help caused her to set up elaborate systems so that she could see as many as possible.

Nor were such practices necessarily confined to holiness churches. A 1950 National Council of Churches survey on spiritual healing practices showed that more than a third of the 460 pastors (Methodists, Episcopalians, Lutherans, Baptists, Disciples of Christ, United Brethren, Congregational, Evangelical, and Reform) responding claimed actual cases of healing. The techniques they used varied from prayer alone to the laying on of hands, anointing with holy oil, and pastoral counseling.[61]

Apparently to her own surprise Kathryn Kuhlman (1907–1976), the last nationally known, twentieth-century woman evangelist, also worked in this tradition.[62] Mystery, contradictions, and ambiguities surround Kuhlman's utterances and her life. Unwilling to credit her mentors and role models and embarrassed about her marriage, she chose not to talk about much of her early career. About her age she was coyly secretive, and her reminiscences of her girlhood did not always tally with the record.

She was born in Concordia, Missouri. People who knew her as a child there have spoken of her dramatic gifts—"She should have been a movie star"—and her leadership and organizational skills. She was, she said, converted at fourteen in a little Methodist church, and in 1924 she left home to join her evangelist sister and brother-in-law on the tent-meeting circuit.

For years she itinerated, first with them, and then teamed up with Helen Gulliford, a more experienced young woman trained as a pianist at the University of Oregon and in scriptures at the Bible Institute of Los Angeles. Gulliford coached Kuhlman in her preaching and later found the team a business manager.[63] Billing themselves as "God's Girls," they thumbed rides and whistle-stopped across the Midwest, often penniless. "I had no money," remembered Kuhlman, who preferred to reminisce in the singular. "It was an event when I got fifteen cents to buy a pair of lisle stockings."[64] A red-headed, beautiful young girl, she attracted people, one preacher said, by "sex and salvation." The "girl evangelist," said Kuhlman, "has no easy time—I work as high as 18 hours a day. She must live in an atmosphere of ever watchful care, for there are so many eager to misjudge. She must always be smiling, happy, eager—the feminine relief of tears is denied her. . . . The life is no bed of roses."[65] God's Girls performed in little country churches that could not afford preachers and in abandoned opera houses.

They succeeded so well that in the thirties they were pastoring a two-thousand-seat redbrick Revival Tabernacle in Denver and running a radio program, while continuing to tour. Then, to the horror of her congregation and Gulliford, Kuhlman in 1938 married Burroughs Waltrip, a traveling evangelist who divorced his wife and deserted his two small children to marry Kuhlman. The marriage did not take: they were soon divorced, and Kuhlman's career was in ruins.

As she reported it, this catastrophe turned her life around:

> I had a sorrow, I had a heartbreak. I remember walking down a dead-end street and realizing that my life was a dead-end street. It was four o'clock on a Saturday afternoon. It was at that time and in that place that I surrendered myself fully to the Holy Spirit. There are some things too sacred to talk about. I will only say that in that moment, with tears streaming down my face, God and I made each other promises.[66]

She turned up again in the 1940s in Franklin, Pennsylvania, the scene of her first healing. As the story goes, one night in 1946 before Kuhlman began to preach a woman stood up and said that during Kuhlman's service the night before she had felt a strange bodily sensation and knew herself suddenly healed, an event confirmed by her physician.[67] Reports of this and successive miracles drew crowds, and the next year Kuhlman moved to Pittsburgh, her base of operations for the rest of her life. She rented the city's Carnegie Auditorium for two weeks that turned into twenty years, after which she moved her "miracle services" to the First Presbyterian Church in downtown Pittsburgh.

A woman of charm and obvious intelligence, who could learn from experience, she handled herself well. She lived more than comfortably, wearing beautiful clothes and furnishing her office with antiques. But she enjoyed a reputation for financial integrity, winning not only adulation from worshipful converts but support from the local Episcopalian bishop, the Roman Catholic mayor, and indeed the Pope himself. Although she liked to tell her staff, "You go against the enemy with the sword of the Lord and with Kathryn Kuhlman," they in fact were running a complex operation of daily radio broadcasts and weekly TV shows, of a worldwide radio ministry to Europe, North Africa, and Australia. The Kathryn Kuhlman Foundation not only supported all this but also dispensed charity to the needy, offered scholarships and student loans, supported a farm for the rehabilitation of drug addicts, and provided subsidies for twenty-two missionary school- and church-related institutions in foreign countries.[68]

Describing herself as one who merely carried a water bucket for the Lord, Kuhlman insisted that everything she did and said was by the inspiration of the Holy Spirit. "In the miracle services, when I walk out on that platform I die a thousand deaths. The longest walk I ever take is the walk from the wings to behind that pulpit. The reason I walk so fast is because I can hardly wait for the anointing of the Holy Spirit to come upon me."[69] Any Christian, she said, could do what she did if he would pay the price of "full surrender and yieldedness."

Ignoring a period at Simpson Bible Institute in Seattle and the advice and training of several evangelists, Kuhlman claimed that everything she knew came from observation: "For years I had a complex because I've got no degrees or seminary training. All I know is what I've learned as I've watched the Holy Spirit at work."[70] She skillfully sidestepped rousing the envy or ire of clergymen:

> You ministers, . . . remember, I'm really not a preacher. . . . When you think of Kathryn Kuhlman, I don't believe anyone thinks of me as a woman preacher—not really. I don't think of myself as a woman preacher—*never!* Nobody refers to me as Reverend Kuhlman. . . . And I don't think of myself in that light, believe me, because I can't preach. All that I know is that I'm somebody who loves the Lord with all my heart. . . . So if you've come here today to hear me preach a sermon, forget all about homiletecs [*sic*] . . . I don't even know what it means. I'm just here talking to you about the Lord and my own personal experiences."

But on other occasions she would announce, "If everybody in the world told me that as a woman I have no right to preach the Gospel, it would have no effect upon me whatsoever, because my call to the ministry was as definite as my conversion."[71]

Kuhlman's pronouncements about healing were almost equally conflicting. She found offputting the routines that McPherson and other healers used: "The long healing lines, filling out those cards, it was an insult to your intelligence."[72] Instead, standing in the pulpit she would proclaim, "Nothing is hopeless in the eyes of God. There is a woman being healed of cancer. Stand up! Claim your healing!" Or she would pray, "I rebuke that cancer in the mighty Name of Jesus." She was, she said, a mere bystander, only watching the healings. She eventually denied that a sufficiency of faith would ensure healing: she had, she said, seen too many nonbelievers cured, and too many believers go unhealed. "No, I do not know why all are not healed physically, but all *can* be healed spiritually, and that's the greatest miracle any human being can know."[73]

Although she was ordained by the Evangelical Church Alliance and considered herself a pentecostal, Kuhlman showed little interest in denominations. She built no church, founded no sect. Despite her disclaimers, she structured her ministry around healing, traveling hundreds of thousands of miles every year to hold her "miracle services," titling books *I Believe in Miracles, God Can Do It Again,* and *Nothing Is Impossible With God.*

For most of her career she was supported by many women, including Margaret Hartner, to whom she referred as her secretary-phone-answerer-letter-writer-fellow-minister. But Kuhlman did little to better the status of clergywomen. She did argue that everyone had the right to expect the same conditions as prevailed in early Christianity, when women preached, and insisted that "Christianity freed women from their subservient role. I could never see how women could reject Christ, because he gave dignity to women." But the self-protectiveness that caused her to deny that she herself was so much as a preacher precluded her from helping her fellow clergywomen. When a reporter for *Christianity Today* asked whether being a woman hampered her work, she answered:

> Let me bare my soul: I do not believe I was God's first choice in this ministry. Or even his second or third. This is really a man's job. I work hard, seventeen hours a day. I can outwork five men put together. I get little sleep. I stand at the pulpit four and a half hours at a time without sitting down once, and I can still leave the stage as refreshed as

when I walked on. . . . God's first choices were men. Someplace man failed. I was just stupid enough to say, "Take nothing and use it."[74]

In feminist terms, Kuhlman was a queen bee. Dispraise herself as she might, she saw to it that Kathryn Kuhlman was the cynosure at any service in which she participated, refusing to appear with other evangelists, using lights, organ fanfares, careful costuming, and theatrical entrances to focus attention on herself. Although she forbade prophesying, speaking in tongues, and other dramatic manifestations among her congregations, Kuhlman used the touch of her hands to render people "slain in the spirit"—falling prostrate at her feet. Whatever other miracles she may or may not have wrought, Kuhlman certainly worked one in creating her own ministry and fame at a time when elsewhere in the holiness and pentecostal movements clergywomen were in eclipse.

The history of clergywomen in America from the seventeenth century until 1960 records women struggling individually and usually in isolation. Despite an occasional effort in the late nineteenth and early twentieth centuries, such as the Iowa Sisterhood or the clergywomen's organizations founded by Madeline Southard and Julia Ward Howe, clergywomen were just too sparse on the ground for much mutual support. The denominational differences among them arbitrated against their networking with each other. The feminist movement of the nineteenth and early twentieth centuries, concentrated on abolition, temperance, and woman suffrage, paid little attention to the women trying to enter any of the professions and almost none at all to clergywomen. Organized church and synagogue laywomen seldom mounted campaigns for women's ordination, and laywomen were as apt as laymen to oppose clergywomen's appointments in their churches.

Thousands of women who might have served as clergywomen could not overcome the combination of societal disapproval, theological naysaying, and institutionalism. They veered away either into one of the channels churches opened to divert them from the ministry, or into secular work.

Came the 1960s.

Notes

1. Ruth A. Tucker and Walter Liefeld, *Daughters of the Church: Women and Ministry from New Testament Times to the Present* (Grand Rapids, Mich.: Zondervan, Academie Books, 1987), p. 288.

2. Letha Dawson Scanzoni and Susan Setta cite three major reasons for this pullback: (1) these churches had never offered women more than a limited equality, permitting them "prophetic" more often than "priestly" roles and insisting that the husband remain head of the household; (2) changes in the secular culture like women's voting and working outside the home alarmed these churches; and (3) they were concerned not to upset the established

order, in which women's place was in the home ("Women in Evangelical, Holiness, and Pentecostal Traditions," in *Women and Religion in America,* ed. Rosemary Radford Ruether and Rosemary Skinner Keller [San Francisco: Harper & Row, 1986], 3:233).

3. Della E. Olson, *A Woman of Her Times* (Minneapolis: Free Church, 1977), pp. 13–14.

4. Ibid., pp. 42–63, passim. Women's participation in preaching and teaching in the Free Church movement peaked just before and after 1900 (p. 77). Thereafter ordained women served in other capacities, usually as foreign missionaries.

5. Lucille Sider Dayton and Donald Dayton, "Women in the Holiness Movement" (prepared for the 106th Annual Convention of the Christian Holiness Ass'n, held in Louisville, Ky.), pp. 20–22. But, the Daytons note, "These women in the western Tennessee Nazarene conference were criticized severely and in 1905, 12 of them defended their right to preach in a book, *Women Preachers,* edited by Mrs. Fannie McDowell."

6. John W. V. Smith, *The Quest for Holiness and Unity: A Centennial History of the Church of God (Anderson, Indiana)* (Anderson, Ind.: Warner Press, 1980), p. 193.

7. Alice J. Dise, "Black Women in Ministry in the Church of God," in *Called to Minister . . . Empowered to Serve: Women in Ministry and Missions in the Church of God Reformation Movement,* ed. Juanita Leonard (Anderson, Ind.: Warner Press, 1989), pp. 60–62.

8. Dayton and Dayton, "Women in the Holiness Movement," p. 21.

9. Rebecca Laird, *Ordained Women in the Church of the Nazarene: The First Generation* (Kansas City, Mo.: Nazarene Pub., 1993), pp. 53ff.

10. Dise, "Black Women in Ministry," in *Called to Minister,* ed. Leonard, pp. 60–61.

11. For information on Crawford, see Tucker and Liefeld, *Daughters of the Church,* pp. 360–61.

12. Susie Cunningham Stanley, "Alma White: Holiness Preacher with a Feminist Message" (Ph.D. dissertation, Iliff School of Theology, Univ. of Denver, 1987), p. 2. See also Ferenc Morton Szasz, *The Protestant Clergy in the Great Plains and Mountain West, 1865–1915* (Albuquerque: Univ. of New Mexico Press, 1988); Tucker and Liefeld, *Daughters of the Church;* and Gertrude Metlen Wolfram, *The Widow of Zarephath: A Church in the Making* (Zarephath, N.J.: Pillar of Fire, 1954).

13. Stanley, "Alma White," pp. 27, 43.

14. Ibid., pp. 81–82.

15. Ibid., p. 114; and Tucker and Liefeld, *Daughters of the Church,* p. 369.

16. Stanley, "Alma White," pp. 101, 99, 332, and 194.

17. Tucker and Liefeld, *Daughters of the Church,* p. 370.

18. For McPherson's life, see Daniel Mark Epstein, *Sister Aimee: The Life of Aimee Semple McPherson* (New York: Harcourt Brace Jovanovich, 1993); and Edith L. Blumhofer, *Aimee Semple McPherson: Everybody's Sister* (Grand Rapids, Mich.: William B. Eerdmans, 1993). McPherson included her reminiscences in *This Is That: Personal Experiences, Sermons, and Writings* (Los Angeles: Echo Park Evangelistic Ass'n, 1923).

19. Blumhofer, *Aimee Semple McPherson,* pp. 6, 77; Epstein, *Sister Aimee,* p. 12.

20. During and since McPherson's lifetime many journalists and physicians have investigated the validity of the healings attributed to her, with the usual mixed results.

21. Blumhofer, *Aimee Semple McPherson,* p. 158.

22. Epstein, *Sister Aimee,* p. 220.

23. Blumhofer, *Aimee Semple McPherson,* p. 191.

24. Epstein, *Sister Aimee,* p. 242.

25. Ibid., p. 263. At the 1995 Pew conference on American religious history at Yale University Edith Blumhofer pointed out that other evangelists of both genders had similar encounters with the Ku Klux Klan.

26. Blumhofer, *Aimee Semple McPherson,* p. 318.

27. Epstein, *Sister Aimee,* p. 320.

28. Blumhofer, *Aimee Semple McPherson,* p. 144.

29. Quoted in *Women and Religion,* ed. Ruether and Keller, 3:245.

30. Blumhofer, *Aimee Semple McPherson,* p. 225.

31. Ibid., pp. 353–55.

32. Cheryl Townsend Gilkes, "'Together and in Harness': Women's Traditions in the Sanctified Church," *Signs* 10 (Summer 1985): 682–83.

33. Barbara Brown Zikmund, in *In Our Own Voices: Four Centuries of American Women's Religious Writing,* ed. Rosemary Skinner Keller and Rosemary Radford Ruether (San Francisco: HarperSanFrancisco, 1995), p. 305. See also C. Eric Lincoln and Lawrence H. Mamiya, *The Black Church in the African American Experience* (Durham, N.C.: Duke Univ. Press, 1990), p. 289.

34. Lincoln and Mamiya, *Black Church,* pp. 288–89.

35. See Lyle Saxon, Edward Driver, and Robert Tallant, *Gumbo Ya-Ya: A Collection of Louisiana Folk Tales* (1945; reprint, New York: Johnson, 1969). "A list of Spiritual congregations . . . indicates that there have been at least 175 in New Orleans over the years, and even though the names of pastors are incomplete or missing for 20, women led at least 60 percent of the total" (David C. Estes, "Ritual Validations of Clergywomen's Authority in the African American Spiritual Churches of New Orleans," in *Women's Leadership in Marginal Religions: Explorations Outside the Mainstream,* ed. Catherine Wessinger [Urbana: Univ. of Illinois Press, 1993], p. 150).

36. *Guide to the Transcripts of the Black Women Oral History Project,* ed. Ruth Edmonds Hill and Patricia Miller King (Cambridge, Mass.: Schlesinger Library, 1991), p. 108.

37. "From 1930 to 1980 the movement of black and white women into the professional ministry has increased 240 percent. But, according to [Delores] Carpenter, the number of black women graduates from accredited theological seminaries increased 676 percent from 1972 to 1984" (Lincoln and Mamiya, *Black Church,* p. 288).

38. *Woman's Pulpit* (April 1923).

39. *Woman's Pulpit* (Jan.-Feb.-Mar. 1986).

40. Uldine Utley, *Why I Am A Preacher: A Plain Answer to an Oft-Repeated Question* (1931; reprint, New York: Garland, 1987), pp. 49ff.

41. *Life and Work of Mary Lee Cagle: An Autobiography* (Kansas City, Mo.: Nazarene Pub. House, 1928), p. 85; and Laird, *Ordained Women,* p. 114.

42. Margaret M. Poloma, *Assemblies of God at the Crossroads: Charisma and Institutional Dilemmas* (Knoxville: Univ. of Tennessee Press, 1989), p. 101.

43. Nilah Meier-Youngman, "Hispanic Women in Ministry in the Church of God," in *Called to Minister,* ed. Leonard, p. 68.

44. Jeanette Hassey, *No Time for Silence: Evangelical Women in Public Ministry Around the Turn of the Century* (Grand Rapids, Mich.: Academie Books, 1986), pp. 5, 140.

45. Betty A. DeBerg, *Ungodly Women: Gender and the First Wave of American Fundamentalism* (Minneapolis: Fortress Press, 1990), p. 79, citing "Why Women in the Pulpit?" *Our Hope* (May 1930): 651.

46. Poloma, *Assemblies of God,* p. 275n.

47. Elaine J. Lawless, *Handmaidens of the Lord: Pentecostal Women Preachers and Traditional Religion* (Philadelphia: Univ. of Pennsylvania Press, 1988), pp. 149, 164.

48. Margaret Lamberts Bendroth, *Fundamentalism and Gender: 1875 to the Present* (New Haven, Conn.: Yale Univ. Press, 1994), chapter 4, n. 19.

49. DeBerg, *Ungodly Women,* p. 124, citing an unsigned article, "The New Woman," *Truth, or, Testimony for Christ* 22 (July 1896): 369–70.

50. On the life of Evangeline Booth, see P. Whitwell Wilson, *General Evangeline Booth of the Salvation Army* (New York: Charles Scribner's Sons, 1948); Victoria Booth Demarest, *God, Woman and Ministry* (St. Petersburg, Fla.: Sacred Arts Int'l and Valkyrie Press, 1978); and especially Margaret Troutt, *The General Was a Lady: The Story of Evangeline Booth* (Nashville: A. J. Holman, 1980).

51. Troutt, *General,* p. 29.

52. Ibid., p. 183.

53. Ibid., pp. 154–59; and Dorothy Schneider and Carl J. Schneider, *Into the Breach: American Women Overseas in World War I* (New York: Viking, 1991), pp. 121–39.

54. Troutt, *General,* p. 174.

55. Ibid., p. 181.

56. *The Honeycomb,* quoted by Troutt, *General,* p. 222.

57. Troutt, *General,* p. 238.

58. Ibid., pp. 228–29.

59. *Woman,* quoted in *Women and Religion,* ed. Ruether and Keller, 3:257–58.

60. Troutt, *General,* pp. 149, 240.

61. Allen Spraggett, *Kathryn Kuhlman: The Woman Who Believes in Miracles* (New York: World Pub. Co., 1970), p. 67. See also David E. Harrell, Jr., *All Things Are Possible: The Healing and Charismatic Revivals in Modern America* (Bloomington: Indiana Univ. Press, 1975).

62. For Kuhlman's life, see Harrell, *All Things;* Helen Kooiman Hosier, *Kathryn Kuhlman: The Life She Led, The Legacy She Left* (Old Tappan, N.J.: Fleming H. Revell, 1976); Spraggett, *Kathryn Kuhlman;* and Wayne Warner, *Kathryn Kuhlman: The Woman Behind the Miracles* (Ann Arbor, Mich.: Servant, 1993), by far the best of the lot. See also William A. Nolen, *Healing: A Doctor in Search of a Miracle* (New York: Random House, 1974).

63. Warner, *Kathryn Kuhlman,* p. 57.

64. Hosier, *Kathryn Kuhlman,* p. 134.

65. *Detroit News Pictorial,* Nov. 28, 1937, quoted by Warner, *Kathryn Kuhlman,* p. 49.

66. Spraggett, *Kathryn Kuhlman,* p. 135.

67. Ibid., p. 136. Harrell notes that healing ministries flourished particularly from 1947 to 1958; during that period several charismatic evangelists established independent ministries and, unlike Billy Sunday, Dwight Moody, and Billy Graham, emphasized healing (*All Things,* pp. 8ff.). After 1958 evangelism turned toward teaching rather than healing, as miracles and frauds became too commonplace, but by 1970 healers had again surfaced. In that year, for instance, Roxanne Brant (b. 1953) became president of the Outreach for Christ Foundation, headquartered in Orlando, advocating a ministry where "the sovereign and unpredictable Spirit of God falls upon certain individuals and sections of the audience, healing people in their seats as their physical problems are called out through the gift of the 'word of knowledge.'" Brant conducted seminars and inaugurated a radio series (Harrell, *All Things,* p. 188, citing "Introducing the Ministries of the Outreach for Christ Foundation," *Logos Journal* [Sept.-Oct. 1971]: 31).

68. Hosier, *Kathryn Kuhlman,* p. 104. Kuhlman's will provided for about a quarter of a million to family members and twenty employees and left all the rest to Tink and Sue Wilkerson, making no provision at all for the Foundation. In 1992 Tink Wilkerson was convicted of fraud (Warner, *Kathryn Kuhlman,* p. 242).

69. Spraggett, *Kathryn Kuhlman,* p. 136.

70. Ibid., p. 134; and Warner, *Kathryn Kuhlman,* p. 34.

71. Hosier, *Kathryn Kuhlman,* pp. 45–46.

72. "Miracle Woman," *Time* (Sept. 14, 1970): 62. Warner describes some of the techniques that Kuhlman deplored (*Kathryn Kuhlman,* pp. 136–40).

73. Hosier, *Kathryn Kuhlman,* pp. 133, 119, 111.

74. *Women and Religion,* ed. Ruether and Keller, 3:242–43.

7 ———————————————————————————

Second Wave Feminism—
in Church and Temple
1960- 🖎

THE WOMEN'S MOVEMENT of the 1960s and 1970s burst on the world, and particularly on the United States, with the accumulated force of almost half a century. Women in 1960 of course looked, acted, and thought of themselves differently from women in 1920, when the first woman's rights movement subsided, but they hadn't been talking much about the changes they had been undergoing, either among themselves or more publicly, and in truth many had not been thinking much about them. A lot of them, by force of economic necessity and/or their own volition, had departed from the life-styles of their mothers and certainly of their grandmothers. Society had bought into the concept that educating women was a good idea, usually on the dubious grounds that education would make them better wives and mothers, all too often without forethought about the effects of education on women themselves and on their ideas about their own roles.

As in the nineteenth century abolitionism spawned the woman suffrage movement, so in the latter half of the twentieth century the civil rights movement gave rise to the women's liberation movement—in both cases by inadvertence. Exactly as nineteenth-century women fighting for the freedom of African-Americans became aware of their own oppression, so with twentieth-century women. Moreover, the civil rights struggle pricked the consciences of a good many churchmen and sensitized them to other forms of deprivation and exclusion. As Sue Hiatt has remarked, "The Philadelphia ordinations [of the first Episcopalian clergywomen] wouldn't have been possible without the civil rights movement."[1]

In 1963 millions responded to the ideas of Betty Friedan's *Feminine Mystique* with that shock of recognition that marks authenticity. Whether or not they read Friedan's book, whether or not they formed consciousness-raising groups, whether or not they joined the National Organization for Women, all sorts of women set about reconnoitering their own positions and resetting their compasses.

Women rediscovered the pleasures and profits of associating with other women and of working in groups familiar to their foremothers from 1880 to 1920 in organizations like the Women's Christian Temperance Union, the General Federation of Women's Clubs, and the National American Woman Suffrage Association. In the interim men who had considered it good sport to derogate women and women's activities had so frequently jeered at women's groups as time-wasting, incompetent, trivial, and gossipy that many women had withdrawn from them. In the 1960s and 1970s they strengthened existing organizations dedicated to improving women's opportunities, like the American Association of University Women, and founded a bewildering array of new ones both general in purpose and specific to particular occupations.

In the academy, women scholars zestily undertook to rewrite history and to refashion their own disciplines, asking, in Carolyn Heilbrun's words, What happens if we place women at the center? Their answers are still rattling academic bones, but they have forced even the *New York Times* to change its language, even the most recalcitrant defenders of the traditional canon to acknowledge the existence of women.

Perhaps above all else the women's movement has rescued women from isolation—within the home, within suburbia, within their own thoughts—and from exclusion—from business, from politics, from sports, from the professions. Late in the twentieth century, black women have developed womanism, criticizing the feminist movement for racism, criticizing the civil rights movement for sexism, and adding their concerns about class.

Unlike the woman's movement of the early twentieth century, the movement of the sixties questioned not just woman's rights but also woman's role. The first movement had argued that women needed the vote to do what society said women were supposed to do: keep their husbands virtuous and bear and raise healthy, virtuous children. The second said women might do things other than what society prescribed. Accordingly, the first movement changed relatively little what women thought about themselves in relation to religion, while the second revolutionized the thinking of both laywomen and clergywomen about themselves in relation to church and synagogue and ultimately about the nature of religion itself, right down to its theology.[2]

For to change woman's role in society required a change in society, and changing her role in religion inevitably changed religion. Thus in 1960 Valerie Saiving Goldstein in "The Human Situation" challenged Reinhold Niebuhr's assertion that "man's greatest sins are pride and lack of obedience," arguing that these may be sins of men but can only be virtues for women crippled by overdoses of humility and compliance. Women might rather be condemned for "triviality, distractibility, and diffuseness; lack of an organizing center or focus; dependence on others for one's own self-definition . . . in short, underdevelopment or negation of the self."[3] In 1837 Harriet Martineau had warned that assigning separate virtues to women and to men suggested the necessity of separate gospels for the two genders.[4] In the late nineteenth century Elizabeth Cady Stanton and Matilda Joslyn Gage, "addressing women in particular . . . repudiated self-sacrifice as a theological and moral good (and one that was, in practice, urged selectively along gender lines) and promoted self-development instead."[5] Now Goldstein was similarly implying that establishment theology had interpreted the gospel for men only, without regard to women's realities. Women were rejecting the authority of religious patriarchies in favor of their own consciences, values, and experience.

Therefore the American Academy of Religion sprouted a women's caucus and theological schools started women's centers and courses on women and religion. Nuns left their orders, women flooded into seminaries and pulpits, laywomen demanded votes and voices in religious assemblies, and Roman Catholic laywomen flouted the teachings of their church about birth control. All these were backed up by the general defiance of authority that was characteristic of the sixties.

Just as this defiance found universities and colleges particularly vulnerable because they are dedicated to examining and reexamining truth, so also with churches and synagogues. As Nelle Morton writes, "The theologians and the religious institutions say how necessary it is to examine faith again and again in each generation, in each new phase of our social order, to remain faithful to that with which they have been entrusted."[6] Transforming religious institutions and changing theology became not just a wish, not just self-serving, but a duty.

Like the American military, many religious authorities have made the resultant crisis and process of change more damaging to everyone, including themselves, by desperately clinging to the patriarchal mode. The military may indeed have accepted change more readily than religious institutions because it is more susceptible to political pressures, its manpower shortage came earlier, and the decline of quality in its manpower supply was publicized by the media.[7]

Ironically enough, at least until the 1990s and even now, the contemporary women's movement has paid little attention to clergywomen. No clergywoman, no modern-day Lucretia Mott or Anna Howard Shaw has been recognized as a leader of the movement. Even though clergywomen are doing jobs traditionally regarded as men's work outside religious circles, they have received neither the sympathy nor the scrutiny awarded policewomen, women engineers, women construction workers, women miners, and academic women. Even today many feminists do not know that advanced clergywomen have advocated the destruction of patriarchal theology; many more clergywomen have confronted the patriarchal church hierarchy and won; and almost all clergywomen until very recently have had to refute the doctrine and/or deny the authority of their institutions in order to respond to the "call" that they recognize as from God.

Rather, like women in the military up until the time of the Gulf War, clergywomen have been ignored or derogated by feminists as having been suborned into a patriarchal, hierarchical, authoritarian institution. In Sara Maitland's words, the women's movement analyzed the historical record of the church and decided that "'The Church is the Enemy'—the perfected tool for the oppression and subjugation of women."[8] Somehow the evil perpetrated by religious institutions that many see as having victimized women rubs off onto clergywomen: they are found guilty of contributing to the perpetuation of patriarchy and/or of cooperating in the exploitation of their sex and themselves.

Perhaps also secular feminists have not recognized a major alteration in religious ideals. In the spirit of the sixties and of feminism, many clergy, women and men, were changing their theology and their concept of their own roles by reworking ideas of what good Christians or Jews owed to God and their community and what to themselves. In the theology of the nineteenth and early twentieth centuries, self-denial was *a*, perhaps *the* Christian virtue, especially for women: language such as "dying to the self" and "being born again in the Spirit" reflected the meanings of not merely doing without, being un*self*ish, sacrificing for others, but of denying one's own selfhood. Jewish theology stressed the duty that women owed to their menfolk over the development of their own religious natures. In the sixties self-advocacy and self-nurture modified or replaced self-denial. Specifically, the justification runs that no clergyperson can adequately serve the community without tending to her/his own mental and spiritual health. Now divinity schools teach prospective clergy the importance of support groups, weekly days off, vacations, and sabbaticals.

All the same, even before or without recognizing the feminism of many clergywomen, the second women's movement has enormously benefited them. Like other women, they raised their consciousness and learned assertiveness. They began to understand the importance to minorities of a critical mass, of networking, and of support systems. People of conscience within the church and especially within the hierarchy, alerted by feminist discussions, took thought not only for women's right to ordination but also for their well-being thereafter.

Unlike almost all other women, however, clergywomen did not directly benefit from the new legislation and the court cases designed to attain equality for women in the workplace. Constitutional separation of church and state meant for clergywomen that they could seldom call on the state for protection of their rights as workers. One clergywoman, Mary Wilson Murphy, did successfully sue in 1993 to overturn a governmental agency regulation requiring military chaplains to be ordained, which closed the chaplaincy to women from denominations that refused to ordain them. Murphy held a master's degree from a Roman Catholic seminary and was working on a doctorate from Notre Dame; she was the widow of two veterans, each of whom had died of service-connected disabilities. She had already served as the Roman Catholic chaplain of a state prison. But despite her court victory she didn't get the job: the military no longer requires ordination but still requires an endorsement from the denomination, which the denomination would not give her.[9]

On the other hand, the admission of other women to the military chaplaincy illustrates the way that the opening of traditionally male jobs to women helped clergywomen. After the Civil War no woman was commissioned a military chaplain again until 1972. Apparently no woman applied in World War I, although the Salvation Army women were in many ways performing the duties of chaplains. In World War II Eleanor Gertrude Collie, an ordained Universalist minister, circumvented a Congressional ruling that barred the chaplaincy to women by getting a commission in the Women's Army Corps (WAC), which assigned her on special duty to the Chaplains' Corps. Though she was not allowed to wear chaplain's insignia and could have been reassigned, she did in fact perform all the duties of a chaplain.[10] The American Association of Women Ministers and other clergywomen lobbied for women chaplains, with little support from clergymen; the War Department countered that not enough servicewomen were based in any one place to justify appointing a woman chaplain, but said that their tables of organization called for a Women's Army Corps chaplain's clerk to act as librarian in larger installations.[11]

After the war military women worked persistently by lobbying and by resorting to the courts to move themselves from auxiliary forces to the regular military, to open more military jobs to women, and to claim their rightful benefits. Accordingly, the 1970s brought women into the several chaplains' corps. In 1973 the Navy commissioned the first full-fledged woman chaplain since the Civil War, Florence D. Pohlman, a graduate of Princeton Divinity School, though the Civil Air Patrol, an auxiliary of the Air Force, had accepted women chaplains in the 1960s.[12] Also in 1973 American Baptist Lorraine Potter became the first female chaplain in the Air Force.[13]

The next year the Army commissioned Alice M. Henderson Harris of the African Methodist Episcopal (AME) church. When she decided to become a minister, she had changed from the Baptist to the AME church "because they had a more progressive attitude toward female ministers." Not all that progressive—Harris's homiletics professor at Turner thought that she would settle for marrying a minister and protested that he could not grade a woman. When on graduation she received no assignment to a church, she turned to the military, not realizing that the Army had no other women chaplains.[14] In 1980 Rabbi Bonnie J. Koppel became the army's first Jewish woman chaplain when she was commissioned a second lieutenant in the reserves,[15] although not until 1992, when Rabbi Chana Timoner went on active duty in the army, did the military enjoy the service of a full-time Jewish woman chaplain.

Chaplain (Lieutenant) Pohlman's earlier clerical career illustrates one reason that opening the chaplaincy was a boon for clergywomen. It showed a familiar pattern: minister of music, interim supply, advisor for youth, lay leader. While the military certainly is not always an equal opportunity employer, it does award equal pay for equal rank and it does afford possibilities of promotion—advantages that Pohlman and most other clergywomen did not and do not enjoy in civilian life. What's more, as one Presbyterian Air Force lieutenant colonel told us, military life offers clergywomen, particularly single clergywomen, an opportunity for friendships among peers (their fellow officers) and social experiences denied them as civilians. The life is varied and adventurous. One day may find the chaplain down at the flight line, pastoring to the pilots before takeoff; the next may see her on her way to Sicily, where a startled Italian will passionately deny the possibility of a female priest. A former peace activist and civil rights worker, the lieutenant colonel has come to terms with the military: "These folks need ministering to like everyone else."

Indeed, as one Episcopalian Navy chaplain told us:

> To me, the chaplaincy is the greatest missionary field. Not to proselytize [which is forbidden], but to be with people. Who in a parish or in a church are with the people all the time? When you go to sea you're living with these people for six months. They are being exposed—God willing—to the grace of God. If they want to be agnostic, that's OK, but you're still living and working with them. You are an integral part of the whole system. They're seeing you at three in the morning if you're up working with them then. In a parish you might know what somebody does for a job, but you're not standing there watching them on the assembly line or being with them in the same conditions.

What's more, in a way this is a virgin field. She continued:

> When I came in about twelve years ago, I'd ask somebody who came to see me, "Do you go to any particular church?" And they'd say, "Well, I don't, but my parents were raised Methodist." But these days, I'll ask a Marine or a sailor the same question. "Don't go to church." "OK. Where did your parents go?" "Oh, my parents didn't go to church." I've had on more than one occasion a sailor or Marine literally walk in to a service for the first time in his or her life. So if you're preaching and you're saying something about St. Paul's letter to the Romans, you might as well be speaking Chinese. "What is holy communion? What's this bread and this wine we got going here?" They don't have a clue. You have to be broad enough to know that you might be preaching to some devout Episcopalian who has always gone to church and the sailor or Marine in the back is there for the first time in his or her life.

✐ Ordination

Of more than two hundred Protestant denominations, about a third had already begun to ordain women before 1965. Among them by 1976 they had about ten thousand ordained women, about 5 percent of clergy. These women were distributed unevenly over the ordaining denominations, with the Salvation Army accounting for about a quarter and pentecostal and holiness churches, many of them black, for another quarter.[16]

In the 1970s, with more churches beginning to ordain and more acceptance of clergywomen, women flocked to the theological seminaries. From 1972 to 1980 female enrollments increased 223 percent against 31 percent for males; female enrollments in ordination degree programs increased 241 percent.[17] In some denominations the gains for women students were even more dramatic: in the Master of Divinity programs at American Baptist church seminaries, for instance, the numbers of enrolled men increased by 9 percent from 1970 to 1980, the numbers of enrolled women by 597 percent. At the same time enrollments fell off in programs leading to the Master of Religious Education and Master of Arts in Divinity, which had formerly attracted women. These figures do not hold, however, for predominantly black seminaries, where during this decade the enrollment of both genders in Master of Divinity programs increased substantially, that of males by 47 percent and that of women by 317 percent.[18]

Theological faculties too were changing. In 1971 seminaries employed only seventy-three full-time female faculty (3.2 percent of the total) and 104 part-time (6.9 percent). By 1980 they had 195 full-time women (7.9 percent) and 386 part-timers (16.3 percent). In 1971 they counted 103 women among their administrative personnel (12.2 percent) and in 1980 193 (18.8 percent).[19]

Even when the numbers of women students reached a critical mass, male professors and students often had trouble adjusting to their presence. As always when schools go co-ed, some male students fought against the decision by attacking individual women. "Some of the seminary students," writes Henrietta T. Wilkinson, "invited college women on dates to 'elevate the girls spiritually.' One of these men invited me to eat at the seminary and to go to student preaching with him. I accepted out of curiosity, and found that his purpose was to let me know that as the newly elected president of the college student body, I was on their prayer list. He let me know that the prayer had to do with their serious doubts about the value of my influence on the students. He cooled my incipient desire to go to seminary."[20] Rev. Barbara Ruth reported an incident in a Methodist seminary in which a professor illustrated two ways to experience God, joyfully and painfully: "Joy is like a perfumed woman who approaches you in a dark room and suddenly kisses you," adding that women could substitute for the perfumed woman a man with shaving lotion. All Ruth's explanations could not make her professor or classmates understand that "a man with shaving lotion approaching me in a dark room would scare me to death."[21] An Army chaplain who had started out in the military as an enlisted woman and become an officer—a challenging achievement—told us: "Honestly, I think it was tougher going to theological school [in 1980] than it was in the Army."

At Princeton a male administrator told Willa B. Roghair that she must drop out of the seminary to put her husband and fellow student through.[22] Even in the 1980s her years at Princeton Theological Seminary could rob a woman of her self-esteem and undermine her faith in the institutional church. "I came out of college an activist, a strong, confident feminist," one alumna told us. "I had been part of significant changes in services for women there. We tried to do the same thing at seminary: we did attempt to tack theses on the seminary doors, but we were always defeated. It was just so entrenched, and we couldn't make any real changes."

But of course women students did make real changes, even when they had to wait a while to see them. "As a student I was innocent and naïve," a rabbi told us.

> I didn't even imagine the seminary would have to change to accommodate me, that I would make contributions that would encourage the seminary to change. Every now and then they would say things in class, like "You shouldn't be here." One professor

said we were making him a sinner because he thought ordaining women a sin. I didn't put much stock in that. I had a practical approach: "I'm here. I won. You can vent all you want and I will graciously listen. Then just give me my grade and let me go."

In this period as earlier, women with earned degrees as Masters of Divinity still faced problems in getting ordained and finding a job. These problems were aggravated for minority clergywomen. Mrs. Mitchell of the National Baptist Convention USA, the largest African-American denomination, could find no church in Los Angeles to ordain her, though she held both a Master of Arts and a Doctor of Ministry; finally an Oakland church agreed to sponsor her, and she and her husband found jobs together at a theological seminary.[23] Perla Dirige Belo, the first Filipina ordained in her Methodist denomination, felt that she was ignored in staff meetings because she is a minority member; the senior pastor told her, "Your position as assistant pastor is only on paper, just a legality since we wanted you ordained." She hesitated to seek another job, "fearing to face the desire of white churches to call a white pastor, and the preference of ethnic churches for a male minister."[24] Jung Mi Han, the first Korean woman ordained by the Presbyterian Church (USA), suffered from the blatant sexism of Korean culture transmitted to the Korean-American church in which she served as assistant to the pastor: a Presbyterian Church in America minister, furious because she argued with him, yelled, "Korean pastors in Korea would not even sit with *chundosa* [assistants] at the same table. How dare you!"[25]

Just as the spadework done in the 1940s and 1950s by military women had paid off in the 1960s and 1970s in more opportunities and more equitable treatment for military women, so with the work done by women in the mainline churches, particularly the church hierarchies, to gain ordination and open seminaries and pulpits to women. With more women seminary graduates knocking on their doors, churches found it more and more difficult not to answer. The last two major mainline Protestant denominations, Lutherans and Episcopalians, capitulated on the issue of ordination for women in the 1970s. In both instances the process was affected by denominational ties to European churches.

European Lutherans set an example for Americans by approving the ordination of women in the 1960s. Among American Lutherans, the Lutheran Church of America led the way in 1970, but the staunchly conservative Missouri Synod Lutherans still refuse to follow, although some synods within the Association of Evangelical Lutheran Churches, a breakaway group from the Missouri Synod, have voted to ordain women.[26]

The dramatic struggle over the issue within the Episcopal church caught the attention of the nation. Never have so many religious leaders and churchmen written and argued so much about so few. Although in such a passionate debate it's hard to estimate their real weight, theoretically Episcopalians faced two complications: their ties to international Anglicanism and the priestly tradition of Catholicism. The mere idea of ordaining women repelled those high-church Episcopalians who still dream of reunion with Rome.

Some Episcopalian clergywomen trace their spiritual foremothers back to the mid-nineteenth century:

> In America, the first ordinations of Episcopal women took place in 1845, without legal sanction by canon law and without precedent. The Episcopal General Convention of 1889 acknowledged and approved the existence of the Order of Deaconesses in the Protestant Episcopal Church in the United States of America many years after the fact.[27]

In the Episcopal tradition members of the diaconate are pastoral ministers, whereas priests are sacramental ministers. But many Episcopalians found it difficult to think of deaconesses as ministers at all. They were, of course, treated differently from male deacons, even after the 1920 Lambeth Conference of Anglican Bishops declared them fully ordained clergy within holy orders—a statement withdrawn in 1930. Usually deaconesses were posted where men were loath to go—to Appalachia, to Indian reservations, to rural ghettos, and to urban slums. Nor, unlike most male deacons, could they expect ordination as priests. But in ordaining deaconesses Episcopalians had nonetheless set foot on a slippery slope. (A slippery slope for some is a window of opportunity for others.)

Slowly and reluctantly, other steps followed. In 1935 a joint Anglican commission allowed that it could find no compelling reason either to ordain women or not to ordain them but upheld the restriction of the priesthood to men for the time being. During World War II the bishop of Hong Kong ordained a woman as priest—presumably because of a shortage of male candidates. But in 1948 the Lambeth Convention voted down for twenty years a proposal for an experimental ordination of women priests. Then in 1958 the Episcopal Theological School in Cambridge, Massachusetts, began to admit women to programs that trained candidates for the ordained ministry. The decision prepared a group of highly qualified women to spearhead the movement for women's ordination.

Next in 1965 maverick Bishop James Pike of California sowed the wind by formally recognizing deaconess Phyliss Edwards as a deacon. In an effort to quiet the resultant whirlwind, the American House of Bishops resorted to the tried and true ploy of appointing another study committee on the issue. That committee lobbed the question to the Lambeth Convention of 1968, which sent it right back to the national churches. So the 1970 convention in Houston, now for the first time including laywomen as delegates, no longer able to duck the issue, voted down priesthood for women—but approved their ordination to the diaconate. In 1971 Suzanne Hiatt became the first woman so ordained.

By this time a lot of people were lined up to support women's ordination. The Episcopal Women's Caucus formed in 1971 with a membership of laywomen, deacons, and seminarians prioritized the issue. Its steering committee later merged with Priests for the Ministry of the Church into the National Committee for the Ordination of Women to the Priesthood. Some male deacons selflessly refused ordination to the priesthood until it was granted to women. Inevitably positions rigidified on the other side, the heated rhetoric revealing interesting motivations. George Rutler declared that the main job of a priest "is to be a *man* at the altar."[28] A priest asked, "How would you react to the presence of a pregnant woman in the pulpit? Giving absolution? How would you, the reader—male or female—react to the sight of a beautiful long-haired woman celebrating the Eucharist? Attractive, yes, but also distracting."[29]

The 1973 convention in Louisville tried again—only to have the will of its majority defeated by parliamentary maneuvering, even though by then the Anglican Consultative Council had given permission for individual dioceses to proceed with the ordination of women. The Louisville decision bitterly disappointed the several scores of ordained women deacons, who had taken the 1970 Houston convention's endorsement of women in the diaconate "on the same basis as men" as a signal that priesthood was just around the corner. One woman deacon pleaded with her bishop: "Oh, I could wait until the General Convention gives me permission to be who I am. I could wait, and I might. But, Bishop, when this permission is someday given and you ordain me to the priesthood, you'll be ordaining only a shell. Because by then, through these years of disobedience to God on my part, I will have lost my soul."[30]

On December 15, 1973, five women deacons, all fully qualified for priesthood, presented themselves at an ordination ceremony for five male deacons, asking for ordination at the same time; when it was refused they walked out of the cathedral, weeping, followed by a third of the congregation.[31] In desperation, advocates began to consider alternative means. Professors and priests challenged individual bishops to ordain women on their own authority—even as the American House of Bishops moved to prevent them. Women candidates, strongly supported by some Episcopalian priests and by many of the laity, finally decided on a *coup d'église.*

On July 29, 1974, the feast of Mary and Martha, at the Church of the Advocate in Philadelphia, Bishops Daniel Corrigan, Robert DeWitt, and Edward Welles ordained as priests eleven women deacons: Merrill Bittner, Alla Bozarth-Campbell, Alison Check, Emily Hewitt, Carter Heyward, Suzanne Hiatt, Marie Moorefield, Jeanette Piccard, Betty Schiess, Katrina Swanson, and Nancy Wittig.[32] All of them had much to lose. The ordinands risked their careers because their own bishops and standing committees had not approved their ordination. The bishops, all retired, risked their reputations, friendships, and whatever peace they might have hoped for in their old age. But each of them perceived a duty not only to women but also to their church. In Nancy Wittig's words: "It is time for the church to move and to be changed, and if there is any way that I can have a part of it, that is what my responsibility is."[33] At their ordination Bishop Welles affirmed that responsibility: "If you're not any different from the men (priests), then I've wasted my time."[34]

They celebrated in a triumphal service attended by a congregation of almost two thousand people. Many in attendance saw in it an acknowledgment of their own calls to the priesthood. In his welcome, the rector of the host church remarked that if an obstetrician tells a woman that she will give birth on August 15 and the baby arrives on July 29, the woman and the baby are right, not the physician; then he announced the opening hymn, "Come Labor On." During a period set aside in the service for those who wished to protest, an angry young priest shook his fist at the ordaining bishops, shouting, "Sirs, you will never again be called bishops, for today you violate the law of God that says *his* priests shall be called *Father.* . . . Today you break the bond between Adam and Eve."[35]

The ensuing storm of theological disputes did little but vent emotions and create misery. More "irregular" ordinations of women followed. Ultimately the accomplished fact carried the day, and in 1976 the General Convention at Minneapolis approved the ordination of women. Some women by this time doubted the benefit of being admitted to the priesthood of an institution that had for so long rejected women, but for others the decision occasioned pure joy. Peggy Bosmyer, called to St. Michael's Mission in Little Rock in 1974, two years before the convention approved women's ordination, wrote:

> Coming home from the Minneapolis Convention, I flew into the Little Rock Airport. And a huge crowd of people were there in the airport waiting area, with iced champagne and a huge sign, ALLELUIA, that went all across the front of the terminal. The whole lobby was just packed with people; Episcopalians cheering, and Roman Catholics too. Someone told us the Roman Catholic nuns had been praying for us all through the convention. Everybody in the airplane was going, "Wow, look at that! What's happening?" And we said, "The Episcopal Church just voted to ordain women." I was so proud to be an Episcopalian.[36]

Ordination for women did not precipitate for Episcopalians the dire consequences foreseen by the naysayers. By early 1978 only sixteen Episcopal congregations had voted to secede, taking with them fifty priests out of nearly thirteen thousand. This schism—if schism it may be called on so minor a scale—resulted in the Anglican Church of North America, which would not accept women priests; it has since divided into five separate churches, who number altogether about fifteen thousand communicants, or less than half of one percent of Episcopalians.[37]

Instead of schism, most opponents of women's ordination resorted to obstructionism. In 1977 the House of Bishops affirmed the right of individual bishops not to ordain women. All this backing and filling continued to occasion legalistic dodges. In Chicago, for example, the diocesan bishop would not himself ordain women but allowed his suffragan to do so. The next year the Standing Committee there refused to endorse women candidates but agreed to "backdoor" ordinations for them whereby women recommended by the Chicago bishop were sent to other dioceses for ordination and eventually transferred back to Chicago—a process at once inconvenient and demeaning for the clergywomen involved.[38]

In 1994 the Episcopal Women's Caucus decided to seek remedies. "If conscience prohibits one from applying the canons equally, one must *in conscience* decline to serve," wrote Carol Cole Flanagan. "After 124 years of dialogue on the role of women in the church, and 18 years of accommodation, enough is enough. It is time to implement the canon."[39] The presiding bishop asked for a year's grace, apparently in the hope that in another twelve months the church could resolve the dilemma it had failed to unknot for the past eighteen years—how to enforce its own law that the provisions of the ordination canons "shall be equally applicable to men and women" and still salve the consciences of dissenting bishops. The caucus reluctantly assented. The designated committee considered such alternatives as transferring a woman candidate from a noncomplying diocese to an "assisting diocese," the candidate to bear all costs and penalties, perhaps having to uproot her family; or setting up concurrent jurisdictions in which a provincial bishop would act on behalf of the diocesan bishop who could not bring himself to ordain a woman. On September 30, 1995, despite the threats of a dissenting bishop to "become a thorn in the flesh of this Protestant sect," Episcopal bishops voted 121 to 15 to compel all bishops to permit the ordination of female priests in their dioceses; however, the decision must be formalized at the 1997 convention.[40]

Whatever the reasoning of the opponents, its clergywomen have immeasurably enriched the Episcopalian church. Consider the remarkable Pauli Murray (1910–1985), who justly laid claim to being a "black activist, feminist, lawyer, priest, and poet." She had every reason to rage against the Episcopalian church in which she had been brought up. When she was a child in Croom, Maryland, the white Episcopal church would not permit her to cross its threshold. In her fifties, an attorney and an outstanding figure in the civil rights movement, she recognized that the church forbade her to preside at the Eucharist because she was a woman:

> I remember only that in the middle of the celebration of the Holy Eucharist an uncontrollable anger exploded inside me, filling me with such rage I had to get up and leave. I wandered about the streets full of blasphemous thought, feeling alienated from God. The intensity of this assault at the deepest level of my devotional life produced a crisis in faith. I had been taught all my life to revere the church and its teachings; now I could only condemn the church as sinful when it denied me the right to participate as fully and freely in the worship of God as my brethren. If the present church customs were justified, then I did not belong in the church and it became a stumbling block to faith.[41]

Yet in 1973 Murray resigned her tenured professorship at Brandeis to enter seminary as a candidate for holy orders. On the day in 1976 when the Episcopal church assembly approved the ordination of women, she celebrated her first Eucharist in the chapel building where her grandmother Cordelia, the daughter of a slave raped by a white man, was baptized. Early in 1977 she was ordained at the National Cathedral in Washington, D.C., by a bishop who had refused to ordain anyone until the church approved women's ordination.

Roman Catholicism

Roman Catholics, priests and laity alike, watched the struggle over women's ordination in the Episcopal church with special interest and with attention to its implications for Roman Catholicism.[42] Ties between the two churches have remained close in theology and ritual. Disaffected communicants move from the Roman Catholic faith to the Episcopalian, and vice versa.[43]

Hopes for women's ordination to the priesthood have flourished at least as long among Roman Catholics as among Anglicans. The "irregularly" ordained Episcopal women priests received many expressions of support from Roman Catholics. A Roman Catholic laywoman wrote Carter Heyward: "Thank you for becoming a priest. I don't want to be a priest; I just want a woman who is a priest so that I may go to her." And a nun, "I want to tell you of my support and admiration. I totally agree with you and your call and I'm proud of your courageous conviction. Do continue 'fighting the good fight.' . . . The time will come when the prophet's voice will be heard." And a priest and monk: "Just a wee word to tell you I remember you, and your cause, every day in my Mass."[44]

In no Christian faith has the attitude toward women been so ambivalent as in Roman Catholicism. Saints of the church throughout the centuries have voiced hatred and contempt for women. Tertullian, in the third century, to women: "Do you not know that you are Eve? You are the devil's doorway. It was you who profaned the tree of life. It was you who disfigured the image of God which is man." In the fourth century St. Ambrose: "Adam was led to sin by Eve, not Eve by Adam." In the twelfth century, Bernard of Clairvaux: "Their [women's] face is as a burning wind, their voice the hissing of serpents." In the thirteenth century, Thomas Aquinas: "In her particular nature woman is something defective and accidental. If a girl child is born it is due to weakness of the generative principle, or imperfection in the pre-existing matter, or to a change produced by external causes, for example by the humid winds from the south, as Aristotle says." In the seventeenth century, Jesuit Gracian: "It is clear that woman is under man's dominion and has no authority, nor can she teach, give evidence, make a contract, nor be judge."[45] Even in the late twentieth century women still sit stony-faced listening to sermons that tell them they have inherited the guilt of Eve in introducing sin into the world.

Yet for all this misogyny Roman Catholics have developed in the Virgin Mary a female image closely associated with God—an image of relatively little force among most Protestants, but powerful among Roman Catholics. As a well-worn joke has it, an old woman comes to church to pray, and the statue of Jesus comes alive and says, "What may I do for you, old woman?" And she says, "You be quiet. I've come to talk to your mamma."

The message in the Eve/Mary dichotomy is clear: either woman is to define herself in a relationship to a man—mother, sister, wife—or she is to be cast into outer darkness. Woman as suffering mother is to be adored, but woman as priest is to be denied and excoriated as unnatural.

Of all the many efforts in Christianity to channel God-centered women away from the priesthood, none has succeeded so brilliantly and for so long as the creation of orders of women religious—usually known as sisters or nuns.[46] They started out, Rosemary Ruether maintains, as clergy: "The present insistence of canon law that nuns are laywomen represents the end process of a long effort by the hierarchy to demote nuns from their original status as members of the clergy."[47] True enough, individual women and their orders have occasionally throughout the centuries threatened the power of the priesthood, as when in the Middle Ages some abbesses could appoint priests, or when women's orders contended with bishops and cardinals for control over the sisters. But by and large the system for centuries supplied Roman Catholicism with large numbers of dedicated, selfless, compliant, and hard-working women to run its schools, hospitals, and charitable enterprises. Moreover, their labor cost the church nothing. In Europe sisters were traditionally supported by the dowries the women brought with them and by gifts. Lacking these supports when they immigrated to the United States, the sisters learned to support themselves by their own labor—as they still do.

Small groups of European nuns began coming to the United States about 1790. In 1809 Elizabeth Seton founded the Daughters of Charity, the first indigenous community of American sisters.[48] In 1829 a French priest founded the first order for black women, the Oblate Sisters of Providence.[49] All of them accomplished thousands of small and not so small miracles: surviving cholera and snakes; overcoming Protestant suspicion and hostility by their good deeds, especially their nursing during the Civil War; building hospitals, schools, and orphanages; rehabilitating prostitutes; teaching African-Americans and Native Americans. "Nuns were really the force holding the church together. By the last half of the [nineteenth] century they outnumbered male church workers in every diocese, were four times as numerous as priests, exercised the major influence on the growing immigrant population, and bore the economic brunt of selfless service—'Catholic serfs,' according to one historian."[50]

In the 1920s and 1930s the concern that the sisters had always shown for the poor and the helpless manifested itself in political action. Despite hierarchical fears of the New Woman and efforts to impose stricter regulations on their communities, sisters lobbied for new legislation and encouraged social action organizations in their colleges. And in the complacent 1950s, before the emergence of the second women's movement, American nuns began to transform themselves. Ironically enough, the Vatican at first aided and abetted them. Pius XII charged women religious to take greater responsibility for their own life-styles and for the problems of the contemporary world.

They took him at his word. In the Sister Formation movement, they undertook a huge educational program that has made sisters the most highly educated group of women in the history of the world. They also built a strong and effective support system: the various orders began communicating with one another, seeking advice, exchanging ideas, and backing one another in confrontations with bishops and with Rome. They gave form to their networking in the Conference of Major Superiors of Women, later called the Leadership Conference of Women Religious.[51]

These remarkable accomplishments have been achieved despite a massive exodus from the orders by nuns who now perceived God's will for them differently, despite the shrinking of incoming postulants to the merest trickle, and despite the increasing hostility between the orders and the Roman Catholic hierarchy.[52] As sisters moved farther out into the world, took graduate degrees, and thought about the best ways to approach contemporary problems, they also redefined themselves and their vows. Obedience became a matter of determining for themselves the will of God, not simply accepting what their superiors or the Roman Catholic hierarchy told them.[53] The Second Vatican Council (Vatican II, 1962–1965), which required orders to look at their charism and define their identity and purpose, affirmed their belief that in seeking new paths of service and a new self-determination they were fulfilling their vows.

While different orders and different sisters within each order came up with different answers, Sister Joan D. Chittister has summed up the basic thinking of many of them:

> For all practical purposes, the task that most communities came to this country to do had—with the accession of John F. Kennedy to the presidency of the United States—been completed. Through the school system, the faith had been preserved in a strange land; Catholics had been inserted into a Protestant culture; the church had a tightly organized catechetical base and major institutional system. But whole new pockets of poor and oppressed people have arisen in this society and women religious are attempting to start all over again with the same bias toward the poor of this generation as we brought to the poor of the last, this time with a commitment to system justice as well as to personal charity. We are beginning to see more and more religious working for full salaries to support their communities so that more and more religious can work again for people who can pay nothing. But to do that we have to put a lot of things down: so-called religious garb, institutionalism, withdrawal, a common apostolate in favor of corporate commitments to the global issue of peace, poverty, hunger, minority concerns, human rights and the equality of women.[54]

The death of Pope John XXIII and the swing of the Roman Catholic hierarchy to the right did not stop sisters from serving where conscience called them, whether to the United States military, to state legislatures, or to governmental administrative posts such as the directorship of social services for Michigan. But it has sometimes put them and their orders (which by and large have loyally backed them) sharply at odds with the hierarchy, which has made them pay and pay, not only by humiliating reprimands but also by laicization. Debra Campbell writes:

> Sisters who signed the 1984 New York Times advertisement affirming a plurality of Catholic positions on abortion have met with reprisals from the Vatican. Sister Margaret Traxler, who served as convener of the Justice Campaign, an interdenominational group that lobbies for federal funding for abortions for impoverished rape and incest victims, has had to resign under strong pressure from the Congregation for the Doctrine of the Faith.[55]

Other sisters have become de facto clergywomen—preaching and pastoring professionally. They have served as directors of religious education, as hospital and prison and campus chaplains, as pastor's associates, as "parish administrators." The

Roman Catholic church is faced with a catastrophic shortage of ordained priests at a time when its church membership in the United States is growing, primarily because of immigration patterns.[56] Accordingly it has resorted to appointing women to leadership positions. In 1994, according to the *New York Times* (May 29, 1994), more than three hundred churches were already led by sisters or lay people. Those churches pastored by women are usually, though not always, small, poor, and in remote areas. Often these quasi pastors do not receive a living wage. They are not ordained; they may not, in Roman Catholic terms, "celebrate the Eucharist or the anointing of the sick or the reconciliation of sinners." That is, a woman pastor may not consecrate the communion wafers and wine, though in the absence of a priest she may distribute wafers and wine that he has blessed. She may not offer priestly assurances of forgiveness to sick and dying people or to people who have confessed their sins. Instead, "I'm sure," she says to the dying man who has "talked" rather than "confessed" to her, "that God forgives you." Although some women pastors may perform weddings and baptisms, when an overseeing priest comes around they must let him take over these ceremonies. Some call it exploitation, but others call it God.

One sister, known variously as a "pastoral associate" or "pastoral assistant," told us about her experiences. She joined her order in the early 1960s, fresh out of high school. After two years of traditional training, she and her order went through a bewildering series of changes, exciting for her but painfully difficult for some of the older nuns. The order sent her through college, and for several years she taught school and trained new postulants. Then she became a campus chaplain at a state college, the first woman so appointed in her diocese—and therefore often taken for a secretary. Working closely with a priest, she involved herself in the life of the college community, preaching, counseling, preparing people for the sacraments and for entering the church, leading retreats, but also offering courses, setting up group counseling programs for freshmen having problems, instituting a parents' weekend. "It was a parish," she said.

In her next appointment, this one at a community college, as the only full-time chaplain she coordinated the Interfaith Campus Ministry and devoted many hours to students of nontraditional age, especially the women returning to school after a lapse of several years, many of them single mothers juggling a job, childcare, and classes—overburdened women who needed reassurance and someone to listen.

After several years there—"When I stopped getting excited about freshman orientation I knew it was time to leave"—she turned down another chaplaincy at a prestigious university. "They couldn't believe it when I said no because I did not want to be the priest's employee. I didn't mind working for somebody, but I wanted to be part of a team."

Instead, after twelve years in the campus ministry she accepted a job in a parish.[57] When she talked with us, she had been pastoring for twenty-five years. She carries the day-to-day responsibility for running the parish; her parishioners, one of them told us, think of her as their pastor; the ordained priest is "just part-time." Nonetheless, some members of the congregation still tell her that they long for a man's leadership, a full-time priest. "Is anything not being done?" she asked. "Oh, no, sister, you're doing a good job, a fine job. But we just need a man."

Under her leadership, it's obvious, parishes thrive, with laypeople assuming much responsibility. "Can we have a moratorium on creativity around here?" one priest plaintively inquired after her first six months. "Next time I'm going to take a parish that won't have money for all these programs." But the sister assured him that it was quite possible to do programs without money: she always had. The laity makes it all possible. "My parish," says the sister, "is not dependent on me. When I can't be here, it doesn't fall apart. They can do very well without me. If you're a good leader, people don't have to be dependent on you. They should miss you. They should notice you're not around, and they might realize that once in a while you give them a good idea."

This conception of a nonhierarchical priesthood working cooperatively with "the people of God" is ideologically based. When we asked her whether she would like to be ordained a priest, she said:

> Part of me identifies with that, and I say yes. And part of me believes that the Catholic church is where I'm at home, and it's not just because I'm used to it. It's that I am nourished in faith. I also believe that the church is not the hierarchy, and I believe that if, not just as a religious congregation of women but as a church, we remain faithful to the gospel in spite of the present leadership, we will have a vital church. In some ways I think the church has to die, and the faster it dies the better. In other words, the leadership is getting worse and worse, and that's OK. Because we're engendering other kinds of leadership, and we're not dependent on priests, and we're not dependent on the elected or paid.

She returned to our question about ordination:

> Do I feel called to be an ordained leader in the church? Yes. Would I be ordained [if I could]? I'm not sure. Would I like to be able to be the principal leader of worship, celebrate the sacraments? Yes, I would. Do I see times when I should be able to do that? Yes, especially in times of sickness and death and in reconciliation with the church. Would I like to be a diocesan priest in the present system? I'd have to think about that a long time. Basically yes, but I'd have a lot of. . . . As a member of a religious congregation, I have a lot more freedom than a diocesan priest has.

Yet by the letter of the Roman Catholic law, this highly competent, intelligent, and caring woman is not the leader of her parish. "The pastor [priest] is that, and I'm not. Legally I can't preach, but I do. Church law says that the pastor can invite someone else to preach when he believes it is a necessity. My pastors have interpreted that to mean that they occasionally needed to be preached to."

Similar dodges and word games justify the appointments and actions of other sisters and laywomen as "parish administrators," under the 1983 Code of Canon Law. At first most pastoral administrators were sisters, but that number is declining as membership in women's communities declines and as active members must earn higher salaries to support older members of their communities: most sisters can no longer *afford* a ministry as a "parish administrator." Some laywomen in this position have to take a second job to support themselves.

Their parishioners customarily, their sacramental priests often, and their bishops sometimes speak of these pastoral administrators as "pastors," as reality asserts itself over regulation. In this euphemistic situation the church assigns the pastoral administrators responsibilities without rank. As the responsible person on the ground, often in remote rural areas visited by a sacramental priest only at distant intervals, it is up to the pastoral administrator to bring the comforts and blessings of the church to its people. But she is not ordained. So what does she do when the stock of communion wafers runs out or when a dying parishioner beseeches her for forgiveness? The best she can, of course.

But it's not easy for her to prepare a couple for marriage and then step aside while the priest officiates at the ceremony. Or to watch a beloved parishioner die, mourn with his family, and then regardless of their wishes hear the sacramental priest conduct the funeral. One woman told us:

> The hardest thing for me is anointing of the sick. Weddings you plan for. You know who's going to do it. But anointing the sick is a harder one, because you care for them, and then—when they're really sick you have to call someone and hope he can get there. We [parish administrators] truly cannot anoint the sick. We can pray with them and bless them, give them the Eucharist, say the prayer for the dying. But you have to be ordained to anoint them. At that point you become a little desperate, because it has to be done now. Funerals can be difficult, because when a person dies, I have to locate the priest and get him set into the time before any funeral arrangements can be made. Just logistically getting it done is difficult. Who is then the real priest?

Whenever the sacramental priest arrives, he is invading her turf—and he is accustomed to being an authority figure. That the system works as well as it does is a tribute to the generosity of both parish administrator and priest. Since both are human, problems and pain often mar the experience. Some bishops ignore the administrator in public ceremonies and forget to invite her to meetings. Some prelates, jealous of their prerogatives, don't want administrators to preach or to sit behind the altar. One priest, said a parishioner, "was very threatened by the fact that we had women doing these [word and Communion] services. Someone said, 'Well, Father, after people start seeing what's going on at the Communion services you may not have as many at your Mass.'"[58]

Considered from the point of view of efficient administration, what's wrong, of course, is not that fellow workers in the vineyard don't always get along, but the system itself. One parish administrator who talked with us, a sister who holds a master's degree in spirituality and another in pastoral ministry (a program which in her class enrolled only women), had nothing but praise for the priests with whom she has worked. But, she says, "there are days when I say, 'I wish I were ordained.' Because the work would be so much easier if I were ordained."

After a happy experience of five years as a "pastoral associate" in Appalachia, she hesitantly agreed to serve with another sister as "pastoral coordinators" in a parish without a "priest-pastor." They started with no church building and about forty-five families who had been meeting in an Episcopal church. They arranged for six priests to celebrate the liturgy in rotation. That way, she remarked, the people didn't identify any of the priests as their pastor but looked to the pastoral coordinators. When her fellow coordinator was called elsewhere by family responsibilities, she found herself serving—and for the first time in her life living—alone. Her people asked the bishop for permission for her to preach; with his assent, she did, and liked it. With her parishioners she also took on and successfully executed the task of building and paying for a church. She left after twelve years, even more reluctantly than she had come. Since then she has worked in another new Roman Catholic community, a little bigger, which also has built and paid for a new church.

Nine pastoral coordinators now labor in her diocese. They meet regularly and lobby for more recognition and an expanded role. They want the privileges of baptizing and performing marriages. "We're trying to push some of these boundaries a little bit," she says. "All of the pastoral coordinators preach. But they also need to have a substantive role in celebrating the sacraments. We just anointed parishioners at mass, senior citizens, and our actively sick, and I laid on hands with the priest and did some of the prayers. To participate in the service as much as is allowed—we always have to be working at that."

As for women's ordination, she didn't always believe in it. She says:

> I have come to it out of simply the need. We need more ministers. And we need ordained women. I think there are some areas where our women parishioners would feel more comfortable. I hear lots of confessions. I can't give absolution. But I'm not sure that some of these women would make the same confessions to male priests. Even if we had enough male priests, I think there is a role for women to be ordained, to serve in that capacity.

If the issue of ordaining women did not first emerge in Roman Catholicism with Vatican II, that council certainly increased its likelihood. For the council reflected the ideas of Pope John XXIII: "human beings have, in addition, the right to choose freely the state of life which they prefer. They therefore have the right to set up a family, with equal rights and duties for man and woman, and also the right to follow a vocation to the priesthood or the religious life."[59] For a short interval the doors stood open to change.

But the hierarchy reverted to conservatism. In 1972 Pope Paul VI issued an apostolic letter excluding women from the priesthood and from the new lay ministries of acolyte and lector; in 1977 he said that "a priest must bear a natural resemblance to Christ"—a statement frequently interpreted as referring to the male genitalia.[60] In 1983 the pope directed American bishops to withhold support from anyone actively favoring women's ordination. And in the mid–1990s Pope John Paul II, whom some of his critics refer to as a "geographical Catholic" who cannot escape the limitations of his traditional Polish upbringing, attempted to cut off all further discussion of the issue.[61]

In the 1990s, however, the issue shows no more signs of disappearing than in the three decades that elapsed between Vatican II and John Paul's attempt to make it go away. In 1979 Sr. Theresa Kane, as president of the Leadership Conference of Women Religious, publicly implored the pope:

> I urge you to be mindful of the intense suffering and pain which is part of the life of many women in these United States. . . . As women, we have heard the powerful messages of our church addressing the dignity and reverence for all persons. As women, we have pondered these words. Our contemplation leads us to state that the church in its struggle to be faithful to its call for reverence and dignity for all persons must respond by providing the possibility of women as persons being included in all ministries of our church. I urge you, Your Holiness, to be open to and respond to the voices coming from the women of this country who are desirous of serving in and through the church as fully participating members.[62]

Strong advocacy organizations that endorse women's ordination enjoy support from priests, sisters, and the laity.

Meanwhile the hierarchy has tried frantically to compensate for the shortfall and shortcomings of priests in some other way. For a time they tried recruiting priests for American parishes from other countries—ignoring cultural differences. Pastoral assistants, pastoral administrators, and pastoral coordinators probably represent the hierarchy's best effort but present their own problems in that their service so frequently persuades both the professional women themselves and their parishioners of how well these women function as pastors and how faithfully they carry out priestly duties. In fact, both unintentionally and intentionally, women are edging into priestly roles.

But the hierarchy stubbornly resists women's ordination, whatever its practical appeal. Mary E. Hunt, a cofounder of the Women's Alliance for Theology, Ethics, and Ritual (WATER), comments: "I always say they should have put the stole over the veils and sent the nuns, two by two, up the aisle to solve the priest shortage. Clerical, celibate, hierarchical nuns to the fore, you see, and they would have become the clerical, celibate, hierarchical priests. And it would have all worked in terms of the system."[63]

About 1980 Elaine Blondin Mello developed an alternative, a face-saving compromise that one would have thought the hierarchy might have seized upon with enormous relief—the idea of "collaborative ministry." Mello, who holds a master's from Yale Divinity School and a doctorate from Hartford Theological Seminary, explains: "Collaborative ministry is an alternative in parish staffing, wherein ordained and non-ordained individuals come together to pastor a parish together. For them 'pastor' is a verb, not a title, not a noun." This arrangement differs from associate pastorships and pastoral administration in that the priest and the non-ordained pastor are equals. Like the priest, the nonordained pastor is appointed by the hierarchy for a fixed term, renewable for another six years. (Pastoral assistants, pastoral administrators, and pastoral coordinators, on the other hand, are hired by the local priest and/or the parish and serve at their pleasure.)

The layperson in a collaborative ministry, male or female, was required to have a master's degree in a relevant field, have experience in the ministry, and have demonstrated a faith commitment for a reasonable number of years. The plan called for someone, that is, whose talents and experience would complement those of the priest and whose education and experience would qualify her or him as a strong and equal partner.

The concept reflected Mello's concern that as a student at Yale she saw so many of her fellow Roman Catholics, both women and men, leaving the church to be ordained elsewhere. She told us:

> These were people who felt that they couldn't agree with the ordination policy being set forth by the Roman Catholic church and were having difficulty finding ways to fol-low their vocation in a fruitful and authentic way. I always felt that it wasn't so much that they were leaving the church as they were taking the church with them and just going to another place. It was not a change in the way they felt about their faith or what they believed doctrinally. It was really a ministerial difference. So it bothered me that all these good people were leaving. I just believed in my heart there was a way of people fulfilling a vocation in the Catholic church, even within the parameters that had been set.

Her concern earned her the nickname among her fellow students of "Mother Church."

For a while it looked as though the Gordian knot had been untied. Mello's bishop agreed to implement the plan and with her help and that of a committee installed several such teams in his diocese. "I was involved in convening that program through Archbishop John Whelan," Mello told us, "and participated in collaborative ministry as a parish minister and co-pastor for more than seven years."

Hopes soared when other dioceses showed an interest in collaborative ministry. Archbishop Whelan sent Mello to a number of different dioceses throughout the United States to explain the plan. The National Council of Catholic Bishops in Washington also asked for information. "However," said Mello, "the recent happen-ings in the Catholic church [including papal pronouncements] have made everyone less apt to take this kind of risk."[64]

Too long denied, some Roman Catholic women no longer wish to serve the church hierarchy. Some have left the denomination and been ordained in the Epis-copal church. Some once desirous of ordination have decided that they could not in good conscience be priests in the Roman Catholic church as it is now constituted. The Women's Ordination Conference has shifted its focus from wanting ordination to demanding a reformed church. Its coordinator, Ruth McDonough Fitzpatrick, says: "We still have to work for the ordination of women. But . . . we women now have our own prayer meetings, our own liturgical celebrations, and our own work-shops. Women are now ministering in a renewed Christian ministry. In some ways we are living out that ministry. We would be reined in if we were ordained."[65] In other words, women are going their own way, inside the church or out. As a sister told us, those in power in Rome "do not get it. And I'm afraid that's their problem, not mine. And I refuse to waste a lot of time and energy trying to convert Rome to my way of thinking, because that's kind of a dead end. I'd rather just go out and do what I feel God has promised to do, and whatever is of the spirit will survive, and what isn't won't."

Sister Camille D'Arienzo speaks for many Roman Catholic advocates of women's ordination when she writes, "My concern for the church is that its sins of sexism and clericalism will catch up with it—like toxic wastes that pollute the waters—and will poison its potential to carry Christ to the world."[66] In the thinking of such Roman Catholics concern for the damage their church is doing itself runs just as deep as their concern for the women who suffer from its intransigence.

Let two women speak for the anguish of thousands of others. The first grew up the epitome of the ideal Roman Catholic girl. From her first communion on she went to mass every day; as a teenager she wanted to enter a junior novitiate, but her mother could not bear to give up her only daughter to a convent life. What she really wanted, she knows now, was to be a priest: she had memorized every movement of the priest, read the mass in Latin, knew it by heart. She married right out of high school, an Episcopalian, and bore four children. But as she recognized her husband's lack of real interest in his church, she returned, with the children, to the Roman church, going to mass every day, saying more rosaries, doing more novenas, hoping to solve her problems.

As her marriage disintegrated over a period of years, she worked her way through college and graduate school, earning a Master of Science in pastoral counseling. Meanwhile she had found help in ecumenical charismatic prayer groups and believed that she had received communications from the Holy Spirit. She herself developed a healing ministry with twelve prayer groups. They met in her church, where the priest barely tolerated them and refused all her invitations to attend, though she pointed out that they were not in competition but supplementing the work of the church. Painfully she learned that she could not stay in an institution that denied the Eucharist to nonmembers.

In her second marriage she has found a husband much like herself; he too had longed for ordination since childhood. Together they have discovered a new church home in independent Catholicism, and both of them are now ordained priests. Leaving the Roman church and accepting ordination was no easy decision for either of them. Both had horrible nightmares the night before they were ordained subdeacons. "I felt like I was committing the worst sin and I was disloyal," she told us. "I was damned to hell. It was the same at every step. When I started to celebrate the mass myself, I thought I was going to be struck dead. But it didn't happen." And conscience did not make cowards of them.

These two married priests run a church of their own under the umbrella of the Orthodox Catholic Church. Ultimately they want to have a church attached to a spiritual development center, which will meet people wherever they are, support them with whatever they need. They want to help, to mediate, but not intervene between the communicant and the Holy Spirit. Yes, money is a major problem, particularly since between them they have seven children. The June before she talked with us their family had seven graduations: she received a doctorate, her husband a bachelor's, two of their children master's, and three others bachelor's degrees.

A very different woman was still enrolled in a prestigious theological seminary when she talked with us. She had always known that she wanted to work in a church; she just hadn't known which one. When she was in college she opted for Roman Catholicism. There she remains, despite two severely disillusioning experiences.

First, in a custody fight, her father brought in a priest to "come in and testify against my mother, a bunch of lies. It hurt her, quashed her so badly, that she's unable to worship in the institutional setting. And she's not alone. Many of us are facing that prospect. If I get squashed by the church, I would like to say I'll hang in there and be faithful regardless, but I can't say that."

Second, during a semester she spent studying as a day student in a Benedictine monastery she experienced sexual harassment from the student candidates for the priesthood so severe that she dared not go alone either to the computer room or to the basketball court. "The first thing that would come out of their mouths was 'You're a temptress. You shouldn't be here anyway.' It's the whole Eve story. I can tell you I wasn't offering any man there fruit off my plate." Equally soul-destroying for her was knowing that these men were indulging in both heterosexual and homosexual experiences.

Still, she remains a faithful Roman Catholic—and a passionate advocate for the ordination of women.

> It's not about ordination. It's about power. They want the power and they don't want women to be involved in it. The social justice teaching of the Catholic church allows so much participation and yet the church itself doesn't practice what it preaches at all by allowing people to be participating in governing themselves. The Pope just said there will absolutely be no debate on women's ordination. I have yet to hear a good sound theological argument against women's ordination. If somebody could give me one, and it was logical, being a reasonable, rational creature maybe I could accept it. But I have yet to hear it. And until I do, I will maintain that humanity is equally called to the priesthood.

᪥ Judaism

Recent Jewish history tells a story quite different from that of the Roman Catholics. It too is a story of impassioned women, but their Reform, Reconstructionist, and Conservative communities have reacted with more flexibility; the Orthodox community continues to block their way—though even among the Orthodox, women are now acting in rabbinical roles, as in Roman Catholicism women are acting in priestly roles. "In Catholicism," says a woman rabbi, "the word 'institution' has more force than it does in Judaism."

You've got the Catholic church, and that's an institution. But with us Jews, you know—two Jews, three opinions. They don't like the shul, they go form their own little one, so you can in a way do your own thing, and you don't have to worry about what the pope says. Institutional Judaism is there, and certainly Orthodoxy is institutionally negative in terms of the way women are treated, but those women have an option. [They can, that is, go to Reform or Conservative or Reconstructionist Judaism.] It's a little different than the Catholic church, where you just can't be a priest, that's all, unless they say so.

The necessary impetus for Jewish women's ordination came from the secular women's movement. A woman rabbi comments, "Some of the strengths of the feminist movement have come from the secular world and gradually wormed their way into the more traditional religious institutions. How many Jewish heroines are there in the Bible? Certainly not in the Talmudic period. One of the reasons that the Conservative movement can go along with women rabbis is that the Talmud says nothing about ordaining women, because it's totally unthinkable."

Jewish feminists of the 1960s struggled for full membership in the community, calling for changes. In the 1970s they were forming groups to celebrate women's events, like Rosh Hodesh, the ceremony of the new moon; publishing new prayers for women; continuing to press for fuller acceptance of women in the Jewish community; and in some synagogues seeing their work of the 1960s rewarded by women's being counted in the minyan.[67] In 1973 Rachel Adler broke ground for Jewish women by praying with a prayer shawl and phylacteries at the first National Jewish Women's Conference. In the late 1970s Orthodox women began organizing their own prayer groups; by 1985 they were joining together in the Women's Tefillah Network to provide resources and support for other Orthodox women forming their own groups.[68]

In the 1970s Jews began ordaining women. A joke told by a rabbinical couple acknowledges the primacy of the Reform Jews in this practice: "How do you know what kind of Jewish wedding you're at? If the bride's mother is pregnant, it's Orthodox. If the bride is pregnant, it's Conservative. If the rabbi is pregnant, it's Reform."[69] In 1972 Hebrew Union College (Reform) ordained Sally Priesand; in 1974 the Reconstructionists ordained Sandy Eisenberg Sasso; and in 1985 Conservative Jews ordained Amy Eilberg.

"When I accepted ordination on June 3, 1972," wrote Sally Priesand, "I affirmed my belief in Judaism and publicly committed myself to the survival of Jewish tradition."

> I did so knowing that Judaism had traditionally discriminated against women, that it had not always been sensitive to the problems of total equality. I know that there has been a tremendous flexibility in our tradition—it enabled our survival. Therefore, I chose to work for change through constructive criticism. The principles and ideals for which our ancestors have lived and died are much too important to be cast aside. Instead we must accept the responsibilities of the covenant upon ourselves, learn as much as possible of our heritage, and make the necessary changes which will grant women total equality within the Jewish community.[70]

By 1993 219 women were ordained as Reform rabbis, and women constituted almost half of the students at Hebrew Union College/Jewish Institute of Religion (HUC-JIR); the Reconstructionist Rabbinical College had ordained fifty-two women rabbis, and the Jewish Theological Seminary another fifty. The days for women students of wandering alone in a wilderness of men had passed; no longer, in Rabbi Laura Geller's words, need they be "lonely for the dancing of Miriam and the women."[71]

By their very presence and their leadership style, whether or not they want to (and many of them do), women are changing the rabbinate and Judaism itself—just as in parallel ways clergywomen are changing Protestant and Roman Catholic ministry and Christianity itself. Rabbi Ellen Lewis has remarked that even without an agenda for change, everything she does comes out differently. Not necessarily better or worse—just differently. At practice for the rabbi's first such ceremony, the thirteen-year-old girl asked, "At my Bat Mitzvah do you think we can wear matching dresses?" Rabbi Deborah Prinz continued her male predecessor's practice of using inclusive language in reading the prayer book—but her first service evoked a congregant's complaint: "See, you hire a woman and the first thing she does is change the prayerbook!" Woman as rabbi startles people into attention. Her presence liberates and empowers congregants both female and male: "If she can do it, I can. I could learn those prayers, I could study Torah, I could lead this service."[72] If on some level they have associated a male rabbi with a male divinity, they speculate in new terms about the nature of God.

Moreover, they may reexamine their own connection to the tradition, their ability as individuals to study and understand it. "Judaism is not an edifice lying behind doors and guards," writes Susannah Heschel, "and we should not have to go through a denomination to reach it. Rather, our relations should be with the diversity and totality of Jewish tradition, unmediated by one of its modern forms."[73] Therefore, she argues, women should not be asking men for permission to enter Judaism.

Noting the ongoing change in the conception and function of rabbis, one woman explained:

> Our functions on the whole are less pastoral [than those of Protestant ministers]. Someone in the assimilated Jewish world takes on more of the pastoral function, but as a classical Orthodox rabbi you really would not have that function. You would have the function of a learned person, a person whom others turn to for judgment, and who would be expected to be very knowledgeable in Judaism. However, as you go along you find many types like myself who increasingly expect to visit the sick and certainly to minister to families, which I do a great deal. But still the rabbi who is learned, who makes a fine sermon, who is provocative intellectually is very much admired and he can get away with not being such a *mensch* in other respects.

As a cantor put it to us, about the turn of the century the role of the rabbi began to change, especially in the United States and especially among Reform Jews, as, borrowing from their new Protestant environment, rabbis modified their roles of legal authorities and teachers to more intimate involvement in synagogue services, including preaching.

Cantors exercise primarily a liturgical ministry. "I'm the authority on liturgical chant in the synagogue," one of them told us. "The rabbi and I become the right hand and the left hand. I put it to music but she paints beautiful pictures with the poetry. The cantor is the intermediary between the congregation and God, who tries to motivate the people so their prayers are carried to God." The rabbi "is supposed to challenge them, get them thinking about who they are Jewishly, get them in touch with their feelings about God, get them in touch with Jewish laws." The same forces that swept women into the rabbinate in the 1970s worked also for women cantors. A Conservative cantor who began her work in 1978 reached the pulpit not through courses at a seminary but through an apprenticeship. "The cantor in my synagogue where I grew up, I used to think when he'd open his mouth God was sitting next to me," she said. She wanted to be like him, always thought that she would. "They didn't tell me when I was a kid that they weren't going to let me into the seminary. I always thought that was where I was going to go. I had a rude awakening." But her mentor told her, "Don't worry. If anybody's going to do it, you're going to do it. I'll teach you."

Like Christian clergywomen, by no means all women rabbis work in congregations. They serve as chaplains and editors of religious publications and as professors and academic administrators—though in seminaries they are usually on the lower levels. In synagogues and temples women rabbis typically are employed either as associates and assistants or as sole clergy in small and relatively poor congregations. A woman rabbi remarks:

> As I find with other women not necessarily in this field, you get the job if it's small and unimportant and then you help to make it bigger. I think of a clergy friend. She was a Congregational minister, and she became the head of the council of churches and synagogues. You see when she got it it was not very prestigious. The person who had preceded her was really not very competent. She was working there, and they knew she was really carrying it; she said, "If you don't give me the job as head, I'm leaving." So they gave her the job, and she built it up to the point where they had umpteen applications for her position and she left because she was offered a position as head of programming at a large, prestigious church.

She might equally well have cited the case of a rabbi who started work in a theological seminary as a volunteer and ascended to its paid presidency.

Jewish clergywomen, like their Christian sisters, receive salaries significantly lower than those of their male counterparts.[74] But, a woman rabbi told us:

> On the whole rabbis are paid better than ministers. Considerably so. I'm not sure why. I think it may be that there's more of a sense in Christianity that it's noble to be poor. I think that people are a little embarrassed about paying their rabbis poorly, and it's easy enough to embarrass them about it. I spoke at a retreat of Christian ministers and they

were discussing their problems, and I was just shocked by how little they earned. Absolutely shocked.

A naval woman chaplain underlined the point: for Protestant clergy to leave the military, she said, means a dramatic drop in pay. But rabbis who go on active duty often must take a pay cut.

Women rabbis also report encountering the same kinds of discrimination as Christian clergywomen. Sometimes it comes from congregants, some of whom show comic bewilderment at the very idea of a woman rabbi. One woman told a story of officiating at a wedding: "The groom's uncle came over to me, put his arm on my arm, and said, 'Are you sure you know what to do?' I'm not a kid after all. So I said in a sort of stage whisper, 'I think so!' He looked very sheepish." At another wedding a supposedly important but obviously obtuse male judge said, "It's so nice to see something so well done by a woman." Hardest to bear is the discrimination by male rabbis. One woman, forbidden by one of her fellows to read from the Torah, told him: "I felt the way you would feel if you encountered an anti-Semitic situation." Generalizing about the old-boy attitude of some male rabbis, she said, "I don't know whether I'm twice a Jew or twice a woman."

As Rosemary Radford Ruether has pointed out, Christian and Jewish women share many problems and agenda, like inclusive language. Other problems are specific to the religion, like the Christian linking of Eve and evil, and the Jewish exclusion of women from the minyan.[75] In an interesting study conducted in the early 1990s, Rita J. Simon compared the perceptions of thirty-five Protestant clergywomen and twenty-seven women rabbis.[76] In many ways, she found, they resemble one another. Both groups believe that they are more approachable and less formal than their male counterparts and more likely than men to preach and conduct religious ceremonies from a personal point of view. In both groups individuals in charge of a congregation reported themselves better satisfied than those acting as assistants or associates. Rabbis said that they derived most pleasure from their roles as teachers, therapists, and counselors; ministers similarly liked their involvement in people's lives, from birth to death. Both groups found administrative chores burdensome.

But the Protestants emphasized their spiritual roles, while the rabbis more often spoke of themselves as community leaders and advocates for social justice, and they reported preaching on social issues more frequently than the clergywomen. A similar difference manifested itself in the subjects' reports of their motivation. Ministers often gave spiritual reasons and spoke of being called by God. Rabbis, however, spoke of a desire for greater involvement in Jewish life and for more influence and higher status than most other helping professions afford.

Our own interviews have evoked some of the same responses. Except when interviewees are explicitly comparing and contrasting themselves with their male counterparts, one suspects that the differences between women rabbis and Christian clergywomen would also show up in interviews with male rabbis and Protestant clergymen—that they are integral to the religion rather than to the genders. It may well signify that Jews pay their rabbis markedly more than Christians pay their ministers and priests, for like it or not we live in a culture where money and status are closely linked. Rabbi Mark Winer, an authority on rabbinical pay, observes that Judaism has never looked upon poverty as a virtue.

Most intriguing is the reported difference in motivation. One rabbi whom we asked about a vocation answered in some puzzlement. She had taught in a high school for some time and had also run for political office, both of which experiences she now sees as steps toward being a woman in a leadership position. Her interest in the community and its needs, she said, continues to manifest itself in the ways that she acts as a rabbi. But did God call her to be a rabbi? "We talk about having a great sense of calling, but I don't know that for the most part we would talk about having it come from God. A call from God—I almost look upon that as being a little holier-than-thou. If the idea of calling is to be used, then my sense of dedication came out of the awareness of the Holocaust and the birth of Israel after 2,000 years." Another rabbi, though, told us that not only did she personally receive a call from God, but that she believes that her seminary students are "powerfully called by God." Perhaps once again the Jewish and Christian traditions are intermingling, influencing one another.

In the Christian tradition the idea of such a call has historically been used as a mark of humility, of the sacrifice of one's own wishes to the divine will. Just as among Christians spiritual autobiographies developed a pattern that was copied from one individual to another and from one generation to another, so also with the religious vocation: almost all Christian clergy have spoken and still today speak in terms of answering a call from God. This concept has served the Protestant clergywoman well, justifying her when she broke with tradition by speaking in public, when she defied the authorities of her church, and when to pursue her career she left her children in someone else's care: God made me do it. The Jewish woman, coming to the rabbinate only in the 1970s, in these latter days has perhaps not needed that justification, or needed it less.

On the whole Jewish clergywomen seem to experience fewer problems than Christians about how people address them. In more formal situations people call them "Rabbi"—though a Conservative rabbi chuckled when she told us about a ninety-two-year-old man who accepted and supported her as his rabbi but could not bring himself to address her thus: instead he called her "Rebbetzin," the Yiddish title for the rabbi's wife. The Christians who have talked to us almost all detest being directly addressed as "Reverend." As an Episcopal priest told us, "Call me anything but late for dinner and anything but Reverend." These days first names solve most of the problems most of the time.

A few, especially Episcopalian priests, use "Mother," usually in combination with their first names. One who doesn't said: "When I was first ordained, I really rejected that kind of parental relationship, but in many ways there is a maternal/paternal relationship. I think the diocese does it because it's easy. If they're going to say 'Father,' they have to say something to us guys, so they just do it. And then

there's 'Mother Sue' versus 'Mother Smith.' I'm sort of a city kid, and the first time
I took a funeral somebody behind a tree said 'Hey, Mother' [laughs]. It didn't mean
what they thought it meant. My shoeman right after I was ordained was from
Guyana, and he said he asked his family what to call an English Catholic priest, and
they said, 'Father,' and he said, 'But she's not.' And so his family said, 'Well ask her
if you can call her Lady Father.' Which I thought was just lovely." And another
priest says her son calls her "My mother, the Father."[77]

✒ Holiness and Other Evangelical Churches

Most Baptist congregations still in the 1990s refuse to ordain women, and the
ever-growing power of the conservatives, especially among Southern Baptists, by
far their largest group, severely limits employment possibilities for clergywomen. In
1984 the Southern Baptist convention spoke against ordaining women by adopting a
resolution encouraging "the service of women in all aspects of church life and work
other than pastoral functions and leadership roles entailing ordination."[78] Legally
the power to ordain and to hire rests in local congregations, but here and there
regional associations have claimed the right to expel "churches that may become
corrupt in faith or practices"—for example, that may ordain women. Even the comparatively moderate American Baptist Churches in the U.S.A., which have ordained
women since 1894, in 1983 had only 261 women ministers out of 5,373 active
clergy, less than a half of one percent, and many of these serve as Christian education specialists, youth ministry directors, or chaplains rather than as pastors.[79]

In some holiness and pentecostal churches clergywomen continued to lose
ground after 1960.[80] In the Assembly of God, for example, by 1990 clergywomen
were well nigh invisible. The few survivors are usually channeled into religious education or music, or sent to churches that men don't want. At the behest of local
clergymen—and, she believed, in accordance with God's will—one such woman
reluctantly abandoned work she loved to revive a church that had closed and consequently could not pay her: to support herself she worked as a secretary. She started
with seven dollars in the church treasury, a five-hundred-dollar debt, and no members. When after eight years she had built a membership of seventy who then
offered her a modest salary, she was pressured to yield her post to a male. One of
only two women pastors in her denomination in her southern state, she still feels
uncomfortable at ministerial meetings outside her area: "I feel like I am breaking up
their playhouse." Its "marriage with non-Pentecostal conservative Protestantism,"
writes Margaret Poloma, "is moving the Assemblies of God away from its historical
ambivalence toward women in ministry and toward silencing its prophesying
daughters." So also with some other holiness and pentecostal denominations, which
have edged away from their earlier stances toward joining forces with right-wing
evangelical and fundamentalist groups.[81]

In the Church of God (Anderson, Indiana) in the latter half of the twentieth century a small number of clergywomen, some of them Hispanic, have endured much to survive. Ordained by the Cuban Assembly but sternly criticized by other men in her denomination, Hilaria Palmer for more than twenty-eight years pastored a Miami Church of God to serve Cuban refugees. Cati Perez-Scrivner with her husband pastored the Ministerio Latino in Portland, Oregon, for eight years because "I saw my people with emptiness in their faces and I had a burning ache in my heart to tell them about Jesus." Cindy Mansfield and her husband in the Albuquerque Hispanic Church of God have had to contend with gang violence.[82]

Some of these clergywomen pay a high price for their ministry. Rev. Ruth M. Smith experimented with seven different denominations, none of which ordained women, before she settled into the Church of God. "The Church of God," she remarks, "does not seem to call women to large churches, so God calls us to small ones and does a large work there." In 1980 she was called to a congregation of thirty-five members, some of whom left because she was a woman, others for different reasons; eighteen remained to help her increase the membership and construct a new building. June D. Strickland says, "I argued with God for months and months. I even 'fell in love' with a minister and bargained with God; I will marry him and he can preach. . . . however, the minister married someone else, and still I was called to preach." She tried to combine ministry and marriage to a layman, only to have him desert her just before the birth of their second child. Then, a single parent with two small children, she served a little parish in Texas for eleven years, erecting two new buildings, tripling the attendance, and increasing the budget by 800 percent. Her story ends happily: she remarried, and her husband sold the business he had owned for twenty-nine years to move with her to a new senior pastorate.[83]

Since these conservative groups hold tight to traditional roles for women, some of the women leaders who emerged among them in the 1960s and 1970s instead of seeking ordination found an outlet for their talents and energies as secular leaders for the Christian Right instructing women on how to function in a conservative lifestyle—preaching the gospel, so to speak, in another setting. Marabel Morgan and Helen Andelien concentrated on ways women could improve their marriages. Phyllis Shlafly, Anita Bryant, and Beverly LaHaye taught them about antiabortion, antigay, and antifeminist political action.[84] Other women even offered a born-again Christian system for fighting fat in groups like Overeaters Anonymous and Overeaters Victorious. Jo Berry of Creative Ministries took to the lecture circuit afforded by the retreats and conferences inspired by the women's movement. As women's Bible studies boomed, Marilyn Kunz and Catherine Schell founded Neighborhood Bible Studies, joining together thousands of small discussion groups worldwide.[85] On the other hand, Jean Thompson copastored the Harvest Church in Mount Rainier, Maryland, an African-American congregation "affiliated with the Reverend Lou Sheldon's Traditional Values Coalition," which sent hundreds of women to Washington, D.C., "Taking a Stand for Righteousness and for [Clarence]

Thomas" during the Senate hearings on Thomas's nomination to the Supreme Court. Thompson told reporters: "Being here today is as important as it was in Harriet Tubman's day."[86]

Yet even among fundamentalists and evangelicals, feminism flickers. A tiny group of feminist evangelicals confessed in the 1973 Chicago Declaration that conservative Christians "have encouraged men to prideful domination and women to irresponsible passivity. So we call both men and women to mutual submission and active discipleship."[87] The next year they established the Evangelical Women's Caucus International (EWC), now the Evangelical and Ecumenical Women's Caucus (EEWC). That year too Letha Scanzoni and Nancy Hardesty, both EWC members, published *All We're Meant to Be: A Biblical Approach to Women's Liberation* (Word Books, 1974) challenging evangelicals to put more women into leadership positions and to ordain them. In 1986 the caucus split on the issue of lesbianism, and a small number broke away to found Christians for Biblical Equality, less liberal in its attitude toward homosexuality. Both these groups are opposed by Concerned Women for America, founded by Beverly LaHaye.

Perhaps even more significant than the feminists of EEWC are the holiness women of fundamentalist theology who flinch at the mention of feminism but who nonetheless forsake all others, husbands included, to cling only unto the divine call. Elaine Lawless describes such pastors in the Assembly of God—poor; ill-educated and distrustful of education; disapproving of smoking, drinking, movies, and dancing; believing strongly in traditional male–female relationships. Despite the general disapproval of clergywomen in their denomination, especially among clergymen, says Lawless, almost "every small town in central Missouri is likely to have one congregation [usually Pentecostal] that will be pastored by a woman, often several." Repudiating feminism, these pentecostal clergywomen conceptualize themselves as mothers tenderly caring for their congregations.[88] Yet many of them endure the criticism of family and friends and endanger their husbands' senses of their own masculinity.

The Salvation Army staunchly holds to its lifetime policy of appointing women officers. Some of its tenets divide it from the secular women's movement, particularly its stand against abortion and homosexuality. Although most women officers who have talked with us shy away from the label "feminist," they take great pride in the Army's record of commissioning women officers. For some, this pride jostles uncomfortably against a belief in biblical inerrancy, particularly in texts about men heading households. One woman dedicated to improving women officers' knowledge of their Army predecessors told us, "Some fundamentalist Christians think that these books now of women in ministry in the church border on heresy. The church has been very afraid of the woman's movement. There is still the fear and the accusation that if a woman reads too much [about women in ministry] she's going to get too pushy and too loud and 'this is not Biblical pattern.'"

All the same, some officers frankly call themselves feminists. One of them told us:

[I am an] evangelical, Christian feminist, which means I believe in the proper Biblical interpretation of the value, worth, and role of women in ministry, in the church, in family, and in society. . . . the fundamentalist viewpoint of the role of women as being quiet, not being allowed to teach, not being allowed to speak, submissive, almost doormat, is absolutely not Biblical, and yet it has invaded the Christian community as the way a woman is supposed to look. . . . When you watch Jesus, He's not buying into that at all. He's talking to [women] publicly, which was a no-no; He's letting them touch Him, which was an abomination; and women are with men at Pentecost when the Spirit comes. You read the list of gifts, and it doesn't say, "These gifts are for men and these gifts are for women."

The Salvation Army is too much of and in the world not to feel the effects of the feminist movement. In 1970 former officer Mrs. Billie B. McClure brought charges against the Army for discriminating against her in assignments on the basis of her sex. She lost her case, the court ruling that the Civil Rights Act does not obtain in the relations between a church and its ministers.[89] Women officers have become increasingly concerned about the terms of their employment. To some degree they have begun to worry about married women's not receiving checks in their own names and not having their own Social Security accounts. "I have knowledge of a lot of Salvation Army women for whom the issue is equal pay for equal work," one officer in her forties told us. "But it's not mine. The issue for me is, when I get to retirement, if my husband should precede me in death by a number of years, I'm going really to be hung out to dry [because after his death benefits will be substantially reduced], and I will have worked a lifetime and have no way to legally deal with that." And yes, she agreed, divorce leaves women high and dry.

Single officers have their own problems, some of them, like too frequent moves, not gender specific. Most officers agree that corps work demands two people. A single woman commanding a corps needs an assistant. Now and then a two-woman team evolves, and the Army tries to assign them together. But until recently the Army has hesitated to put a male officer under a woman's direction. Now the Army would send a man to assist her, a major told us in some amusement, "because we have an apartment in the building. I live in a house separate from the building. And since I will be 50 in October, I'm fairly safe now."

Other single women feel that the Army slights them because they are women and because they are single.

I had a divisional leader say to me just a few years ago that because I don't have a college degree other than my [Salvation Army] training school work, because I am a single woman, I am more and more and more in a minority and will be harder and harder and harder to place, even in a corps, because most corps want married couples. Now I haven't found that that's true, because in most of the corps I've been in they don't care if you're purple as long as you're willing to work. But we do have a struggle, because we have some chauvinists at the top who are very old-fashioned in some of their ideas, and I hope that before we move into the next century we'll move into this one as far as the place of women is concerned.

Another said: "I've spent my whole career moving to places just like this. [In this corps] I have almost a hundred thousand dollars in debt. I have no leadership to speak of. There is no youth program going on. There are property problems to be solved. We're trying to do some expansion with our child day care. And I go in and improve the staff and train the leaders and build the congregation and pay off the bills and glue the building back together, and then normally I am off and running to the next assignment, and they would not necessarily do this kind of thing to a married man." A familiar statement, whose like we have heard from clergywomen in many other denominations.

Another single officer commented on the Army's responsibility to talk realistically about their future to young women entrants. "We need to tell them," she said, "if you get to the other side of the commissioning platform at the end of training without a serious attachment, if you're going to be an officer for life, there is every possibility that you are going to end up single. How do you feel about that? The fact that you might be moved more often than other officers, because you are easier to move. The fact that you might be held back because you are a single woman. . . . when we start getting young people ready for training, they hear from the divisional youth secretary and divisional commander and all those guys about this wonderful glory road to heaven, but I think we need to start telling them there are a few potholes in the glory road."

But despite their clear-eyed awareness of these potholes, the Salvation Army women who have talked with us are strikingly, fiercely loyal to their denomination. Nonetheless—like their sister clergy in other churches—Salvation Army women are concerned about the ways in which in the past their assignments have limited their usefulness and the full exercise of their talents. And until very recently the Army has indeed seriously underused highly talented women. In an all-too-frequent pattern, even women who stood out for the high quality of their performance in positions historically held by men could not move up, nor could they set a precedent for the appointment of other women.

The Army has begun to respond to women's concerns— naturally tackling first and enjoying most success with the easier, more cosmetic changes. Married women are now known as "Captain Susie Smith" instead of "Mrs. Captain John Smith." No longer must a married woman assume her husband's rank, whether it is lower or higher than hers; as of May 1995, when a couple marry they take the higher of their two ranks. Some women have recently been appointed to more responsible jobs in the higher echelons. Some married women officers report that their own talents are now being considered when new assignments are made. The Army has experimented with giving married officers separate assignments, so that a husband may work in Army administration while a wife commands a corps (pastors a church) —though they continue to live together. Officers are now sometimes consulted about their own preferences in assignments.

General Paul A. Rader, elected in 1994, and his wife have a good record on women's issues, and women officers vest a lot of hope in them for changes. General

Rader has strengthened the Woman's Committee, which addresses women's issues—founded not by a grass-roots movement but by the hierarchy. "Well, anything that happens is from the top, unfortunately," commented one young officer. "Anything else would have just been considered the coffee break, I guess. This is the problem with the Salvation Army's being a church and running a hierarchal structure. The two are diametrically opposed. I don't know how we've been able to stay alive this long." And she laughed.

But armies are hard to move and hard to change, and even the Salvation Army with its many women officers finds it difficult to shrug off outmoded practices and ways of thinking. Its structure still invites territorial commanders to think first of its men: "Outside the corps," said one young "Daughter of the Regiment" who has grown up in the Salvation Army, "it's just absolutely unacceptable to move a couple into a certain situation because the woman would really do well in a certain divisional role, and then, well, we'll just find something for the guy to do, because we really need that woman's expertise. That's not how it happens. It's always, we need this guy here and we'll find something for the woman to do. She can fit in somewhere." Even in the corps, "the appointment is that the husband is the corps commanding officer. He is the signature on the checks. He is the responsible person." And a prejudiced regional commander can for a time frustrate the good intentions of his superiors. "The Raders are definitely pro-woman," one woman told us. "But if your commissioner in your immediate territory is not pro-woman, it won't matter." Another joked that "a lot of territorial commanders feel that God only speaks to their ears."

Some women officers consequently look skeptically at reform, suspecting tokenism or setups. "They were doing a trial run to find out if a woman could handle administration. [The woman they appointed] was programmed for failure, so that a year later they could say, 'Oh, we tried her.' I honestly believe that the earliest attempts of the Salvation Army to put women in a leadership position were absolutely sabotaged, and I believe were designed to be sabotaged, because men's egos are so big and so strong that they couldn't really believe that a woman could do work of this kind." Moreover, the performance of Eva Burrows as general in the 1980s and early 1990s disappointed them. This second woman general and first elected woman general in the history of the Army did not do much for other women officers. "She placed one or two of her very best friends in great positions," said an experienced officer who found Burrows pleasant to deal with. "But for the rest of us in the United States, there was nothing."

At a 1994 meeting on the Army's future, a woman delegate thanked "national leaders for making the issue of women in leadership a priority but expressed concern that 'Alas, your rhetoric has given way to reality.' Supporting her premise, she contrasted the list of first names of the program participants in the opening session with those assigned as table hosts for meals. The first listed all males, the second all females. She asked, 'Do you see a pattern here?' She concluded her remarks by exhorting leadership to stop talking about the issue and . . . 'Just do it!'"[90] Another woman told us about a resolution to ask divisional commanders to place women in leadership positions *if appropriate,* which "passed by something like 57-43. There must have been 57 women in that room," she said, laughing. An older officer nearing the end of her career said, "I honestly feel that the Army shortchanged me, that I had the ability and the desire and the intelligence. And I believe that they have lost out in certain ways, because they did not allow me to advance." Still, even the most wary women officers demonstrate a noteworthy loyalty to the Army ethic, express their pride in their officer daughters, and believe that those daughters will enjoy opportunities of which they were deprived.

The Salvation Army needs more officers—a situation that Protestant mainline churches may envy. "There just are not enough officers coming through the ranks any more to provide assistant officers for the corps who need them," says a senior woman, "because the Army's losses have far exceeded the number of officers coming in in the last what? Ten, twenty years at least."

The secular women's movement and institutional churches and synagogues still stand in an uneasy relationship with one another. For their own political, theological, and ideological reasons, some leaders of the women's movement suspect religious institutions as they suspect the military. In a kind of guilt by association, they blame servicewomen for the sins of the military and clergywomen for the sins of religious institutions. Religious institutions such as fundamentalism and Orthodoxy, which vigorously advocate traditional roles for women, think of the women's movement in much the same terms that Senator Joseph McCarthy thought of Communism.

But religious institutions are one thing and their members and clergy another. These days it's hard to find a monolithic church or synagogue. Even Mormons and Missouri Synod Lutherans have a few women members who unabashedly speak of themselves as feminists and more who endorse the ordination of women.[91] Thousands of Roman Catholic women, especially nuns, publicly proclaim the necessity for it; some of these women stand on the radical side of other women's issues and have bravely risked their careers, their lifelong attachments, and their church membership to advocate for them. Diana Hochstedt Butler describes her own painful situation as an academic evangelical theologian. Her secular feminist colleagues "view Christianity as chief of all male-constructed oppressors. In the eye of many female academics, a woman who is both a Christian and an academic is suspect. To proclaim to be an *evangelical* academic woman is tantamount to heresy."[92]

❧ Gospel Singing and New Age Religions _____

Meanwhile, in the twentieth century charismatic women deeply interested in religion have crossed revivalism and gospel music concerts, assuming some of the tasks and authority of clergywomen. African-American Dorothy Love Coates, a minister's daughter raised as a Sanctified Baptist, formed the Harmonettes, who won wide popularity. A consummate showwoman, she has had a colorful career, working with Martin Luther King, Jr., and enduring the Newark riots. With the Harmonettes she appears as narrator, reporter, counselor, preacher. At their concerts she addresses sinners of all kinds: "We got some lying addicts, can't get through a day without telling a lie on somebody. We've got some church-going addicts, but going to church will not get you into heaven. . . . And we got some home-wrecking addicts. They say if I can't have peace in my home, I'm sure gonna make hell out of yours. . . . Jesus Christ came down through forty-two generations, hung on a rugged cross, suffered, bled, and died for your sins and mine. That was two thousand years ago, and some folks *still* ain't got the message."[93]

Concert/revival services like these originated in the worship of black holiness churches, where song and dance made for "good church." Coates and others of her kind follow a tradition that started in the 1930s, when professional gospel music groups began traveling. Thomas A. Dorsey, his partner Sallie Martin, and their protégée Roberta Martin set out on tour expressly to revive churches. Making converts wherever they went, they built a circuit of churches and auditoriums where gospel groups performed. Ordained evangelist Mother Willie Mae Ford Smith, a member of the Church of God Apostolic, also began traveling in the 1930s. She used to "talk it up," setting a precedent for the mini-sermons used by later gospel singers. Indeed she taught herself to preach by introducing her songs.[94]

The evangelist/gospel singer known as "Amazing Grace" (DiBicarri) with her group Grace 'N Vessels performs in the northeast, reportedly for twenty thousand people each month. Her followers, drawn particularly from the Vatican II Charismatic Christian Renewal movement, attribute to her the powers of a Kathryn Kuhlman: when she touches people at her services, they keel over; later they come to themselves, sometimes speaking in tongues, sometimes allegedly cured of ills ranging from cancer and arrhythmia to drug addiction. If physical healing does not occur, she says, spiritual healing does.[95]

Dancing on the fringes of both religion and feminism, but at least for a time attracting large numbers of adherents, is New Age spirituality—a rather remote descendant of New Thought. Thanks largely to Emma Curtis Hopkins's institutionalization of female leadership, women continue to minister in the surviving New Thought organizations, constituting more than half of all ministers and practitioners. The movement still gives women a shot at the top jobs: in the 1990s women have presided at least nominally over the Unity School, the United Church of Religious Science, the Universal Foundation for Better Living, and the International Association of Churches of Truth; and the board of the International New Thought Alliance seats half women and half men. But once again the familiar pattern of decline forms: more and more women at the entry level, fewer and fewer at each succeeding level of leadership.[96]

As for New Age religions, Gary Dorsey writes of them as part of "the American psycho-religious carnival" that he and his fellow baby boomers, "women and men less interested in religion than in 'spirituality,'" have been experimenting with.

National data analyzed by sociologists at Hartford Seminary showed that, while one-third of babyboomers had settled into traditional church memberships and another third spurned religion entirely, the rest of us—apparently fussier than our parents—shopped like heathens in a cafeteria of broadening options. A full twenty percent of us attended spiritual growth seminars or sought personal fulfillment through new forms of meditation, Eastern traditions, New Age techniques, and amalgams of science and mysticism.[97]

But the New Age movement is not confined to baby boomers. Some experts think that some 40 percent of all those involved in cultlike New Age groups are over fifty.[98]

As J. Gordon Melton points out, in the 1960s when all this originated, a widespread religious hunger coincided with a disillusionment with existing churches and the presence in American society of a number of eastern religious and mystical-occult gurus who flavored their teachings with eastern derivations.[99] And Rachel Musleah ventures: "Some Jewish women who have turned to paganism seem to be frustrated rabbis, born too soon, who saw no option for a feminine-centered cosmology within the Judaism of their generation."[100]

In this mishmash, which derives as freely from Native American and Eastern religions as from Judaism and Christianity, as freely from psychology as from religion, women have assumed or created positions of leadership in some ways analogous to those of clergywomen, in others to those of 1960s flower children, and in still others to those of successful public relations drumbeaters. Among the more famed of these are Marianne Williamson and African-American Susan Taylor, editor-in-chief of *Essence,* both of whom offer survival techniques for the contemporary world.[101]

Williamson's pitch to the women's market emerges clearly in *A Woman's Worth,* in which she urges women to resurrect the Goddess: "The world despises you. God adores you," she assures women. "It is God's will that we be beautiful, that we love and be loved and prosper in all good things."[102] Shades of Mary Baker Eddy! Catherine Ponder, another spiritual daughter of Eddy and a veteran of Unity Church pulpits for more than two decades, gained renown by touting Bible millionaires: Joshua, Moses, Christ. "The Bible," she said, "is the greatest textbook on prosperity ever written." Mind-cure will protect its practitioners against mugging and melt away their fat.[103] "The Rev. Terry [Cole-Whittaker] is the evangelist of the yuppies," writes Earl Gottschalk in *The Wall Street Journal.* "Bubbly, bouncy and relentlessly upbeat, she preaches a gospel of 'happiness now' to her congregation of young, urban professionals. Wealth is good, not bad. Money is only an energy flow."[104]

Many of the seekers surfing the New Age web keep their affiliation with the faith of their childhood but choose to "enrich" it with beliefs, myths, and rituals borrowed from shamans, crystals worshippers, ecologists, psychics, holistic healers, and spirit channelers.[105] Most of these searchers are educated, high-achieving, and affluent. Estimates of the numbers of New Age followers vary absurdly, from the eighteen thousand Americans attached seriously to New Age groups discovered by a 1991 City University of New York Graduate School survey to the up to twelve million active participants, with another thirty million seriously interested projected by other authorities.[106] But their subculture includes hundreds of churchlike congregations, dozens of institutes, radio stations, magazines, publishing houses, resorts, hotels, healing centers, restaurants, shops, and a flourishing music industry. New Agers have taken over towns like Carbondale, Illinois, and Boulder, Colorado.

Although women don't seem to be making it bigtime as evangelists these days, they're doing just fine in the New Age movement, where if they don't find a ready-made religion to their liking they create one free-lance. One of their women leaders, Elizabeth Clare Prophet, known as Guru Ma, leads the Church Universal and Triumphant. In 1990 her crystal ball perhaps clouded by shades of Miller and Woodworth-Etter showed her a forthcoming Soviet nuclear attack, whereupon some two thousand of her followers left their homes and jobs to move to Montana, where they established a community of bomb shelters.

Georgia Gandalf, brought up a Lutheran, found that "the church teaches intolerance and judgment, and it didn't hold much of a place for women."[107] So, studying astrology, numerology, reincarnation, Tarot cards, ESP, and fire-walking, she cut her cloth to a faith of her own. Her pupil Page Bryant, guided by a power she terms "Albion," acts as a psychic counselor and a predictor of the future. In 1979 declaring Sedona, Arizona, the site of the most powerful collection of natural "vortexes" on earth, places where the earth either emits or receives special energies, she began its transformation into a New Age town. She worked on a radio show, wrote a book, put out an audiotape, and built a following. To her distress some of her followers, establishing themselves as vortex guides, have exploited—she says perverted—Albion's information.

Louise Hay, a movement star as a healer, has attracted a huge group of followers. She too rejects traditional religions, on the grounds that they inspire feelings of guilt and were created to control people. The daughter of a Christian Science practitioner, Hay believes that she has cured herself of cancer. Within the movement she has done it all: pastored in the New Age church Science of Mind, formed a support group for people with AIDS, written a book that sold more than a million copies. She runs her own publishing company, her own nonprofit educational Hay Foundation, and a mail-order catalogue business that grosses millions annually. Her books and audiotapes advocate repetition of sentences like "Today I give love and I receive love because I am love."[108] Hay preaches personal responsibility not only for one's own actions but also for external conditions: each person, she says, chooses every circumstance of his/her own life, body, and family.

Other New Age women function more quietly, often supporting themselves with secular jobs. One who talked with us identifies herself as an interfaith minister. Born into Reform Judaism, at thirteen she converted to Roman Catholicism. During her thirty-one years in that faith, she longed for priesthood. Ultimately she responded to an ad for the New Seminary, an institution founded by an Hassidic rabbi sometimes called "the New Age rabbi," who teaches "Never instead of, always in addition to," honoring the validity of all religions. "When I was ordained," said our informant, "my friend who walked down the aisle with me was a Yorba priest, which is a Puerto Rican earth religion. There was a man who was Wiccan and there were people who were Episcopal and people who were in Native American traditions. All of us were together in this group learning from each other and understanding that we're all part of this force. I believe that everyone has their own path and every path is just as valid."

Expressions of New Age spirituality take a variety of forms. Nelle Morton, at one time a professor at Drew theological seminary, describes the ice cream store opened in San Diego by two former theological students. Around its walls they have printed the names of goddesses, foresisters, foremothers, and women friends. Every year, Morton says, they celebrate their opening anniversary in a ceremony with impressive spiritual overtones.[109]

Whatever the numbers of New Agers, they influence not only the American economy but also the American ethos. For instance, in 1992 J. Z. Knight, a "spirit channeler," presented a dilemma for both the Internal Revenue Service and a divorce court lawyer. Knight's Ramtha School of Enlightenment enabled her to build a two-million-dollar house and breed Arabian horses. The IRS had to figure out how to tax her church, which was also a business. And the divorce court judge called to the stand her alleged spirit channel, a Cro-Magnon warrior named Ramtha.[110]

New Age ideas and techniques spill over into the larger society: meditation, mind-body theories, environmentalism, and visualization of a desired end (as in sports and healing). But, Michael D'Antonio says, they exercise their greatest influence on organized Christianity, which now acknowledges the religious significance of environmentalism, emphasizes spirituality and the mind-body connection, and adopts (or re-claims) such techniques as meditation. A renewed interest in healing is manifesting itself in both Christianity and Judaism. To an ancient Jewish tradition of spiritual healing, modern-day Jews are adding borrowings from Buddhism, Native American religions, and psychotherapy; the Academy for Jewish Religion now offers courses in healing.[111]

Certainly the New Agers have popularized such ideas and increased knowledgeability about them. Certainly some of them have been incorporated into feminist theology, where the terms "Christian feminism," "Judaic feminism," and "feminist spirituality" are now forces of transformative potential within churches and synagogues.

Notes

1. *The Witness* (July 1994).

2. See Elizabeth Cady Stanton, "Address Delivered at Seneca Falls and Rochester N.Y." in *Second to None: A Documentary History of American Women,* ed. Ruth Barnes Moynihan,

Cynthia Russett, and Laurie Crumpacker (Lincoln: Univ. of Nebraska Press, 1993), 1:257; and Anne Todd, "The Woman's Bible: 100 Years Ahead of Its Time," *Daughters of Sarah* 21 (Fall 1995): 47–51.

3. For a discussion of Goldstein's article, see Nelle Morton, *The Journey Is Home* (Boston: Beacon, 1985), p. 3; and Naomi R. Goldenberg, *Changing of the Gods: Feminism and the End of Traditional Religions* (Boston: Beacon, 1979), p. 116.

4. Harriet Martineau, *Society in America* (New York, 1837), 2:233, quoted by Dorothy C. Bass, "'Their Prodigious Influence': Women, Religion and Reform in Antebellum America," in *Women of Spirit: Female Leadership in the Jewish and Christian Traditions,* ed. Rosemary Ruether and Eleanor McLaughlin (New York: Simon & Schuster, 1979), p. 287.

5. Susan Hill Lindley, *"You Have Stept Out of Your Place": A History of Women and Religion in America* (Louisville, Ky.: Westminster John Knox, 1996), p. 296.

6. Morton, *Journey Is Home,* p. xxiii.

7. For comparisons between the military and religious institutions vis-à-vis women in their midst, see Margaret C. Devilbiss, "Women in the Military and Women in the Church: Historical Parallels, Organizational Impacts, and Institutional Implications" (Master's thesis, Lutheran Theological Seminary, Gettysburg, Penn., 1991); Mary Fainsod Katzenstein, "Feminism Within American Institutions: Unobtrusive Mobilization in the 1980's," *Signs* 16 (Autumn 1990): 27–54; eadem, "Organizing on the Terrain of Mainstream Institutions: Feminism in the United States Military," in *Coming to Power,* ed. Mary Fainsod Katzenstein and Hege Skele (Oslo, Norway: Institute of Social Research, 1990); and Marjorie H. Royle, "Using Bifocals to Overcome Blindspots: The Impact of Women on the Military and the Ministry," *Review of Religious Research* 28 (June 1987): 341–50.

8. Sara Maitland, *A Map of the New Country: Women and Christianity* (London: Routledge & Kegan Paul, 1983), p. 16.

9. *Christian Century* 110 (May 19–26, 1993): 547.

10. Dorothy Emerson, *Compendium of Resources,* 4th ed. (Medford, Mass.: Unitarian Universalist Women's Heritage Society, 1992), p. 12.

11. *Woman's Pulpit* (Jan.–Feb. 1944).

12. Edward I. Swanson, "The Navy Commissions Its First Woman Chaplain," *The Chaplain* (Fall 1973). Phyllis Ingram of the United Church of Christ was the first woman chaplain in the Civil Air Patrol, and Rita Sutt of the Christian Churches (Disciples), accepted in 1966, the second (*The Chaplain* [Fall, 1973]).

13. Eleanor Hull, *Women Who Carried the Good News: The History of the Woman's American Baptist Home Missionary Society* (Valley Forge, Penn.: Judson, 1975), p. 92.

14. *Black Women in the Armed Forces* (Hampton Inst., 1974); "Woman Chaplain Breaks Barrier," *Ebony* (October 1975): 44ff.

15. *Journal of Jewish Communal Service* 56 (Spring 1980): 282.

16. Donald Meyer, *The Positive Thinkers: Popular Religious Psychology from Mary Baker Eddy to Norman Vincent Peale and Ronald Reagan* (Middletown, Conn.: Wesleyan Univ. Press, 1988), p. 360.

17. Edward C. Lehman, Jr., *Women Clergy: Breaking Through Gender Barriers* (New Brunswick, N.J.: Transaction Books, 1985), pp. 10–11.

18. Edward C. Lehman, Jr., "Organizational Resistance to Women in Ministry," in *Women and Men,* ed. Hestenes, p. 197.

19. Lehman, *Women Clergy,* p. 15.

20. Henrietta T. Wilkinson, "Bridges," in *Voices of Experience: Lifestories of Clergywomen in the Presbyterian Church,* ed. Alice Brasfield and Elisabeth Lunz (Louisville, Ky.: Presbyterian Pub. House, 1991), p. 29.

21. Sharon Mielke, "Women Want Ministry Call Upheld: Seminarians Cite Psychological Harassment in Their Training," *Texas Methodist/United Methodist Reporter* (March 21, 1980), in *Women and Men,* ed. Hestenes, p. 205.

22. Willa B. Roghair, "Icebergs," in *Voices of Experience,* ed. Brasfield and Lunz, p. 77.

23. "Despite Obstacles, Women Ministers are on Rise Among Black Baptists," *Los Angeles Times,* Part II, Sept 17, 1983, quoted in *Women and Men,* ed. Hestenes, p. 200.

24. "Perla Dirige Belo, "Empowered and Excluded," in *Voices of Experience,* ed. Brasfield and Lunz, pp. 125–27.

25. Jung Mi Han, "A Guiding Hand," in *Voices of Experience,* ed. Brasfield and Lunz, p. 92.

26. John Henry Paul Reumann tells something of the history of Lutheranism on the issue of women's ordination, though he devotes most of his book to rehearsing the arguments for women's ordination pro and con (*Ministries Examined: Laity, Clergy, Women, and Bishops in a Time of Change* [Minneapolis: Augsburg, 1987]). For the Association of Evangelical Lutheran Churches, see Virginia Lieson Brereton and Christa Ressmeyer Klein, "American Women in Ministry: A History of Protestant Beginning Points," in *Women of Spirit,* ed. Ruether and McLaughlin, p. 321.

27. Alla Bozarth-Campbell, *Womanpriest: A Personal Odyssey* (New York: Paulist Press, 1978), pp. 105–6. On the history of ordination for Episcopal women priests, see also Norene Carter, "Entering the Sanctuary: The Struggle for Priesthood in Contemporary Episcopalian and Roman Catholic Experience," in *Women of Spirit,.*ed. Ruether and McLaughlin.

28. George Rutler, *Priest and Priestess* (Ambler, Penn.: Trinity, 1973), p. 35.

29. Carter Heyward in *Ms. Magazine* (December 1974) quoted a more explicit statement of fear: "I've had priests talk to me about a seminal mass, where the priest, as the living representative of Christ, engages in a sex act with the 'bride of Christ,' the church. A woman can't provide the semen; she commits a lesbian act instead. That's what some priests worried about during the last convention—'cosmic lesbianism.' It's the most absurd thing I ever heard. I resent it as a put-down of women and of gays, and as sick, foundationless theology."

30. Quoted by Carter Heyward, *A Priest Forever* (New York: Harper & Row, 1976), p. 41.

31. Ibid., p. 60.

32. Piccard (b. 1895) stands out even in this group of high-achieving, independent women, first, because she was seventy-nine years old when she finally achieved her childhood ambition to become a priest, and second, because forty years earlier she had piloted a stratosphere balloon to the altitude of 57,579 feet, the first woman ever in space. For information on her, see Betsy Covington Smith, *Breakthrough: Women in Religion* (New York: Walker, 1978).

33. Mary S. Donovan, *Women Priests in the Episcopal Church: The Experience of the First Decade* (Cincinnati, Oh.: Forward Movement, 1988), p. 106.

34. John H. Morgan, *Women Priests: An Emerging Ministry in the Episcopal Church (1975–1985)* (Bristol, Ind.: Wyndham Hall Press, 1985), p. 166.

35. Bozarth-Campbell, *Womanpriest,* p. 140.

36. Donovan, *Women Priests,* p. 42.

37. Ibid., p. 10; see also Smith, *Breakthrough.*

38. *Episcopal Women: Gender, Spirituality, and Commitment in an American Mainline Denomination,* ed Catherine M. Prelinger (New York: Oxford Univ. Press, 1992), p. 599.

39. Carol Cole Flanagan, "Women in Waiting?" *The Witness* 78 (June 1995): 36.

40. *New York Times,* Oct. 1, 1995; and *The Witness* 78 (Sept. 1995).

41. Pauli Murray, *The Autobiography of a Black Activist, Feminist, Lawyer, Priest, and Poet* (Knoxville: Univ. of Tennessee Press, 1987), p. 370.

42. Because of the close connections between the Anglican/Episcopal church and the Roman Catholic church, the Roman Catholic hierarchy found the Episcopal about-face disconcerting, at the same time that Roman Catholic advocates of women's ordination found it especially heartening.

43. Episcopal and Roman Catholic priests also move from one denomination to the other. The Roman Catholic church will in some cases ordain married Episcopalian priests with families and permit them to function without ending their marriages. (Theological students sometimes refer to this practice as an "end run.") When the Episcopal church began to ordain women, some of their priests who disapproved sought to serve as Roman Catholics; at least one returned to the Episcopalian flock when he found that he must be reordained.

44. Quoted by Heyward, *Priest,* pp. 126, 115, 120.

45. Marcelle Bernstein, *The Nuns* (Philadelphia: Lippincott, 1976), p. 132.

46. In the strictest usage the term "nuns" is used only for enclosed women religious, but popular parlance has almost destroyed the distinction.

47. Quoted in Weaver, *New Catholic Women,* p. 72.

48. On the history of American women religious, see *American Catholic Women: A Historical Exploration,* ed. Karen Kennelly (New York: Macmillan, 1989); Mary Ewens, "The Leadership of Nuns in Immigrant Catholicism," in *Women and Religion in America,* ed. Rosemary R. Ruether and Rosemary S. Keller (San Francisco: Harper & Row, 1981), vol. 2; James J. Kenneally, *The History of American Catholic Women* (New York: Crossroad, 1990); Elizabeth Kolmer, *Religious Women in the United States: A Survey of the Influential Literature from 1950 to 1983* (Wilmington, Del.: Michael Glazier, 1984); *Midwives of the Future: American Sisters Tell Their Story,* ed. Ann Patrick Ware (Kansas City, Mo.: Leaven, 1985); Marie Augusta Neal, *Catholic Sisters in Transition: From the 1960s to the 1980s* (Wilmington, Del.: Michael Glazier, 1984); eadem, *From Nuns to Sisters: An Expanding Vocation* (Mystic, Conn.: Twenty-Third Publications, 1984); and Lora Ann Quiñonez and Mary Daniel Turner, *The Transformation of American Catholic Sisters* (Philadelphia: Temple Univ. Press, 1992).

49. Lindley, *"You Have Stept Out of Your Place,"* p. 177.

50. Kenneally, *History,* pp. 58–59. Mary Ewens writes: "I estimate, based on the Catholic Directory figures of 1,344 sisters in 1850, 40,340 in 1900, and 177,354 in 1963, that possibly as many as 220,000 sisters have served the church in America since the foundation of the republic" ("Women in the Convent," in *American Catholic Women,* ed. Kennelly, p. 18).

51. In 1954, for instance, they founded the first journal by and for sisters, the *Sister Formation Bulletin,* which became a vehicle for change (Kenneally, *History,* p. 197). They also established various organizations of women religious, including the National Assembly of Women Religious, the National Coalition of American Nuns, Las Hermanas (Hispanic nuns), the National Black Sisters Conference, the Sister Formation Conference, the National Sisters Vocation Conference, and the Association of Contemplative Sisters. "Each of these organizations enabled members to become painfully aware of the subservient position of Catholic women" (Jeannine Grammick, "From Good Sisters to Prophetic Women," in *Midwives of the Future,* ed. Ware, p. 232).

52. In 1966 there were more than 180,000 American sisters; in the early 1990s, about 128,000. Raw numbers continued to rise into the 1960s, but the rate of increase slowed and began to decline in the early 1950s. In 1992 only one percent of them were under thirty (Quiñonez and Turner, *Transformation,* p. 192n, p. 141). The fastest growing group of "reli-

gious" women in the United States is a lay organization composed mostly of former sisters: Sisters for Christian Community (*American Catholic Women,* ed. Kennelly, p. 46).

53. In the words of Sister Mary Agnes Mansour, who distinguishes between *obedience and compliance,* "We should define obedience, especially after Vatican II, as a sincere attempt to discern what God's will is for us" (quoted by Annie Lally Milhaven, ed., in *The Inside Stories: 13 Valiant Women Challenging the Church* [Mystic, Conn.: Twenty-Third Publications, 1987], pp. 71–72).

54. Sister Joan D. Chittister, "No Time For Tying Cats," in *Midwives of the Future,* ed. Ware, p. 17.

55. Debra Campbell, "Reformers and Activists," in *American Catholic Women,* ed. Kennelly, p. 180. See also *Inside Stories,* ed. Milhaven.

56. Forty-six percent fewer priests were ordained from 1980 to 1984 than from 1966 to 1969; by the year 2005 46 percent of average diocesan priests will be fifty-five or older but only 12 percent will be thirty-five or younger (Ruth A. Wallace, *They Call Her Pastor: A New Role for Catholic Women* [Albany: State Univ. of New York Press, 1992], p. 9). Richard A. Schoenherr has written: "[W]hile the diocesan priesthood population will have declined by 40 percent between 1966 and 2005, the lay population is increasing by 65 percent. The laity-to-priest ratio, a fairly accurate measure of supply and demand, will double betwen 1975 and 2005 from 1,100 to 2,200 Catholics per active priest. Furthermore, this is a conservative estimate because it does not account for the growing Hispanic-American population, which is increasing five times faster than the general population. At the same time, recruitment and retention will remain chronic problems and the number of retirements and deaths will soar" ("Numbers Don't Lie: A Priesthood in Irreversible Decline," *Commonweal* [Apr. 7, 1995]: 11–14).

57. The interviewee explained that her order leaves her free to choose jobs but must approve her choice. While this approval is not necessarily automatic, getting it has never been a problem for her, since she checks her bases along the way. She knows that she must choose a ministry that enables her to contribute to her order economically. (At fifty, the interviewee has in her community of eighty-three only six sisters younger than she.) And she makes sure that her colleagues will be like-minded people. In her diocese, and in many others, the priest makes the decision about whether or not to hire her, sometimes with the advice of a committee; he informs the bishop, who may approve or disapprove.

58. Wallace, *They Call,* p. 138.

59. O. John Eldred, *Women Pastors: If God Calls, Why Not the Church?* (Valley Forge, Penn.: Judson, 1981), p. 106.

60. Ibid., pp. 106–7.

61. See, for instance, Colm Toibin, "The Paradoxical Pope," *The New Yorker* (October 9, 1995).

62. Sr. Theresa Kane, in *Inside Stories,* ed. Milhaven, p. 6.

63. Mary E. Hunt, in *Inside Stories,* ed. Milhaven, p. 122.

64. See Robert Dunne, "4 Down 1 To Go: Trying to Save a Team" ; and Jay (John) Montalbano, "Collaborative Ministry at St. Elizabeth Seton," both in *The American Catholic, Northeast* 3 (Dec. 1995/Jan. 1996).

65. Ruth McDonough Fitzpatrick, in *Inside Stories,* ed. Milhaven, p. 32.

66. Sister Camille D'Arienzo, "My Pact with Camillus," in *Midwives of the Future,* ed. Ware, p. 35.

67. See Ann Braude in *In Our Own Voices,* ed. Keller and Ruether, p. 121; and Judith Plaskow, *Standing Again at Sinai: Judaism from a Feminist Perspective* (San Francisco: Harper & Row, 1990).

68. Braude, in *In Our Own Voices,* ed. Keller and Ruether, pp. 121–23.

69. *New York Times* (Sept. 24, 1995).

70. Sally Priesand, *Judaism and the New Woman* (New York: Behrman House, 1975), pp. xvi, 67. See also Gershon Winkler, "They Called Her Rebbe," *Moment* 19 (Dec. 1993): 56.

71. Laura Geller, "From Equality to Transformation: The Challenge of Women's Rabbinic Leadership," in *Gender and Judaism: The Transformation of Tradition,* ed. T. M. Rudavsky (New York: New York Univ. Press, 1995), p. 244.

72. Ibid., p. 244.

73. Susannah Heschel, *On Being a Jewish Feminist* (New York: Schocken, 1983), p. xxxiii.

74. See Mark Winer, "Are All Rabbis Equal?" *Reform Judaism* 18 (Summer 1990): 12.

75. Rosemary Radford Ruether, "Growing Pluralism, New Dialogue: Women in American Religions," in *In Our Own Voices,* ed. Keller and Ruether, p. 431.

76. Rita J. Simon, *Rabbis, Lawyers, Immigrants, Thieves: Exploring Women's Roles* (New York: Praeger, 1993).

77. Morgan, *Women Priests,* p. 140. Many women clergy have perforce given serious thought to what people call them. An Episcopalian priest told us, "I think that when the clergy are called by familial names, like 'Father' and 'Mother,' it tends to keep the congregation children. You often counsel the people who have had the most difficulty with their parents, and I don't want to replace their parent as a good parent, as opposed to a bad one. I will not be other people's mother, because they don't need another mother; they need a priest. I'm mother to four people and that's enough. I want the people that I counsel to learn to be adult, and I don't think they're going to do that with a mother figure or with a father figure. Mother and father to some people are both authorities; father certainly is. Sometimes mother is not an authority figure, and if that detracts from the authority that I have that's dangerous too. The title to me is much more significant than people ever realize. But some people say I have to have a title, and what one do I want, and then they struggle with it, because I say 'Pastor.'"

78. *Women and Men,* ed. Hestenes, p. 210.

79. *Los Angeles Times,* Sept. 17, 1983, in *Women and Men,* ed. Hestenes, pp. 200–201.

80. "The Stained Glass Ceiling," *Christianity Today* (May 16, 1994): 52.

81. Margaret M. Poloma, *Assemblies of God at the Crossroads: Charisma and Institutional Dilemmas* (Knoxville: Univ. of Tennessee Press, 1989), pp. 109–11, 119, 237.

82. Nilah Meier-Youngman, "Hispanic Women in Ministry in the Church of God," in *Called to Minister. . . Empowered to Serve: Women in Ministry and Missions in the Church of God Reformation Movement,* ed. Juanita Leonard (Anderson, Ind.: Warner Press, 1989), pp. 75–76.

83. Ruth M. Smith, "Contemporary Profiles of Women in Ministry," in *Called to Minister,* ed. Leonard, pp. 107, 115.

84. See, for instance, Cathleen M. Falsani, "Personal Power in Political Action: CWA and the Feminist Movement," *Daughters of Sarah* 21 (Summer 1995): 17–22.

85. Ruth A. Tucker and Walter Liefeld, *Daughters of the Church: Women and Ministry from New Testament Times to the Present* (Grand Rapids, Mich.: Zondervan, Academie Books, 1987), pp. 397–98.

86. Jane Mayer and Jill Abramson, *Strange Justice: The Selling of Clarence Thomas* (New York: Plume/Penguin, 1995), pp. 288–89.

87. Nancy A. Hardesty, in *In Our Own Voices,* ed. Keller and Ruether, p. 217.

88. Elaine J. Lawless, *Handmaidens of the Lord: Pentecostal Women Preachers and Traditional Religion* (Philadelphia: Univ. of Pennsylvania Press, 1988), pp. 13, 152.

89. Edward H. McKinley, *Marching to Glory: The History of the Salvation Army in the United States of America, 1880–1980* (San Francisco: Harper & Row, 1980), p. 203.

90. *The War Cry* (June 18, 1994): 12–13.

91. See Mary Farrell Bednarowski, "Widening the Banks of the Mainstream: Women Constructing Theologies," in *Women's Leadership in Marginal Religions: Explorations Outside the Mainstream,* ed. Catherine Wessinger (Urbana: Univ. of Illinois Press, 1993), pp. 216–17, for a discussion of ways in which Mormon women are studying Mormon scriptures and history to rethink the place of women in the religion; and Sonia Johnson, *From Housewife to Heretic* (Garden City, N.Y.: Doubleday, 1981).

92. Diana Hochstedt Butler, "Between Two Worlds: Evangelical Female—and a Scholar," *Christian Century* 110 (March 3, 1993): 231–32.

93. Tony Heilbut, *The Gospel Sound: Good News and Bad Times* (Garden City, N.Y.: Doubleday, 1975), pp. 187–96.

94. Ibid., pp. 224–32; and Jualyne E. Dodson and Cheryl Townsend Gilkes, "Something Within: Social Change and Collective Endurance in the Sacred World of Black Christian Women," in *Women and Religion,* ed. Ruether and Keller, 3:85.

95. Elizabeth Fuller, *The Touch of Grace* (New York: Dodd, Mead, 1986).

96. J. Gordon Melton, "Emma Curtis Hopkins: A Feminist of the 1880s and Mother of New Thought," in *Women's Leadership,* ed. Wessinger, pp. 96–97.

97. Gary Dorsey, *Congregation: The Journey Back to Church* (New York: Viking, 1995), pp. 3, 97–98. For New Age religions and leaders, see Michael D'Antonio, *Heaven on Earth* (New York: Crown, 1992).

98. Catherine Collins and Douglas Frantz, "Let Us Prey," *Modern Maturity* (June 1994): 24, quoting Kevin Garvey, "a Connecticut-based expert who specializes in helping businesses deal with the impact of cults."

99. J. Gordon Melton, *Encyclopedic Handbook of Cults in America,* rev. ed. (New York: Garland, 1992), p. 164.

100. Rachel Musleah, "When the Goddess Calls Jewish Women Answer," *Lillith* 18 (Fall 1993): 8.

101. Taylor sets forth her teachings in *Lessons in Love* (Fall 1995) and Williamson hers in *A Return to Love: Reflections on the Principles of A Course in Miracles* (New York: Harper Collins, 1992).

102. Marianne Williamson, *A Woman's Worth* (New York: Random House, 1993), pp. 21, 26–27.

103. Meyer, *Positive Thinkers,* p. 369.

104. "The Rev. Terry Has a Gospel to Cheer the Me Generation," *Wall Street Journal,* August 23, 1984, quoted by Meyer, *Positive Thinkers,* p. 371.

105. D'Antonio helpfully surveys the New Age movement (*Heaven on Earth*). See also Ruether, "Growing Pluralism"; and Wendy Hunter Roberts, "In Her Name: Toward a Feminist Thealogy of Pagan Ritual," in *Woman at Worship: Interpretations of North American Diversity,* ed. Marjorie Procter-Smith and Janet R. Walton (Louisville, Ky.: Westminster/John Knox Press, 1993).

106. R. Laurence Moore, *Selling God: American Religion in the Marketplace of Culture* (New York: Oxford, 1994), p. 257; and D'Antonio, *Heaven on Earth,* pp. 13–14.

107. D'Antonio, *Heaven on Earth,* p. 25.

108. Ibid., p. 68.

109. Morton, *Journey Is Home,* p. 160.

110. Moore, *Selling God,* p. 262.

111. D'Antonio, *Heaven on Earth,* pp. 399–400. See also Gary Dorsey, *Congregation,* pp. 256–57. A woman rabbi associated with the National Center for Jewish Healing told us of their effort to recapture spiritual responses to illness. Judaism, she said, used to have a tradition allowing for spiritual response to physical illness, "not necessarily to effect a physical cure, although there are people who think that spiritual responses can assist in the physical recovery—that's fine too. But there's a value in just responding to the spirit when the body is ill." Similarly an Episcopal priest spoke of her church's renewed interest in healing.

8

Liberation or Heresy?

UNDENIABLY, FEMINISM AND WOMANISM are shaking up the theology, ritual, and governance of synagogues and churches. Equally undeniably, synagogues and churches are resisting. This interaction between feminists and traditionalists within religious institutions sometimes whispers, sometimes shouts the differences between those who insist on full participation for women and those who long to preserve patriarchy.

The bewilderment of William F. Buckley, Jr., on the *Firing Line* telecast of September 23, 1995, epitomizes the lack of understanding of feminist theological scholarship. Invited to discuss "What's Ahead for the Catholic Church? The Role of Women" were two men: Thomas Fox, editor of the *National Catholic Reporter* and author of *Sexuality and Catholicism,* and Father Richard McBrien, professor of theology at Notre Dame University and editor of the *HarperCollins Encyclopedia of Catholicism.* The picture of three men discussing women's future in the church visually demonstrated precisely what women theologians and clergy complain about—their exclusion.[1] True enough, the two guests were notably understanding of the need for change and cognizant of the contributions that women have made to theology, but their sensitivity hardly compensated for the absence of any of several notable Roman Catholic women theologians—or, indeed, of any woman at all. Fox commented that this "is the first century in which educated Catholic women are sharing their stories . . . and have become the first generation of Catholic theologians who are women in the history of the church. And so they are bringing a whole perspective to the faith that has been denied the faith for 20 centuries." But Buckley just didn't get it: "I don't completely understand your point, because *I wouldn't have thought of theology as being affected by the sex of the person who explores theology.*"[2]

Editors of *Daughters of Sarah* see the matter differently: "The dogmas and doctrines of the church have been decided and written by men for thousands of years. It's time for us [women] to direct *ourselves* in worship."[3]

226

✍ Feminist Theology

To that end American feminist and womanist theologians have been pursuing their work in the latter half of the twentieth century, particularly since the 1960s. African-Americans often identify their work as "womanist" rather than "feminist," taking into account considerations of race and class as well as of gender. They interpret the Bible, that is, in the light of black women's experiences—just as white men have for centuries interpreted it in terms of their own perceptions. Womanist and feminist ideas are now finding their way into secular and religious magazines published for lay readers. For instance, an article by Cullen Murphy in the *Atlantic Monthly* (August 1991) titled "Women and the Bible" thoughtfully surveyed the work of a number of respected women theologians and biblical scholars. Again, the March 1995 number of *Presbyterian Survey* included under the heading "Women Doing Theology" three articles: "What's All the Fuss About Feminist Theology?" by Shelley C. Wiley; an interview with Roberta Hestenes by Eva Stimson, entitled "The Bible—Not Patriarchal But Liberating"; and "Resisting and Rising Above" by Delores S. Williams, dealing with the contribution of African-American women through womanist theology.[4]

Of course, for some people the words "feminist" and "womanist" are anathema. But just as many women in the secular world flinch at the terms yet believe that the women's movement has helped them, so with women clergy. Guarded though some clergywomen are in dealing with feminism's vocabulary, many acclaim its agenda of equal opportunity and equal pay for equal work. Their exclusion from full participation in their religious institutions has made them feminists whether they like the term or not. Similarly for clergywomen and for many Jewish and Christian laywomen feminist theology is opening fresh possibilities for women in religion and fresh insights for all believers into the nature of religion itself—possibilities and insights that many of them, regardless of age, class, or race, perceive with excitement.

With increasing insistence, feminists within and without religious institutions have been demanding reformation, not simply acceptance of the rights of women to be ordained, to preach and to pastor. By the 1990s feminists in church and synagogue had shifted their emphasis from gender equality to a new theology—some would say *thealogy* to emphasize the feminist perspective—that would repair the damage done to women by centuries of patriarchy, male-dominated biblical interpretation, and masculine imagery and language.[5] The range of theological issues coming under review from a feminist perspective is extensive, and much is common to both the Christian and Jewish faiths.

Inclusivity, perhaps the most important of these issues, makes manifest what is happening in churches and in American society generally. Immigration is rapidly shifting the ethnic balance of the country. In the mainline churches, membership has been dwindling among longtime Americans but growing among immigrants. The *New York Times* (April 14, 1996) quotes the Rev. Avelio De Leon: "The United

Methodist Church has lost around two million in more than a decade. Growth is taking place, however, in the ethnic churches: Koreans, Caribbeans, Africans and other Asians." The message is clear: integrate (include) or die. The immigrating descendants of Asian, African, and Caribbeans converted by Christian missionaries in the late nineteenth and early twentieth centuries are now attacking Eurocentric Christianity. Inclusivity—both ethnic and gender inclusivity (which combine in womanist theology)—dominates theological discussion.

Feminist theologians worry about shutting out the poor, shutting out people of different ethnic origins, ignoring single people in favor of catering to families, shutting out gay men and lesbian women, and denying the Eucharist to people of other denominations or faiths. Most of all they object to the ways in which religious institutions have excluded and in some cases still exclude women, theologically, liturgically, historically, and professionally. How, they ask, are women to worship a God presented in all His manifestations as male—Father, Son, and Holy Spirit? Why do some twentieth-century churches still preach the inferiority of women and their guilt as originators of sin? Why has the history of women in the early Christian church been suppressed?

Women and ethnic groups alike seek in religion what Rita Nakashima Brock calls "theological mirrors that reflect ourselves back to us." As an African-American pastor explained to us, "When you think of everything that's religious, the figures are all white, then what does that do to you? Makes you think you were a second thought." Going on to identify black ancestors in Christ's genealogy, she continued, "See, that makes the black women feel better. Hey, we love this thing so much, we love the Bible so much, where am I in here?"

Accordingly, biblical scholars are devoting attention to the women of scriptures and the early church, finding in their roles as prophets, heads of religious communities, and teachers sources of revelation and inspiration for contemporary churchwomen. These scholars are engaged in "a project of retrieval and reconstruction of positive [female] elements within Judaism and/or Christianity in the attempt to find a 'usable past' in scripture and tradition."[6]

Feminist and womanist theologians also seek gender-neutral language ("brothers and sisters" rather than "brethren") or feminine terms to describe the attributes of the divinity ("Mother-Father God"). The proposition that God cannot be adequately represented by male language and symbols alone has advocates in all sectors of the denominational spectrum, from Mary Baker Eddy to Lois Roden, leader of the Living Waters Branch, who in 1977 began her crusade to persuade the world that the Holy Trinity consists of the Father, the Son, and the Mother (the Holy Spirit).[7] "At worst," writes a rabbi, "people still think of God only as male. Why else would they scream 'Idolatry!' when a female image is used? Why else would my own five-year-old daughter settle her friend's question, 'Is God a boy or a girl?' with the pronouncement 'Look, "God" is a boy's name!'"[8] Some womanists argue that since Christ has always been a symbol of the poor and the oppressed, the Christ figure may properly be represented by a black woman. "Christ can be seen," writes Kelly

Brown Douglas, "in the face of a Sojourner Truth, a Harriet Tubman, or a Fannie Lou Hamer. . . . Christ is inside of my grandmother and other Black women and men as they fight for life and wholeness."[9]

Language and symbols inclusive of both genders and all ethnicities take an important first step toward eliminating the androcentric fallacy (spelled "phallacy" by some). For many women, both clergy and lay, inclusive language touches a nerve: Mary Pellauer writes of women who wept the first time they heard God addressed as "Mother."[10] Beyond those, though, feminists and womanists are trying to think in a new way, to articulate a theology that incorporates women's experience as an essential element in spiritual growth and understanding.[11] Moving women from the periphery toward the center of theological concern may necessitate redefining sin and adopting new attitudes toward women's bodies and sexuality.

In academic circles feminism has breached the ramparts: feminist theological scholarship is burgeoning; courses in feminist theology are proliferating in seminaries and divinity schools across the country; and continuing education programs for clergy include work in feminist theology and spirituality. To encourage an open dialogue on sexuality, gender, and religion, the divinity school at Vanderbilt University in 1997 is instituting conferences, a book series, and other forums involving primarily Christian and Jewish leaders but also Islamic, Hindu, and New Age representatives.[12] The intellectual environment in which clergy are trained is richer and more variegated than ever before.[13]

Their studies have driven the most radical feminists (such as Mary Daly, a quondam Roman Catholic who now calls herself post-Christian) into despair about their religious institutions and out of church and synagogue (though not necessarily out of seminaries). A professor at a distinguished divinity school says flatly, "The radical feminists are long gone from the church's pews." But the overwhelming majority of Jewish and Christian feminists labor faithfully on within the gates. Of course as they push at the boundaries of inherited belief, their findings and hypotheses strike traditionalists (often ignorant of their earlier scholarship) as ever more deviant and outré.

❧ Feminist Spirituality

Some of the ideas set out by academic feminist theologians take root among other clergywomen and among laywomen, both those disaffected with their own denominations and those who simply seek a deserved place within them. Clergy and laywomen who with the coming of the feminist movement in the 1960s had begun to think about women's status within their own churches and synagogues responded empathetically to feminist theologians. They listened when these theologians recognized a female element in the godhead, denied the depiction of women as unclean temptresses responsible for all sin in the world, and reclaimed the significance of women's experiences for church and synagogue. Out of this ferment came feminist spirituality.

Feminist spirituality has been and remains amorphous, protean. Some see it as enabling mild, gradual reform; for others it necessitates outright and outraged rebellion; for still others it demands abandoning familiar religions for a "post-Christian" or "pagan" faith. The range of its voices is wide, but they sound a common note of challenge to patriarchal religion and its institutions, combining "a reverence for [their] culture's religious values with an absolute irreverence for the cultural and religious icons that have been used against [them]."[14]

The ideals of democracy and inclusivity in religion are of course not gender-specific. Many clergymen advocate them. But spiritual feminists believe that women have a special contribution to make in achieving them. For good historical reasons clergywomen are not as heavily invested in the status quo of religious institutions as are clergymen. During much of the American past, the profession offered men position, security, and a degree of power, putting many a poor boy on a track to upward mobility. An up-and-coming young man could answer the call of both the Holy Spirit and ambition. Aspiring clergywomen could not; instead they could expect to be denounced as heretics and as unnatural women. Facing incredulity, opposition, even persecution, they have had to be risk-takers, pioneers, and entrepreneurs. And some of their independence and pioneering spirit survives among clergywomen today.

Abandoning Eurocentrism, they embrace ecumenicity—an ecumenicity stretched to a new breadth, not merely to other denominations of Christianity or Judaism, but to other faiths.[15] It's not so much that they ignore differences as that they leap over them. To enrich their worship, they borrow from Islam, from Buddhism, from Native American religions, from goddess religions, even from witchcraft, neopaganism, and New Age notions. For some of them, all of these represent merely different manifestations of one God. They would learn about the divinity (whoever and whatever that might be), when and where they can, from whomever they can.

Some invoke Sophia, conceptualized either scripturally as a feminine personification of God's wisdom or as a Gnostic goddess. Churchwomen may listen to Starhawk, a self-proclaimed witch and medicine woman who preaches a woman-centered, goddess-centered religion, without accepting all her ideas.[16] Rather they improvise, borrow, and adapt. They "explore new spiritualities through the worship of the goddess, in matriarchy cults or in debates about androgyny. Feminist voices of spirituality also speak about our relationship to nature and about peace as a goal of political and human liberation."[17]

Clergywomen influenced by feminist spirituality and feminist theology in turn influence their parishioners. "You see it in the children already," a Lutheran pastor told us. "In my confirmation class, the girls will talk about God as Mother, they'll talk about a female god. That's not an embarrassment for them. And the boys don't even snicker and laugh."

Besides inclusive language, these clergywomen introduce into worship rituals that pertain especially to women, that celebrate the achievements and crises of a woman's life. Sometimes they write new rituals to mark the onset of menstruation or of menopause; sometimes they resurrect old ones. Rabbi Nina Beth Cardin has dug up "Italian Jewish women's liturgy, pretty much from the 1700s and 1800s, prayers in Hebrew with Italian directions."

> These prayers deal specifically with women's experiences, with the three commandments that women take on as their premier commandments, in addition to those they share with men: lighting the Shabbas candles; throwing a pinch of dough into the oven when preparing the Shabbas bread in remembrance of the sacrifices given in the temple and gifts of food to the priest who served in the temple; observing family purity laws, most notably refraining from sleeping with one's husband when a woman has her period. I've looked at a host of prayers associated with these three commandments; they focus on family, childbirth, pregnancy, health. Then there's a whole other genre of the Yiddish tradition of Jewish women's prayers. These establish a whole parallel religion for women showing that women experience Judaism in a different way.

Feminist spirituality exhibits two strong and contradictory impulses, one toward the individual spiritual quest and the other toward community, both of which threaten institutional religion. As a Unitarian-Universalist clergywoman told us, "My sense is that people aren't moving only to change the church's structure, but we are reaching for something in ourselves that we find at different places and at different rates. It's not like a committee of women from different denominations got together and said, 'Let's do X, Y, and Z, and then take it to the people.' It's that women are on individual odysseys and occasionally we come together at the same time and place and say, 'You've discovered that? I've discovered it too!' Or 'Let's take this home. Let's rattle some cages.'" As Elinor Lenz and Barbara Myerhoff comment,

> In place of leadership there is networking, with women of various denominations coming together to explore and exchange ideas. Instead of transcendence there is immanence—women looking into themselves and building on their own life experience; thus, unity of mind and body, of human beings and nature, replaces dualism and polarization. The theology, if there can be said to be one, is open-ended, a process theology consisting of a responsible search for truth as it unfolds rather than a commitment to absolute truth for all time. There is no formal church or ministry; the "church" may be a woman's home or a retreat in a rural setting where nature serves as the ministry.[18]

To satisfy their need for community, spiritual feminists have banded together in hundreds of loosely organized denominational, interdenominational, and interfaith networks, small and large, as clergywomen or with laywomen. They welcome all comers—Jews, Christians, Muslims, Buddhists, and New Agers.

Most Christian and Jewish spiritual feminists of whatever degree accept a few basic propositions in whole or in part:

1. Traditional biblical scholarship (if not the Bible itself) is overwhelmingly androcentric and deals unfairly with women, wrongly subordinating them to men. If there is one point on which all Christian feminists agree, it is that St. Paul was either wrong or has been misinterpreted.

2. Naming is powerful: since language shapes reality, changing language changes

patriarchal traditions and structures. The naming of God is more than a matter of inclusive language, of "he" not including "she." God is genderless, or there is a feminine side to God (Mother) represented by names used in the Old Testament like Sophia, Shekinah, and El Shaddai. (The problem is complicated by the absence of a neutral gender in Hebrew.)

3. The male-dominated authority structure in religion has aborted the egalitarian possibilities embedded in scripture and serves only the interests of a sexist society. "Priesthood is for people, not for men." Religion must acknowledge the equality of all the people of God; it must not assert the authority of men over women, clergy over laity.

4. Religion must abandon dualities, especially that of body and soul, recognizing sexuality, including women's sexuality, as part of God's creation and therefore good.

5. All life is sacred. All forms of oppression, suffering, and injustice contravene God's will. Spiritual feminists therefore recognize responsibility to combat poverty, militarism, ecological destruction, and the exploitation of marginal people. Women are particularly challenged to a ministry of healing and sharing, of caring and nurturing.

6. Women need their own rituals and celebrations, both inside and outside conventional religious settings, to celebrate their own life experiences. Dance, painting, and song help to overcome the restraints of language.

7. Ecumenical and interdenominational fellowship liberates and empowers women's religious life.

✑ The Re-Imagining Conference

Most of all, it is time to state clearly and dream wildly about who we are as people of God, and whom we intend to be in the future through the power and guidance of the spirit of wisdom whom we name Sophia.

—Re-Imagining Conference program and liturgy

The Re-Imagining Conference of November 4–7, 1993, is a metaphor for spiritual feminism. Organized to celebrate the midpoint of the World Council of Churches' "Ecumenical Decade: Churches in Solidarity with Women 1988–1998," the conference dramatized feminist theology and spiritual feminism in evolution—and in action. The World Council created the Decade for Women to address the plight of women around the world. In effect, the council did not just authorize efforts to study women's problems and to help them but imposed this task on churchwomen as a moral duty.

The Re-Imagining Conference, which met in Minneapolis, undertook this work through "a global women's theological colloquium that addressed the goals of the

Decade."[19] The conference was some three years in the planning, involving nearly 150 people, clergy and laity, representing six denominations. Thirty-five women from ten denominations, twelve countries, and eight ethnic backgrounds made up the roster of speakers and artistic facilitators, among them several Third World theologians and clergywomen.

The conference was supported by most of the mainline Christian denominations, most prominently by the Presbyterian Church, USA, and the United Methodist Church. Would-be participants competed for the twenty-two hundred tickets. The attendants were almost all women, only a third clergy. They were *churchwomen:* "I wouldn't have gone to Re-Imagining," one of them said, "if I'd been a feminist who had given up on the church completely. In that case I would have gone to a Woman-church celebration, a Wicca conference or something. This was women still in the church and women refusing to be defined out of the church." They came from all states except Nevada, from as far away as Australia, Brazil, New Zealand, and Korea. They represented sixteen denominations, ranging from 405 Presbyterians and 391 Methodists to two Moravians, one Jew, and one Buddhist. Unlike previous women's conferences and conventions, which attracted little attention outside their own constituencies, the Re-Imagining Conference became a *cause célèbre* across the country, spawning charges of heresy and blasphemy.

"Re-Imagining"—the very term welcomes the unorthodox, the nontraditional. A member of the planning committee remembers:

> Naming the conference was important, and many names were suggested, among them, "re-imaging." Our retreat facilitator (whom we accuse of not being able to spell) wrote it down on the board as "re-imagining." This prompted us to discuss the nuances of the two words. The name was chosen out of our growing understandings that theology is imaginative work and that we are responsible for our theologies, for plumbing their depths and their possibilities, for meeting the crises and issues of our own time in history.[20]

The conference was crafted as a continuum of worship, responsive readings, speeches and workshops, song, dance, art, and drama. Audience participation was expected (but not enforced, as some critics later charged). The physical arrangements, modeled on theater in the round, engaged the audience. As speakers made their presentations, they slowly turned to face successive quadrants of the audience, seated in groups of ten at small tables around the center platform.

These small groups, identified as "talking circles," remained together throughout the conference. "There," one clergywoman reminisced, "we talked about our lives and faith, bounced around responses to presentations, and asked questions. . . . Strangers, we formed a unique community, a safe place where we could lay our burdens down and lift our joys up, where we could explore, question, affirm, and simply hang out with friends—friends who love the same God and struggle to be faithful."[21]

Group singing and dancing were infused into the program, before, after, and sometimes during presentations, meals, and rituals. Theater, dance, and song were integrated into nontraditional worship, rituals, and liturgies. As Pamela Carter Joern explained to us, "It was our conviction that all that we do, all of life, is sacred and theological, so we tried very hard to have speakers and singing and ritual all of one piece, so you didn't go off in a room and hear a lecture and then come back to another room and do a worship service." Much of the music was written especially for the conference or drawn from other cultures (Hawaiian chants, African freedom songs). A play commissioned for the event, written by Joern, was performed on two successive evenings, as was a concert by the singing group Sweet Honey in the Rock. Everywhere art commemorated women's suffering and experiences in the Bible and throughout the world, including a set of large wood figures representing Minnesota women killed by domestic violence during 1990. Art was also made on the spot: "Nancy Chinn and conference participants will be creating four murals on the stage as we are gathered in plenary sessions, one for each day," the conference program announced. "Some of our table work will be included. Artists gathered at the conference may want to consider collaborating with Nancy in this work of re-imagining."

The work of the conference was accomplished in four interrelated activities:

1. Three plenary sessions with major addresses by women theologians, each developing a particular theme: "Religious Imagination," "Re-Imagining God," and "Re-Imagining Community." These, especially Delores S. Williams's critical assessment of orthodox teachings on Jesus' death and the doctrine of atonement, later drew fire from conservatives.[22]

2. Discussions within the "talking circles." As one clergywoman explained to us: "There were times when your table was asked to fellowship in different ways. For example during the time that you were listening [to a speaker on the platform] you were encouraged to respond by drawing." A lay participant at first thought, "Forced personalization? Will it work? [But it did. Our table joined our individual doodles and drawings together], connecting our lives through shared experience. The conference planners wanted us to have a new paper tablecloth the next day and later to tear it into individual pieces to carry away from the conference. Not this table. The tablecloth had become a sacred symbol of our connection to God and our connection to each other."[23]

3. Seminars featuring theologians from different cultural or national backgrounds. Each focused on a particular topic: Jesus, Creation, the Church as Spiritual Institution, Sexuality, Language-Word, Women-Arts-Church, Ethics-Work-Ministry, and the Church as Worshipping Community.[24] Participants chose among four simultaneous sessions, each with three presenters. One clergywoman "went to the Jesus seminar that first day thinking, 'What am I doing here? They've got all these other seminars on sexuality and creation and all these imaginative seminars, and I'm sitting here in a seminar on Jesus! Must be because I'm Mennonite!' There were about five hundred other people there too. These three women, Delores Williams and another one from Taiwan [Kwok Pui-Lan] and Barbara Lundblatt from New York City just

wove this incredible fabric of what it means to be a people of Christ. I'll never forget it. It's like leaven, a lot of leaven, released into the church."

4. Rituals and liturgical elements designed especially for this conference to respond to women's experiences, needs, and life cycles. Critics later attacked these as heresy and paganism—especially the frequent invocations of Sophia and the "milk and honey" ceremony on the last day of the conference.

In many ways the Re-Imagining Conference comes across as a religious Woodstock—a liberating, empowering, and joyous communal experience. The tapes of the proceedings record the audience's bursts of laughter, roars of approval, and voices raised in song. The conference offered more than an exercise in feminist theology; it also provided an *enactment* of nontraditional formulations of human–divine relationships from a feminist viewpoint. Conferees were giving visible and audible form to theological concepts.

Above all, in the words of a Lutheran seminary student, the conference "challenged the participants to 're-imagine' God. Not *change* God, or *forget* God, or *profane* God (contrary to what you might have read in the newspaper), but to open our minds to a more expansive vision of God. All of this was done in a wonderfully safe environment which encouraged risk and creativity, but didn't demand it."[25]

Not every participant delighted in every aspect of the conference. "Some things were said that were not especially helpful to me," a Presbyterian clergywoman reported. "But what I received far outweighs any distress caused by some 'radical women.'"[26] Some women had trouble dealing with the invocations to Sophia but found the other parts of the conference helpful and empowering. So also with the final ritual of milk and honey. "Certainly not all women . . . felt comfortable with this actively embodied meeting, worshipping, sensual celebrating. . . . However, for many women the celebration of women's bodies felt like coming home after a long, dry, hard journey."[27]

A music minister started out with qualms. "As I attempted to recruit women for the 'dream team' from within my own African-American culture, I found myself warning that they would need to have a comfort level with the pronoun *She* associated with God. In retrospect, it was never an issue. The beauty of the music, dance, and artistry brought forward such a sense of warmth, gifts, service, and life force that the political agenda stood still."[28]

Some were troubled about lesbianism and lesbian militancy. At the conference Melanie Morrison, co-chair of the Coordinating Council of CLOUT (Christian Lesbians Out Together), who felt "uneasy" because at the plenary sessions "no one was speaking in a lesbian voice," asked for a few minutes to invite lesbians, bisexuals, and transsexuals to come forward. As soon as she had issued the invitation, she later wrote, "women in every part of that great hall left their tables and started moving toward the center of the room. At least 150 women [others estimated about 100] circled the stage three rows deep and spilled up onto the platform. I intended to ask the people remaining at their tables to stand in solidarity with us. But when women began to stream to the center, a roar went up from the crowd as people rose spontaneously to their feet and gave the women a long thunderous ovation."[29] But others reacted differently. A Methodist chaplain told us, "I personally find it quite difficult to be supportive of lesbian women coming out forward as pastors, chaplains. That's a personal faith issue for me and an understanding of my scripture faith walk. Many times at women's conferences there is an element of lesbianism that is difficult for me. It's very aggressive, actually. But I knew that up front: I haven't gone to a woman's conference where that didn't happen. The rest of it was very nice for me."

Despite the multicultural emphases of the conference, some complained that conference participants were "too white and too middle class." An African-American Baptist minister wondered about the other women at her table: "We gained a superficial knowledge of one another in the several days we were together. Although I could not accept or understand all the words of my sisters on the platform or in the seats next to me, I could listen and rejoice with them when crippling spirits disappeared or diminished at the end of our days together. I joined with the crowd on that last day in dancing and rejoicing for the good things Christ had done in our midst."[30] At least one *mujerista* theologian thought that Hispanic-Americans were inadequately represented: "As the conference unfolded, I waited in vain for the voices of Latinas—for the voices of women from Latin America to dream the vision, to share the wisdom that is ours with the gathered sisters at the conference."[31]

Though a liturgical dance minister "loved the procession dance and the dance with the bread," the speeches transgressed her theology. "The more I listened, the more I realized I was in the wrong place. Although some good was said, most of it was against my beliefs. . . . I believe it is wrong to pray to our Maker, Sophia. Our Maker is God, and our Mother is Mary, Jesus' mother."[32]

Participant critiques like these pale before the bitter assaults on the conference and its participants orchestrated by conservative groups within major denominations—particularly Presbyterians and Methodists. These foiled the efforts of conference organizers to "create a safe space where people (regardless of gender, race, age, physical ability, class, or sexual orientation) could engage freely in dialogue."[33] The many references to "safe space" in both the literature and our own interviews testify to its importance. Several of our interviewees spoke of usually having to hold their tongues, lest they offend parishioners or colleagues who disagree with them, of seldom being able to speculate freely and openly. Local pastors and parish priests are particularly at risk if they introduce to their congregations the kinds of theological issues that animated the Re-Imagining Conference. As a Lutheran pastor wrote, "There is so much in worship and theology that I cannot explore because I feel responsible for too many. In trying to respect the place where others are, in trying to bring people along slowly in seeing new images, I often feel exhausted. . . . There are so many concepts that get hidden or silenced because one needs a safe place to explore and experiment." For her the conference was "like a long drink of cool, refreshing water," a place "to hear voices more radical than mine, to be challenged. So often I feel that I am pushing others."[34]

Women *felt* safe during the conference. They saw it as an arena where everyone was free to discuss and speculate about spiritual matters without being confronted with a friend/foe situation that defeats genuine dialogue. People spoke out boldly. A group of Church of the Brethren women eager to change the name of their denomination to include women mounted the platform to shout: "We're not waiting for permission any longer!"[35]

But for some women the Re-Imagining Conference turned out to be not so safe. Peggy Halsey, a laywoman with the United Methodist Board of Global Ministries, said: "We thought [the conference] would be a safe place, and it wasn't. . . . Women felt they could really be themselves—how naive."[36] In the backlash to the conference Mary Ann Lundy lost her position as director of the national Women's Unit of the Presbyterian Church, and others felt threatened. The governing board of an American Baptist congregation, its pastor wrote, received "a photocopy of the two-page synopsis of accusations leveled by the *Presbyterian Layman*, with a highlighted paragraph about me as a leading lesbian heretic." The attack boomeranged, for this first openly lesbian pastor in her denomination had told her congregation of her sexual orientation before they called her to their pulpit.[37]

Most of the participants understood the Re-Imagining Conference as a valued opportunity for women to think, speculate, and worship together, each in her own way, each respecting the way of others. They didn't go to the conference expecting to receive ultimate truth, but to share a religious experience with other women, including women different from themselves and from each other. For a Lutheran clergywoman, "the worship . . . did what it intended: it got us to imagine, What if. . . . People could take away from it what they wanted. It wasn't a Council of Trent: it wasn't intended to come up with a definitive doctrine defending oneself against heresy." And a United Methodist chaplain told us: "In the military I get really isolated from women in the ministry and from women's life in general. I'm really living very much in the male world. I loved being in a woman's environment [at the conference]—it was a feeling environment. Women are different in the way that we approach God and in the way that we worship and when you have a lot of women together who are doing women's worship we tend to do it differently."[38]

Perhaps the most reassuring reaction for doubters about the conference came from the wife of a rather traditional Presbyterian pastor in Iowa; we know her only as Mabel Victoria. In her seventies, she was killed in an automobile accident soon after the conference, but not before she had told her family so much about how the conference had nurtured and empowered her that they dedicated contributions in her memory to funds that had paid for the conference.

❧ Christian Anti-feminism and the Reaction to Re-Imagining

The nonconformity involved in the kind of investigation the conference undertook terrifies a lot of people. First, it forces conservative, traditionally oriented men to confront changes in the attitudes of women that threaten male primacy; and it forces conservative, traditionally minded women to confront possible changes in their own status and responsibilities. Worse still, it does all this in the name of religion. Second, religious traditionalists are not among the few people of any stripe who find uncertainty and change tolerable, and feminist spirituality opens the door to all sorts of uncertainties and changes. What excites and challenges spiritual feminists frightens people who believe in absolute and unchanging truth—in creedal doctrines. Debates between the two groups, like most debates on the eternal verities, are usually couched in win/lose terms, where compromise is impossible.

The conference raised hard theological questions about God and Christ and the church, about the doctrine of atonement, about the prophetic and pastoral responsibilities of the clergy—questions that conservatives prefer to regard as settled. They have caused quarrels among the faithful for the past two thousand years and promise fair to provoke more in the next millennium. Now these issues are presented from another viewpoint—feminist theology is demanding a hearing, and doing so in language that strikes the conservative ear as dangerous to faith and belief. Is nothing sacred? Are there no firm foundations? Are there no limits?[39]

Denominations have not seized on the raising of these questions as opportunity to confront difficult theological issues. Nor have they acknowledged that the conference achieved a goal to which they give ardent lip service—making the Christian church more ethnically diverse. Nor, most critically, have they paused to ask themselves why the orthodoxy they have been preaching is failing to meet the needs of so many women.

Instead they—particularly Presbyterians and Methodists— have been caught up in a power struggle. Immediately after the conference, conservatives vigorously protested the use of denominational funds to support a conference that in their view promoted heresy, paganism, blasphemy, apostasy, goddess worship, and lesbianism. One Presbyterian clergywoman speculated to us that conservatives were finally coming to understand that women's ordination meant real change, whereas earlier they had assumed that clergywomen would simply act in the same patterns as clergymen.

At any rate, this onslaught must be understood as part of an ongoing conservative assault on churchwomen who do not unquestioningly accept traditionally patriarchal practices and theology. For example, since the early 1990s—perhaps significantly, a time when a United Methodist woman bishop was beginning to appoint women to major pulpits—Professor Heather Elkins of Drew Theological Seminary and the Rev. Susan Cady of the United Methodist Church have been drawing fire for the liturgical use of the name of Sophia, even though the liturgy in question employed only scriptural passages. The mere mention of Sophia was heard as implicitly referring to interpretations that have treated her as a goddess, hence an underhanded means of worshiping a goddess. Three years before the Re-Imagining Conference the "brewing storm over Sophia Worship" rumbled in the pages of the conservative Methodist publication *Good News*.[40] As feminist theology explored "diverse images of God, the meaning of a multi-racial, multi-cultural church, ecumenical commitment, equal participation of women, and the dynamics of control and power," conservatives scented danger.[41]

So although little that happened at the Re-Imagining Conference was new or without mooring in serious theological and scriptural scholarship, radically conservative elements in the mainline denominations seized on this gathering as a fresh opportunity to attack liberalism in general and feminism in particular. In most denominations women meet every two or three years nationally, and of course they have had controversial meetings before.[42] Mary Hague Gates, a Re-Imagining planner, said, "The issues weren't new, but somehow we were blamed for bringing them up."[43] Reta Finger asked in bewilderment, "Didn't they know anything about the theology of big names like Rita Nakashima Brock, Beverly Harrison, Chung Hyun Kyung, Delores Williams, Ada Maria Isasi-Diaz and others? . . . Of course you're going to hear some things from these speakers that push hard against traditional theological boundaries."[44] But of course "they"—the attacking conservatives—knew little about feminist theology and detested what they did know.

In 1993 the timing was propitious for an all-out assault on feminist influence both because of the turn to the right in the nation generally and because of other problems within mainline denominations—notably declining memberships, declining contributions, and liberal/conservative rifts. The most vigorous attack was launched by the *Presbyterian Layman* and the Methodist *Good News,* both organs of constituencies often critical of the national church leadership; both partially financed by the Institute on Religion and Democracy, a conservative think tank with a long record of opposition to the National and World Councils of Churches.[45] Both journals had sent reporters to the conference. The intemperance of their language is a measure of the opposition's passion.

James Heidinger II, editor of the Methodist *Good News,* censured the conference as "the most theologically aberrant I have ever read about, far removed from Christian tradition." A retired United Methodist Church bishop said that "no comparable heresy has appeared in the church in the last fifteen centuries."[46] The January-February 1994 issue of *Good News* featured articles with the message: "'Re-Imagining' Rejects Historic Christianity" and "Shocking Conference Challenges Orthodoxy." In their organ *United Voice* (March 1994) the Episcopalians United For Revelation, Renewal & Reformation charged that the Re-Imagining conference "Drops Christ for Sophia." The *American Family Association Journal* (February 1994) weighed in with an article titled "Mainline Churches Sponsor Radical Feminist Conference: Pagan Worship Encouraged, Lesbianism Praised." And the Biblical Witness Fellowship, a conservative "renewal" group within the United Church of Christ, published in August 1994 a pamphlet whose title says it all: "Uncloseting the Goddess: A Look at Emerging Feminist, Neo-Paganism in the Church through the Open Door of Re-Imagining." The *Presbyterian Layman* headlined Susan Cyre's conference report: "PCUSA funds effort to re-create God," describing the "recurring themes" as "destroying traditional Christian faith, adopting ancient pagan beliefs, rejecting Jesus' divinity and his atonement on the cross, creating a god(dess) in their own image, and affirming lesbian lovemaking. . . ."

The reporters from these journals focused on conference events most likely to inflame readers who knew nothing of the context nor of feminist theology. Their reports had an effect similar to what one could evoke by telling someone completely ignorant of Freud only that he believed all little boys want to sleep with their mothers and to kill their fathers. They made much, for instance, of the use of Sophia, Wisdom, as the feminine element in God. Similarly they highlighted the closing worship service, a milk-and-honey ceremony that included words reminiscent of the Song of Solomon: "Our Sweet Sophia, we are women in your image. With the nectar between our thighs, we invite a lover, we birth a child; with our warm body fluids we remind the world of its pleasures and sensations."[47] The reporters interpreted this ceremony not only as parody of the Eucharist but also as goddess worship and pornography. They denounced the theology expressed at the conference as rejecting the atonement of Jesus. They condemned the liturgy and ritual as non-Christian. They presented the format of the conference as coercive and destructive of free inquiry, and they accused the conference "of endorsing lesbianism."

Predictably, the homophobic theme runs throughout their catalogue of conference iniquities. Attacks on women commonly include charges of lesbianism, regardless of fact or relevance, and some Christian fundamentalists come close to equating feminism with lesbianism. A Unitarian minister spoke to us of "the far-out rhetoric that I've heard from people like Pat Robertson. You know, feminists want all women to be lesbians, disobey their husbands, and leave the church. That's such a hoot!" But it's also a case of double vision: what seems to conservatives to be endorsing lesbianism seems to others simply to be accepting fellow Christians, whatever their sexual orientation.

Critics of the conference demanded disciplinary action against staff responsible for denominational support of the conference—apologies and assurances that in the future no such deviations from orthodox theology would be tolerated. Readers of the *Presbyterian Layman* and *Good News* were deluged with denunciations of the conference and appeals to withhold contributions.

The Presbyterian attack was arguably the most vigorous and most effective. Among others, it convinced a Presbyterian military chaplain who did not attend the conference; she commented to us, "What a scandal! I'm proud to hear that my church has enough sense to fire people that advocate things like that. They kind of remind me of rebellious children that want to show up their daddy or whatever authority figure it is that they feel enthralled to and have to rebel against, and all I can say for these people is that I hope like most teenagers they don't get into so much trouble that they can't come back to where we truly find spiritual nurturing before they do too much damage." This tendency to treat churchwomen as irresponsible, errant youngsters to be corrected showed up also in the proposal at the Presbyterian General Assembly of June 1994, to have monitors at all future women's assemblies; it was defeated.

The *Layman*'s appeals to wield the financial stick also worked: the Presbyterian General Assembly Council (the executive arm of the Assembly, which is the national governing body) was confronted with "an expected $2.4 million loss in giving, created in part by congregations protesting the church's involvement" in the Re-Imagining Conference.[48]

Reportedly, by early 1994 the council had received more than one thousand letters complaining about the conference, "two judicial complaints had been lodged, and more than 100 local church councils had sent resolutions demanding investigation of the conference or the disciplining of staff members involved."[49] Twelve Presbyterian congregations from six states (Kansas, Missouri, New Jersey, Ohio, Pennsylvania, and Wisconsin) brought suit, demanding that the denomination's Permanent Judicial Commission "publicly disavow" views expressed at the conference. The complaints charged that the council had "failed to discipline agencies and individuals involved" in the conference, and that members of the council had, in violation of church law, "affirmed" the ordination of practicing gays and lesbians. The denominational court dismissed these charges, stating that "there was no evidence the council had violated the denomination's constitution."[50] However, the Presbyterian Theology Office found the "pervasive invocation" of Sophia to be "a particularly problematic aspect" of the conference because it amounted to "an alternative employed in distinction from the triune God." Also, according to the office, the milk-and-honey ritual, though not explicitly cast as a communion service, "functioned clearly as an alternative to the Lord's Supper."[51]

Presbyterian conservatives particularly targeted Mary Ann Lundy, director of the denominational Women's Ministry Unit when the conference was being planned (and, incidentally, the great-niece of Orlena Weese, who pastored her own church in a denomination that had broken off from the Baptists). On the initiative of the Women's Ministry Unit the Presbyterian Church (USA) contributed an initial planning grant of $66,000 to the Re-Imagining Conference budget of $400,000—more than any other denomination. Later, as associate director of the General Assembly Council (GAC), Lundy served as liaison from the U.S. Ecuminical Decade committee to the conference planning committee. Some twenty Presbyterian national staff members attended the conference.[52]

When the right-wing complaints poured in, the GAC leadership, Lundy's colleagues, meeting in Dallas in February 1994, conducted an investigation. At one point they interrogated her for two hours, "looking for something to pin on me. Afterward they distributed their findings, their personnel report about me, to everyone, at an open meeting including the press. This was clearly against GAC personnel rules. I was not allowed to talk on my own behalf—effectively silenced." Then she was asked: "Don't you admit to bad judgment in not having anticipated that this [conference] would be controversial?"[53] Whatever leads to controversy, the question implied, must be the result of bad judgment.

In its decision the GAC tried to compromise—after all, it had a duty to avert schism. While reaffirming the Presbyterial heritage, the council also recognized "that faithful Christian women and men will have varying understandings" of that heritage; it faulted much of the criticism of the conference as based on prejudices, stereotypes, and oversimplification. By a narrow margin (thirty-two to thirty-one) it found no reason to demand a special review of the work of Mary Ann Lundy, but allowed that perhaps she had shown bad judgment. According to the *Christian Century,* "Council members said people voted as they did for a variety of reasons— some voting against the review because they preferred a statement of support for Lundy, others voting against it because they wanted her fired outright."[54] The council left the question of Lundy's continued employment to her immediate superior.

There followed eight months of seesawing, with Lundy refusing to resign, enduring "horrible" phone calls and a flood of critical letters, many of them form letters, many from the Southeast, and some focused on other issues such as dislike of the union between southern and northern Presbyterians. Predictably her mail also bore accusations of lesbianism, adultery, and fornication. ("Not true, but why say so?") Encouragement also poured in: good letters and phone calls, her favorite flowers. Many people warned the leadership that her departure would put all staff members in jeopardy from right-wing groups. Finally in May, Lundy and her previously supportive superior issued a statement "that Ms. Lundy will leave her position as of July 1, 1994. Circumstances have made her goal of effective service to the church unattainable."

In June 1994, the Presbyterian General Assembly passed a resolution condemning certain Re-Imagining Conference rituals as using "language, including the term 'Sophia,' in ways that imply worship of a divine manifestation distinctly different from 'the one triune God.'" The assembly also affirmed the right of women to do theology, but called for more careful scrutiny of future conference funding.[55]

Even so, the attack on feminists did not abate. In the spring of 1995 a group of conservative Methodists formed a "Confessing Movement," charging "that some Methodists have been 'experimenting with pagan ritual and practice,' enjoying wealth without regard for the poor and accepting sexual promiscuity, divorce, homosexual conduct and widespread abortion. At a news conference officials of the group said about 13,000 people had signed the movement's manifesto."[56] In May 1995, the male editor of publications of the Southeastern Minnesota Synod of the Evangelical Lutheran Church in America wrote of "the tide of reactionary, anti-woman drivel I am daily bombarded by."[57]

Meanwhile supporters of the conference did not stand silent. They too have produced a substantial literature, repudiating accusations of heresy and paganism, defending their efforts to re-imagine God through language and symbols—language and symbols with biblical and early Christian roots. For example, they assert that "Sophia" was used to denote a feminine attribute of God—hardly a new idea as the scriptures personify wisdom in Sophia.[58] What the conference was doing, they say, was neither to substitute a goddess for a god nor to create a new god. Rather, the conference assumed the existence of a God so complex as to be beyond the capacity of any one human being or any one group to know completely. By approaching this divinity from the woman's perspective, naming divinity in new ways, participants would contribute further insight into that majestic Being.

Some of the forty-eight members of the United Methodist Commission on the Status and Role of Women (COSROW) have alleged a deliberate conservative strategy to cripple the Women's Division; they warn against letting conservative critics set the church's agenda, asking "Are we being taken off the track of dealing with the critical issues of violence and abuse toward women?"[59] Early in 1994 the United Methodist Appalachian Development Committee protested the charges of heresy and goddess worship as "deeply troubling to us, particularly because a common experience of women in Appalachia is that theology has been used to silence, limit and oppress women."[60] More than a thousand United Methodist women, clergy and lay, signed "A Time of Hope—A Time of Threat," a document supporting the aims of the Re-Imagining Conference. Bishop Susan Morrison, one of the signatories, found the attack on women in Methodist leadership hardly surprising, given the disagreements in the denomination in recent years over such issues as the ordination of women, inclusive language, and reproductive rights. She summed up: "We can talk about God as a mineral—Rock of Ages—but when we speak of God as feminine, it creates a crisis."[61]

Do the conference and the furor that followed offer useful insights into the world in which American clergywomen must live and work? We think so. At base they were part of the current power struggle between religious conservatives and liberals, between patriarchs and feminists. The underlying issues are not so much theological as political.

Conservatives have good political reason to view feminist theology with alarm. Feminism, by definition, is not reverential, dutiful, and submissive. Feminist theology and feminist spirituality radically modify or overturn patriarchal theology. The feminist reading of scriptural texts and church history and feminists "doing" theology challenge deeply held traditional religious beliefs—beliefs slow to change, emotionally buttressed, and typically passionately defended. The opposition to the Re-Imagining Conference was a political event, in which conservatives accused national denominational leadership of capitulating to a liberal agenda.

But more than liberalism is involved. Underlying all else is the gender issue. Re-Imagining was a woman's conference, its agenda an exercise in feminist theology and feminist spirituality. The pockets of resistance to women's ordination continue to hold traditional ideas about women's role in the church. The reaction to the conference, says Carter Heyward, discloses "a real antifeminist movement that is very much in keeping with where we are in Washington these days and where we are with the Christian right." The demonization of the conference is a sign of the times as represented by the Christian Coalition and the pervasive swing to the political right.

Some fear that the whole controversy, besides further polarizing denominations, may exercise a chilling effect. United Methodist Bishop Judith Craig received letters about the conference that left her feeling "attacked and threatened."[62] Some women candidates for pulpits have been asked, "Did you attend the Re-Imagining Conference? And if so, what do you think about it?" A Presbyterian clergywoman who did not attend the conference worries for fear that people will be afraid to be creative in worship services, to use inclusive language, to introduce new rituals. Remembering worship services she herself has done where she has "used Wisdom" (Sophia) now makes her wonder about her own vulnerability. It was scary, she said, to encounter at an ecumenical student conference the same woman reporter who blew open the whole Re-Imagining controversy; here she was again, recorder in hand, writing everything down. It is dreadful, said this minister, to feel such fear within one's own church; if Mary Ann Lundy could be punished by her own denomination, who is safe?

The chill factor was clearly exposed in the question-and-answer column of the *Presbyterian Survey* (March 1995): when a reader asked for an unemotional explanation of the Re-Imagining controversy, the columnist answered: "Remember the 1988 presidential debates on TV? Dukakis was asked a 'what if' question about his wife being raped. He gave an 'unemotional' reply. His candidacy went downhill from that moment. I wish not to follow him into oblivion!" Again, a woman newly hired into her denominational hierarchy withdrew her name from an innocuous story, because its use might identify her as having attended the Re-Imagining Conference. A clergywoman whose pastoral experiences have been profoundly unhappy said that she first thought seriously about leaving the pastorate when she saw the reaction to the Re-Imagining Conference. "I thought, My goodness, if the church doesn't have room for other images for God, then am I really in the right place?"

As we write, political clashes continue as conservatives devise new means of preserving the traditions they value. They are mounting an effort to revise Methodist doctrine, so that anyone not baptized explicitly in the name of "the Father, the Son, and the Holy Ghost" may not be regarded as a true Methodist and therefore not entitled to ordination. Consternation ensues among those clergywomen baptized with the use of inclusive language—and puzzlement arises among those Methodists (mostly African-Americans) who have traditionally baptized in the name of Jesus. And the Board of Directors of *Good News*, in January, 1995, describing the Re-Imagining Community as a "non-Christian cult," has thrown the gauntlet: "We question whether one can maintain with integrity the doctrines of the United Methodist Church while at the same time participating in the new 'Re-Imagining Community.'"[63]

❧ The Future of Feminist Spirituality

You can't go backwards from that kind of experience [the Re-Imagining Conference]. It's as if you shifted in a paradigm and you're in a new paradigm and you cannot shift back and see it the other way.

—A Mennonite clergywoman

The spirit of the Re-Imagining Conference lives on, notably in a continuing Re-Imagining Community of women and men fired by the experience of the 1993 gathering. It defines itself as a "global ecumenical community of acceptance where exploration, discussion, study and practice of the Christian faith are carried out freely and responsibly to seek justice, honor creation, and call the Church into solidarity with all people of God." Its quarterly newsletter sustains the fellowship created by the original conference and the work of reforming the church. The group has been holding small conferences each November.[64] It continues to receive from participants letters evidencing the "deep hunger for renewal."[65]

Many other groups—like the Evangelical and Ecumenical Women's Caucus; the Women's Theological Center in Boston; the Resource Center for Women and Ministry in the South; the Women's Alliance for Theology, Ethics and Ritual (WATER); and the Women's Ordination Conference—hold conferences similar in form and spirit to Re-Imagining. As Mary Hunt suggests, the various women's conferences may be "but the tip of a very big iceberg."[66] Clergywomen today work in a world where a significant minority of the women they pastor are dissatisfied with orthodox theology and are seeking new ways to understand and to worship the deity. Were it not so, the Re-Imagining Conference would never have happened.

Both Christianity and Judaism have alienated thousands of women by condemning them as unclean beings and the source of original sin, subordinating them to men's authority, counseling them to put up with abusive men, and shutting them off from altars, pulpits, and institutional power centers. Yet few women in churches or synagogues are so completely alienated that they simply pronounce themselves agnostics or atheists and have done with it. To such women as these, the life of the spirit matters supremely. They cannot just write off their religious institution as a lost cause or a venture that they tried and didn't like. When their rage or their grief mounts high enough, they may shift denominations; they may "defect in place," continuing membership in a church or synagogue but living their spiritual lives apart from it; or they may seek consolation outside established religious institutions.[67]

Refusing to be driven out of "their" own church or synagogue, those who defect in place hope to transform those institutions by establishing their presence and representing women's concerns, by networking, by providing forums for the discussion of issues, by developing their own sense of community—that they are not alone in their concerns for the role of women in the church or synagogue. Some such spirit has informed the protests of many Roman Catholic sisters, bringing them and their orders into confrontation with the patriarchal hierarchy, even while they remain intensely loyal to their church.

Curiously enough, those who defect in place often distinguish between religion and spirituality, asserting "Spirituality is not religion" and "My religion is in one place; my spirituality in another." They thus distinguish between the institutions they belong to—their religion—and their personal pilgrimages—their spirituality. And these may well conflict. Their religion, they suggest, matters to them because it provides their families with a community, or because through it they can work more effectively toward social reforms, or because they believe the ideas that inform the institution outweigh the patriarchy that has corrupted it, or simply because it is familiar and long-loved. But that religion often fails to support their quests, often condemns them for continuing to search, and often leaves them frustrated and embittered. What kind of religion is it, they ask, that preaches a God that denigrates woman's sexuality, that preaches gender inequality?

Not all clergywomen feel these concerns: only a minority react with such passion to the flaws in their religious establishments. But, for several reasons, attention must be paid. First, the clergywomen of this mind are among the most highly educated and most articulate in the nation. Second, they voice objections some of which a majority of other clergywomen share, silently but deeply. Third, even more laywomen share their sense of alienation. Fourth, they hold positions of influence, particularly in theological seminaries and in institutional administration. Fifth, they have impact; they are being heard; they are effecting changes. All in all, they temper the climate of the world in which the clergywoman works.

To wit. Item: An African Roman Catholic bishop recommended that the church find a way to allow women into the College of Cardinals. Item: American Roman Catholic bishops supported removing masculine language from church textbooks and allowing more women into the top ranks of theologians, administrators, and activists.[68] Item: Santa Clara University, a Jesuit institution, appointed Denise L. Carmody, a former nun, head of its religious studies department.[69] Item: Oxford University Press published a version of the New Testament "unique in how far it carries the principle of inclusion," and Viking published a new edition of the Union Haggadah in which the "English translation has been further revised: 'forefathers' is replaced by 'ancestors,' and 'He,' or 'The Lord' by 'The Almighty,' in accordance with the intentions of the Central Conference of American Rabbis."[70] All of these items signaling meaningful shifts of attitude were reported in November 1994.

To be sure, critics have greeted the new biblical edition with the same cries of outrage bestowed successively on every new version of the Bible issued in our lifetimes; the same cries, we assume, that greeted the King James Version of the Bible in 1611 ("Forsooth, Tyndale's translation was good enough for my sire and he's good enough for me").[71] But the very debate the new edition has provoked calls attention to the position of women in religion.

A good deal of pain is in store as women strive to strengthen that position. Even mild interest in this movement among churchwomen can set off tremors within religious institutions. These are hardly surprising among the doctrinaire Mormons, who have already disciplined several women exploring theology, including Lynne Kanavel Whitesides, whom her bishop disfellowshipped for apostasy and warned against publicly criticizing church leaders or talking about her belief in praying to a Mother in Heaven.[72] But shock waves radiate into mainline churches as well. With much fanfare, an appeal to the bishop, and a threat of a student protest a Methodist church in Champaign-Urbana, Illinois, in the early 1990s denied its own women members permission to use its premises for a lecture by Starhawk, a spiritual feminist guru; moreover, the church also cut off the funding for the proposed event, even though the moneys in question had been left in a bequest specifically to provide speakers for the women's group. The women thereupon found other quarters and raised the money themselves; Starhawk lectured in Champaign, to women whose ties to their church were not strengthened by the incident.

The old order is changing, slowly and agonizingly. Reaction against women in church leadership is charged with religious fervor, laden with terror of change and the economic fears of competition of unhappy clergymen, and aggravated by the tradition of bringing charges of blasphemy and heresy against those within the same institution with whom one disagrees. Church heresy trials spin out into defamation of character charges in civil courts. The academic freedom of seminaries is threatened by withdrawal of funding. A seminary professor speculates that conservatives in mainline churches, having failed to gain majority backing on issues like abortion, are now seeking a viable enemy. They may find that enemy, she thinks, by recreating the image of the heretical woman, which originated in the fourth century in tandem with the concept of heresy. Women, the argument then ran, are soft-headed, unreasonable, easily misled into error, hence likely victims of heresies.

All this misery, of course, gets mixed up with secular anti-feminism. Rush Limbaugh attacks women as "feminazis"; conservative churchmen talk about "feministlesbianwomanists [one word]." Religion clearly does not always stifle the impulse to attack the object of one's dislike by sexual innuendo. Whether or not the attack succeeds in silencing the woman or getting her fired or forcing her out of her profession, it certainly causes her intense pain. Contemporary Christian churches still have their martyrs, as well as their heresy trials.

Yet making martyrs probably threatens the feminist spirituality movement less than its own diffuse nature. Women in its midst suspect structure, fear hierarchy. One has to wonder whether purposive, effective change can issue from a movement so splintered and so insistent on the right of each individual to go her own way?

Some clergywomen argue that feminist spirituality is currently passing through an amorphous stage, a necessary preliminary to self-definition. A Roman Catholic sister remarked:

> Feminist spirituality is continually evolving through a process that is Spirit-led. It is a worldwide phenomenon. Women everywhere are taking similar initiatives, moving toward some common understandings, even though we remain disconnected from one another. In one sense, however, we are already connected, energetically rather than structurally. The first step toward coalescing this energy more intentionally is to go public. We feminists and others who support feminist values in religion and spirituality need to declare what it is we believe in spite of the threats that have intensified since Re-Imagining. There's enormous risk for some to say, "I too believe in Sophia. For me, that is simply another name for God." More and more women and men need to speak up and speak out, so that others who have been silent will say, "I have always felt that way, but I was afraid to say anything." Then it will become clear how widespread the

movement really is and how much it holds in common. Meanwhile, small circles of initiative, interacting from time to time, are foundational to the process. At the moment, that's my preferred way. When the time for a more formal global networking arrives, I will be ready to join it.

But in the past, as the woman suffragists found, reform has demanded institutionalization. Only when women joined in the National American Woman Suffrage Association and the Woman's Party, only when leaders like Harriot Stanton Blatch, Carrie Chapman Catt, and Alice Paul firmly controlled their organizations was the Nineteenth Amendment passed and ratified. Without institutionalization, groups may influence, but can they transform?

Nevertheless, the spiritual feminist movement, loose and unorganized as it now is, potentially embodies the most significant alteration in the Judeo-Christian tradition since the Protestant Reformation. Clearly, most clergywomen, like most laywomen, do not subscribe to feminist spirituality without reservation. How could they, indeed, when the movement is so heterogeneous, so much in process, so much in flux? Few agree even on a definition of it. But it is generating (or resurrecting) and disseminating ideas among which individual clergywomen and laywomen pick and choose. Even if they say, as many do, "That's not for me," its echoes reach them, now and then touching a nerve.

"That's not for me," a rabbi in her sixties told us. "I'm not into that at all. It's very fringy and very minimal, numerically. They try to include whatever they think is new, so they would have feminist symbols, goddess things, stuff like that. But as far as I'm concerned, that's not of interest." Still, later in the interview she told us, "You know the prayers we say, 'Our Father, our King,' well that's a male image, and I change it where I can. I'll say 'ancestors' instead of 'fathers' and I'll include mothers as well as fathers, but it's not a big issue with me."

A Roman Catholic commented, "I can't pray to a goddess. The whole goddess movement is somehow not Christian. But on the other hand I can think of God as feminine, and I do. I do believe that the present Scripture as it comes down to us is only half there. In preaching I was talking about the story of Martha and Mary, and I said, 'I wonder who was telling the story. I wonder if Martha or Mary was telling the story, would it have changed? Would Jesus have gotten up and gone into the kitchen and both of them discussed it and fixed the vegetables and washed the pots?' People get really nervous about it, and think you're rewriting Scripture. You're just talking about the spirit that's there. Because I think so much of what Jesus did and said got lost."

Another moderate, an Episcopalian rector in a good-sized parish, told us, "I had to laugh. Sunday's gospel was the healing of Peter's mother-in-law. She has a fever, and the disciples come, and they grab Jesus and they pull him in and he raises her up, 'and then the fever left her, and immediately she served them.' The minute she got up she got dinner for the boys!"

As ever, far-out ideas gradually become familiar, move toward the center, grow acceptable. Just as scholars are changing our reading of history by adding women's points of view, so clergywomen both inadvertently and intentionally are inevitably changing both theologies and hierarchies.

Notes

1. See *Concilium* (Dec. 1985), special issue, "Women—Invisible in Church and Theology," ed. Elisabeth Schüssler Fiorenza and Mary Collins.

2. Transcript of program. Italics added.

3. Editorial, *Daughters of Sarah* (Fall 1994).

4. A convenient overview of Christian feminist theology is *Feminist Theology: A Reader*, ed. Ann Loades (Louisville, Ky.: Westminster/John Knox, 1990). See also Valerie Saiving, "The Woman Situation: A Feminine View," *Journal of Religion* 40 (1960): 100–112; and Elisabeth Moltmann-Wendel, *I Am My Body: A Theology of Embodiment* (New York: Continuum, 1994). On Jewish feminist theology, see Judith Plaskow, *Standing Again at Sinai: Judaism from a Feminist Perspective* (San Francisco: Harper & Row, 1990); Sally Priesand, *Judaism and the New Woman* (New York: Behrman House, 1975); and *Gender and Judaism: The Transformation of Tradition,* ed. T. M. Rudavsky (New York: New York Univ. Press, 1995).

5. See, for example, Charlotte Caron, *To Make and Make Again: Feminist Ritual Thealogy* (New York: Crossroad, 1993).

6. Susan Hill Lindley, *"You Have Stept Out of Your Place": A History of Women and Religion in America* (Louisville, Ky.: Westminster John Knox, 1996), p. 425. See also Karen Jo Torjesen, *When Women Were Priests: Women's Leadership in the Early Church and the Scandal of Their Subordination in the Rise of Christianity* (San Francisco: HarperSanFrancisco, 1993).

7. The Living Waters Branch is a reformist group with a background in the Seventh Day Adventist and the Davidian Seventh-Day Adventists. It was founded by Lois Roden's husband in 1955. Lois Roden is quoted as saying that "I'm not a feminist. because I base my concept of the femininity of the Holy Spirit strictly on the Scriptures" (*The Whig-Standard,* Kingston, Ontario, February 28, 1992, in *Shekinah* Second Anniversary edition). Roden's theology calls for the ordination of women.

8. Margaret Moers Wenig, "A Birthday Wish: Celebrating Twenty-One Years in the Rabbinate" (papers of the Women's Rabbinic Network Conference [March 1993], p. 36).

9. Kelly Brown Douglas, *The Black Christ* (Maryknoll, N.Y.: Orbis, 1994), pp. 108, 117. See also Delores S. Williams, *Sisters in the Wilderness: The Challenge of Womanist God-Talk* (Maryknoll, N.Y.: Orbis, 1993).

10. Mary Pellaur, "On Remembering and Re-Imagining," *The Well Woman* (1994).

11. See Lynn N. Rhodes, *Co-Creating: A Feminist Vision of Ministry* (Philadelphia: Westminster, 1987), pp. 31–36; Elizabeth A. Johnson, *She Who Is* (New York: Crossroad, 1994); and Ursula King, *Women and Spirituality: Voices of Protest and Promise,* 2d ed. (University Park: Pennsylvania State Univ. Press, 1993).

12. *Chronicle of Higher Education* (March 22, 1996).

13. Immaculate Heart College Center in Los Angeles offers a master's degree program in feminist spirituality.

14. Barbara Kingsolver, review of Maria Elena Lucas, *Forged Under the Sun/Forjado Bajo et Sol: The Life of Maria Elena Lucas,* ed. Fran Leeper Buss (Ann Arbor: Univ. of Michigan Press, 1993) in *Women's Review of Books* (Feb. 1994).

15. See, for example, Diana L. Eck, *Encountering God: A Spiritual Journey from Bozeman to Banaras* (Boston: Beacon, 1993); and Naomi R. Goldenberg, *Changing of the Gods: Feminism and the End of Traditional Religions* (Boston: Beacon, 1979).

16. Starhawk, *The Spiral Dance: A Rebirth of the Ancient Religion of the Great Goddess* (San Francisco: Harper & Row, 1979).

17. King, *Women and Spirituality,* pp. 10–11. See also the entry for "spiritual feminism" in Mary Ann Warren, *The Nature of Woman: An Encyclopedia and Guide to the Literature* (Inverness, Calif.: Edgepress, 1980).

18. Elinor Lenz and Barbara Myerhoff, *The Feminization of America: How Women's Values Are Changing Our Public and Private Lives* (Los Angeles: Jeremy P. Tarcher, 1985), pp. 155–56.

19. Sally L. Hill, "The Planning Process at the Local Level," *Church and Society* 4 (May–June 1994): 117.

20. Hill, "Planning Process," p. 117.

21. Mary Jo Cartledge-Hayes, "Re-Imagining Revisited," *Update, Newsletter of the Ecumenical and Evangelical Women's Caucus* 18 (Summer 1994): 9.

22. According to a report issued in 1994 by the conservative Biblical Witness Fellowship Renewal Movement of the United Church of Christ, Williams, a professor at Union Theological Seminary, said, "I don't think we need a theory of atonement at all [applause]. I think Jesus came for life and to show us something about life and living together and what life was all about. Atonement has to do so much with death. I don't think we need folks hanging on crosses and blood dripping and weird stuff" (*Uncloseting the Goddess: A Look at Emerging Feminist, Neo-Paganism in the Church through the Open Door of Re-Imagining*). The last sentence here attributed to Williams is frequently quoted out of context.

23. Katherine Juul Nevins, "Womb of the Mountain," in *Re-Membering and Re-Imagining,* ed. Nancy J. Berneking and Pamela Carter Joern (Cleveland, Oh.: Pilgrim Press, 1995), pp. 41–42.

24. These sessions were supplemented by a wide variety of workshops ("Multi-Format Option Groups") such as: Quality of Life for Women, Women in Political Crisis: Refugees and Victims of Torture, Theology of Children, and Dancing the Way of the Beatitudes.

25. Sandy Larson, "Reflections from the Seminary," *The Well Woman* (1994): 13.

26. Barbara Price-Martin, "In a Foreign Land," in *Re-Membering and Re-Imagining,* ed. Berneking and Joern, p. 38.

27. Elizabeth Bettenhousen, "The Power of Women's Theology," *The Well Woman* (1994): 11.

28. Gloria A. Taylor-James, "A Musical Tapestry," in *Re-Membering and Re-Imagining,* ed. Berneking and Joern, pp. 9, 10.

29. Melanie Morrison, "Here's to you, Mr. Robertson," in *Re-Membering and Re-Imagining,* ed. Berneking and Joern, p. 53. See also Morrison's letter to the *Christian Century* 111 (April 6, 1994).

30. Cheryl Dudley, "Standing Up Straight," in *Re-Membering and Re-Imagining,* ed. Berneking and Joern, pp. 77–78.

31. Ada Maria Isasi-Diaz, "Where Were the Latina Voices?" in *Re-Membering and Re-Imagining,* ed. Berneking and Joern, p. 99.

32. Kathie Bomsta, "A Different Dance," in *Re-Membering and Re-Imagining,* ed. Berneking and Joern, p. 120.

33. *Re-Imagining,* newsletter to Participants in the Re-Imagining Conference, no date, but before Feb. 1, 1994.

34. Kristen Schlauderaff, "More Power to Her," *The Well Woman* (1994): 8.

35. Dolores Costello, "Moving Right Along," in *Re-Membering and Re-Imagining,* ed. Berneking and Joern, pp. 216–17.

36. *Christian Century* 111 (February 16, 1994): 160.

37. Nadean Bishop, "A Series of Miracles," in *Re-Membering and Re-Imagining,* ed. Berneking and Joern, p. 24.

38. Six years before the Re-Imagining Conference Lynn N. Rhodes wrote: "Feminists claim that authority for ministry must be situated in honest and reflective discourse of women about their *own* experiences-in-relationship" (*Co-Creating,* pp. 33–36 passim). Cf. Laura Geller, "From Equality to Transformation: The Challenge of Women's Rabbinic Leadership," in *Gender and Judaism,* p. 251.

39. Thomas C. Oden, "Can We Talk About Heresy?"; Lewis S. Mudge, "Gathering Around the Center: A Reply to Thomas Oden"; and Thomas C. Oden, "Can There Be a Center Without a Circumference? A Response to Lewis Mudge," *Christian Century* 112 (Apr. 12, 1995): 390–403.

40. Randy Petersen, "Wisdom's Feast or Gospel's Famine," *Good News* (July/August 1990): 11–16. This article centers on the work of Susan Cady, who with her fellow Methodist pastor Hal Taussig and Roman Catholic writer Marian Ronon had in 1986 published *Sophia: The Future of Feminist Spirituality,* a revised and expanded edition of which later appeared as *Wisdom's Feast: Sophia in Study and Celebration.* Cady's interest in Sophia got her into trouble with some of her parishioners.

41. "A Time of Hope—A Time of Threat," a statement eventually signed by more than a thousand United Methodist churchwomen, released March 8, 1994, at a New York City press conference.

42. See Mary E. Hunt, "Another Fine Women's Conference," in *Re-Membering and Re-Imagining,* ed. Berneking and Joern, p. 190; "Discipleship of Equals, Breaking Bread/Doing Justice," WOC Gathering '95, pp. 7, 3; June Steffensen Hagen, "EEWC Members Freewrite For Our Future," *Update* 18 (Fall 1994): 6; and *Update* 17 (Summer 1993): 6.

43. Mary Hague Gates, "Lingering Impressions," in *Re-Membering and Re-Imagining,* ed. Berneking and Joern, p. 75.

44. Reta Finger, "If You Want My Opinion . . . Cassette Tapes and Theology," *Daughters of Sarah* 20 (Fall 1994): 25.

45. Leon Howell, "The Role of the Four Sisters, Funding the War of Ideas," *Christian Century* 112 (July 19–26, 1995): 701–83. Four foundations supply financial support for organizations and think tanks that lead the attacks on liberal Protestantism: the Bradley Foundation, the John M. Olin Foundation, the Smith Richardson Foundation, and the Sarah Scaife Foundation. "The neo-conservative organizations generate a steady stream of invective against non-conservative Christian activity. For example, press reaction to the 'Re-Imagining' Conference held in Minnneapolis in 1993 was based entirely on reports by three participants representing neo-conservative publications" ("Homeland Ministries" supplement to *United Church News,* CONNtact Edition, 11 [April 1995]).

The Re-Imagining Conference attracted little or no media attention until it became an object of controversy. The *Christian Century* (Dec. 21–28, 1994) named the controversy, not the conference, as its number 2 news story of 1994, and Donna Schaper (United Church of Christ area minister) faulted the *Christian Century* for failing to "prohibit the publication of two stories about the extent of the protest before one on the conference itself appeared" ("A Strategy for Interpreting the Re-Imagining Conference in Our Parishes," *Congregations*

[Jan.–Feb. 1995]). In retrospect it seems that the leaders of the conference were unwary in managing press relations. See Judy Weidman, "Re-Visiting Media Issues from Re-Imagining," *HeadsUp* (May 1995).

46. *Christian Century* 111 (Feb. 16, 1994): 160–61.

47. Convention Liturgy Book.

48. *Christian Century* 111 (May 18–25, 1994): 522.

49. *Chrsistian Century* 111 (Mar. 16, 1994): 275.

50. *Christian Century* 111 (Oct. 19, 1994): 945.

51. *Christian Century* 111 (Mar. 16, 1994): 275.

52. Ibid.

53. See also Mary Ann W. Lundy, "Departure under Fire," in *Re-Membering and Re-Imagining*, ed. Berneking and Joern, pp. 121–23.

54. *Christian Century* 111 (Mar. 16, 1994): 275.

55. Sandra Valentine, "The *Re-Imagining* Community," *Daughters Of Sarah* 20 (Fall 1994).

56. *Christian Century* 112 (June 7–14, 1995): 600.

57. Letter from John Bachus II, Lanesboro, Minnesota, *Re-Imagining* newsletter (May 1995).

58. See Proverbs 8:9, Luke 7:35, 11:49. Catherine Keller, "Inventing the Goddess, A Study in Ecclesial Backlash," *Christian Century* 111 (Apr. 6, 1994): 340–42; and Johnson, *She Who Is*.

59. *Christian Century* 111 (Mar. 16, 1994): 275f.

60. *United Methodist News Service* (May 4, 1994).

61. *Christian Century* 111 (Mar. 23–30, 1994): 307.

62. *United Methodist Newscope* 22 (July 22, 1994). In early 1996 the Re-Imagining Community office received information that a Presbyterian clergywoman in California had been censured by her presbytery for her association with the community.

63. *United Methodist News Service* (Feb. 2, 1995).

64. Attendance at the 1995 Conference was limited to four hundred and was sold out by mid-August (*Christian Century* 112 [Dec. 20–27, 1995]: 1239–40).

65. *Re-Imagining* (May 1994). In the February 1995 issue of the quarterly newsletter, the editor announced memberships in all fifty states, Canada, and several other countries. The issue of May 1996 notes the second annual gathering of a group of Presbyterian women and men called Voices of Sophia, "an intentional feminist community."

66. Mary E. Hunt, *Re-Membering and Re-Imagining*, ed. Berneking and Joern, p. 192.

67. The best known of the spiritual feminists who have abandoned the Christian church completely is former Roman Catholic Mary Daly, who terms herself post-Christian. See her book *Gyn\Ecology: The Metaethics of Radical Feminism* (Boston: Beacon, 1978). We owe the felicitous expression "defecting in place" to Miriam T. Winter, Adair Lummis, and Allison Stokes, *Defecting in Place: Women Claiming Responsibility for Their Own Spiritual Lives* (New York: Crossroad, 1994). "The status of Jewish women continues to prompt some women to leave Judaism, others to press for change within Judaism, and still others to fight against changes in roles which they have found meaningful and fulfilling" (Ann Braude, "The Jewish Woman's Encounter with American Culture," in *Women and Religion in America*, ed. Rosemary R. Ruether and Rosemary S. Keller [San Francisco: Harper and Row, 1981] 1:143).

68. *Christian Century* 111 (Nov. 2, 1994).

69. *Chronicle of Higher Education* (Nov. 23, 1994).

70. *Chronicle of Higher Education* (Nov. 16, 1994). Quotation on Haggadah from Daedalus Books catalogue, Fall 1995.

71. "There was scandal among the clerisy when William Tyndale published his translation of the New Testament in 1526 and thus opened it up to those of a vulgar tongue; he was arrested for heresy, strangled, and burned. When the Revised Version appeared, in 1885, many readers considered that it traduced rather more than it revised; more controversial still was the determinedly unpoetic New English Bible, which came out in 1961. If you are issuing a new version of the Good Book, a bad press is part of the deal" (Anthony Lane, *The New Yorker,* [Oct. 2, 1995]). Lane goes on to give the Inclusive Version a bad review.

72. *New York Times* (Sept. 19, 1993).

9

Church and Synagogue
as Workplace
🦅

Where Clergywomen Are and What They Do

WHERE CLERGYWOMEN ARE depends above all on their denominations. To over-simplify a situation chaotic to the point of absurdity, we may summarize thus: most of the mainline Protestant denominations and three of the four Jewish denominations now ordain women, with varying degrees of enthusiasm. Many holiness and pentecostal churches, with the outstanding exception of the Salvation Army (which unhesitatingly ordains women), hold to the principle but waver in the practice. Most fundamentalists, most Mormons, Orthodox Christians, Orthodox Jews, and Roman Catholics refuse women ordination.[1]

Whether ordained or no, women clergy at the end of the twentieth century still think of themselves as pioneers. In status, in pay, and in numbers they lag behind their sisters in other traditionally male professions, particularly medicine and the law. Ironically, in parts of the United States clergywomen are still less familiar to the public than women firefighters and construction workers, while in other parts clergy worry about the feminization of the profession. In the mainline Christian churches, the sizable depression caused by declining membership and in some cases declining contributions limits the upward mobility of all clergy, a limitation that clergywomen feel disproportionately.

As a group, clergywomen today are among the best and the brightest in their profession, a fact related to their small proportions within it: it's easier to recruit x good women than 10x good men.[2] With women occupying more than half the seats in some theological seminaries, this situation may have already begun to change, though change is slowed by the backlog of talented older women for whom the clergy has become a possible choice only late in their lives. Meanwhile, in all denominations to one extent or another, clergywomen are underemployed.

In the recent past, American businesses in a frantic effort to increase efficiency have been painfully learning the wisdom of putting their best people in key positions. Hardly a whisper of this lesson has penetrated into churches and synagogues, where jobs for women are talked of, if at all, in terms of equal rights and social justice rather than in terms of productivity. This tendency is encouraged by the many Christian feminists who talk about the *sinfulness*, not the *impracticability* of the religious institutions' treatment of women.

Yes, a few women are moving up in denominational hierarchies. Yes, women bishops preside in several denominations.[3] Yes, more churches and synagogues are hiring clergywomen: they now constitute 11 to 12 percent of all clergy.[4] But almost invariably women find jobs only in the poorest, smallest, most remote pastorates, or as assistants, or in noncongregational jobs; put up with long delays in moving; and hit the glass ceiling at their second move. A Harvard study conducted from 1977 to 1987 revealed that an Episcopalian clergywoman has a better chance of being elected suffragan bishop of a large urban diocese than of being chosen as rector of a prestigious, well-financed congregation in the same diocese.[5]

Most clergy, including most clergywomen, want to be sole or senior pastors. In a 1993 survey, for instance, Presbyterian clergywomen showed solo pastor, co-pastor, and head of staff as the positions in which they could make best use of their gifts for the ministry, though only about a third of them held such a position. Almost all those clergywomen who do hold such pastorates serve small churches or several small churches simultaneously—three, four, even as many as nine.[6] Laura Geller noted in 1995 that of the 189 Reform women rabbis already ordained, none serves as head of a thousand-member congregation.[7]

Are clergywomen satisfied with their smaller congregations, delighting in their intimacy, pleased to avoid the myriad administrative tasks imposed on the clergy of larger churches and synagogues, concerned to save time for their families? Some are. One pastor who has the credentials to teach in a theological seminary but instead serves a tiny congregation explained to us: "If I were only at Yale or Harvard I would just totally lose touch. To me part of being here is a witness. I'm going to stay here and show you that the local church is important. I think the hope of the mainline churches is that women are trying new things that haven't been done; the congregations are growing and becoming vital, even though the numbers are still tiny."

Rabbi Arnold Sher, director of the Reform Movement's Rabbinic Placement Commission, says: "It's very clear that women in 'AB' congregations (166–300 members) are not seeking larger pulpits."[8] In the words of one woman rabbi, "Men seem to be really hung up on size. You'll hear guys at rabbinical conferences say 'How big are you?' or 'How big is yours?' and you know they mean how many member families do you have? To a woman it sounds like the boys in the playground." But another rabbi told us, "We [women] ask ourselves, are we fooling ourselves, changing our expectations to match reality? Are we saying we're happy with smaller pulpits—sour grapes? Or are women in fact saying 'No, no. Our true love is to develop an alternative model to what a pulpit rabbi can be, should be, and in fact the way synagogues should be structured and function and how big they should allow themselves to be?"

Associate and assistant pastorates are considered good ways to start out for males; for women they go on and on and on, yea unto the third and fourth appointments. As a Lutheran clergywoman told us, "The church is now congratulating itself for being able to place so many women right out of seminary, and I'm saying, 'That's good, but after 25 years that's nothing to brag about. What you need to worry about is the women who are 56 and 42. It no longer works for us to be sweet young things, the associate you can pat on the head and send off with the youth group. Taking an ill-paid position is OK when you're first out, because you think it will get better. When it doesn't after ten years, you have to say, 'Now wait a second. If I were working for a taxi company I'd get more respect.'"

Occasionally by choice, more often for lack of anything better, many Christian and Jewish clergywomen take nonparish jobs or "special ministry" jobs: in chaplaincies, in denominational and interdenominational administrations. But funds for all these special ministries are evaporating—except, comments Barbara Brown Zikmund, for prison chaplaincies, unfortunately a growth industry.

The burnout rate among chaplains, whether on campus, in prisons, in hospitals, or in the military, flares high. "I learned real quickly that I don't want hospital chaplaincy," an Episcopalian priest told us. "It's all crisis ministry. You lose a quarter of your parish every year." Nor is campus ministry all beer and skittles these days: "In campus ministry money has dried up and positions have become more tenuous, more part-time, they've used more women, and I think women are more exploited," said a Presbyterian woman with long experience in the field. "Ten years ago you usually had to have had some parish ministry experience; positions now are entry-level positions, just because of the pay. Now in a lot of positions you don't even have to be ordained."

Tight church and college budgets are squeezing campus ministries into different shapes. Many a campus chaplain is spending more and more time raising money for activities. Or if she's paid by the school, she may be seen as just another student services person, the necessity for whom faculty question, so that she spends time and energy justifying her own presence, her own job, and responding to the question, "Why do we need an ordained person in that job?" Somehow the chaplain, whether military or hospital or campus or prison, must work ecumenically, ready to serve people of all religions and denominations, or none—yet resist being thrust into a purely secular position.

Military chaplaincies afford peer support and opportunities for promotion, but they're not for everyone. Some clergywomen as a matter of principle refuse to join the military and others cannot meet military standards of age and physical fitness. Chaplain Major Janet Y. Horton has described the drawbacks: "In the PX, spouses and civilians want to know if you're a *real* chaplain. Even though you're obviously wearing rank insignia on your uniform, other officers ask if you're a chapel activities specialist [a position for enlisted troops, not officers]. Some men resent it when you don't receive the *tough* assignments, others resent it when you do." The woman chaplain, says Horton, forfeits her private life and takes an incoming fire of suggestive comments and rumors.[9] On the other hand, she enjoys financial security, varied assignments, a standard of living well above that of most clergywomen, and the prospect of a healthy pension after twenty years of service.

But as the American military downsizes, senior chaplains are clinging to their commissions, well aware of the near impossibility for Protestant clergy of finding equal pay in the civilian ministry. Accordingly, the military is recruiting few chaplains of either gender. What's more, fewer slots and shrinking opportunities for promotion inevitably further politicize career advancement. "You get the senior people being very competitive, looking out after their own faith groups and their friends," a lieutenant-commander told us. "They write evaluations of junior people, and if they didn't like them or had been confronted on an issue, . . . all you have to do to take somebody out of ministry is to give them a C evaluation or rank them as third out of three, even if they're the best, and they'll never get promoted. And it's going to get even more competitive: the projected future is to try to contract as many of the shore billets as possible to hungry local clergy—and for fewer hours, so that they won't have to be offered benefits." Worldwide the Air Force has never had more than about twenty women chaplains on active duty at any given time; the Army never more than about forty; and the Navy and Marines never more than about sixty. No wonder that many women chaplains feel severely isolated.

Editorships of religious publications and administrative appointments in denominational headquarters or in the National or World Council of Churches or in the Central Conference of American Rabbis can put women on the cutting edge of change. ("But remember," a Roman Catholic sister warned us, "you can get cut on the cutting edge.") Some seek the academic world on the faculties of theological schools or in departments of religion. Recently women have begun to specialize in interim ministries, looking for new jobs and shifting locations every year or two. As search processes for new pastors have lengthened and sophisticated, interim jobs have come to demand specialized skills, for which some denominations now offer special training. Some clergywomen find these jobs more accommodating of their family responsibilities than regular pastorates. But it's hard, one of our interviewees noted, to build a career or economic security as an interim: the moves are lateral, and periods of unemployment often lengthy.

In fact clergywomen as a group have to anticipate extraordinarily long job searches. The 1993 Presbyterian survey reports: "For their first call, [only about] one quarter (24%) of women searched less than one year. . . . Additionally, 38% of women searched for one to two years, 13% for two to three years, 7% for three to four years, 4% for four to five years, 13% for five to nine years, and 1% for ten or more years. . . . the patterns of search time are similar for the second, third and fourth calls."[10] "It's called, 'Be a Rabbi and See the World,'" a Conservative rabbi quipped as she told us of her moves from California to Arizona to Connecticut in search of work, finding it either as an assistant or in small congregations.

As among American women workers generally, it's hard to read the ambiguities of the growing part-time segment. Some women, of course, deliberately choose part-time work to allow time for domestic responsibilities. But industrial down-sizing in the general populace and declining memberships and contributions among mainline churches force many into part-time jobs—even more women than men, both in the general populace and among the clergy.[11] One woman described herself to us as "a half-time consulting minister—That's a discreet way of saying, 'We're not paying this person enough.'" In any case, most part-time workers, including clergy-women, lose benefits. The problem is exacerbated because in at least some denom-inations the church pension fund is structured around *full-time parish ministry*.

Given all this unemployment and underemployment, what do clergywomen do? Some women imaginatively stitch together several responsibilities. "Women are re-defining the contours of the rabbinate," said a woman who combines teaching in a seminary, administration in a religious organization, and editing a religious jour-nal. "We are expanding what can be seen as authentic ways of performing ministry in the rabbinate. We're very adamant about calling these our rabbinates. With the numbers of large pulpits dwindling in the Conservative and Reform movements if we all say we are going to be pulpit rabbis, a lot of men are going to be affected. And cobbling together part-time positions delights me, though sometimes I'm crashing under the diffused responsibilities on me. But it allows a cross-fertilization that is extraordinarily fruitful."

Other clergywomen resort to combining part-time paid or volunteer work in a religious institution with supporting themselves by a secular job. Indeed a 1988 assembly of the International Association of Women Ministers focused on ways clergywomen can support themselves in secular occupations. "We may all eventu-ally almost have to find other work," an Episcopalian priest told us. "Many clergy get counseling credentials and do counseling either on the side or as part of their job so they can have some other income. Some are lawyers. I know one person, a woman, who is a secretary, who works Sundays in a cluster of churches. I know one who gave up and went to work for Habitat. I know one who is a nurse and a chap-lain—two different jobs."

Presbyterians call such clergy "tentmakers," after St. Paul, who subsidized his vocation by leatherwork, including tentmaking. Other denominations speak of dual-career, bivocational, and nonstipendiary clergy, voluntary ministers, and worker priests. As tentmakers point out, the practice of clergy supporting them-selves in whole or in part by working in secular occupations goes back a long way, even in this country. Almond H. Davis wrote about Salome Lincoln (1807–1841), "After she began to travel and preach; as she received but little from others, she was accustomed to work with her hands to clothe herself; and then go out on her mis-sions of love, till it was expended; being too sensitive to say anything in relation to her circumstances, and the church too *covetous* to inquire."[12]

Both history and common sense, some say, support this mode of living for clergy: all believers, lay and clergy alike, are called to minister; clergy who earn at least part of their living from other work will better serve their congregations, better under-stand their parishioners who labor in other vineyards, and empower the laity by developing opportunities for congregational teamwork.[13] "God is not calling us to choose between our tent and our church or ministry situation," writes Rev. Linda Kuhn, "as if the latter—the church, the spirit, and religious realm—is the only truly important work, the faithful work, the religious work. We are in a unique position to take professional ministry and the realm of the spirit off a false pedestal as if it is more worthy, more faithful, more noble, in and of itself—and bring it to ground level, rooted in the real stuff of existence, where most people live, with all its demands."[14] And of course historically some denominations, including for many years the Quakers, have not had a paid professional clergy.[15]

Faced with unemployment or underemployment, a good many clergywomen—particularly, though by no means exclusively, African-Americans—respond entrepreneurially. Some simply create their own jobs, taking on some small responsibility and building it into importance, or hanging up a shingle as a spiritual director. An African-American woman in the Church of God told us about starting out as a lay minister. Gradually she made a reputation as a speaker in schools and to women's groups; then the denomination, seeing her as a representative to the public, urged her to be ordained. Now she has a part-time appointment in a local church but earns her living mainly by writing for Church of God publications and developing religious education materials.

Partly for cultural reasons like *machismo* and the black community's conception of the clergy as a roadway to upward mobility for black men, ethnic clergywomen have an even harder time than whites. Such a hard time, in fact, that many black clergywomen leave black denominations for better opportunities in predominantly white denominations. As Delores Carpenter wrote in the *Washington Post* of September 12, 1985, African-American women comprised more than a third of female seminary enrollment in accredited theological seminaries, and more than 60 percent of black women seminary graduates were joining mainline white denominations, thereby enjoying better opportunities for ordination and employment.[16] In the mid-1990s, with the influx of churchgoing immigrants, mainline predominantly white churches need to meet the demands of their burgeoning ethnic congregations for ethnic clergy. Thus in 1993 the United Church of Christ (UCC), more concerned for an ethnic than for a denominational match, appointed a Lutheran Native American clergywoman to pastor a Native American UCC congregation.[17] On the other hand, minority clergywomen face racism as well as sexism. Renee Hill reported that at the Episcopalian General Theological Seminary she found an unwelcoming atmosphere: "One person in the class looked at me and asked me if I was a Baptist—never assuming that I might be an Episcopalian!" And when she was job hunting in New York City, "Most of the other parishes where I interviewed never even bothered to get back to me. There's a real old boys' network out there."[18]

Perhaps partly for such reasons, black clergywomen have distinguished themselves by the numbers of churches they have founded and continue to found. Besides all the formal and informal mentoring that goes on among African-American clergywomen, at least one of them is taking direct action to open opportunities for her young sisters. Dr. Suzan JohnsonCook, senior pastor of the Mariners' Temple Baptist Church in New York City, is undertaking to back qualified black clergy-women who want to start their own ministries. She told us: "What I hope to do is raise funds, so if someone comes with a project and says, 'I really feel called of God. I just need some start-up seed money,' I'd be in a position to do that for them. If there are enough women who've been through it, we can say, 'Look, we're here for you, and this is the way you can get a building, this is the way . . . ,' it cuts off a lot of the pressure, and you start being able to minister."

Another African-American marvels that more clergywomen don't set off on their own. Of her original denomination she remarks, "I found myself going one direction and they were going another. So I just simply split with the church, and I started my own church." Why, she wonders, do clergywomen stay in such difficult situations, which make them so angry and load them down with psychological baggage? African-American Baptist clergywomen "have to kowtow to get what they want." She comments: "I don't need you [men] to ordain me. I don't need you to give me a church. And I tend to be more accepted, because I'm not in [male preachers'] hair."

A white clergywoman, Dr. Lillie McCutcheon of the Church of God, expresses similar concerns. Her mother early in the twentieth century "planted" four churches. Dr. McCutcheon took over one of them: "I took a church that had—oh, I would be stretching it to say 20 people," she told us. She served it for forty-three years; eventually she was supervising a staff of five, black and white, women and men. "I would advise any lady that's going to go into ministry to choose to start a church of her own," she says. "This saves her the difficulty of having anybody fighting against her being a lady minister."

The Church of God and several other denominations help women who would take McCutcheon's advice by giving them experience, assisting church planters, and in effect doing market research to identify good sites for new churches. Other would-be founders launch out more or less on their own.

Finally, unemployment, underemployment, and desperate economic necessity fuel higher burnout among clergywomen than among clergymen. "This is especially true in black congregational-polity churches, especially in Baptist churches," says Prathia Hall Wynn, Associate Dean for Spiritual and Community Life at United Theological Seminary in Dayton. "Very often they must go back to teaching or typing or whatever they were doing before or can find to do, because there are no placements for them." The critical time usually arrives some eight to ten years after ordination, when a woman realizes that she simply is not going to get the opportunity to do the work to which she believes God has called her.

So women drop out of their profession more often than clergymen—though this fact is difficult to interpret.[19] For one thing, women workers in all occupations show more checkered career patterns than men, at least partly because of family responsibilities and societal expectations. For another, experts speculate—though the proposition is hardly capable of proof—that women enter the clergy with less realistic expectations than men. Some of them think of it, that is, *solely* as a dedicated life of service, and not at all as a career, an idealism that readily lends itself to disillusionment.

Again, the helping professions generally attract more than their share of people who themselves need help emotionally. "Some people say," a Lutheran clergywoman told us, "that some women go into the ministry because of unresolved issues with their fathers, deliberately choose a male-dominated role in order to keep working at that unresolved relationship." A knowledgeable laywoman who serves on a screening commission for clergy comments, "I am reluctant to generalize, but when it comes to intelligence and insight and grasp, I have seen some women who are way above the norm. I have seen few men who are above the norm. But when it comes to people that don't have their act together I have seen quite a few women and some men too. I think that we have some very wounded folks [aspiring to the clergy] that are looking for the church to save them. I have seen more women than men in that category." When things go wrong on the job for such people, dropouts increase.

But the healthiest of clergywomen may find that she simply has no choice, economically speaking, but to drop out. In the 1993 Presbyterian study a woman computer system engineer and business owner commented, "I am forthright in saying I cannot afford to work more than half time for the church." And another wrote, "I am actively seeking a new career direction—not for lack of a continued sense of call, but for lack of opportunities with decent conditions and pay."

Leaving a profession, particularly the clergy, entails a painful, complex decision, usually taken for a mixture of reasons. To the outsider the vocation to the clergy sounds much like that to teaching or any other of the helping professions, to which people are drawn out of a desire to serve and because they find the work congenial. But many if not most clergy believe, and their institutions encourage them to believe, that their call is different, that by accepting it they are doing what the divinity wants them to do. Giving it up imposes a psychological penalty, as well as a sense of having wasted lots of money and much effort in preparing for work now denied. Some people who leave the clergy are angry; some are heartbroken; almost all of them bleed for more than a season.

To survey or speculate about their reasons is inevitably to oversimplify. The 1993 Presbyterian survey found feelings of isolation the most commonly given reason for leaving. These may spring from being placed in remote country churches where no one in the congregation shares their interests or political view, or from finding no one in their congregations of backgrounds similar to their own. Their sense of having to suppress their opinions and beliefs particularly troubles and isolates clergywomen. One respondent in the 1993 Presbyterian survey wrote, "One of the hardest things for me is walking on the boundary between caring for people who have a very different theology and philosophy than I, and finding a place where my views—openly stated—are valued. I feel like I am living with a mask on—always guarded in my words, for fear of alienating people with my 'liberal' ideas. At the same time, I feel judged by more ardent feminists (and some clergywomen among them) for capitulating to my congregation—I don't stand up enough for my views. Tight wires are lonely places!"

"It's bringing people along is the struggle that's so hard," a United Church of Christ clergywoman told us. "Trying to make some changes in people's thinking is something that you just battle with until you're worn out. Not necessarily on the gender issue: on peace issues, redefining families, even I guess theological points, like questioning the atonement or what that means for women. Asking tougher doctrinal questions, where a lot of folks aren't ready to go along with you yet. Your woman's experience leads you to feel something real different. The only place you can articulate it is with other clergywomen, because your congregation isn't ready yet for that." No wonder such women found relief at the Re-Imagining Conference: "It was an absolutely safe place to be a feminist and to explore that. But it was feminism within the church context. Many of us women are so *terribly* responsible and we're so *terribly* respectable in our denominations, and we're so very *careful* not to offend people."

In the Presbyterian survey of reasons for leaving the ministry, the sense of isolation was closely followed by underuse of one's abilities: "I sense very strongly," one woman wrote, "a longing and need to be moving into something else with perhaps less resistance and more valuing of my gifts." A former clergywoman now in medical school described to us a typical mixture of motives: "My denomination has grown more conservative; I'm no longer comfortable with their theology [i.e., she feels isolated within the denomination.] The denomination's reaction to the Re-Imagining Conference stunned me. I went into the ministry in the first place because I believed the church could effect social change. Now I realize that I am not going to be in a position to do the things I've always felt called to do. I am not going to be called to an urban church as a social justice person, working with housing projects, food pantries, homeless shelters, getting people involved in Habitat for Humanity, doing educational programs about hunger and poverty. I'm not going to be called to be head of staff. I see no future. The four seminary classmates I've kept in touch with, very gifted women, have always been underemployed. I just had a call from one of my presbytery friends, saying she can't stand it any more and wanting to know how I feel about my decision to leave. This seems to happen to a lot of women about the seven- to ten-year mark. The church ends up losing many good people. They're so gifted. They have so much to offer. And the church just can't make room for them. It's so sad to me."

✑ What's Holding Them Back? _____

What causes the limitations on clergywomen's job opportunities? Who's to blame? No one and everyone.

Societal and institutional sexism contribute. "In some ways [the church] still seems like a labor union dominated by men," said a knowledgeable laywoman, "and the women are not in that game. The men protect each other, and they protect behavior that shouldn't be protected, and at the same time they haven't quite accepted women as insiders."

In most mainline denominations that ordain, theological seminaries and hierarchies have started campaigns to reduce sexism. Every alumna whom we have asked agrees that the environment for women at her seminary is now more welcoming than it was for women in the 1960s and 1970s. As one rabbi phrased it, "There is now equal opportunity—maybe not equal enthusiasm, but equal opportunity on the part of the teachers." Denominational hierarchies hold consciousness-raising classes for clergy on sexual harassment and suggest women candidates to congregations seeking pastors. Some of these efforts work well and some don't. As a Lutheran minister remarked, "When a bishop says to a congregation 'Well, would you take a woman?' it's like saying, 'Well, would you take something damaged? Would you take something inferior?'" An Episcopalian priest told us, "Whenever the women went to the bishop, talked about a problem, and suggested correction, he assented and acted, but he never saw the connections among problems, the common source. He was known to say very loudly and very firmly, 'There is absolutely no problem with women in this diocese.' We finally gave up." A district superintendent told one woman about a job opening for which she was well qualified, but, he said, "There's nothing I can do. They just don't want a woman." Surely he had enough influence to get her an interview? she suggested. He did, and she got the job. As a rabbi commented, "Where the problem rests now is in the hearts and souls of those who are at the heads of those institutions."

But it rests also in the hearts and souls of congregations. In almost all denominations they have a lot of say-so about who their pastor will be—though much less so among Methodists, and somewhat less among Episcopalians. Even in Methodist churches where hierarchies assign ministers to specific pulpits, a black clergywoman told us, "There are still churches that will tell the superintendent or the bishop, 'We don't want a woman. We don't want an African-American.' In some districts that's a pretty good way to get one. But not always."

On occasion congregational autonomy can help women: as Mila Frances Tupper has observed, churches with centralized governments have been slowest to ordain women, while more congregation-centered denominations have allowed for greater diversity. Some Southern Baptist congregations have ordained women at the risk of denominational discipline. On the other hand, a few members who oppose women in the pastorate can easily end a candidacy. Some clergywomen believe that women are more vulnerable than men to these "clergy-killers," because the church does not give women the same sense of authority. Another woman wondered whether clergywomen's being "into making connections among people" might "become threatening, even though in forming those connections we're not thinking about getting power."

"Many Conservative congregations," a rabbi told us, "won't even consider *inter-*

viewing a woman." A Christian clergywoman also commented on this result of local control: "They are still capable in many places of saying 'No, we're not ready for a woman pastor,' and they say it outright, and the bishop can say until doomsday, 'We don't have men pastors and women pastors, we have pastors of the church.' And they say, 'OK, but we're not ready for a woman pastor.'" An African-American minister in the Church of God told us of being asked to recommend a candidate for a church in which she had often preached. "When I mentioned a friend," our informant said, "one of the ladies burst out, 'But she's a woman! I don't think that a woman would make a pastor!' She was embarrassed, so she looked at me and said, 'But I don't mean any harm.' They've had two men since then, and they've had bad luck, because they didn't get a woman!"

Even among young people this rejection of clergywomen may show up. "My worst experience," a Presbyterian minister told us, "was in campus ministry, where a leader of the main student group walked into my office the first week and said, 'I don't believe you are called to ministry. I don't think what you're doing is Biblical, and therefore I am resigning my position and I'm going to boycott anything that you or this campus ministry is involved in from now on and I'm going to spread the word,' and then walked out of the office." The clergywoman still bears the scars of the resulting conflict. A minister in the African Methodist Episcopal Church writes of a young man who "loudly declared as he turned to leave [when he saw her in the pulpit], 'A woman can't tell me nothing.'"[20]

Congregational autonomy and the separation of church and state enable churches to reject women solely because of their gender—like the late-nineteenth-century mission parishioners in North Dakota who concluded that "if it had come to that pass when a woman must fill the pulpit they had better shut up altogether before they were disgraced."[21] As a farmer remarked of an able woman candidate, "I'd ruther have a man that wa'nt so good."[22]

Attitudes toward women generally rather than theological beliefs usually dictate congregational attitudes.[23] Donna Schaper thinks that familial relationships carry over into antagonism toward clergywomen: "Whatever feelings people have about their mothers—and most people, male and female, have enormously complicated feelings about their mothers, even more confused than those they have towards their fathers, which are confused enough—they also have about women clergy. Mothers are practically the only experience people have with female power. Put a woman in a vestment and it looks as if she has power; thus all the associations are maternal."[24] At any rate, even in the late twentieth century some men find women professionals threatening. "A lot of men work for women bosses now," a Lutheran pastor remarked to us. "They have new threats and they're in competition with women. It's real hard for them to cope with it. Even the clergy—almost all clergy groups in my area have some men with this sort of Promise-Keepers' idea that men are the head of the household. None of them have actually said women shouldn't be ministers, but when push comes to shove, some of them feel that the problem with this culture is that men haven't asserted themselves and that if we [men] only asserted our dominant role, things would be better."

Then, too, sexuality hovers around male rejection of clergywomen. The more naïve overtly say, "I can't stand the idea of looking at a woman in the pulpit. I might get sexually aroused and that would embarrass me." To which a forthright woman occasionally snaps, "What do you think has been going on with women looking at men up there all these years? Welcome to the world!" In another context Carol Marie Noren remarks that awareness of gender is heightened when a woman preaches: she represents women although male preachers do not represent men. Maybe not: maybe a preaching woman heightens men's perception of gender status; maybe for the women in the congregation preaching men have always represented men in general and male authority.[25]

Women in the congregation as well as men may oppose clergywomen, though on the whole, as an observant laywoman remarked, women's opposition "reflects the men's view of things. There are many women who still reflect the view that men have. It's been the safest way through the years." An African-American clergywoman expanded on this point: "This whole socialization of self-less-ness, which I think is diabolical, is extremely destructive in terms of women's esteem and standing—the standing that they give themselves. Consequently very often the most vocal opponents of the ministry of women are other women. That is part of what I call the pathology of oppression, that women have internalized the hate and therefore cannot themselves be comfortable with things that women do unless they are things that women do with the approval of men. It's internalized misogyny." As Barbara Brown Zikmund points out, it's also easier for women to express whatever doubts they have without being labeled sexist.

Some older women resent women professionals of any stripe, envying the opportunities these women have enjoyed that were denied them in their own youth. Some widows look to the clergyman as a kind of substitute spouse. A laywoman on a synodical committee that screens candidates for the ministry says flatly, "Some women like a male pastor as sort of a safe sex symbol." A clergywoman in a working-class parish believes that some of her women parishioners view all single clergywomen as potential threats to their marriages.

And some parishioners of both genders have theological scruples or simply cannot bring themselves to feel that a woman can be a "real" minister or priest or rabbi. All too rare are parishioners like the sweet elderly woman who said to her new woman pastor, "My dear, I have a problem with the idea of a woman in the pulpit, but that's my problem, not yours."

Given a chance, a clergywoman can often dispel doubts. "Most of the old women—you know churches always have a lot of old women—at first think that women ought not to be ordained," observed a laywoman, "but they're so glad to have anybody there to minister to them that they soon become really staunch supporters." One woman reported to the 1993 Presbyterian survey, "When I was hired as interim in my most recent position, they were leery of having a woman. When they interviewed my replacement they told her—We're prejudiced about women ministers—we prefer them." Once or twice we have heard of a small congregation experienced with clergywomen that will interview *only* women candidates.

Clergywomen describe rejection by clergymen as hurting them most, hardest to bear. Not all clergymen, they hasten to add, eagerly naming those who have supported them, taught them, opened doors and pulpits to them. But rejection from clergymen ranges from discomfort at having women around at their meetings to fear of competition to fury at the invasion of "their" territory. Usually subtle, it occasionally expresses itself overtly and vulgarly, even in pushing and shoving.[26] In any form it leaves women feeling betrayed by the group to which they belong and the people they have trusted. A Mennonite clergywoman painfully described a retreat where a brother minister refused to take communion because she was present.

An American Baptist spoke of her denominational clergy association, where she is the only woman senior minister: "I feel like those guys like me a lot and I think we get along well. It was at one of those meetings, however, that one of their number walked up to me and said that there were rumors going around the state that I was a lesbian, and how glad he was that my roommate Chana [a rabbi] was getting married and dispelling those rumors. I realized at that moment that that was not a support group for me and never could be. Many of them even knew my boyfriend at the time. I was just shocked."

Insightfully, a clergywoman remarked on the greater support she received from older men—and the greater opposition from her peers in age: "Those who are moving in life in the direction of giving up power, as we all do as we age, [can contemplate sharing power], but those who still believe that they have the right and privilege to control are very adamant against giving up that power or sharing that power with those who have not been empowered in the past." As a retired bishop commented, some senior ministers "are comfortable surrounded with a covey of women serving them and carrying out their programs, but when you put a woman on the *ordained* staff, John Wayne falls off his horse."[27]

Even clergywomen themselves may contribute to gender discrimination by accepting positions where the employing institutions are clearly exploiting them. Idealism and naïveté about handling one's own career help to account for this co-optation. Episcopal priest Elizabeth Canham warns, "I am a little worried when I hear women denying any interest in 'status' as priests, saying they simply want to be demonstrating the servant role. My concern arises from the fact that women have been perceived as offering a supportive servant ministry for so long that we need other images."[28] In the 1990s, a sizable number of second-career or empty-nest women are entering the clergy; many of them can afford to take a low salary either because they have already achieved financial security or because their husbands are supporting them. Other women just don't know how to negotiate for better salaries and benefits.

But still others are caught in a bind: despite excellent qualifications, they simply cannot find decently paid jobs in the work to which they feel called. In a way they're comparable to the many college and university adjunct professors who piece together some sort of living by teaching multiple courses at various institutions for a few hundred dollars a course because they "love to teach" or think of teaching as their vocation. That is, they cooperate in their own exploitation by staying in a profession that cannot/will not support them.

Further, in denominations with an oversupply of clergy two principles clash: Do they give the job to the person who can do it best or to the one who needs money more? A rabbi told us about her experiences in seeking a hospice chaplaincy. She went on two interviews. After the first, "They ended up giving the job to some . . . excuse the expression, but some hack who happened to be a male. And the second time, someone said to me, 'Look, let's face it. If I have a choice between giving it to you and giving it to someone who needs bread on the table, 'I will give it to the person who needs bread.' I can't argue with the concept. I'm blessed and I don't need it. But I feel I have a lot to give. And I also feel, to be honest with you—your husband's listening?—I do think that women have a certain sensitivity to the job."

✒ Professional Problems

Besides the major problems of underemployment and unemployment, clergywomen of course face many other on-the-job difficulties. Most of these they share with others.

They share with clergymen the problems of the profession. For instance, Protestant Christian clergy as a group receive egregiously low compensation—so low that some men leave the profession because they cannot support their families in it, let alone educate their children. Their pay is notably lower than that of rabbis.[29] The compensation of clergywomen is even lower—profoundly lower. The 1995 Hartford Seminary survey shows a range of *average* compensation, including salary and benefits, from $27,000 annually for Wesleyan clergymen to $46,000 for their Episcopalian peers; Wesleyan clergywomen average $19,500 and their Episcopalian colleagues $37,000. "A woman," the report says, "is likely to receive a salary $5300 lower than a man even when we control for [other variables]. Net of everything else, a woman is likely to be paid almost 20% less than a man." It is poor comfort that this discrepancy between the genders is a little less than in the population at large, where women earn some 72 percent as much as men.

Among rabbis the same gender pattern appears. Rabbi Mark Winer, who monitors salary data for the Central Conference of American Rabbis, finds "an alarming disparity in wages between men and women in the rabbinate, with the wage gap getting larger the further one is removed from entry-level positions. At the middle-size congregation, over three hundred families, for example, there is no woman even close to the median salary."[30]

Just as clergywomen get lower salaries than clergymen, so they enjoy fewer benefits—partly because of the proportionally larger numbers of part-time women, partly because of women's frequent relegation to small, poor parishes, partly because of the numbers of women in nonparochial positions. John H. Morgan notes that some 38 percent of Episcopalian women priests neither live in a rectory nor receive a housing allowance—a longtime prerogative of the clergy. In effect, the churches these women serve are being subsidized by the women themselves or the husbands (or parents) who provide their housing. Morgan was obviously appalled by his discovery that in 1985 only 37 percent of Episcopalian women priests were participating in the church pension fund: "What about retirement! What about plans for life after active ministry! What about the institutional Church's responsibility to care for the professional clergy who give their lives in service to the institution!"[31]

Although not being married frees up time for work, single clergy experience problems in placement. "I think that all single people, male or female, have a very difficult time getting work in the church," says a single woman priest, "because people are afraid of what they may do sexually. I think there's also the 'We want to call somebody just like us' kind of thing. Or a 'family person.' I interviewed in a parish and got down to the final three, and was telephoned by the chair of the calling committee. 'We're really not going to call you because you're not married. I guess we decided we needed to have somebody just like us.' The reason there was a vacancy was that the married rector had run off with somebody in the vestry. So they called somebody just like them, who went and did the exact same thing."

Being single also aggravates the sense of isolation common among clergy, male or female. "I'm largely in a working class parish, as many clergywomen are," one pastor told us. "They may not have grown up in working-class communities. I didn't. So learning all those norms of those communities has been really a test, really different. I don't feel at home."

Gay and lesbian clergy of course face special problems. Except in the most liberal denominations, it's almost impossible for clergy to be out of the closet, but few authorities doubt that gay men have always constituted and still constitute a significant presence in all ranks of the clergy, and lesbians undoubtedly are represented among clergywomen at least in proportion to their presence in the general population. Some speculate that gays and lesbians are distributed in greater numbers within the helping professions, including the clergy, than in the population at large.[32] Christian lesbians are just beginning to function as a group: in 1991 Protestant and Roman Catholic clergywomen and laywomen organized Christian Lesbians Out Together (CLOUT).[33]

A good many denominations have pronounced the case closed: homosexuality is unnatural and forbidden, and that's that. Though they may treat gays and lesbians in their congregations "compassionately," they still regard them as sinners and do not even consider ordaining them. Of this double standard lesbian clergywoman Rose Mary Denman writes, "I'm not sure who should be more angry: the ministers, who, in fact, do have different expectations placed upon them by the Church, or the laity, who are, in reality, being told that their standards don't count as much as do those of the clergy." She quotes an African-American acquaintance: "Women, gays, and lesbians are good enough to raise money for you [the Church] by making pies and serving chicken dinners, teaching your children in Sunday school, and directing your choirs, but we're not good enough to share the Word of God with you."[34]

Most other denominations follow the same line as the military: don't kiss, don't ask, don't tell. For example, the United Methodist discipline reads, "No self avowed, practicing homosexual may be accepted as a candidate, ordained, or appointed to a ministry in the United Methodist Church."[35] In Judaism "no openly gay or lesbian rabbi has been successfully placed in a UAHC Congregation other than in those congregations that have predominantly gay and lesbian members."[36] Nelle Morton writes that this attitude of the monkey covering his eyes has created "one of the most obscene and dishonest situations within religious institutions as one woman after the other has been fired from top church boards or teaching positions for being lesbian and the reason attributed to other causes."[37]

The issue stubbornly refuses to go away; disagreement over it erupts with the regularity of Old Faithful. Conservative Methodists in the summer of 1995 tried to force the church hierarchy to take action against an ordained clergywoman who had come out of the closet. Both her bishop and the general secretary came to her defense, commending her for her courage, denying any violation of church discipline, and affirming her right to disagree with church teaching.[38] Sometimes the authorities interpret church law generously: when in 1994 a Michigan Episcopalian bishop ordained to the priesthood a lesbian in a committed relationship, a majority of a committee of his peers ruled that he had not violated church law, because the 1979 resolution of the General Convention that states "we believe it is not appropriate for this Church to ordain a practicing homosexual person" is not necessarily mandatory.[39]

A few denominations do allow the ordination of practicing homosexuals. Once ordained, gay or lesbian clergy must find a church to serve—no easy task. One lesbian told us about the vain search that she and her partner made for a co-ministry: "I think churches looked at us in the early 80s and thought, Huh? Not one woman, but two, in relationship, and wanting to do something called co-ministry? I think that as good as we are, and probably as good as we even were 15 years ago, it wasn't enough, and we didn't know enough to assuage people's fears about what looks like a triple whammy."

In the United Church of Christ individual congregations may announce themselves "open and affirming" in acceptance of gay people. "That movement with different names again crosses all the mainline denominations," a lesbian pastor told us. "The Methodists are 'reconciling congregations.' I think the Unitarians are 'welcoming congregations.' The Disciples are 'open and affirming.' And I think the Lutherans are 'reconciled in Christ' or some such thing. In the Presbyterians they're 'warm light churches.'" By the spring of 1994 130 United Church of Christ congregations, 2 percent of the total, had so proclaimed themselves.[40] Other congregations who have not so identified themselves occasionally knowingly call a gay or lesbian clergyperson. In 1995 when Tracy Lind, rector of St. Paul's Episcopal Church in Paterson, New Jersey, "came out" from the pulpit, "Parishioners received the sermon with tears and a standing ovation."[41] Metropolitan Community Churches form a primarily gay and lesbian denomination, which claims thirty-two thousand members in sixteen countries—but the National Council of Churches has not admitted it into membership.[42]

In the divisive atmosphere of late-twentieth-century America, the complexities of this issue multiply. One United Church of Christ clergywoman living openly in a committed relationship told us that she thought she had made her sexual orientation clear by telling a calling committee that for eight years she had been living with a woman who coparented her children. "But I wasn't heard," she said, "because I didn't use the big 'L' word. When it became clear people then felt betrayed." Many of her parishioners didn't care; others cared passionately; and the divisions among them did not improve the health of the church. Though she has since found a half-time position in a parish indifferent to her lesbianism, she still cannot get her health insurance extended to cover her partner. "The denominational insurance board is adamant that they will not do that, that it would split the church wide open, that the conservative wing of our church, which has generated huge amounts of money, would leave."

Hostility toward homosexuals, she says, comes much more from institutional policy than from personal encounters. With remarkable detachment, she comments;

It's interesting to me as a gay person how magnetized people get in churches around issues and concerns of sexual morality, and particularly around gay issues. There are 43,000 verses of scripture; there are five passages, I think it's something like .08 of one percent of the Biblical text is dedicated to talking about so-called homosexual practices. We can get so exercised about that. And the most frequent moral issue in the gospels is economic, and we hardly are exercised about that at all.

All in all, the homosexual issue is a tangled web for religious institutions, whether or not they tacitly encourage deceit about it. Lesbian clergywomen who dare not declare themselves live in anguish, particularly because the silence forced upon them strikes many of them as sinfully dishonest. As one of them writes, "The closet is silent, dark, and lonely."[43] Many straight clergy are uncomfortable with church policy. Administrators worry about lawsuits alleging sexual exploitation that might be brought against a lesbian clergywoman by an estranged partner who belongs to her church. And ecclesiastical courts and hierarchies turn and twist in an effort to reconcile denominational policy with Christian charity. Take the case of an out-of-the-closet lesbian who in 1990 was serving a United Church of Christ congregation in Milwaukee. She fell in love with a man but decided not to marry him, out of solidarity with gays and lesbians, who cannot marry their chosen partners. Nonetheless, she informed the church hierarchy, she intended to live with her lover. They warned her that by moving in with him she would risk her standing; she gave in so, she said, that she would not endanger the financial support that her church received from the conference. She did indeed marry and bore a son. Some of the gays and lesbians in her congregation indignantly left, insisting that she had betrayed them because she proclaimed herself a bisexual, and that's a copout.[44]

More recently, in 1996, an Episcopal church court dismissed heresy charges against a bishop who had ordained a gay man, ruling that "there is no discipline of the church prohibiting the ordination of a non-celibate homosexual," but declining to render "an opinion on whether a bishop and diocese should or should not ordain persons living in same-gender sexual relationships."[45]

Besides the problems specific to individual clergy, like the preference for married people and the reluctance to hire homosexuals, clergywomen and clergymen share a host of problems common in an era when people seeking to renew their spiritual lives no longer turn automatically to church and synagogue but thumb through New Age experiments or explore Zen and Islam.

Among the most omnipresent and oppressive of these problems is the vulnerability that results from too many bosses—most immediately a whole congregation of them, and/or a whole hierarchy of them. As William Grimes observes, "Academic politics are vicious, it is said, because nothing is at stake. In clerical politics, however, everything is at stake, in this world and the next."[46] Clergy who want to hold on to their jobs, even more clergy who aspire to better jobs, sail between the Charybdis of congregational disapproval and the Scylla of hierarchical disapproval, with their own draconic consciences hovering above, always ready to swoop.

One clergywoman who had endured such a Gethsemane told us about the agony of her final church service the Sunday after her American Baptist congregation had fired her out of hand for participating in a campus debate on homosexuality and Christianity: "We love you, but we can't have a gay advocate for a pastor." They did not doubt that she was straight; they just could not tolerate her expressing her beliefs. Eight months afterward, now pastoring part-time a tiny Metropolitan Church congregation, she grieved as she relived the experience in its narration.

Another woman ran into trouble as an associate pastor with her notorious senior minister. In the job that she had entered with high hopes and in which she loved the congregation, she found him cutting off her opportunities for service one after another and misrepresenting her performance. How was she to fight back without looking like a hysterical, ultrasensitive, paranoid woman? In the end she decided to resign rather than further to divide the congregation, a majority of whom supported her—a frequent concern for conscientious clergy in such a position. "One of my biggest fears for women now," she says, "is that women who are competent become threatening, and we don't have enough men who are secure enough in their roles. I think the better I did the worse it got." At the seminary where she is now employed (three hundred miles away from her husband and four-year-old son), an older woman student who knew nothing of her experience except that she had worked as an associate minister asked her, "How do you keep from throwing gutter-balls in ministry? When I was in high school and would go bowling with guys, and I bowled better than they did, I would throw gutter-balls so that they would like me. Now as a youth director, I realize that I'm threatening the pastor, and I'm wanting to throw gutter-balls again."

Whatever the extra vulnerability of clergywomen in facing these problems, the fact remains that clergymen too encounter them; they go with the territory. In at least one particular, clergywomen may be better off than clergymen: while some churches still expect to get free the services of the clergyman's wife, apparently few if any expect much from the spouses, or indeed the families, of clergywomen. Clergywomen have cheerfully told us that their spouses attend their churches only rarely, and that their children abhor the thought of listening to them preach, though we've also heard about husbands who bake for church suppers and fairs, and children who are their mothers' staunchest supporters. In any case, the conduct of spouse and family does not seem to concern overly either the clergywomen or the congregations they serve.

Clergywomen share a different set of problems with other women professionals, many of them so familiar as to need no expounding: for instance, double-duty with job and family, the lack of decent affordable childcare facilities, and the anger against professional women of some laywomen who have elected (and can afford) to be full-time homemakers. In some ways clergywomen are better off, in some ways worse off than other working women. In scheduling, for example, they have more freedom than women with nine-to-five jobs, but they also are bombarded with more emergency demands. Sometimes, of course, their problems take different forms. An American Baptist pastor chuckled as she talked about her relationship with her three-year-old and nine-month-old: "It's an interesting dynamic, because I'm the pastor but I'm the mommy. On Sunday they see the other kids sitting with their moms. So we've had to try to build in time during worship when I can actually hold them for a moment or two."

Yes, clergywomen too, especially the younger ones, must deal with sexual harassment, as surveys demonstrate.[47] Though to a woman our interviewees practice caution in counseling situations, most of their anecdotes concern the advances of other clergy—and they resent them more. For instance, one rabbi wrote off to the generation gap an incident in which an old man after kissing the Torah she held remarked: "I'd rather touch her breasts than the Torah." But she was upset when her colleagues laughed about it the next morning.[48] Some comments from clergymen are clearly wrought, consciously or subconsciously, to deny the woman her professional status and reduce her to a sex object, like the remark directed to a woman who had just preached at an interfaith service: "Sweetheart, you were beautiful. If you give the invitation, I would come forward every Sunday!"[49] "Ironically," said an Episcopalian priest, "all of the men I've had trouble with are clergy or bishops. What was once the boys' club is now mixed company, and 'What do we do with the girls?' There were a couple of people for whom that was a really big issue, and they had to be spoken to. Yes, the bishop did act. I've never had any problem with any parishioner." And she knocked wood.

By far the most brutal, vulgar, and overt sexual harassment of clergywomen that we have heard or read about has been inflicted on military chaplains. No doubt this happens partly because they belong to a small minority of women in a man's world, partly because of a failure of will among the leadership to prevent it. As commissioned officers women chaplains usually have little trouble with enlisted personnel, but their peers and superiors are another matter. "When I reported aboard [my ship]," a naval officer told us, "the officers in the wardroom said, 'Oh, a woman chaplain! Well, Chaplain, women who come into the military are either sluts or bitches. What are you?'" Unfortunately, she said, some of the harassment comes from male chaplains, especially from denominations that disapprove of ordaining women. "After a couple of tours, and you've been called a slut or a bitch, somebody spat in your face, if you've had a senior male chaplain make comments about the size of your breasts and call you 'Ironpants' and give you lower grades because you're not putting out, most women say, 'Why am I doing this?'"

For clergywomen, as for other women executives, lack of mobility and conflict with partners' careers present major obstacles. Some clergywomen married to clergymen try for hard-to-come-by co-pastorates, which often necessitate their sharing one salary and each finding part-time work elsewhere. Others avoid co-pastorates at least until their marriages are well-established, feeling that they may strain marital relationships. Like other professionals, these couples sometimes must resort to the hardships of commuting marriages; who takes major responsibility for children may depend on who lives nearest the better childcare facilities.

Inevitably, solutions are catch-as-catch-can. No amount of planning can anticipate the vagaries of life and work. "My husband and I have a fixed policy about taking turns choosing locations," a Presbyterian clergywoman in her late thirties told us, "and we keep violating it."

> We have never gone through really significant times when we've felt tremendous sacrifice. However, I don't think we've ever been quite on the same wave length in terms of both being totally fulfilled by what we were doing at the same time. The good part has been that we have had ministries in areas that we probably would not have considered if we had not been location bound by a spouse's appointment. But my husband's resume especially looks odd, spotty, with a list of churches like yo-yos; it certainly doesn't show a normal progression. He has followed me more than I have followed him. I feel that he has been more generous, but part of it too is that he's a white male, a very capable white male, and both of us have always known that in some ways he has more possibilities than I do.

Besides the many problems that they share with clergymen, with other professional women, and with the working population generally, clergywomen confront difficulties specific to them.

First, their "sacred calling" and their upbringing as women may combine to heighten their vulnerability, their inability to defend themselves when congregations or colleagues or senior ministers or the hierarchy begin to play hardball. Second, because of the separation of church and state, clergywomen (except military chaplains) presumably enjoy none of the governmental protections afforded women in other jobs—though this presumption still may be tested if and when clergywomen choose to resort to the courts.[50] Church hierarchies and individual clergywomen alike shudder away from discussion of this fact, because for other reasons both treasure the separation principle. Moreover, even more than other working women some clergy dislike the whole idea of relying on governmental protection against their employers—their churches. "I don't like to use affirmative action terminology because it's legalistic," one clergywoman told us. "Lutherans don't function well on that legalism. We do better by responding to the grace of God and God's love in the world."

But the absence of governmental protection for clergywomen strikes women's historians forcibly. No academic institution, no corporation, would dare to say openly to prospective, present, or past employees the words that congregations fling at clergywomen without a thought. "One male member of a [pastoral search committee] told me that 'if I were a man, I'd really be something!'" reported a respondent to the 1993 Presbyterian survey. When a boorish member of a search committee leads off an interview by asking, "What are you going to do about your sex life?" the clergywoman has no recourse. Women rabbis at their interviews hear questions like, "What kind of clothing do you intend to wear on the bimah? What is your husband's income? Will you ask members of the congregation to set you up on dates?"[51]

The power of the state has in fact since the 1960s forced secular employers to change their behavior, and changes of attitude have followed, particularly as the courts interpreted the provision of a nonhostile work environment as the employers' responsibility. Not, however, in a good many churches and synagogues.

Some have changed both behavior and attitude toward women as a matter of conscience, faith, and justice. The Episcopal General Convention of 1994 tried to make amends for past transgressions against women, adding commemorations for several women, including Sojourner Truth, to their calendar; authorizing a Standing Liturgical Commission to continue developing supplemental inclusive language texts; using a litany celebrating many women, including those "irregularly" ordained to priesthood in 1974 and 1975; and praying: "For the subordination of women and the church's complicity in that subordination, God of infinite mercy, forgive us."[52]

But congregations and denominations that interpret conscience, faith, and justice differently remain intransigent, and the state is not stopping them, perhaps constitutionally cannot stop them. Presently it's an untouchable subject. But does a *Brown v. Board of Education* or a *Roe v. Wade* lurk in religion's future? What if a clergywoman brought a sexual harassment case against her bishop or a member of her board of trustees? Would the principle of the separation of church and state cause the court to deny her the legal right to a nonhostile work environment?

In 1993 Professor Dierdre Good, an unordained faculty member at the Episcopalian General Theological Seminary (GTS), filed a complaint with the New York City Commission on Human Rights. The institution required faculty to live in seminary housing but stipulated that any faculty member living with another person as a couple must be married; when Good informed officials that her woman partner would be moving in with her, she was told that she would have to vacate her apartment. Eventually GTS settled the matter by adopting a new policy barring students and faculty members from living together unless they are married *or in a committed same-sex relationship.*[53]

The *Christian Century* (Sept. 13–20, 1995) reported the Rev. Raye Nell Dyer's suit against the Baptist General Convention of Texas and the Galveston Baptist Association after she was fired in August 1994 from her position as Baptist Student Union director at a branch of the University of Texas. She alleged gender discrimination in violation of Texas law both in the firing and in the wage paid her. In May 1995 the Roman Catholic St. Meinrad School of Theology fired tenured professor Carmel McEnroy, allegedly because she signed a Women's Ordination Conference letter in the *National Catholic Reporter* asking that conversation continue on women's ordination; McEnroy then announced that she would sue the seminary.[54] The conflict between laws against gender discrimination and sexual harassment on the one hand and the separation of church and state on the other remains unresolved.

Anyway, the lack of state protection seriously handicaps clergywomen today. As one woman wrote on the 1993 Presbyterian surveys: "My own presbytery doesn't follow EEO guidelines and out of the last 12 pastors called 10 were men to fill the positions with [salaries of] $35,000 to $95,000. Two women were called to part-time positions of $15,000–$25,000. Tell me that doesn't indicate a problem!!"

Clergywomen have gained much during the twentieth century. But as compared to women in other professions Christian clergywomen still at the end of the twentieth century are failing to flourish. Though many of them are highly and expensively educated, as a group they are underpaid to the point of penury. They typically hit the glass ceiling on their second placement. They periodically suffer long periods of unemployment in their chosen profession. Unhappily, *except for the Salvation Army,* churches presently most open to clergywomen—the old, mainline churches —are losing members and financial support. Holiness and pentecostal churches that at the beginning of the twentieth century welcomed women into their pulpits no longer have significant numbers of clergywomen. Fundamentalist Protestant churches, Orthodox churches, and Roman Catholic churches, which ban clergywomen, are gaining membership. As one clergywoman told us bluntly, "No profession is perfect, but people somehow often have the idea that the church comes as close as you can get, and that's hogwash."

The very recent beginnings of women rabbis complicate generalizing about them. Like most rabbis, they are better paid than their Christian peers, but so far they show the same tendency to hold jobs in smaller and poorer congregations or as associates and assistants or in nonpastoral positions.

We have found no evidence at all that the presence of clergywomen in any way causes or contributes to the decline of the mainline churches. To the contrary, clergywomen have revived a good many of their congregations that would otherwise have died. Anne Cox, writing in *The Witness* (July 1994), noted other benefits that women priests have conferred on the Episcopal church: they have improved its health, particularly in its ability to deal "with the old secrets of sexual abuse and harassment"; they have ministered to other women in ways that men could not, particularly in incest and spousal abuse cases; and few people tend to mistake the woman priest for God. Women rabbis have fulfilled the prophecy of Martha Neumark's father: "The rabbinate may help the woman, and the woman rabbi may help the rabbinate."[55]

Notes

1. On the status of women in the Orthodox church, see Elisabeth Behr-Sigal, *The Ministry of Women in the Church* (Redondo Beach, Calif.: Oakwood, 1991).

2. Both in 1983 and in 1995 studies were conducted at the Hartford Seminary, the first by Jackson Carroll, Barbara Hargrove, and Adair T. Lummis, the second by Barbara Brown Zikmund, Adair T. Lummis, and Patricia Mei Yin Chang. Both found that Christian women clergy tend to come from higher status families than Christian male clergy.

3. By 1992 Methodists had elected eight women bishops and more than eighty district superintendents. By 1995 Lutherans had elected two women bishops; Episcopalians four (Susan Hill Lindley, *"You Have Stept Out of Your Place": A History of Women and Religion in America* [Louisville, Ky.: Westminster John Knox, 1996], p. 423).

4. Ibid., p. 422. Women are represented among the clergy in just about the same proportions as in the American military.

5. Article by Sally M. Bucklee in *The Witness* (July 1994). See also Mary S. Donovan, *Women Priests in the Episcopal Church: The Experience of the First Decade* (Cincinnati, Oh.: Forward Movement, 1988), p. 18.

6. "Presbyterian Clergywomen Survey," Research Services, Congregational Ministries Division, Presbyterian Church (U.S.A.). Deborah A. Bruce, "Presbyterian Clergywomen: A Profile," *Monday Morning* (Dec. 20, 1993), summarizes the Presbyterian Clergywomen Survey.

7. Laura Geller, "From Equality to Transformation: The Challenge of Women's Rabbinic Leadership," in *Gender and Judaism: The Transformation of Tradition,* ed. T. M. Rudavsky (New York: New York Univ. Press, 1995), p. 246.

8. Quoted by Geller in *Gender and Judaism,* ed. Rudavsky, p. 247.

9. *Military Chaplains' Review* (Winter 1981). But see also Judith Ann Craig Piper in *Our Struggle to Serve: The Stories of 15 Evangelical Women,* ed. Virginia Hearn (Waco, Tex.: Word, 1979).

10. A 1987 survey on clergy employment and unemployment conducted in the United Church of Christ by the Board for Homeland Ministries shows 38 percent of clergywomen as against 24 percent of clergymen answering affirmatively the question "Since ordination, have you ever been unemployed?" The clergywomen responding identified discrimination against women as the first reason for their unemployment, whereas clergymen listed conflict with church.

11. The 1993 Presbyterian survey of clergywomen reports about a third in part-time work.

12. *The Female Preacher: or, Memoir of Salome Lincoln* (1843; reprint, New York: Arno, 1972), pp. 49–50.

13. Lynn K. Rhodes, *Co-Creating: A Feminist Vision of Ministry* (Philadelphia: Westminster, 1987), p. 117.

14. Worship service, 1991 Association of Presbyterian Tentmakers Conference.

15. Churches in the National Spiritualist Association, some of which define themselves as Christian, do not pay their pastors.

16. Rosemarie Green, "Gender Parity in the Black Church: Daughters of Thunder Struggling for Two Centuries," *Daughters of Sarah* 21 (Summer 1995): 35–38. See also C. Eric Lincoln and Lawrence H. Mamiya, *The Black Church in the African American Experience* (Durham, N.C.: Duke Univ. Press, 1990), pp. 298, 307.

17. *Christian Century* 110 (March 3, 1993): 235.

18. *The Episcopal New Yorker* 159 (Jan/Feb/Mar., 1994): 13.

19. Despite vigorous efforts to locate "dropouts," the 1995 Hartford Seminary study of clergy, funded by a grant from the Lilly Foundation, found difficulty both in defining the term and in putting together a significant sample. The study notes that "14% of the women ended up in secular work immediately after graduating from seminary as compared to 10% of the men," and that close to a third of active clergy surveyed, women (31 percent) and men (28 percent) alike, sometimes "thought seriously about leaving church-related ministry for some other kind of work." The first and second preliminary reports of this study reach no conclusion on the relative rates of dropout for women and men.

20. Annie Ruth Power, "Hold On To Your Dream: African-American Protestant Worship," in *Women at Worship: Interpretations of North American Diversity,* ed. Marjorie Procter-Smith and Janet R. Walton (Louisville: Westminster/John Knox, 1993), p. 48.

21. Helen D. Lyman papers, A-33, Box 2, Folder 3, p. 60, Schlesinger Library, Cambridge, Massachusetts.

22. Lois A. Boyd and R. Douglas Brackenridge, *Presbyterian Women in America: Two Centuries of a Quest for Status* (Westport, Conn.: Greenwood, 1983), p. 113.

23. See Edward C. Lehman, Jr., and the Task Force on Women in Ministry of the Ministers Council, American Baptist Churches, 1979, "Project Swim: An Overview: A Study of Women in the Ministry," in *Women and Men,* ed. Hestenes, p. 181; and Sam Justice, "Women Ministers: How Are They Being Accepted," *Ministries* (Fall, 1984), reprinted in *Women and Men,* p. 210H.

24. Donna Schaper, *Common Sense About Men & Women in the Ministry* (Washington, D.C.: Alban Institute, 1990), p. 13.

25. Carol Marie Noren, *The Women in the Pulpit* (Nashville, Tenn.: Abingdon, 1991).

26. See, for instance, Martha B. Kriebel, *A Stole is a Towel: Lessons Learned in the Paris Ministry* (New York: Pilgrim Press, 1988), p. 14: "When a clergywoman dressed in a clerical shirt and suit walked into a meeting of ordained ministers, one man wearing a similar clerical shirt forcefully pushed her out of the room, shouting, 'You have no right to be here!'" Episcopalian clergywomen serving communion have had their arms scratched. One African-American minister had to fight valiantly against the efforts of three brother clergy to shove her off the bench they were "sharing."

27. Martha Long Ice, *Clergywomen and Their World Views: Calling for a New Age* (New York: Praeger, 1987), p. 141.

28. Elizabeth Canham, *Pilgrimage to Priesthood* (London: SPCK, 1983), p. 95.

29. The Central Conference of American Rabbis (CCAR) has been gathering salary data on Reform rabbis for more than twenty-five years. Although these data are not made public, Mark Winer, who has supervised the CCAR's recent surveys, dealt with the subject in "Are

All Rabbis Equal?" *Reform Judaism* 18 (Summer 1990): 12. Our generalizations herein on the differences between the salaries of women and men rabbis and the disparity between the salaries of Protestant and Jewish clergy are based on a 1996 conversation with Rabbi Winer. The compensation of Roman Catholic priests is extremely difficult to figure because of the many perquisites and fees that come with the job. One of our interviewees noted that the priest need "never cut a lawn, never buy a lawnmower, never pay a tax, never pay home-owner's insurance . . . Catholics are used to the fact that Father of course has to have a house-keeper, has to have a cook."

30. Quoted by Geller in *Gender and Judaism,* ed. Rudavsky, p. 248. See also *Woman's Pulpit* (Jul.-Aug.-Sep. 1993); and *United Church News* (May 1995): 13.

31. John H. Morgan, *Women Priests: An Emerging Ministry in the Episcopal Church (1975–1985)* (Bristol, Ind.: Wyndham Hall Press, 1985), pp. 49–50.

32. See, for example, Rose Mary Denman, *Let My People In: A Lesbian Minister Tells of Her Struggles to Live Openly and Maintain Her Ministry* (New York: William Morrow, 1990), p. 248.

33. For CLOUT's manifesto, see *In Our Own Voices: Four Centuries of American Women's Religious Writing,* ed. Rosemary Skinner Keller and Rosemary Radford Ruether (New York: HarperCollins, 1995), pp. 289f. For denominational organizations of gays and lesbians, see Lillian Faderman, *Odd Girls and Twilight Lovers: A History of Lesbian Life in Twentieth-Century America* (New York: Columbia Univ. Press, 1991), p. 226.

34. Denman, *Let My People,* p. 156.

35. Quoted by Denman, *Let My People,* p. 161.

36. Stacy Offner, "Homophobia and Heterosexism" (papers of the Women's Rabbinic Network Conference [March 1993], p. 50).

37. Nelle Morton, *The Journey Is Home* (Boston: Beacon, 1985), p. xxv.

38. *Christian Century* 112 (Jul. 19–26, 1995; Aug. 30–Sept. 6, 1995).

39. *The Witness* (Jan/Feb 1995): 78.

40. *WAVES,* Natl Newsletter of the United Church Coalition for Lesbian/Gay Concerns 21 (June 1994).

41. *The Witness* 78 (Dec. 1995): 36.

42. *Christian Century* 111 (July 13–20, 1994). The Metropolitan Community Church was founded by Troy Perry, a homosexual fundamentalist minister. For the story of Army Reserve Captain Carolyn "Dusty" Pruitt, pastor of the Metropolitan Community Church in Long Beach, California, in the early 1980s, see Randy Shilts, *Conduct Unbecoming: Lesbians and Gays in the U.S. Military, Vietnam to the Persian Gulf* (New York: St. Martin's, 1993), pp. 435–36.

43. Denman, *Let My People,* p. 213.

44. *Women's Pulpit* (July-Sept. 1993).

45. *Christian Century* (May 22–29, 1996).

46. William Grimes, "Crisis at an English Country Church," television guide, *New York Times* (Oct. 22, 1995).

47. A 1983 survey of United Church of Canada clergywomen showed that 35 percent of the 238 women reported being victims of sexual harassment as theological students or as women in professional ministry (remarks and jokes, pornographic pictures, gestures, sexual advances, physical assaults). A 1986 survey of 138 ordained women in the United Church of Christ showed 43 percent (Kriebel, *Stole,* pp. 38–39). Jennifer Cowan reports a survey by the Religious Issues Task Force of the American Jewish Congress Commission for Women's Equality, which used as a standard the EEOC guidelines defining sexual harassment ("Survey Finds 70% of Women Rabbis Sexually Harassed," *Moment* 18 [Oct. 1993]: 34).

48. Cowan, "Survey," p. 34.

49. O. John Eldred, *Women Pastors: If God Calls, Why Not the Church?* (Valley Forge, Penn.: Judson, 1981), p. 88.

50. An interviewee told us that in the negotiated settlement when she left a church under unhappy circumstances the church required a promise from her not to sue—an indication that churches may be beginning to worry about gender discrimination suits.

51. Cowan, "Survey," p. 34.

52. Elizabeth G. Maxwell, *The Episcopal New Yorker* (Aug./Sept./Oct. 1994).

53. *New York Times* (July 25, 1993); *Chronicle of Higher Education* (Aug. 4, 1993; Jan. 26, 1994).

54. *Re-Imagining* (Nov. 1995): 22; and letter from Women's Ordination Conference dated July 1995.

55. In *Women and Religion in America,* ed. Rosemary R. Ruether and Rosemary S. Keller (San Francisco: Harper & Row, 1986), 3:164.

10

Approaching the Millennium

❧

What They Want

CLERGYWOMEN ARE NOT A MONOLITHIC GROUP. Overall they're probably more likely to want change than clergymen: after all, they are still a pioneering minority. But different clergywomen want different things for their institutions and for themselves. Denomination does not necessarily limit or determine their visions of their churches and synagogues or of their own roles: though Unitarian and Reform Jewish clergywomen as groups are more liberal than Southern Baptists and Conservative Jews, women from each denomination differ among themselves, and Roman Catholic women frequently outdo them all in their revolutionary visions of the future. Nor does degree of education necessarily predict their views, though in general the more highly educated the clergywoman, the more change she wants and thinks possible. But all (except those who have given up on religious institutions as hopeless) agree on one point: they want acceptance by their denominations, by their hierarchies, by their clerical colleagues, and by their congregations.

In their desires for their institutions and themselves clergywomen range along a spectrum. At one extreme they want simply to act and be recognized and affirmed as clergy in religious institutions as those now exist. They want to lead and pastor their congregations, support their communicants on their spiritual journeys, and with the laity help needy and suffering people. "Just let me get on with that ministry—doing what God has called me to do." It's easy to understand their feelings. Who needs more hassle? Some of these are older women, often married to well-off husbands, women who can't believe their own good fortune in being admitted to the clergy and rejoice over whatever appointments they receive. At this end of the spectrum clergywomen see themselves primarily, if not exclusively, as pastors.

In pentecostal and holiness churches that do not ordain or where during the twentieth century women's ordinations have dwindled, even in those newer ones founded by women, clergywomen tend toward this end of the spectrum. In her 1987 interviews with fifty-three of them Susan Kwilecki found "a deliberately passive, charismatic approach to the ministry." These twenty-seven black and twenty-six white women served in such churches as the Assembly of God, the Church of God of Prophecy, and the Church of God (Cleveland, Tenn.) They are characterized, Kwilecki says, by "principled passiveness," claiming that they didn't choose the ministry, but rather God chose them, thus mitigating women's natural incapacity for leadership. Most of them insisted that the Bible says that the husband heads the house, that the woman who steps out ahead of a man steps out of the will of God, and that woman's first duty is to her home and family. Even so they differ in their methods and styles. Kwilecki contrasts two women, one white and one black. The first, a sixty-two-year-old who co-evangelized and co-pastored with her husband until his death, now as solo pastor flatters and pushes responsibility onto males. The second, a sixty-seven-year-old, fought back when the pentecostal church she had founded wanted to put a man over her, persisting even when all but five of her parishioners departed. But all of these clergywomen focus primarily on doing their jobs.[1]

At the other extreme impassioned Jewish and Protestant clergywomen long to transform their churches and synagogues. These women, writes Sara Maitland, rather than "demanding simply a right to their fair share of the cake, . . . are saying that the churches got the recipe wrong in the first place, the cake is not worth the eating, and that a new deal is necessary—not merely to give women what they want, but to serve God as God wants." As women, such clergy believe, they can bring to their institutions a new theology, new visions of divinity and humanity to meld with the old, making them truly inclusive and open to all, enriching the religious life of their institutions and their people. These clergywomen see themselves as prophets, as Maitland says, with the duty "to recall the community to its own roots in its central truth."[2] They envision their institutions as the hope of the world, with the power to transform society in the name of social justice.

So also with Roman Catholic clergywomen. Some of them wish that they could be ordained simply so that they could do their parish work more efficiently. Others who earlier longed for ordination now are not so sure. "When we asked the question, 'Would you be ordained, if you could be?'" said Allison Stokes, referring to the survey she, M. T. Winter, and Adair Lummis reported in their 1994 book *Defecting in Place,* "it was amazing to me how many came back and said again and again, 'Not in the church as it presently is.' They're not interested in hierarchy and women becoming priests and working to become bishops and then angling to be the pope. They really feel that the church has to be totally reformed and then maybe they would be interested in serving in an ordained capacity."

Carter Heyward, one of the eleven Episcopal priests "irregularly" ordained in 1974, talked with us about what happened when in 1975 she and Sue Hiatt joined the faculty of the Episcopal Theological Seminary:

> Right in the beginning some of the men on the faculty basically said, 'Well, we accepted your ordination, we're glad you're here, but now let's just get on with the business of the church and forget about this woman's thing.' My colleague Sue Hiatt

and I said 'No, no, that's not really what this is about.' That's been our perspective from the beginning, that it's not simply about joining a boys' club and becoming one of the guys. In my experience the most creative, liberating, and liberated men agree with that; they don't want to be part of the club either. So the question is can we continue to help the church open up and become more and more what we can be when we are open to the spirit moving in new directions and trying to take stock of who is still left out.

Clergywomen like these raise hard questions for church and synagogue; they are not the easiest of colleagues.

Most clergywomen, of course, position themselves toward the middle of the spectrum rather than at either end, doing their best to combine pastoring and prophecy. As Carter Heyward puts it, "I don't think you can be either/or a pastor or a prophet; I think you have to somehow mix them." That's no easy task. There's always a parishioner who wants to gag her/his pastor on anything "political," like abortion or homosexuality, or who reels in horror at a change in the liturgy. There's always a bishop who disapproves of letting Starhawk speak within the sanctuary. In Heyward's words, "churches institutionally really discourage prophetic voices. Therefore the churches teach on the whole in their seminaries pastoral care and conciliation and compromise as important Christian virtues. Up to a point they are, of course, but only to a point." So most clergywomen like most clergymen walk carefully within the politically possible, introducing a new concept here, a new phrase there, ready to retreat when protest rises too high, sensitive to the possibility of giving offense.

Hard as it is for clergywomen to find good jobs, and difficult as it is for women to challenge old ideas without being labeled aggressive and destructive feminists, the political pressures on them weigh even more heavily than on clergymen. And the newer and younger clergywomen at the end of the twentieth century, most of whom found it comparatively easy to get ordained, are greatly tempted to accept the status quo, in Maitland's words, to "take the definition of 'proper ministry' not from their own spiritual experience nor from the theological fact of their ordination, but from precisely that male model in opposition to which women fought for ecclesiological authorization. The clerical model is a very old and very powerful one. By inviting some of the most able and enthusiastic women into its power structures institutional Christianity may be able to evade the more profound issues of in-built sexism and dualism."[3]

To avoid raising hackles, to be permitted to continue their work, some women even unblinkingly accept a second-class priesthood. Heyward observes, "The younger generations have any number of women who do, I think, make peace with their own oppression too readily. Yes, some have become just members of the boys' club. When I relate to them individually I am very committed not to being harsh about this, because I think in most cases these are women who are doing the best they can, trying to make a living, trying to maintain some integrity, but they are still willing to settle for less than what would be to me the optimal."

Because of their different situations, clergywomen ordained a generation or two ago may lean more toward the prophetic aspects of ministry, and those ordained recently more toward the pastoral.[4] Women from both groups recognize these differences and the reasons for them. A Conservative rabbi told us, "I have lived in the Jewish feminist world for twenty years or so. A significant number of the women students are not looking to shake things up and to change things. Their agenda is just to be the best rabbi that they can be and get the most out of their studies that they can get. This fire in the belly for change that many of us had when we came in and many of the current students still have is not shared by all—absolutely."

An Episcopalian priest newer in the clergy acknowledges, "Part of the reason I'm here [as rector of a good-sized, prosperous church] is that [women ordained early] got so bloodied that they became bitter. I'm walking on their murdered bodies, as it were. On the other hand, I think there's probably a self-selection of the women who chose to be those early pioneers in this denomination. They were women who were more ready to seek martyrdom, to be rejected, and to fight the good fight." And a still younger woman remarked, "I was born the year that women started to be ordained in the Presbyterian church. I think that for women to stake out new territory, they have to be very courageous and very vocal and outspoken, so there's a radical leading edge. For those of us who follow, we can afford to be not as outspoken. We can look at other issues, because that one's already been taken care of for us to some extent."

Despite such differences among them, despite the conservatism of a few, most clergywomen work in some degree to change their institutions. Some are willing to pay a higher price for change than others: for some the pain and shock of a parishioner at liturgical or linguistic change is too expensive, even at the cost of continued pain for another parishioner who has felt excluded by the traditional liturgy and language.[5] But when push comes to shove—as it often does—most of them labor, albeit inch by inch, for more inclusiveness, more breadth of vision.

One middle-of-the-road Presbyterian clergywoman told us, "At my interview the committee asked, 'Are you going to call God *Mother* from the pulpit?' When I said no, one person on the committee said, 'Thank God,' and another 'I'm sad.' During my internship I had found that it just pushed way too many buttons for people, and I could find other ways of presenting God that were less emotionally laden and still would get at feminine imagery. [My congregants are] exposed to it all the time, but they would never label it as feminist theology. It's just who I am."

❧ Will They Get What They Want?

If the first woman God ever made was strong enough to turn the world upside down, all alone—these together ought to be able to turn it back and get it rightside up again; and they are asking to do it.

—Sojourner Truth

Despite all their difficulties, most clergywomen, whatever their denomination, not only find enormous satisfactions in their own work but predict better days ahead. Those whose denominations already ordain them foresee more clergywomen, more upward mobility, and freer acceptance and recognition. Sometimes it's a matter of faith, as with the Roman Catholic sister who told us, "Under the present leadership nothing will change. We'll keep regrinding the same wheels and we'll accept inferior candidates for the priesthood. And yet there are millions of people deprived of the Eucharist every day. . . . But the present pope is not going to be around for too long. It all depends on who replaces him." When we asked how she reads the politics of choosing the next pope, she answered, "Well, you know, the Holy Spirit has a funny way of not following the politics. The next pope could mean ordination for women."

Others point to the gains clergywomen have already made as predictors of the future. A clergywoman scarred from hitting the glass ceiling hard nonetheless insisted:

> There are more and more of us, and we can't be stopped. In Montana maybe 12 or 13 percent of our clergy [in the Evangelical Lutheran Church in America] are women—a lot of our best and brightest are women. I think that some of the congregational resistance will break down. I think some of the collegial resistance will break down. I think some of the synodical resistance will break down as women are just more and more involved in all aspects of ministry. That's got to happen. Our neighboring synod, South Dakota, now will have a woman as bishop. Our superstar women used to run for bishop and not be elected. Now a woman elected bishop has to be very, very good, but not necessarily the very best and brightest. Somehow it seems to me that it's becoming less of an odd thing and it's more of a normal thing. I think that that's just happening at all levels of the church and all levels of congregational life.

We venture now out of history into prophecy—as Schlegel remarks, "A historian is a prophet in reverse." As for survival, clergywomen are almost certainly right in their assertion that "We're here to stay." They're probably right in their belief that their numbers will increase. As one Reform rabbi told us, "I think women are only going to make more and more inroads into the Jewish community." And quite possibly sooner or later Roman Catholics, Orthodox Jews, and even Christian fundamentalists will begin to ordain women.

In any case women of all these denominations will independently claim their right to preach and pastor, often with support of male colleagues, as when in 1992 Rose Marie Vernall, a former Roman Catholic nun, a widow, and the mother of two adopted children, was ordained a priest in the African-American Catholic Congregation. The ordaining bishop, who founded that denomination in 1989, was a former Roman Catholic priest.[6]

Despite the conservative backlash of the 1980s and 1990s, women continue to move into the workplace and into occupations formerly reserved for men. The demographics say that white males are soon to become a minority in the work force, and the population is getting used to seeing women in all kinds of new places doing all kinds of new work. In "Yentl" Barbra Streisand familiarized movie audiences with the possibility that women might aspire to be rabbis. The telltale television has ventured to fashion a series around a clergywoman and run ads centered on clergywomen (Proud father: "This is my daughter's first wedding. She has another one at 4:30.")—an indication of fascination with or increasing acceptance of women in this role.[7] Broadway has presented Diane Shaffer's play *Sacrilege*, about a nun who would be a priest. And every Sunday the *New York Times* in its wedding announcements reports clergywomen performing the ceremonies.

The very presence of ordained clergywomen in the Jewish and mainline Protestant denominations makes a difference elsewhere. For one thing, these denominations still attract a membership from the dominant upper and upper-middle classes with a disproportionate influence on mores and values.

Our own village during the past fifteen years has been discovering clergywomen. First we had one somehow holding things together in an impoverished Congregational church. Then the Baptists hired a charismatic woman who not only livened up the congregation but became the talk of the town by starting a soup kitchen and by taking as her housemate and exchanging pulpits with a woman rabbi from a synagogue in a neighboring town. At about the same time the United Church of Christ congregation employed a woman with long experience in state and national hierarchies as assistant minister. Now the Episcopalians boast of their new rector, a highly educated, high-achieving second-career woman named Hope. Jews, Christians of all denominations, and nonbelievers all know her or know about her. Asked when he closes on Sundays, our news vendor tells us, "Oh, about noon. It all depends on when Hope stops talking."

The presence of clergywomen like these speaks loudly to women in nonordaining denominations. Mormon women and sympathetic Mormon men hear—they can after all look to the example of the Reorganized Church of Jesus Christ of Latter-Day Saints.[8] Whether or not they choose to defect, Roman Catholic women who think about being ordained often interact with Episcopalians, perhaps taking Episcopalian clergywomen as mentors or spiritual directors, or acting in those capacities for the Episcopalians. "Even in the Orthodox Jewish community," one Reform rabbi told us, "there's been an enormous effect on women. Now they have women leading study groups and prayer groups and even some Orthodox women have what they call a Bah't Mitzvah, although they don't do what I might do for a young woman becoming Bah't Mitzvah in terms of access to prayers and stuff." The numbers of Orthodox Jewish women who have mastered the texts necessary for ordination are multiplying.[9] "Theologically I might be more comfortable in Orthodoxy," a Conservative woman rabbi told us, "but Orthodoxy won't allow me to read the Torah, not in public. It won't let me chant the Torah. Not to be able to do that . . . spiritually I would wither."

One wonders just how long Rome can continue to close down churches, operate "priestless" parishes, deny the presence and services of a priest to many communicants, and flout the opinions of a majority of their American membership on ordination for women—though Mark Russell jokes, "When we can get all the priests into a

Dodge minivan, then maybe the church will begin to think about ordaining women." The Vatican in 1994 acknowledged actual practice in American churches by approving altar girls.[10] And some hints suggest that the hierarchy may allow the ordination of women as deacons, though not as priests. In 1995 the Canon Law Society of America found such an ordination in keeping with Roman Catholic history and theology and endorsed it as "desirable" for the United States. Peter Steinfels in the *New York Times* of November 12, 1995, noted: "The Pope and the Vatican have carefully refrained from ruling out ordination of women to the diaconate, even in major pronouncements against ordaining women to the priesthood." Ordination as deacons would theoretically empower women to preach at liturgies, administer baptism, officiate at marriages, and conduct funeral services and burials and other rites. Common wisdom has it that Roman Catholics will ordain married male priests before they ordain women. But painful shared experiences have made many of those men ardent supporters of the women who seek ordination; their priesthood might increase the pressure for women's ordination.

The declining number of priests must constantly haunt the Vatican. Richard A. Schoenherr predicts: "The laity-to-priest ratio, a fairly accurate measure of supply and demand, will double between 1975 and 2005 from 1,100 to 2,200 Catholics per active priest. . . . The bottom line shows about 21,000 active diocesan priests in 2005, or 40 percent fewer than the 35,000 registered in 1966. This priestly cadre, diminished not only in size but in youthful vigor, will be burdened with overwork."[11]

Nor should we underestimate the strength of belief and the dedication of those who struggle to re-form the Roman Catholic church to ensure greater justice within its walls for all—women included. They want not only ordination for women but also a democratization of the whole church structure. Although many of them believe that the hierarchy would like nothing better than to see them depart, they persist in the belief that the church is defined not by the hierarchy but, in accordance with Vatican II, as the people of God. As David Riesman remarked of one case in which sisters had followed their consciences rather than the dictates of the hierarchy, "This disturbance is being described as a little squabble among nuns. It reminds me of the fact that the problems raised by Luther were dismissed at the time as a little squabble among monks."[12] And Thomas C. Fox in *Sexuality and Catholicism* wrote, "Approaching the outer edge of the beginning of the twenty-first century, an exclusively male Catholic priesthood is the most painful, most intractable, most divisive, and potentially most damaging issue facing the church."[13]

As the Vatican hardens its position against women's ordination, declaring the pope's ban on the subject infallible dogma, will its proponents leave the church? Will they continue their watchful waiting for a new pope? Or will some maverick bishop follow the Episcopalian precedent, ordain a woman, and confront the pope with an accomplished fact? Or, as Colm Toibin speculated in *The New Yorker* of October 9, 1995, is there one among the College of Cardinals, "cunning and secretive, who is planning a quiet revolution in the Catholic Church. It could happen overnight: suddenly, without warning, the Berlin Wall of clerical celibacy could be destroyed; the bans on contraception, on women priests, and on divorced people who have remarried receiving the Eucharist could be overturned."

As for fundamentalist churches, the ultimate resolution of the issue may be more in doubt. Disagreement about ordaining women, some say, may ultimately provoke schism in huge and heterogeneous denominations like the Southern Baptist and National Baptist Conventions.[14] Certainly it has been causing more and more disputes in recent years between extreme fundamentalists and moderates, not to mention considerable embarrassment. In 1995 over faculty protest the president and trustees of the Southern Baptist Seminary decreed that in the future they would hire only professors who believe that the Bible prohibits women from preaching. As Martin Marty writes: "It happened that literally a week after these trustee actions, the seminary held its annual preaching contest. A panel of two faculty members and six students (all men) read the 28 submitted manuscripts, which did not identify the name or gender of the authors, and picked the three best. Then they listened to audio tapes to determine first-, second- and third-place rankings. To their surprise, to the horror of the trustees and president, and to the delight of us observers, the voices were those of three women: Kimberly Baker, Mary Beth McCloy and Dixie Petrey. They now all stand accused of violating scripture for preaching the pure word of God better than did the other 25 contestants."[15]

At times fundamentalism and feminism have jostled along well enough together. In the nineteenth century Alma White declared her aim to combine in the Pillar of Fire Church "feminism and ultra-fundamentalism." In the late twentieth century evangelists Daisy Osborn and Marie Brown admix fundamentalism and feminism in their teachings. Some contemporary fundamentalists of both genders display the traditional fundamentalist willingness to support women in professional roles *if* they acknowledge these as secondary to their roles as wives and mothers, and *if* their menfolks approve. They honor women like Dorothy Ruth Miller (1873–1944), who taught at Nyack Bible College and the Prairie Bible Institute but turned down the offer of the chair of Bible at Wheaton because, she said, that was a man's place.[16]

Historically fundamentalists have tended to moderate their tone and accommodate their practices as they involved themselves more in society. Only when they have sharply separated themselves, or when they have dominated society regionally (like the Mormons in Utah) have they held firm against the values and ethic of mainline society. Of course should they seize control of society or attain sufficient power to control major political figures, they will impose their own morality, with its subservient status for women. But their inevitable association with mainline thinking and practice as they struggle for political control exposes them to the possibility of compromise, even in the form of women's ordination.[17] What are we to make of the ambivalences reflected by an Evangelical Free Church of America pastor when one of his women parishioners went to him and said, "God has called me to be a Navy chaplain." He responded, "Perhaps so, but you can't stay here because God doesn't call *our* women to that kind of work."

Despite backlash, despite the high audibility of the religious right, of late here and there in fundamentalist churches women have successfully asserted themselves. Life experience often persuades women that it's necessary to insist on women's rights, and the combination of vocal feminism in society and their own experience of religious institutions occasionally persuades fundamentalist women that it's necessary to insist on including women. As a missionary evangelist commissioned by the Osborn Foundation told us, seeing the movie "Yentl," attending to the words of her mentor, and observing the realities of African women's lives changed her attitudes:

> I had always thought, 'Why should Dr. Daisy [Osborn] preach to women? We know we've heard the Bible, and it was always masculinized, but I appropriated it for myself.' I would listen to her and kind of laugh. But then at a women's conference in New Guinea I was just bowled over. These women within their own cultural context had been put down. Dr. Daisy told me the truth! They really can't appropriate the Bible for themselves. Now I figure if it helps women I'll go with it. I believe that what God wants to do He can't do until women fully do what they're called to do.

Mormon women, writes Maxine Hanks, whose "church conveys priesthood power to women yet insists that women do not have it and cannot use it," are reclaiming that power in women's blessing circles, retreats, and feminist organizations.[18] But the end of the twentieth century affords bleak and wintry prospects for clergywomen in fundamentalist denominations.

Among holiness churches, the Assemblies of God stand out with 4,600 women, 20 percent of their 26,000 licensed clergy.[19] Among those that in their heyday encouraged women's ministries but where during the twentieth century the numbers of clergywomen have dwindled, some show signs of reversing this trend. The same societal forces are at work among them as within the mainline churches. The tiny Evangelical Women's Caucus, which began to function independently in 1975, regularly makes feminist voices heard.[20] In 1994 in an effort to reverse the trend away from clergywomen, women organized the first International Wesleyan-Holiness Women Clergy Conference, its theme "Come to the Water: A Celebration of Our Call," with plans for more such conferences to follow. They also launched several newsletters for women clergy.

In 1973 the Women of the Church of God under the leadership of ordained minister Nellie J. Snowden called the church to accountability about the role of its women; in 1974 its General Assembly resolved to consider more women for positions of leadership.[21] One ordained African-American clergywoman in the Church of God told us, "I think I see a future that may not have been possible in years past. Years ago women became pastors if they 'preached out' [founded] a church. But [in] churches that were already in existence, in many instances, people were reluctant to call women as pastors. In the 1970s or 1980s, only about 3 percent of the larger churches in the Church of God were pastored by women. I think that the future is going to necessitate that that number increase, because women are becoming prepared, and many of the younger women have a more demanding type personality. Yes, there's a shortage of male ministers. I might see some resistance [to women pastors], but I don't think there's going to be an alternative."

Even members of the hierarchy within pentecostal churches do not always think alike on women's ordination. "The Church of God in Christ as a national church does not ordain women," an African-American clergywoman told us. "Individual bishops do. Bishop O. T. Jones has advocated for women and was only allowed by the national church to do special ordinations for seminary graduate women who were being placed in institutional chaplaincies. After he'd done nineteen or twenty-some—very significant number for one bishop—of them, the national church told him to stop and asked him not to do any more women's ordinations until they have a national ruling. So that's a struggle within one of the pentecostal churches."

Then too, women members sometimes fail to conform—like Lois Roden, ordained minister, president, and bishop of the Living Waters Branch Church founded by her husband in 1955. That church splintered from the Branch Davidian church, itself splintered from the Seventh Day Adventists. Roden believes that the Holy Spirit is feminine. She tells the story of a woman who asked, "My Father in heaven, where is my mother?" And God answered, "My daughter, I thought you would never ask."[22] Some pentecostal women are calling into question the concept of the husband's headship of the household. As one woman in her sixties pithily remarked to us, "We're beginning to see that we both share in this relationship. There are some things that I take lead in as a woman, and there are some things that he will take lead in. I think you take lead based on your understanding. If you don't know what to tell me to do, how can you tell me to do it?"

In the mainline denominations tentmaking or its moral equivalent, now on the increase, will doubtless continue to multiply in the foreseeable future. Though some hierarchies and indeed some tentmakers fear that the practice of employing part-time clergy may erode the educational standards for ordination and even the use of ordained clergy, the harsh economic facts of mainline denominational life necessitate it. The need for part-time clergy, at least in the short term, may be met in large part by empty-nest women and second-career women and men. Often they can afford to do the work they love. As one part-time rabbi told us, "My circumstances are such that I don't require the money, so I generally give it to charitable purposes." Seminaries in the 1990s are enrolling many people well above traditional student age who seek religious training. Such students populate the classrooms of the Hartford Theological Seminary, which no longer offers the Master of Divinity. Their existence, along with the proliferation of part-time ministries, provides yet another sign of a possible major shift in American religious life, with greater emphasis on individual spirituality, lay responsibility for the operation of the religious institution, and a changed role for the clergy, away from authority, toward enabling.

Economic as well as social factors engender Mary Daly's speculation that "it is quite possible, many would say inevitable, that the distinction between hierarchy and laity as we now know it will disappear. Since our age is characterized by the emergence of oppressed minorities, it is unlikely that the Church can hold out against this rising tide. The existence of a separate and superior priestly caste, of a hierarchy, appears to modern man [sic] as a quaint leftover from an earlier stage of human development." The clergy's tasks, she says, touch "many areas requiring special competence: theology, teaching, preaching, social service, counselling psychology, business administration, recreational leadership. Any of these areas of work can be handled by qualified members of the laity, men and women, and any of them can be handled better by lay specialists than by clerical non-specialists."[23] Or, as one Episcopalian priest remarked, "There are people all over the congregation who can do better any one thing that I do."

Just as clergywomen are gaining a foothold in the profession, the ground is shifting under their feet—ironically enough, in some of the very directions advocated by feminist theology. It's possible that economics may increase the willingness of the churches to employ women. At Buffalo Gap, Texas, early in the twentieth century one old layman described the situation succinctly: informed at a church meeting that his pastor, Mary Lee Cagle, was thinking of leaving, he asked: "What do we want to change pastors for? This is the cheapest thing I know of. I have been a member here three years and it has only cost me twenty-five cents."[24] As one woman wrote in the 1993 Presbyterian survey, "I think it's ironic that the PC(USA) is more open to women than ever as we stand on the brink of financial and ecclesiastical crisis." In the words of Michael and Susan Carter, "Women get a ticket to ride after the gravy train has left the station."[25]

So far economics show little sign of encouraging the hiring of women rabbis. At any rate one Conservative woman rabbi told us that while theoretically a shortage of rabbis in that denomination should open up more pulpits to women, "it doesn't really work that way, because most congregations—I'll have to be honest with you—would still prefer to have a man. They still have that bias. My sense is that for the greater part, money is not the factor that would determine. They would prefer a man. They would pay more money for a man just to have a man."

Will the profession of the clergy feminize? In some senses, feminization is already well advanced. Feminist theologians and parish clergywomen are giving Christians and Jews new understandings of their faiths with the fresh theological insights afforded by women's eyes, experience, and scholarship. In many denominations inclusive language is startling congregations into awareness that the people of God or even divinity may comprise feminine as well as masculine elements.

Some evidence indicates that more and more clergy, regardless of gender, are adopting a more "feminine" style of ministry—if, indeed, such a thing exists. Clergywomen generally believe that their styles of ministry differ from those of men, just as theoretically in business women manage differently than men. These alleged gender differences are epitomized in the film "Dead Man Walking," with its legalistic, authoritarian priest and its loving, empowering sister.

Edward C. Lehman, Jr., in *Gender and Work* reports on his study of clergy in mainline Christian denominations, in which he sought to test this hypothesis, examining interpersonal styles, theology, career goals, thought forms, power and authority, and ethics.[26] His sample comprised two hundred ordained clergywomen and two hundred ordained clergymen, supplemented with one hundred ethnics and twenty-three women senior ministers in relatively large churches. He asked them three kinds of questions: whether statements about approaches to ministry fitted the interviewee; how much time was spent in various activities; and how important each of several roles was to the clergy member. He found few significant differences among men's and women's modes of operating. White clergy manifested more feminine scores; other groups more masculine scores, regardless of gender. Greater differences in style showed up for women and men who had recently finished seminary, and for those with shorter job tenure than for the rest of the sample. (This may suggest that regardless of gender the longer the tenure the more pressures congregational and denominational demands exert on the clergyperson.) Differences most often appeared in willingness to use power over congregation (masculine), desire to empower congregation (feminine), preference for rational structure in decisions (masculine), and legalistic tendencies on ethical issues (masculine). Men were more involved in sermonizing, formal classes, and church visitation; women in funerals, working in church structures beyond the local congregation, and social justice issues. *But overall Lehman found slight gender differences, and all of these were affected by other variables, particularly co-pastoring, senior ministering, and seminary cohort.*

Elaine J. Lawless in her nonquantitative study reached opposite conclusions. When she began, Lawless writes, "I believed [women] ministered differently and uniquely *because they were females:* that they preached differently; saw God, religion, and spirituality differently; and, by their very presence and persistence, were changing the focus of religion toward a more process-oriented, liberation-defined, humanistic endeavor. [With the study complete] I believe this more than ever...."[27]

Much as their conclusions conflict, however, both Lehman and Lawless found a movement toward a "feminine" style of ministry among men. Lehman notes a tendency for his whole sample to characterize their styles in relatively feminine terms.

Some clergywomen, particularly younger women with growing families, argue that the presence of women in the clergy can and should lead to better balance between work and personal responsibilities. Rachel Adler writes of the overburdened rabbinate, where "rabbis are always on call. They extol Shabbat and work seven days a week, preach family and put their own family second, offer others serenity and are always in a tizzy."[28] And some of our interviewees have told us that they believe their insistence on allowing time for family and a personal life will change things for clergymen. But in our own observation workaholics come in both genders; the many part-timers tend to work more than they are paid to; and numbers of women, particularly older women, are so delighted to be clergywomen that they go flat out.

Whatever the impact of clergywomen on ministerial style, some more or less remote possibility exists that the clerical profession will come to be dominated numerically by women. Whenever this has happened in a traditionally male occupation, once the process has started it has gone fast, as with grammar-school teaching in the Civil War period, as with clerical work at the turn of the twentieth century, as with pharmacy and veterinary science at the end of the twentieth century. "Yes, absolutely, I think the ministry will be feminized, and for all the wrong reasons," an Episcopal priest told us. She sees the ministry as spiraling down from a low-stress, high-status profession to a high-stress, low-paying, relatively low-status job—maybe in part because women are entering the profession. "I do think there's a possibility that clergywomen will come to outnumber clergymen," says a faculty member at a theological seminary. "I certainly do have women colleagues who actively do believe that that's what's happening, that it happens every time women begin to make inroads: their presence so devalues the profession that men basically leave it."[29]

Another clergywoman sees the situation completely differently. "I would read it that you're not going to get the same kind of women going into the profession. Women might say, 'Gee, I'd like to go into the ministry, but when I look at this, I can't afford it.'" However, that pattern has not emerged in the course of feminization of other professions, and the concepts of selfless dedication and a divine call arbitrate against its emerging with the clergy.

No one wants to feminize the clergy. So far as we know, even the most ardent religious feminists deplore the possibility. Most clergywomen work from the premise enunciated in the nineteenth century by African-American Anna Julia Cooper: "I claim . . . that there is a feminine as well as a masculine side to truth; and that these are related not as inferior and superior, not as better or worse, not as weaker or stronger, but as complements— complements in one necessary and symmetric whole."[30] Clergywomen see as ideal churches and synagogues in which clergywomen and clergymen, laywomen and laymen labor together. One told us about her concerns for her own congregation, where laywomen are exulting in new opportunities and new roles: "It's scary to me, because we're losing the balance between men and women, rapidly. And I don't want people to start saying, 'Oh that women's church,' especially because I'm so involved in all this feminist stuff."

Discerning hierarchies in Judaism and Christianity show equal concern about the possibility of the feminization of the clergy. Episcopalians are exerting extra efforts to attract young men into the priesthood—not necessarily for patriarchal reasons but at least in part because the authorities fear that it will become a woman's profession. Highly placed men in Reform Judaism overtly worry over this problem—even though women still constitute such a tiny proportion of rabbis. Both the clergywomen themselves and the responsible church and synagogue authorities have reason for this concern. Professions tagged as women's occupations nosedive, losing status and lowering pay. Moreover, such an outcome would indicate a failure of the important theological argument that religious institutions need both clergywomen and clergymen to include all human experience, to represent the unity in the divinity of both genders.

But the economic signals of occupational feminization are already flying: low pay, loss of status, a shortage of clergymen in some denominations, and the increase of part-time positions. Slots in theological seminaries are filled with women aspiring to ordination, and women qualified for ordination on every ground except biology exist in numbers. Absurd though it seems to speculate about the possibility at a time when so many powerful churches and synagogues will not ordain women at all, the possibility of clerical feminization cannot be ignored. But it's highly speculative. Will the special, mystical nature of religion differentiate the clergy from other professions? Will most congregations insist on conceptualizing clergy as male? Will the Christian Right's repudiation of women's leadership dominate the religious picture of the future?

Much more immediately and much more probably, clergywomen may be relegated to a different track than clergymen, with fewer and lower material rewards and less upward mobility. It's quite possible that even if women come to outnumber men the profession will still reserve its best-paid, highest-status jobs for men, as among librarians and in public school systems. Such a practice would simply wear one more rut in the rough road of the history of clergywomen. The October 1964 issue of *Renewal* commented on the treatment of "Christian educators and pastors" as "second-class citizens." John Morgan in a 1985 survey predicted that the Episcopal church was creating a second-class priesthood: "women priests are being directed away from the traditional role as Celebrant and Confessor and directed into assisting in institutions as either chaplains or administrators and in parishes as religious educators."[31] The 1993 Presbyterian survey remarked that the denomination is rapidly developing a de facto two-tier career system, "with women serving the poorest and most difficult congregations while males serve the prosperous and prestigious mega-churches."

This situation constitutes a clear and present danger for clergywomen and for the profession. Women and men concerned for the future need to think long and hard about how to handle it, for once established a two-tier career system damages the profession itself, traumatizes individual women, and lowers their professional status. Men within it feel the need to prove their masculinity to themselves and the world, sometimes by derogating women. A battle of the sexes may ensue; so far as we know, in the past women have always lost—as they lost when "muscular Christianity" shouldered its way into the churches at the turn of the twentieth century.

It may well be that women whose temperaments and talents incline them toward the pastoral more than the prophetic mode of ministry, those not eager to fight for theological change, those ambitious to build their own careers should be encouraged to involve themselves in denominational politics, to seek out mentors, to network with those who can help them, to study the techniques for getting ahead, just as women lawyers and businesswomen do, just as many clergymen do. The tendency of some younger and newer clergywomen to join the boys' club may yet serve the profession and its women well.

American women gained the vote only because the National American Woman

Suffrage Association under Carrie Chapman Catt conciliated, persuaded, compromised, played politics, and lobbied professionally while simultaneously the National Woman's Party under Alice Paul made a spectacle of themselves, picketed the White House and the Congress, went to jail, went on hunger strikes, and targeted for defeat all Congressmen whose party did not support woman suffrage. Obviously prophetic clergywomen are not going to adopt such tactics. Equally obviously, the profession and their religious institutions need both pastoral clergywomen to work within the system and prophetic clergywomen to change it—to go the "Re-Imagining" route.

However, the clergywomen of the future, like those of the past, may well laugh at commonsense, economics-based prognostication. Some indications suggest that clergywomen are actually altering clerical practices toward a more egalitarian relationship with their congregations; that clergymen too are coming to value more a position that leaves time for their families and to yearn less for large congregations. Rabbi Arnold Sher of the Reform Movement's Rabbinic Placement Commission "argues that the definition of success is starting to change as men as well as women are choosing more often to stay in middle sized congregations, preferring continuity and intimacy and the pleasures of organic growth to the more traditional rewards of prestige and power."[32] This trend may help to account for the similarities that Edward Lehman found between men's and women's styles of ministry in mainline Christian denominations, with both leaning toward "feminine" values and practices.

As the first eleven "irregularly" ordained Episcopalian women priests irrefutably demonstrated, the fait accompli wields power: in Ellen Goodman's words, "We deal with the *fait accompli* better than with fantasies. . . . As a species we are remarkably resistant to the idea of change—and remarkably adjustable to its reality."[33] The presence of clergywomen in American society is already very much a fait accompli. Whether or not they occupy the seats of power, many clergywomen are in fact using new liturgies, gender-neutral language, and a new theology that responds to the needs of women as well as men. Outside as well as inside churches and synagogues, women are preaching and pastoring. Ordained women hold services in other women's homes. At their own communion suppers, in house churches or on factory floors, unordained clergywomen pray, "Lord Jesus, if it be Thy will, be present in these wafers," relying on Christ's promise that where two or three are gathered together in His name, there He is in the midst of them. Roman Catholic Hispanic women at their conferences not only deliver the homilies but use a liturgy they themselves have prepared, in which only women have leadership roles.[34] Jewish women gather in their own minyans and say *kaddish* for their own dead. New congregations of lesbians and gays call clergywomen they themselves empower. Widespread ecumenicity common among New Age experimenters, among the mainline denominations, and among Jewish and Christian feminists weakens denominational barriers to women's ordination.

We still puzzle about the difficulties of communication and misunderstandings between feminist clergywomen and other late-twentieth-century feminists, particularly considering the radical transformations that some clergywomen have wrought in their lives and work and the courage with which they have defied patriarchal institutions. It's ironic that two groups so deeply interested in value systems and morality, both of whom are becoming increasingly impatient, should have said so little to each other.[35]

On the one hand, it's true, most clergywomen have to watch their tongues because of their plethora of bosses and their vulnerability to minority opinion in their congregations and denominations. Most feminist clergywomen can safely talk with complete openness about their views only to each other, a situation aggravated by the tendency of academicians—and many of their leaders are academicians—to address only each other. By and large their publications and innovations simply do not reach secular feminists.

What's more, many secular feminists have closed their eyes, ears, and minds to clergywomen, branding them guilty by association with patriarchal institutions, hence politically incorrect.[36] Now some are beginning to look and listen. At the 1995 United Nations Fourth World Conference on Women in Beijing "Bella Abzug join[ed Betty] Friedan in begging the women theologians to be in deeper conversation with the feminist movement."[37] As an African-American senior pastor put it, "Myself I think [neither] black womanists nor white feminists have done enough sitting down with black women who are pastors, to say 'You reach them on this level and I reach them on this level. Where can we come together?' I hope that that conversation will happen. I think that we're very much on two different tracks. One's not better than the other. Scholarship is important: people who argue on that level and create new places for women are very important, but what I've done to create places for women, being in a male-dominated traditional pastorate, is equally important. We've got to find ways to be cooperative and collaborative."

Clergywomen frequently express the same need in their relationships with laywomen. This felt need goes beyond their desire to interact democratically with their congregations, to level the barriers between clergy and laity. As Nina Beth Cardin writes, "the struggle to become clergy is only one element of the larger question of women's roles in religion, but this most obvious point is often ignored and the divide between clergywomen and women becomes almost as large as between clergywomen and men."[38] The history of laywomen within their churches and synagogues displays many of the same difficulties as those that clergywomen have confronted. All too often the differences in their vocations have masked the similarities in their situation. They have been divided; neither clergywomen nor laywomen have conquered; and women's status in religion remains under attack.

As we think back on the history of clergywomen, as we survey the diversity of clergywomen at the end of the twentieth century, we discern common, interwoven threads of experience. Feminists or advocates of traditional "family values," post-Christians or fundamentalists, sophisticates or semiliterate women, they share priorities, especially in positioning the relationship with a deity (even though they can't agree on which deity) at the center of their lives. For that relationship, and for the task of bringing others to it, they stand ready to sacrifice everything else—

societal and institutional approval, prosperity, health, friends, and sometimes even family. That passion distinguishes them. As Susan Conrad writes, "The story of the American woman is, in many ways, the record of her attempts to be an American."[39] And the history of the American clergywoman is the record of her attempts to be faithful to her religion.

If it's true that it takes only about 2 percent of a population to make a revolution, one may be brewing among Jewish and Christian feminist clergywomen, well-supported by laywomen of all denominations. Instead of accepting the limits set by their religious institutions, some clergywomen will walk around them, their pilgrim feet beating new thoroughfares to freedom and service to God and their fellow human beings.

Notes

1. Susan Kwilecki, "Contemporary Pentecostal Clergywomen: Female Christian Leadership, Old Style," *Journal of Feminist Studies in Religion* 3 (Fall 1987): 57–75.

2. Sara Maitland, *A Map of the New Country: Women and Christianity* (London: Routledge & Kegan Paul, 1983), pp. 4–5. See also Janet Marder in *Reform Judaism* (Summer 1991); Laura Geller in *Gender and Judaism: The Transformation of Tradition,* ed. T. M. Rudavsky (New York: New York Univ. Press, 1995), p. 245; and Martha Long Ice, *Clergywomen and Their World Views: Calling for a New Age* (New York: Praeger, 1987), p. 149.

3. Maitland, *Map,* p. 104. See also Constance H. Buchanan, "The Anthropology of Vitality and Decline: The Episcopal Church in a Changing Society," in *Episcopal Women: Gender, Spirituality, and Commitment in an American Mainline Denomination,* ed. Catherine M. Prelinger (New York: Oxford Univ. Press, 1992), p. 323.

4. "There is a key generational difference among women clergy right now, with the younger trusting way too much in the women's movement to guarantee security and the older generation much too burned by the trouble we've already seen. There are so many interesting ways to be mistaken" (Donna Schaper, *Common Sense About Men & Women in the Ministry* [Washington, D.C.: Alban Institute, 1990], p. 13).

5. For documentation of this sense of exclusion among laywomen, see Miriam Therese Winter, Adair Lummis, and Allison Stokes, *Defecting in Place: Women Claiming Responsibility for Their Own Spiritual Lives* (New York: Crossroad, 1994). Gary Dorsey's *Congregation: The Journey Back to Church* (New York: Viking, 1995) also documents this reaction; see especially p. 92, where the church secretary/religious education specialist says, "I won't sing a lot of the hymns anymore. I just sit there and count all the men in those songs. He's, Hims, Fathers, Lords, fellows. . . ."

6. *Woman's Pulpit* (Jan.-Feb.-Mar. 1992).

7. The series featured Patty Duke as a divorced single mother. It flopped, as it deserved to—perhaps at least in part because it told too little about the clergywoman and her professional problems. Her life and problems as told in the series did not stem from or center on her work.

8. Constant H. Jacquet, Jr.'s "Women Ministers in 1986 and 1977: A Ten Year View" (New York: National Council of Churches, 1988), shows that in 1986 the Reorganized Church of Jesus Christ of Latter Day Saints had 860 clergywomen.

9. Blu Greenberg, "Is Now the Time for Orthodox Women Rabbis?" *Moment* 18 (Dec. 1993): 50ff.

10. *New York Times* (Apr. 15, 1994).

11. Richard A. Schoenherr, "Numbers Don't Lie: A Priesthood in Irreversible Decline," *Commonweal* (Apr. 7, 1995): 11–14.

12. Quoted in Ritamary Bradley, "The Truth Shall Make You Free," in *Midwives of the Future: American Sisters Tell Their Story*, ed. Ann Patrick Ware (Kansas City, Mo.: Leaven, 1985), pp. 79–80.

13. Quoted in Colm Toibin in *The New Yorker* (Oct. 9, 1995). See also "Teaching on Women's Ordination Infallible?" *The American Catholic* 3 (Dec 1995/Jan 1996): 5, 10.

14. "Indeed, the question of women's ordination may be the catalyst which ultimately brings schism to a diverse and increasingly disoriented denomination" (Bill Leonard, "Good News at Wolf Creek," *Christian Century* 101 [May 2, 1984]: 455–56). See also "Despite Obstacles, Women Ministers are on Rise Among Black Baptists," *Los Angeles Times* (Sept. 17, 1983).

15. *Christian Century* 112 (June 21–28, 1995): 663. See also Bill J. Leonard's report of the seminary president's forcing the resignation of its last tenured woman faculty member by threatening her with heresy charges ("Seminary Crackdown," *Christian Century* 112 [May 10, 1995]).

16. L. E. Maxwell, *Women in Ministry: A Historical and Bibliographical Look at the Role of Women in Christian Leadership* (Wheaton, Ill.: Victor, 1987), p. 114.

17. On the other hand, association with more conservative churches frequently strengthens bans against women in the pulpit. Historically when a church that does not ordain women has united with one that does, more often than not women have lost out. See Jeanette Hassey, *No Time for Silence: Evangelical Women in Public Ministry Around the Turn of the Century* (Grand Rapids, Mich.: Academie Books, 1986), p. 55; and Margaret M. Poloma, *Assemblies of God at the Crossroads: Charisma and Institutional Dilemmas* (Knoxville: Univ. of Tennessee Press, 1989), p. 119.

18. Maxine Hanks, *Women and Authority: Re-Emerging Mormon Feminism*, ed. Maxine Hanks (Salt Lake City, Utah: Signature, 1992), p. xxvii. Mormon feminism shows the same patterns as Roman Catholic feminism. Some Mormon feminists argue that the church long since has empowered women as priests (D. Michael Quinn,"Mormon Women Have Had the Priesthood Since 1843," in Hanks, *Women and Authority*). Others urge women to exercise their priesthood without waiting for male approval (Margaret Merrill Toscano, "Put On Your Strenth O Daughters of Zion: Claiming Priesthood and Knowing the Mother," in Hanks, *Women and Authority*). Still others urge that priesthood in a faulty system is not worth having; as Marian Yeates writes, "I see women's ordination to Melchizedek priesthood as a kind of 'tune-up' when I believe what is needed is an overhaul of the vehicle or church system" ("Why Shouldn't Mormon Women Want *This* Priesthood?" in Hanks, *Women and Authority*, p. 358). See also Susan Hill Lindley, *"You Have Stept Out of Your Place": A History of Women and Religion in America* (Louisville, Ky.: Westminster John Knox, 1996), pp. 270–71, 339–43.

19. James W. Davis, "More Women Than Ever Are Entering Ministry," *Fort Lauderdale Sun-Sentinel*, reprinted in *The Hartford Courant* (Feb. 23, 1996).

20. Richard Quebedeaux, "We're on our Way, Lord!: The Rise of 'Evangelical Feminism' in Modern American Christianity," in *Women in the World's Religions, Past and Present*, ed. Ursula King (New York: Paragon, 1986), p. 141.

21. Juanita Evans Leonard, "Women, Change, and the Church," in *Called to Minister . . .*

Empowered to Serve: Women in Ministry and Missions in the Church of God Reformation Movement, ed. Juanita Leonard (Anderson, Ind.: Warner Press, 1989), p. 157.

22. *Sekinah,* 2nd anniversary ed., p. 11.

23. Mary Daly, *The Church and the Second Sex* (New York: Harper & Row, 1968), pp. 165–66.

24. Mary Lee Cagle, *Life and Work of Mary Lee Cagle: An Autobiography* (Kansas City, Mo.: Nazarene Pub. House, 1928), p. 107.

25. Barbara F. Reskin, "The Feminization of Book Editing," in *Job Queues, Gender Queues: Explaining Women's Inroads into Male Occupations,* ed. Barbara F. Reskin and Patricia A. Roos (Philadelphia: Temple Univ. Press, 1990), p. 107.

26. Edward C. Lehman, Jr., *Gender and Work: The Case of the Clergy* (Albany: State Univ. of New York Press, 1993).

27. Lawless, *Holy Women,* p. 1. See also Celia Allison Hahn, "Is There a Feminine Style of Religious Leadership?" in *Especially for Women: The Best of Action Information* (Washington, D.C.: Alban Institute, 1992).

28. Rachel Adler, "A Stumbling Block Before the Blind: Sexual Exploitation in Pastoral Counseling," *CCAR Journal* 40 (Spring 1993): 28.

29. However, Reskin and Roos expect significantly more women to enter the clergy, but they do not anticipate its becoming predominantly a woman's occupation (*Job Queues,* p. 318).

30. Gerda Lerner, *The Creation of Feminist Consciousness: From the Middle Ages to Eighteen-Seventy* (New York: Oxford Univ. Press, 1993), pp. 218–19.

31. John H. Morgan, *Women Priests: An Emerging Ministry in the Episcopal Church 1975–1985* (Bristol, Ind.: Wyndham Hall Press, 1985), pp. 22–23. Catherine M. Prelinger in reporting a 1988 survey notes the absence of straight clergywomen in inner-city churches, which increasingly are pastored by women and gay men ("Ordained Women in the Episcopal Church: Their Impact on the Work and Structure of the Clergy," in *Episcopal Women,* p. 292).

32. Laura Geller, "From Equality to Transformation: The Challenge of Women's Rabbinic Leadership" (papers of the Women's Rabbinic Network Conference [March 1993], p. 25).

33. Ellen Goodman, *Close to Home* (New York: Simon & Schuster, 1979), p. 99.

34. Ada Maria Isasi-Diaz, "The Birthing Stool: Mujerista Liturgy," in *Women at Worship: Interpretations of North American Diversity,* ed. Majorie Procter-Smith and Janet Walton (Louisville, Ky.: Westminster/John Knox Press, 1993), p. 192.

35. See the feature story in Metro Report of the *New York Times* (July 12, 1992), linking spiritual and secular feminists.

36. "In evangelical churches, feminism is a dirty word, and for many feminists, Christian is a dirty word. We [the Evangelical and Ecumenical Women's Caucus] help bridge a big gap" (June Steffensen Hagen, "EEWC Members Free-write For Our Future," *Update* 18 [Fall 1994]: 6).

37. *United Church News* (Oct., 1995).

38. Letter of March 19, 1996, to the authors.

39. Susan P. Conrad, *Perish The Thought* (New York: Oxford Univ. Press, 1976), p. 237.

Index